Franziska Klose

DETROIT

FIELD NOTES FROM A WILD CITY

Spector Books

When somebody asks me:
"Will the city ever come back?"
I tell them, "It's back, it never
went anyplace. You've left
maybe, but the city never did."

Jerry Herron in: Bredow (2006). High Tech Soul

PLANTS

S

T

V

W

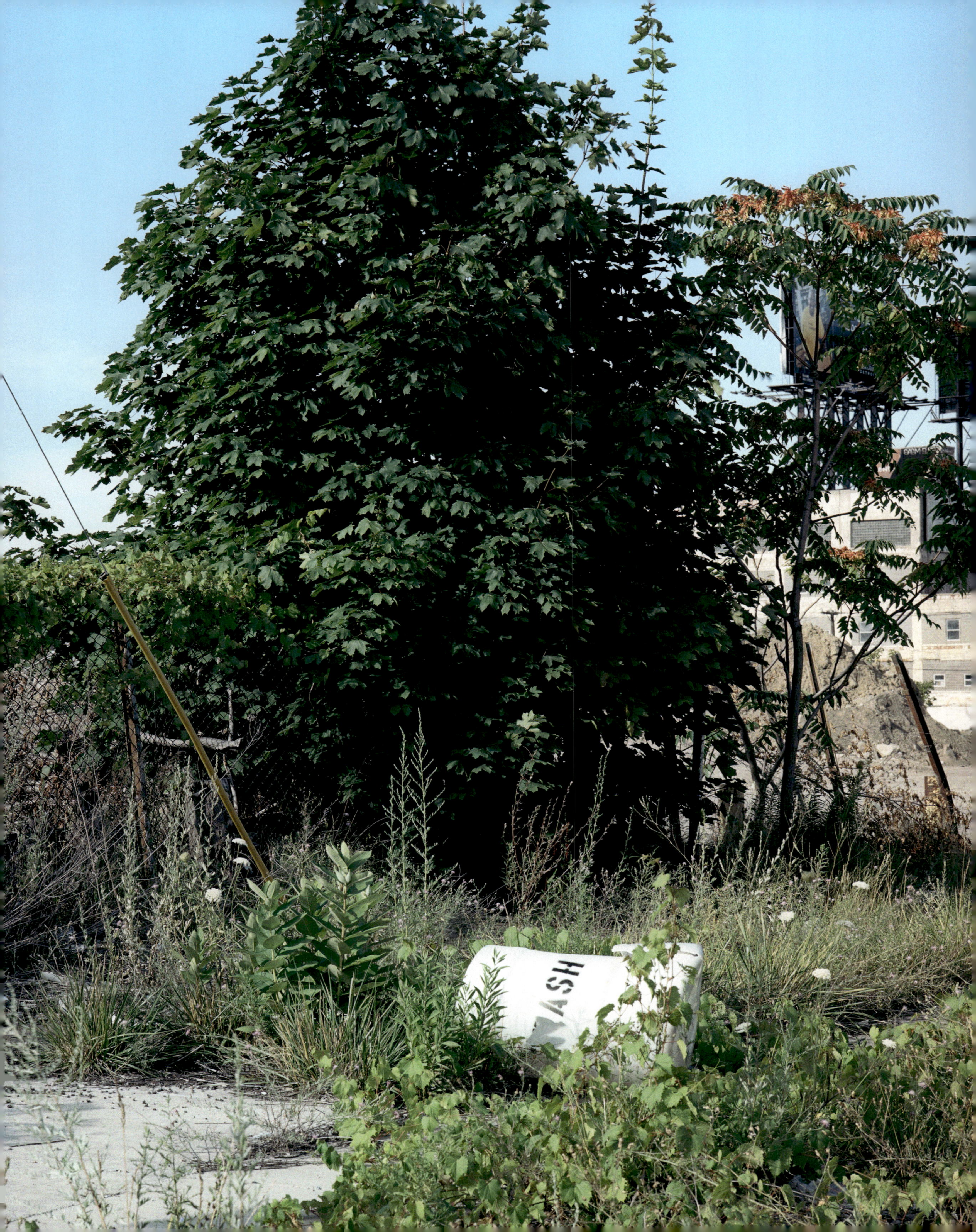
ASH

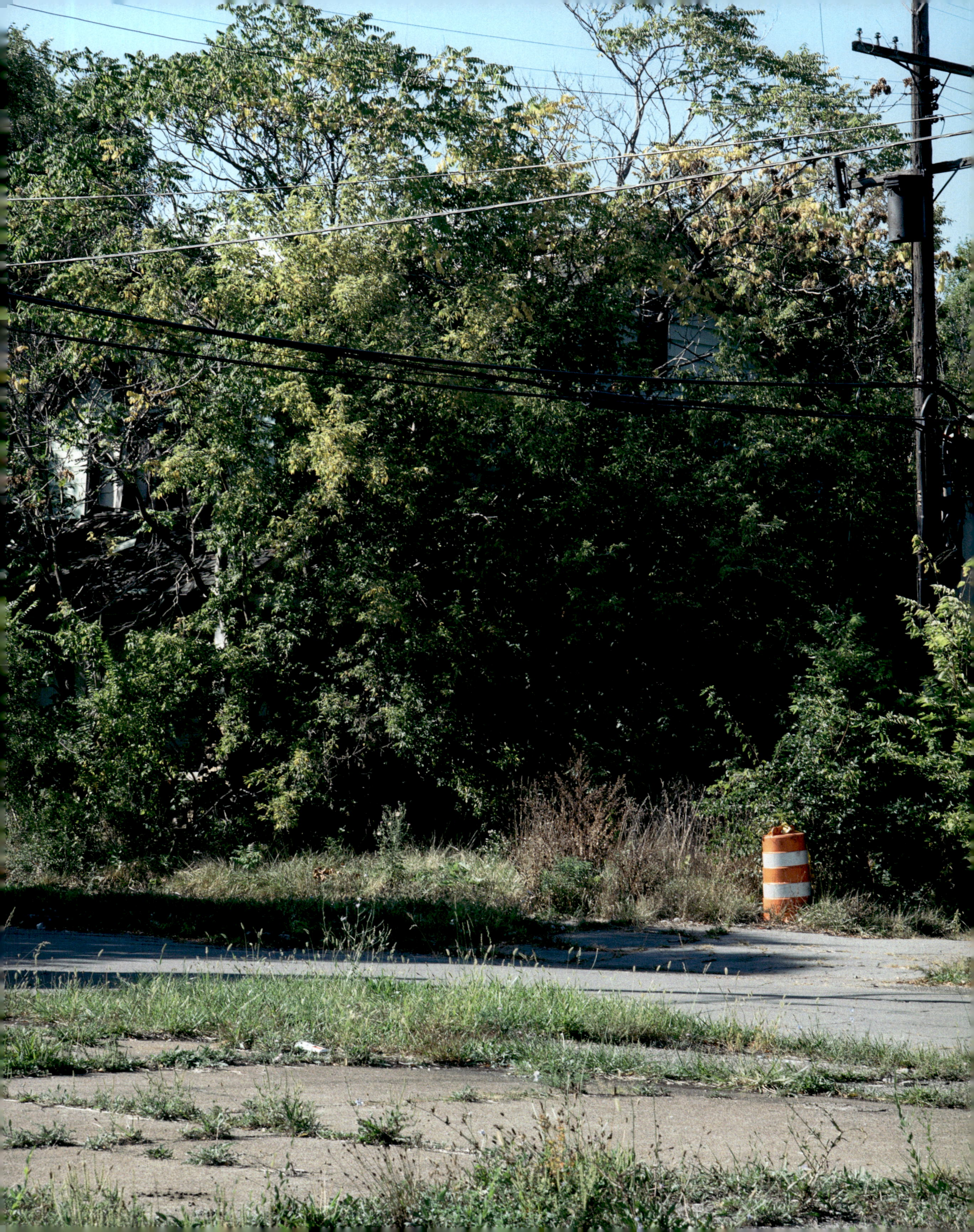

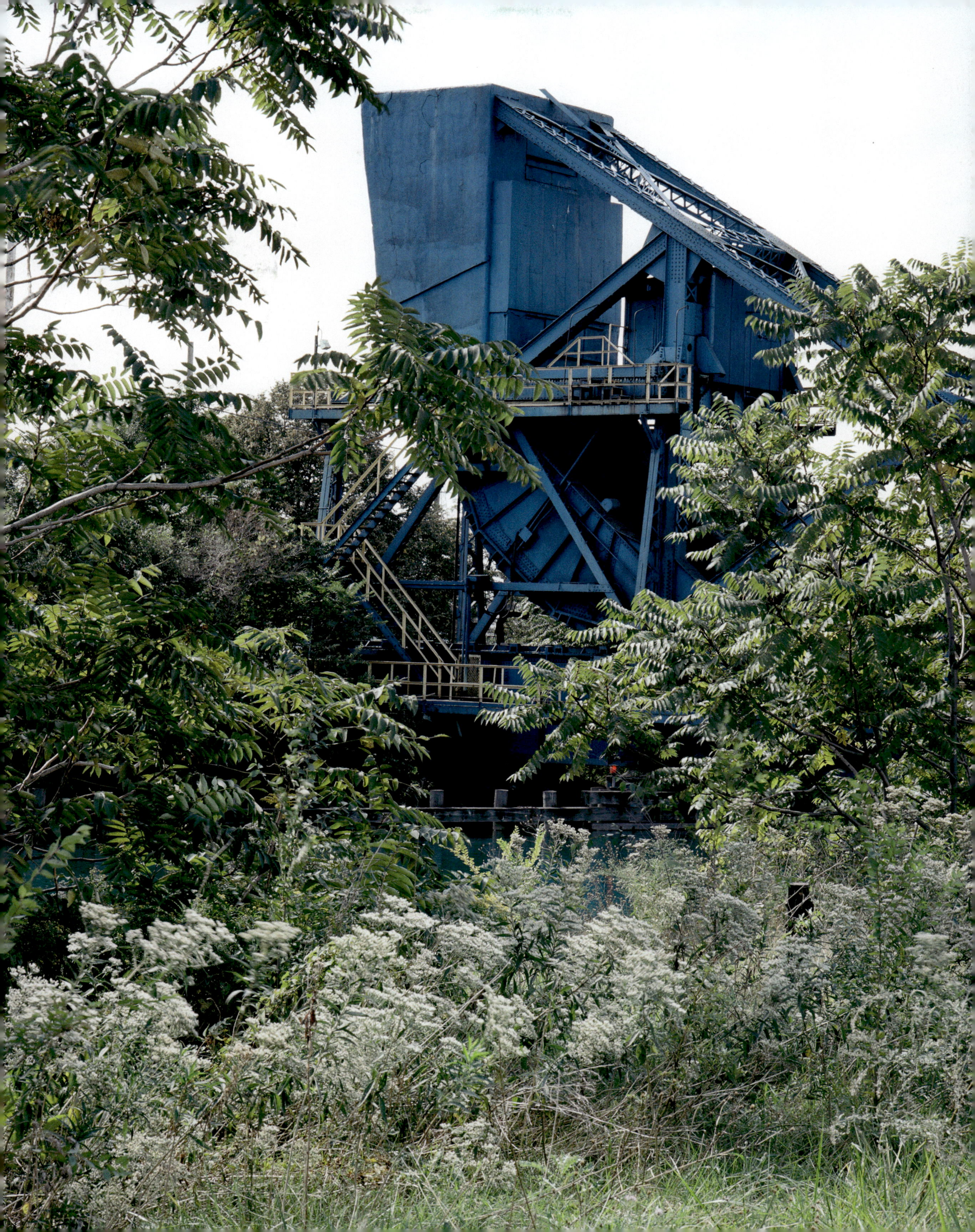

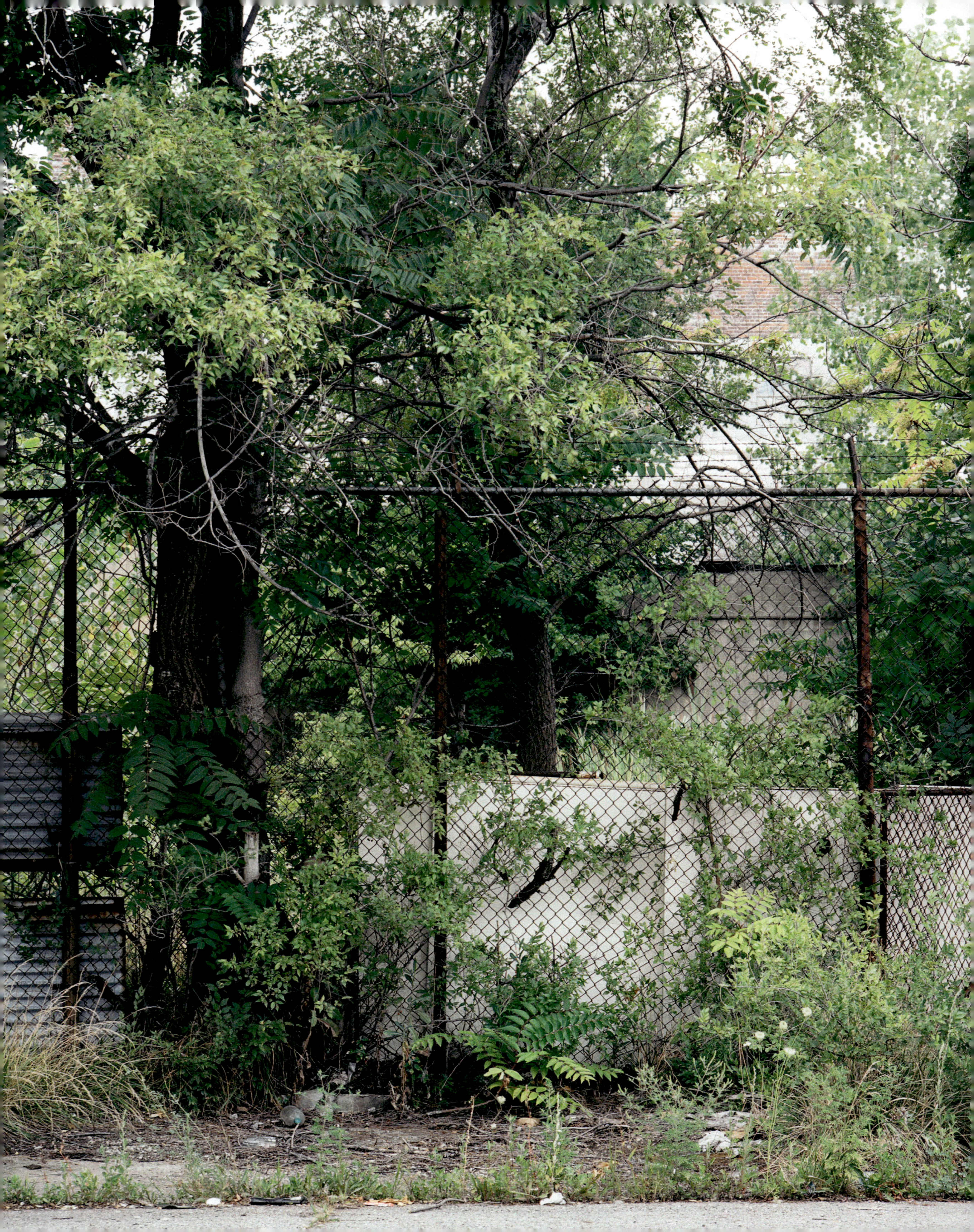

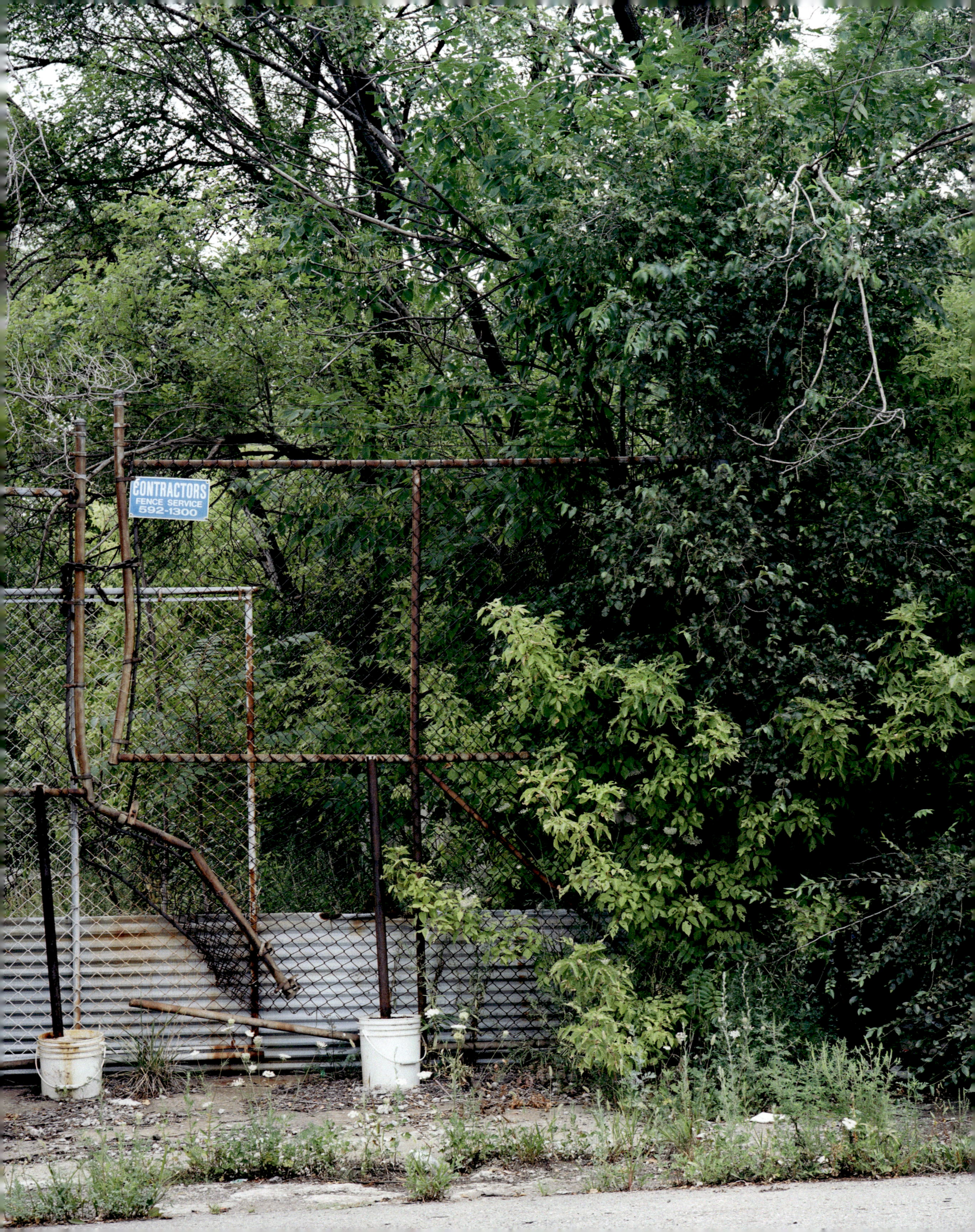
CONTRACTORS
FENCE SERVICE
592-1300

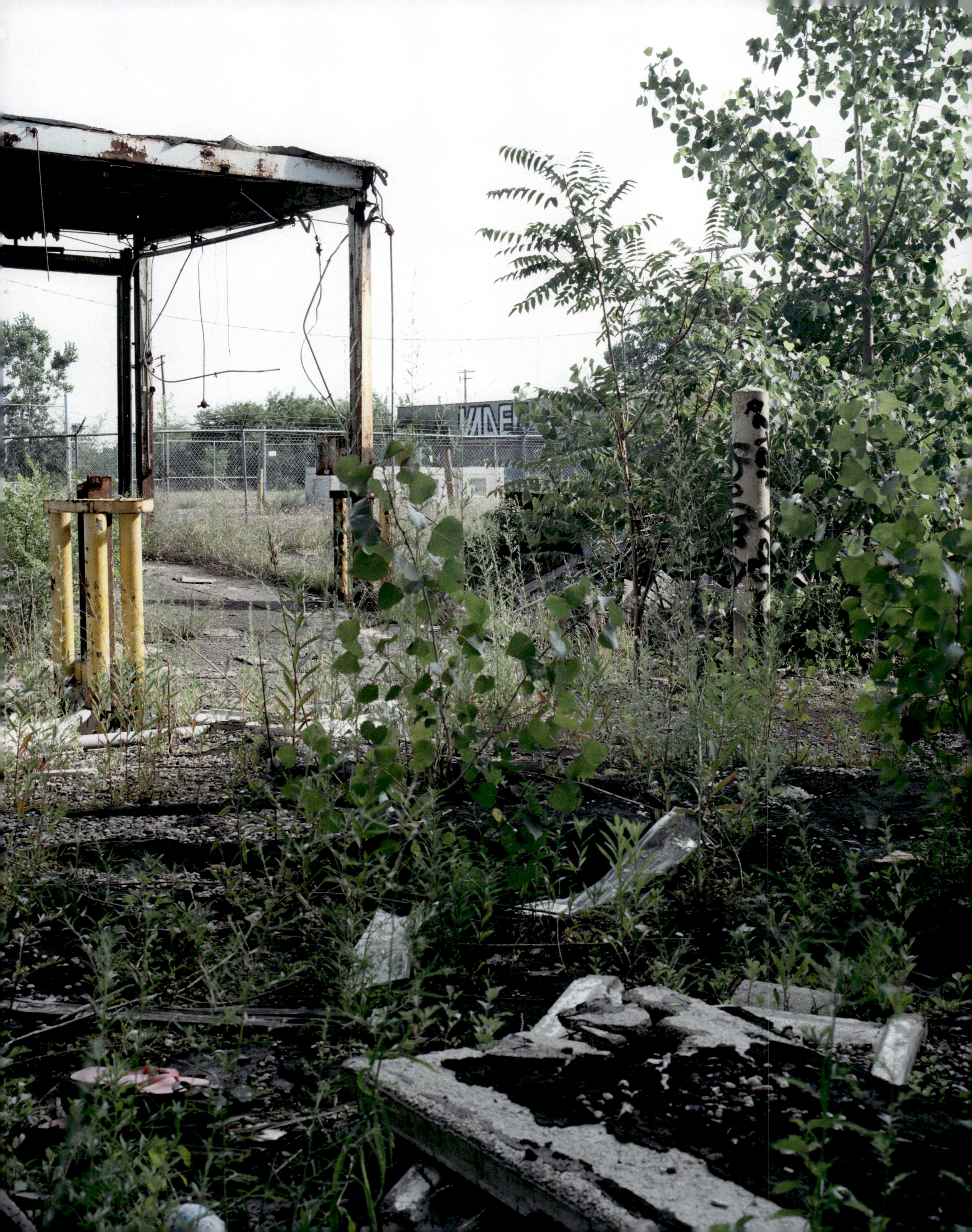

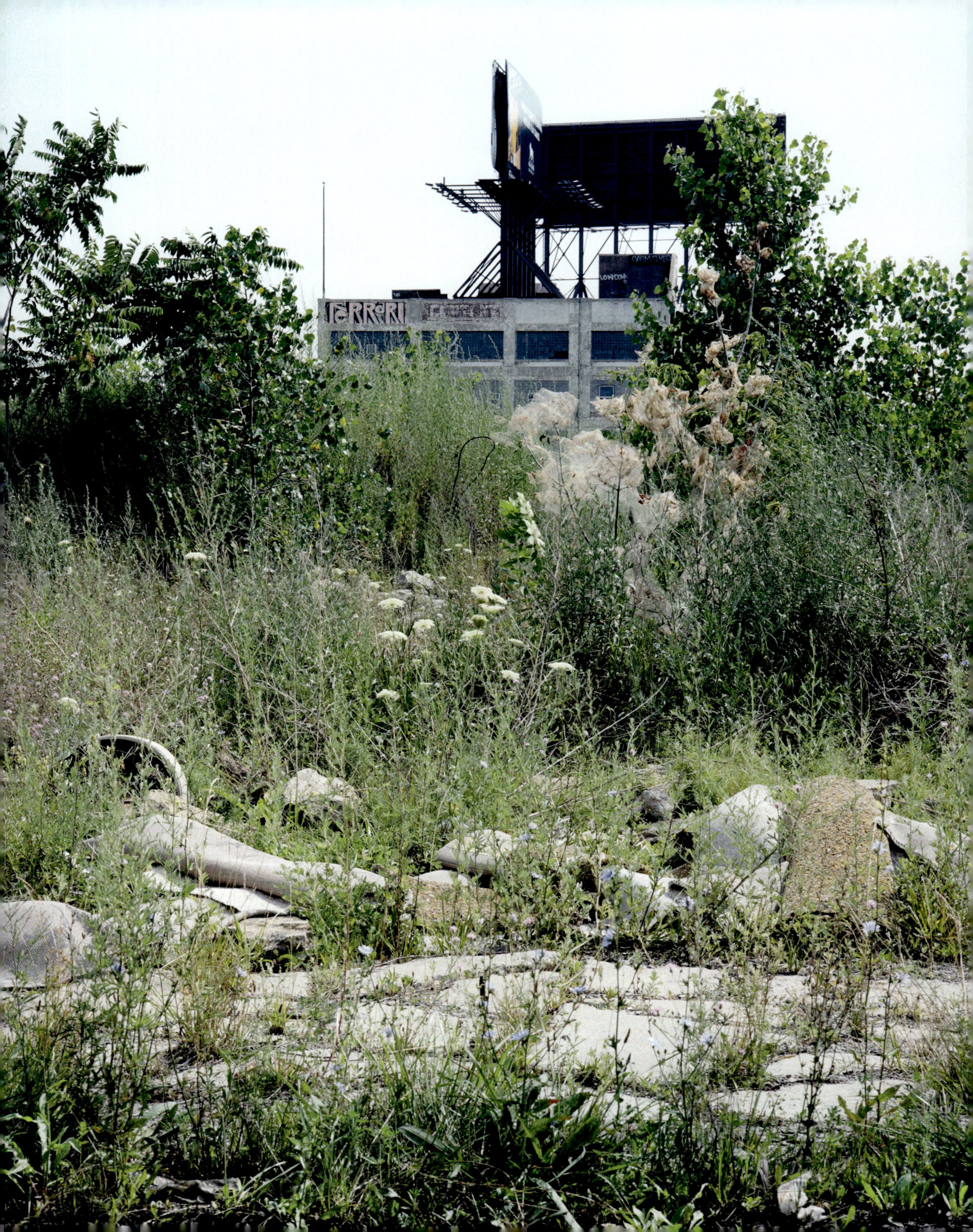

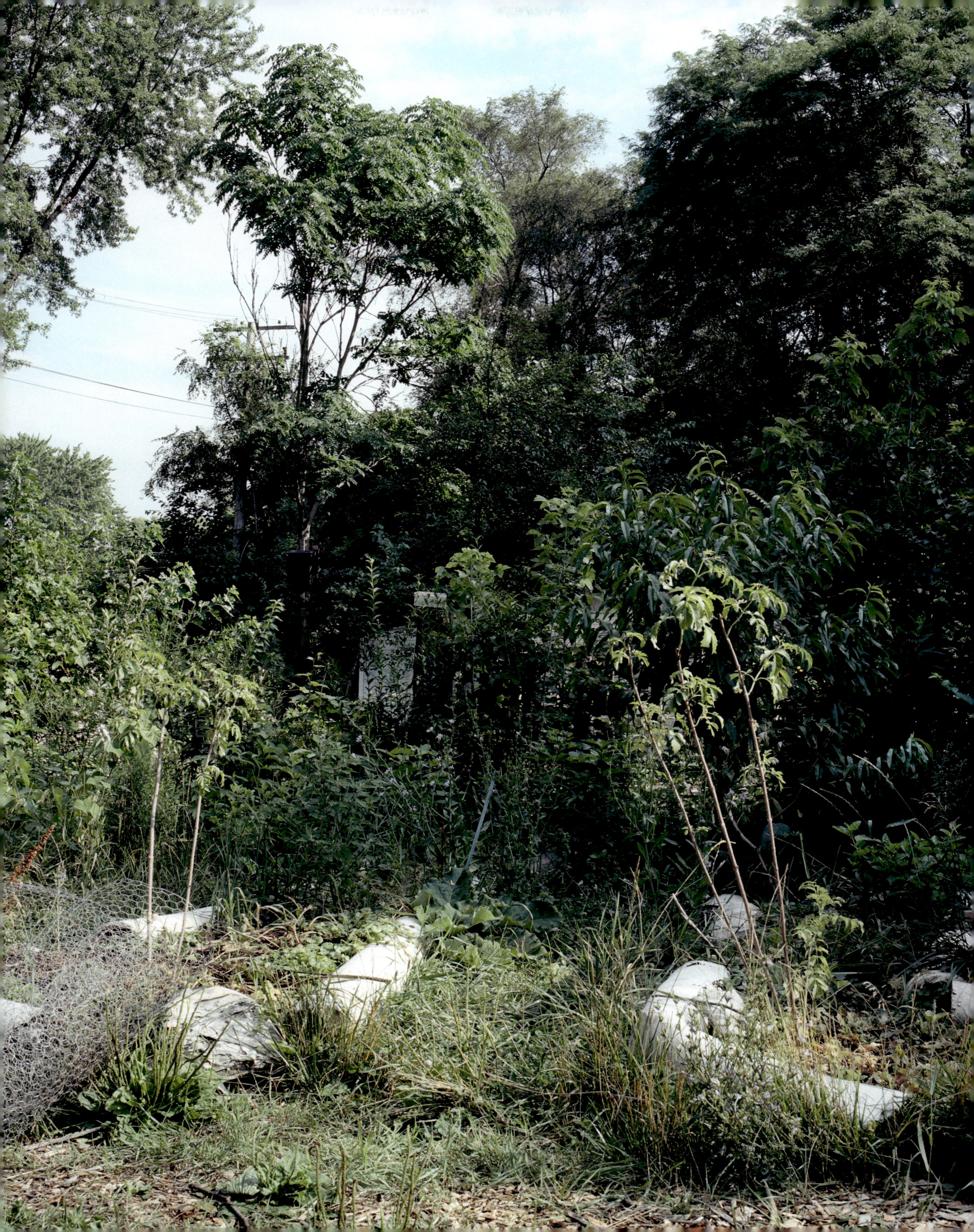

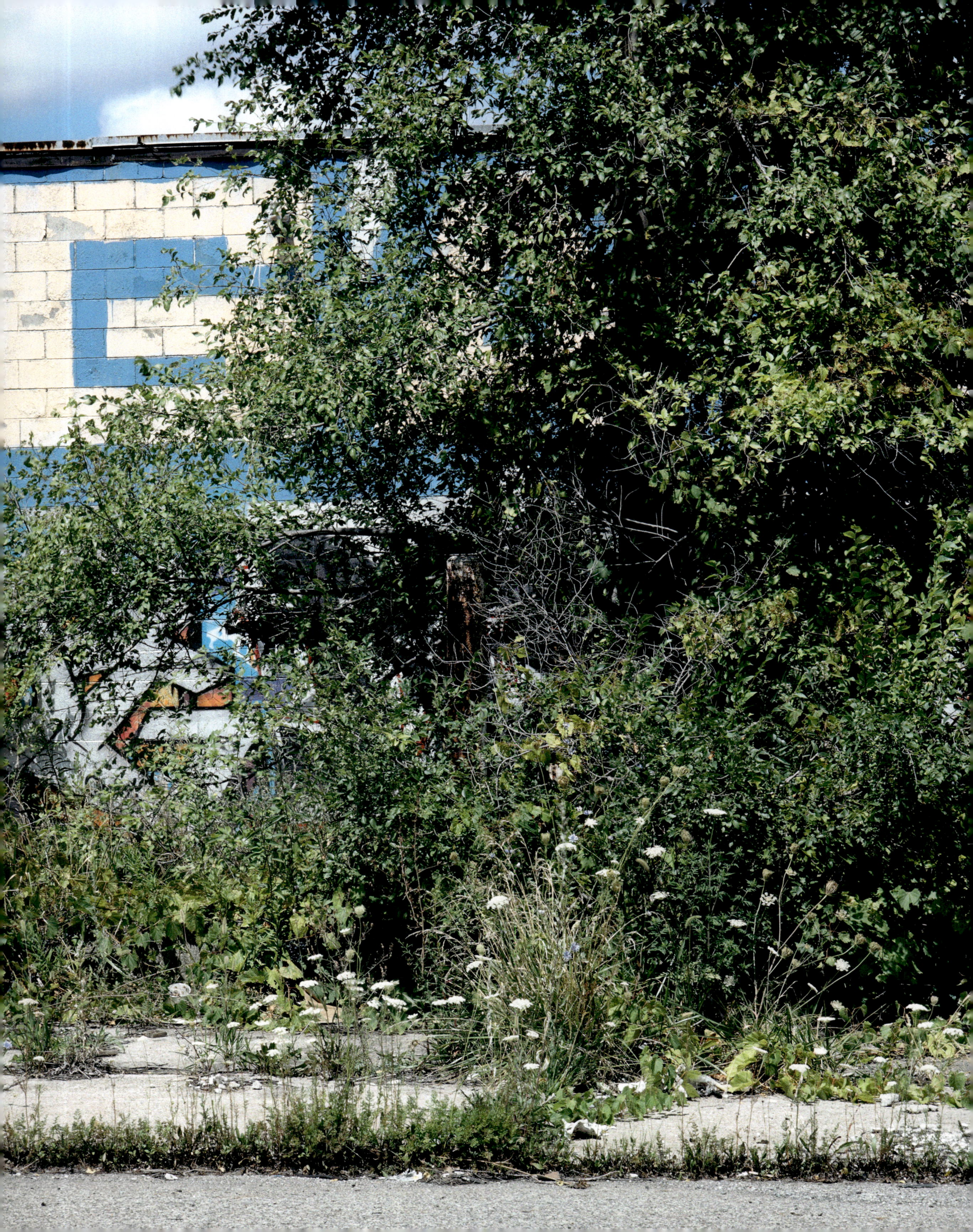

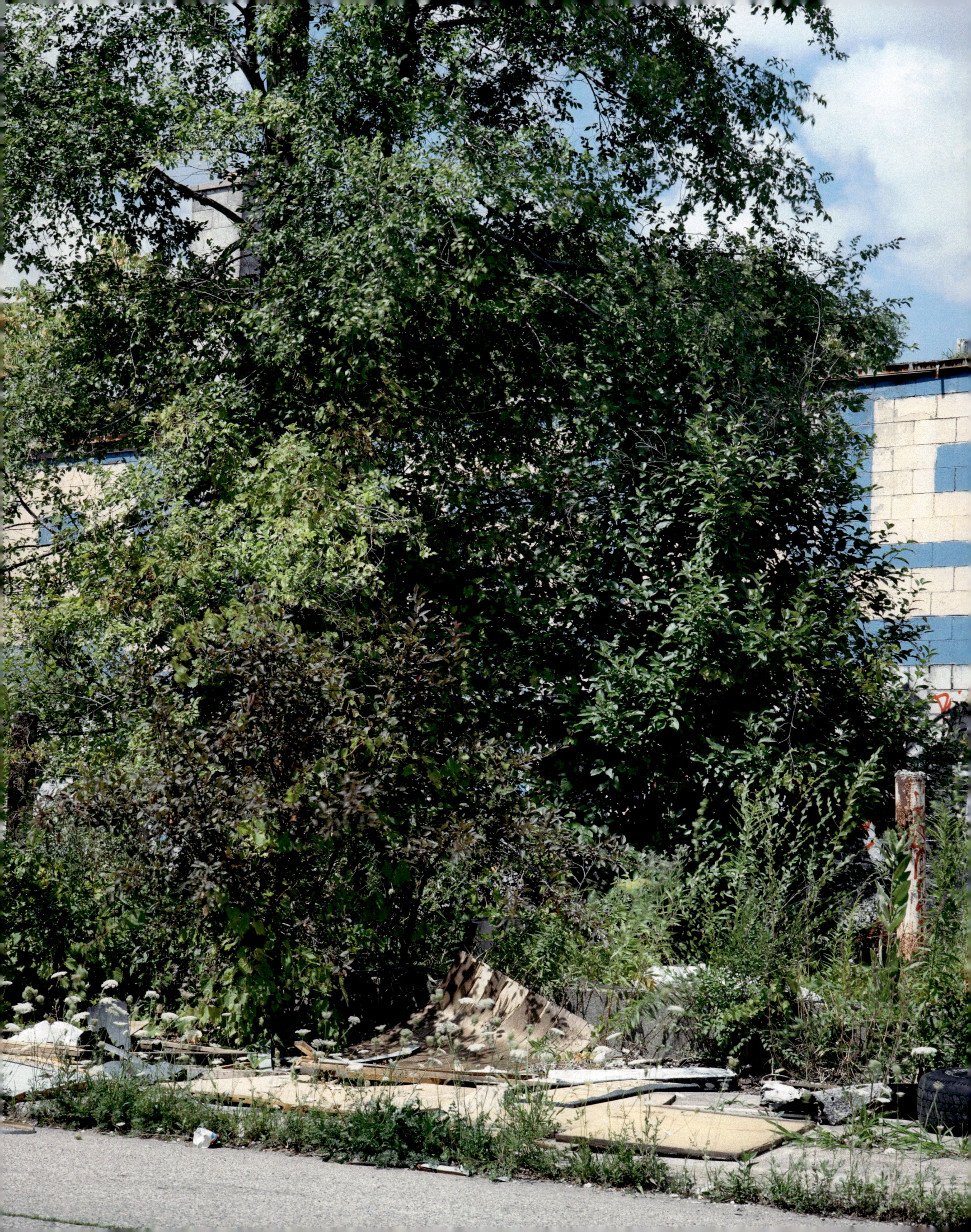

One day after a brief thunderstorm, when the rain had cleared away and chunky white clouds dotted the sky, I wandered into a neighborhood, or rather a former neighbor-hood, of at least a dozen square blocks where trees of heaven waved their branches in the balmy air. Approximately one tattered charred house still stood per block. I could hear the buzzing of crickets or cicadas, and I felt as if I had traveled a thousand years into the future.

Rebecca Solnit (2007). Detroit Arcadia

1

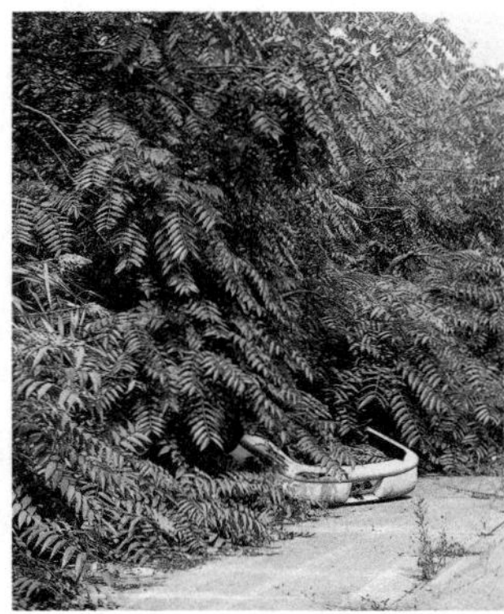

2

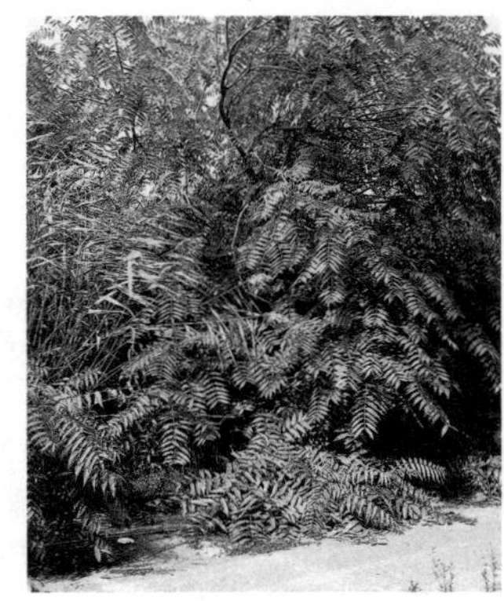

2550 East Grand Boulevard, 2015

Milwaukee Junction Neighborhood

2550 East Grand Boulevard is located in Milwaukee Junction, the cradle of Detroit's auto industry. It was here that virtually all of the first automotive manufacturers started out. The photographs were taken within sight of the General Motors Hamtramck Assembly Plant, which opened in 1985. During one of Detroit's economic recessions, the city granted General Motors a tax break for the construction of the new plant, expropriating the residential and church properties in the Poletown East district where the facility now stands. The demolition took place under protest of the residents and at the taxpayers' expense.

The expropriation of private property for the benefit of urban development was made possible by recent changes in Michigan state law. While General Motors President Francis James McDonald stated in an interview in 1981: "The eighties are going to be a very exciting decade. I feel that government, labor, and industry and management must really get together to take on challenges that face us. And I see that happening." ° Father Francis Skalski of St. Hyacinth's Church criticized: "… it was a shame that people like General Motors were coming in and taking over the area from poor people. It reminds me of a medieval king — there's a massive area, a nice big fence in front of the property, beautiful landscaping, and behind they have their castle — their plant." °°

In November 2018, General Motors announced the closure of the Hamtramck Assembly plant to "take proactive steps to improve overall business performance, including the reorganization of its global product development staffs, the realignment of its manufacturing capacity and a reduction of salaried workforce." °°°

Two years, one 40-day national strike, and 800 layoffs later, GM is retooling the plant in 2020 for the production of electric pickup trucks.

° Wylie (1989). Poletown, 29
°° Wylie (1989). Poletown, 72
°°° General Motors press release in: LaReau (2018)

3

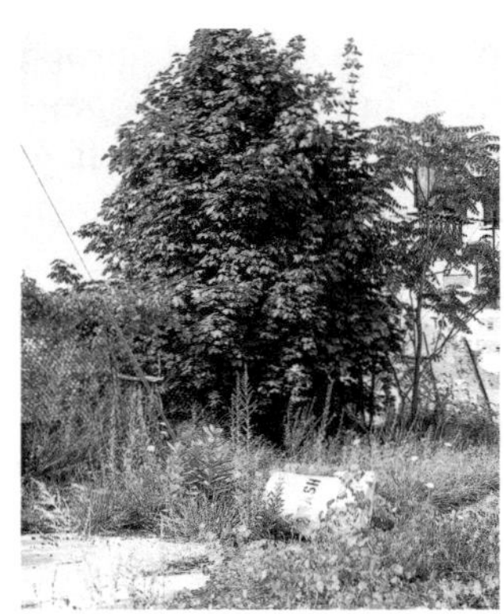

Fisher Body Plant 21 (Bucket), 2015

Milwaukee Junction Neighborhood

The factory premises of the former Fisher Body Plant 21 are located in the Milwaukee Junction district where the first car manufacturers were established around 1900. Of the initial 43 manufacturers there were only eight left in 1926. Like many others, Fisher Body was bought up by one of the Big Three.

In 1919 the factory was built to a design by Albert Kahn. With the exception of the Great Depression era, when the factory served as a soup kitchen and shelter for the homeless, for 80 years car components were produced here: chassis (at first still made of wood), parts for its limousine, ambulances, and buses as well as, in war production, components for airplanes, anti-aircraft guns, and tanks. In 1983, General Motors closed down the site and outsourced production to Flint. The factory building has stood empty since 1993. Like the Packard Automotive Plant, the Fisher Body building has become an icon of Detroit's ruin porn.

The photographs were taken on the property opposite the factory site, which originally served as a warehouse.

→ 8 Fisher Body Plant 21 (Poplar Tree), 2015
→ 9 Fisher Body Plant 21 (Rugs), 2015

4

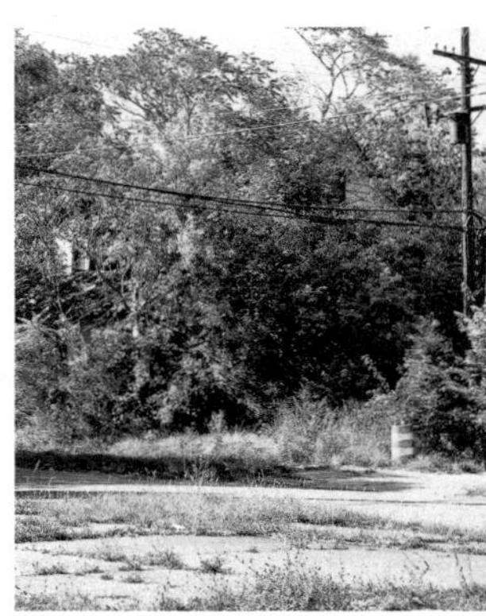

6203 Marcus Street, 2015

Airport Sub Neighborhood

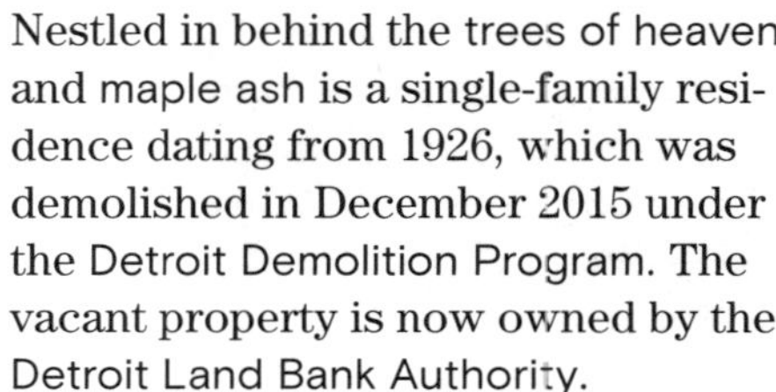

Nestled in behind the trees of heaven and maple ash is a single-family residence dating from 1926, which was demolished in December 2015 under the Detroit Demolition Program. The vacant property is now owned by the Detroit Land Bank Authority.

While Detroit of the 1920s is often described as a "total industrial landscape,"° in which factories, workshops, and residential areas fused densely into one another, only a few decades later the view is quite different. Vacant industrial complexes, abandoned houses, and vast expanses of grassland can be seen everywhere — like a cityscape that has been decimated by industry.

° Zunz (1982). The Changing Face of Inequality, 3

5

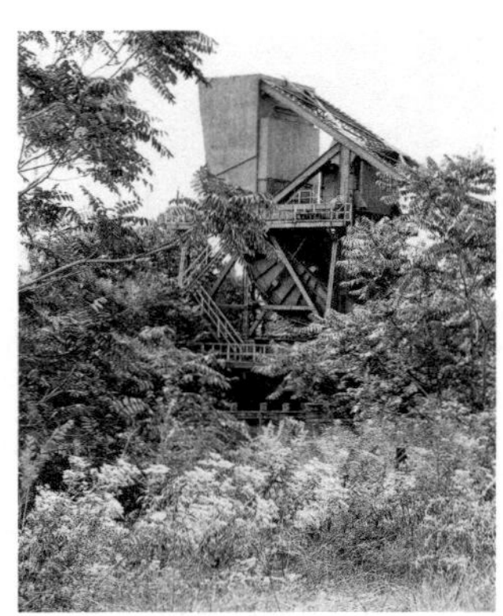

Zug Island (Steel Mill), 2015

River Rouge

Zug Island is an artificial island at the confluence of the River Rouge and Detroit River on the southwestern city limits of Detroit. Since 1901, heavy industry has been smelting steel and producing coke here. The blue tower is part of a steel mill operated by United States Steel. The island is not open to the public. It is located across from of the Ford River Rouge Complex. Even today, the busy shipping traffic, plumes of smoke, and the pounding of hammers give the impression of an industrial Detroit. Despite the brackish river water, lead poisoned soil, and solvent polluted air, the shores around Zug Island are popular fishing spots. They are lined with "Chemicals in the Food Chain" signs warning which species of fish should not be eaten.

The island is named after the furniture entrepreneur Samuel Zug, who bought the swampy piece of land in 1879. It was created in 1891 by a canal that was made to navigate around rapids. Long before the Europeans settled here the marshland was used as a burial ground by indigenous peoples in the area.

Big Three
Ruin Porn
Detroit Demolition Program

A winter Tuesday, the city pouring fire, / Ford Rouge sulfurs the sun, Cadillac, Lincoln / Chevy gray. The fat stacks / of breweries hold their tongues. Rags / papers, hands, the stems of birches / dirtied with words. ... One brown child / stares and stares into your frozen eyes / until the lights change and you go / forward to work. The charred faces, the eyes / boarded up, the rubble of innards, the cry / of wet smoke hanging in your throat, / the twisted river stopped at the color of iron. / We burn this city every day.

Philip Levine. Coming Home, Detroit 1968

6

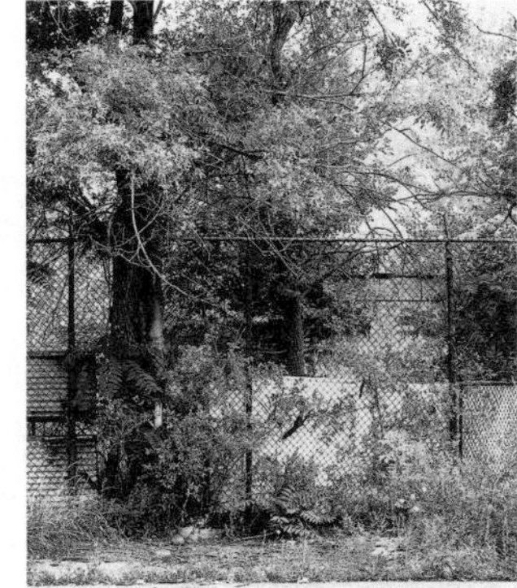

7

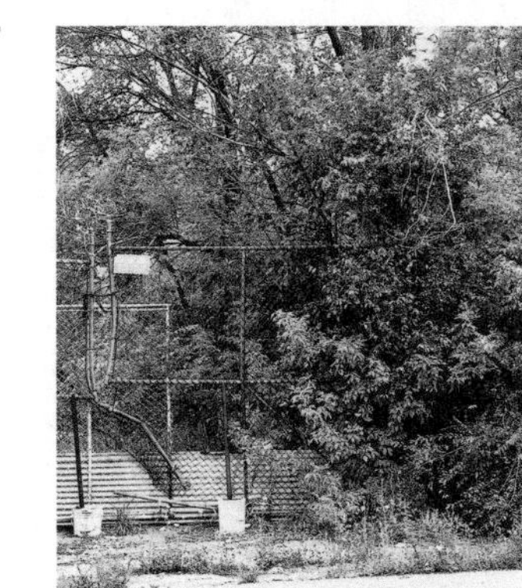

6437 East Palmer Street, 2015

Gratiot Town / Kettering Neighborhood

The two photographs show the fence in front of a workshop area adjacent to Trinity Cemetery, Packard Automotive Plant, and the Detroit Belt Line railroad tracks. Not far from here, I met Allan Hill in 2015, an older man wearing a Jesus baseball cap. The former auto worker lived next to the Packard plant for eleven years, in a workshop where he repaired bicycles and cars. In agreement with the owner he had been a kind of caretaker of the complex and had occasionally shown people around. Recently he even gained some fame through international newspaper articles and a small documentary film. In 2019, the city's Building Safety Engineering and Environmental Department closed down his workshop for "various violations of property maintenance codes." °
Allan Hill was evicted at the age of 74.

° Williams (2019). "I haven't had my day in court"

→ 11 / 12 East Palmer Street (Balsam Poplar), 2015
→ 27 / 29 Packard Automotive Plant, 2015

8

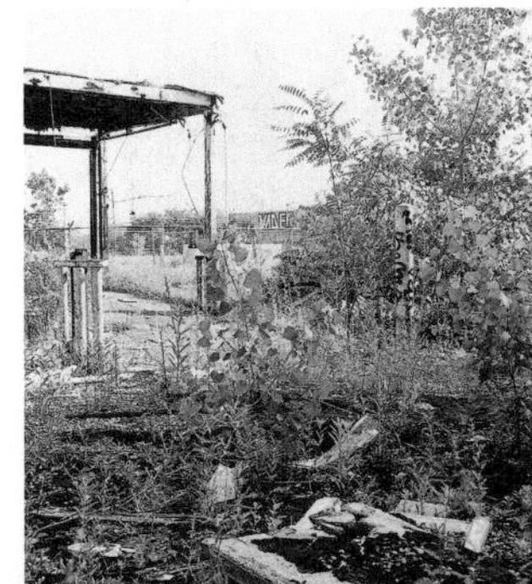

Fisher Body Plant 21 (Poplar Tree), 2015

Milwaukee Junction Neighborhood

9

Fisher Body Plant 21 (Rugs), 2015

Milwaukee Junction Neighborhood

→ For a description see
3 Fisher Body Plant 21 (Bucket), 2015

10

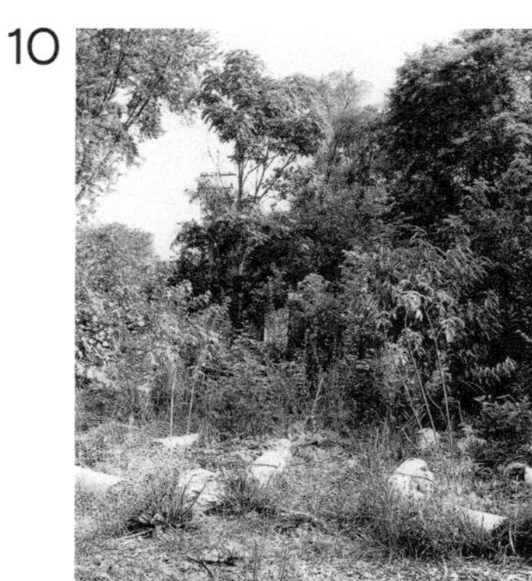

Beaverland Farms (Elderberry Trees), 2016

Brightmoor Neighborhood

Beaverland Farms is a small-scale agroforestry project in Brightmoore Detroit. It was founded in 2015 by Brittney Rooney and Kieran Neal as a self-sustaining homestead and a farming testing ground. Unlike many other urban gardens, which often grow kale, squash, and other summer vegetables, they started growing perennial plants, which will grow back every year, and crops that are rich in calories and easy to store such as potatoes, corn, and cereals. The beds are planted in such a way that successive crops can be harvested over several years with very little effort. Berry bushes will form living fences and a few years from now fruit and nut trees will provide shade and save water. When I visited the farm again in 2018, the experimental field had been adapted for more commercial usage. Brittney and Kieran had founded a company with a holistic farm management in which profitability, quality of life, and sustainable conservation of the land have equal priority. In addition to their market stand they also supply restaurants with vegetables.

The photographs are from 2016. Picture 10 shows small elderberry trees planted in recycled paper tubes. Picture 24 shows car tires that were lying around in the neighborhood and are now used to grow quinoa plants. In picture 61 a newly planted vegetable field is being irrigated.

www.beaverlandfarms.com

For Beaverland Farms and Brightmoor see also
→ 24 Beaverland Farms (Quinoa), 2016
→ 61 Beaverland Farms, 2016
→ 21 14409 Burgess Street (Pray Hope and Don't Worry), 2016
→ 62 Beaverland Street (Neighbors Building Brightmoor), 2015

11

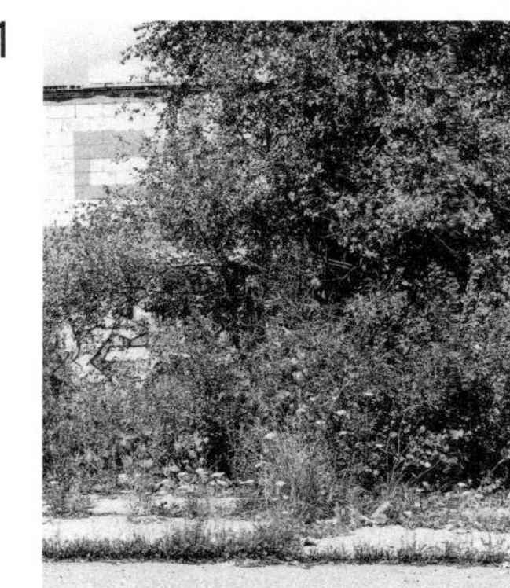

12

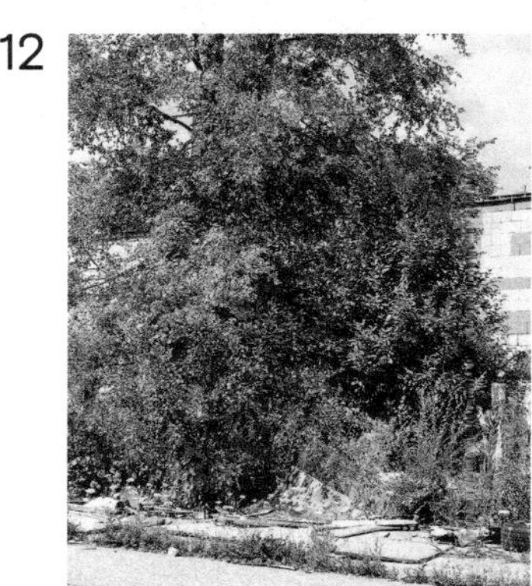

East Palmer Street (Balsam Poplar), 2015

Gratiot Town / Kettering Neighborhood

Both pictures show a balsam poplar tree, overgrown with vines and flanked by goldenrods, common milkweed, wild carrot, and a small Siberian elm. The balsam poplar is also called hackmatack or tacamahac poplar. Both names come from the indigenous Algonquian language. They refer to a dense forest or the resin of the balsam poplar.

In 2018, three years after I took these pictures, the flat building in the background had been painted over and all the plants had been removed. Only the balsam poplar tree was still there. The tree is located next to the Packard Automotive Plant.

→ 6/7 6437 East Palmer Street, 2015
→ 27/29 Packard Automotive Plant, 2015

The belief that an industrial country has to concentrate its industries is not, in my opinion, well-founded. That is only a stage in industrial development. ... Industry will decentralize.

Henry Ford (1924). My Life and Work, 191–193

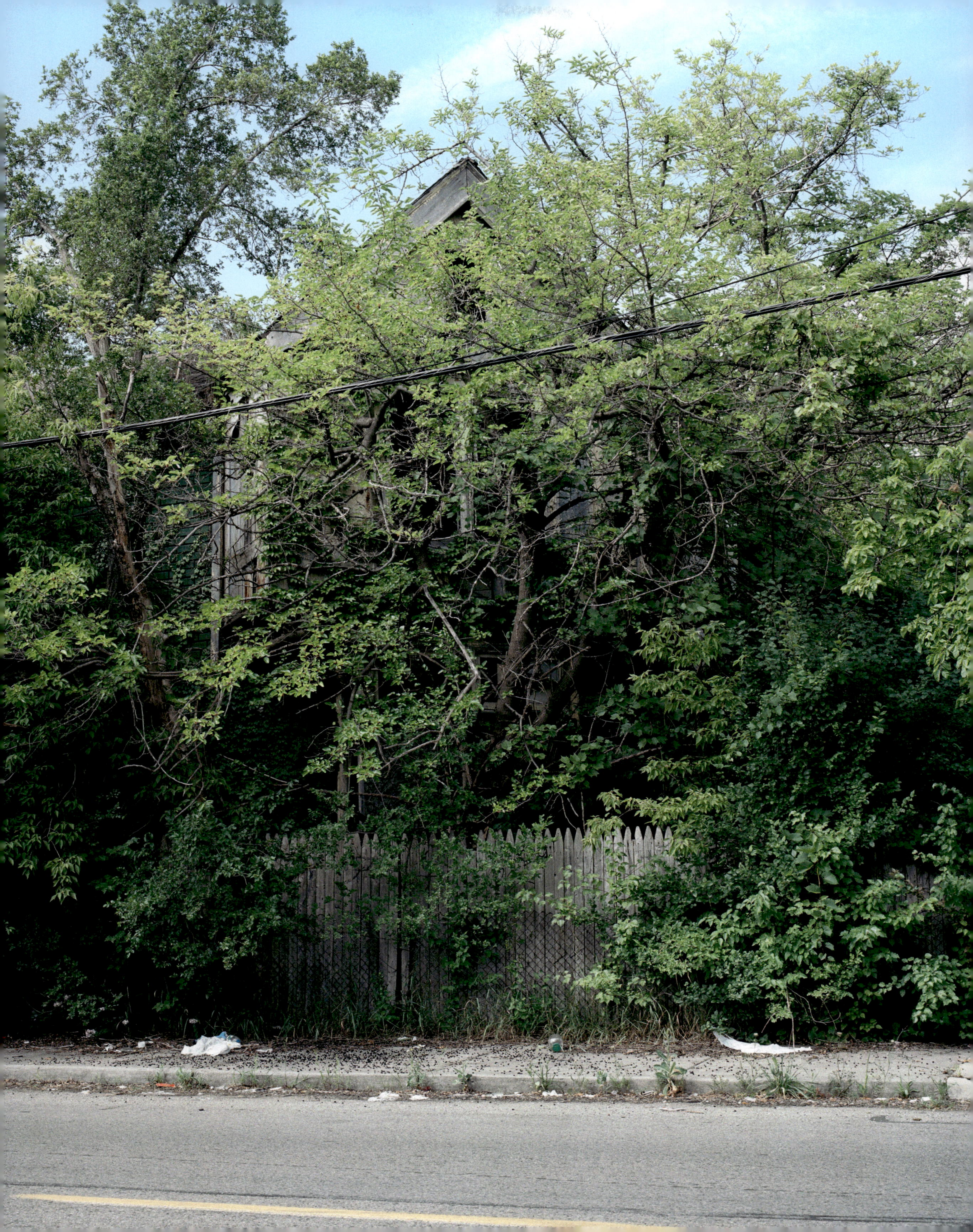

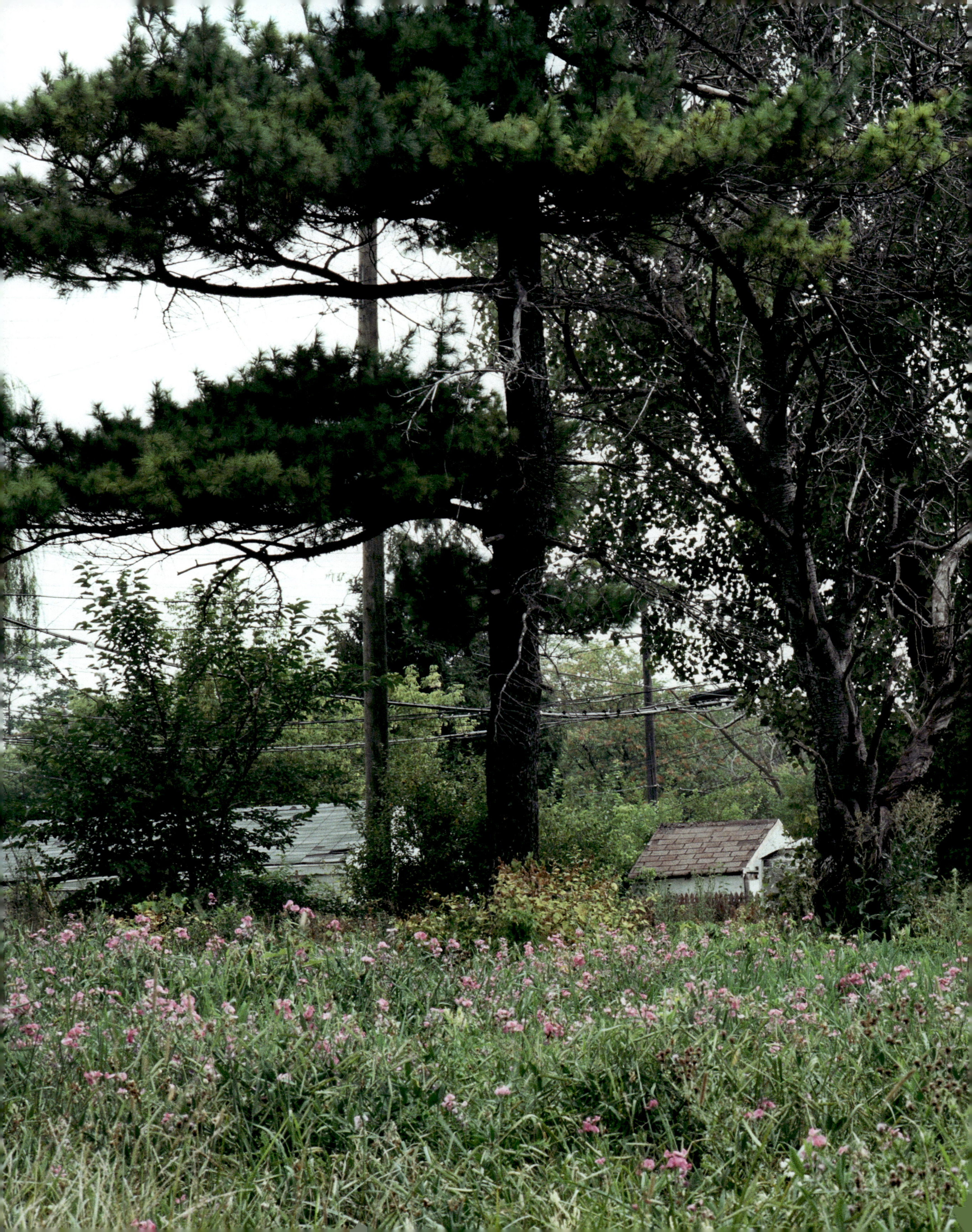

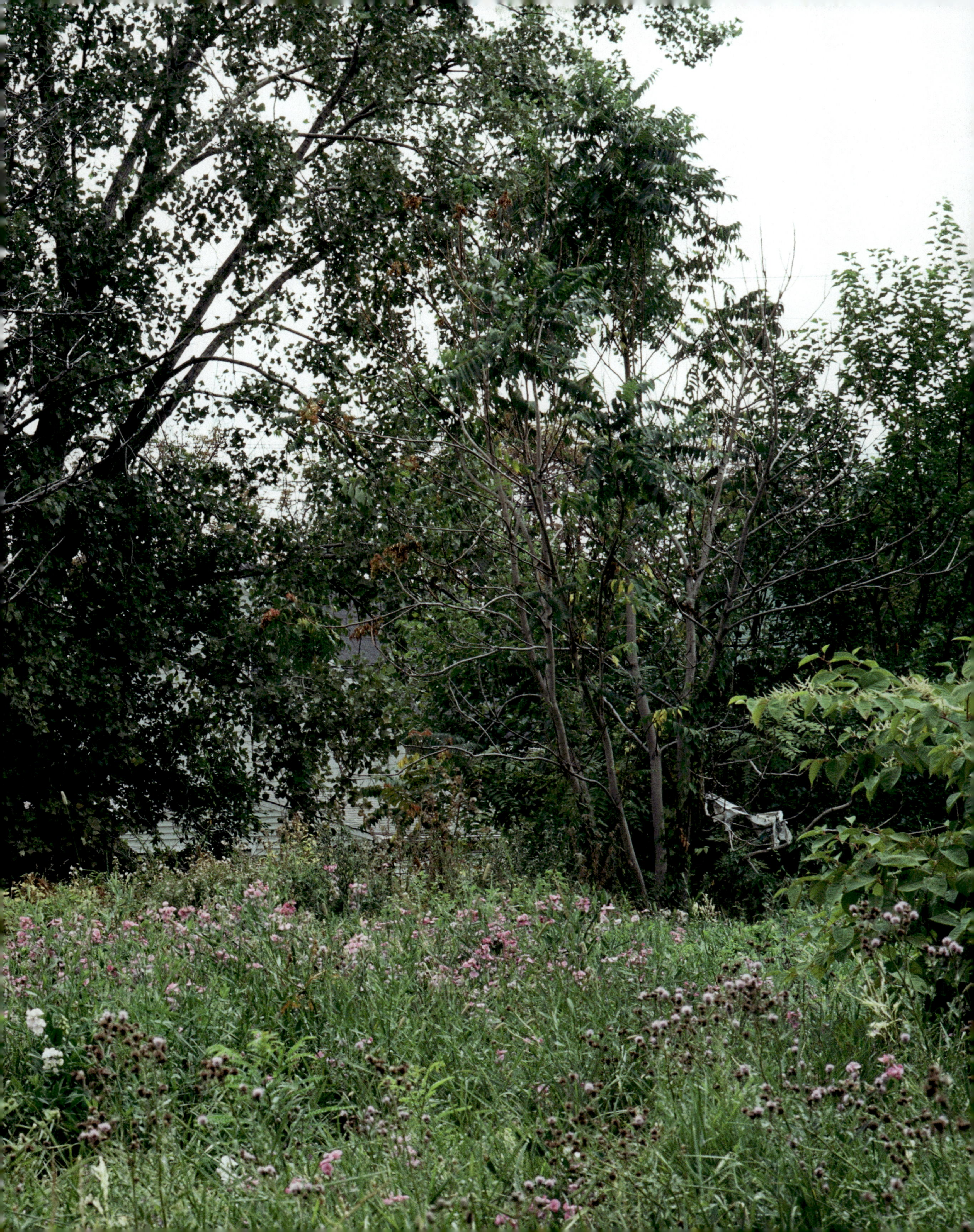

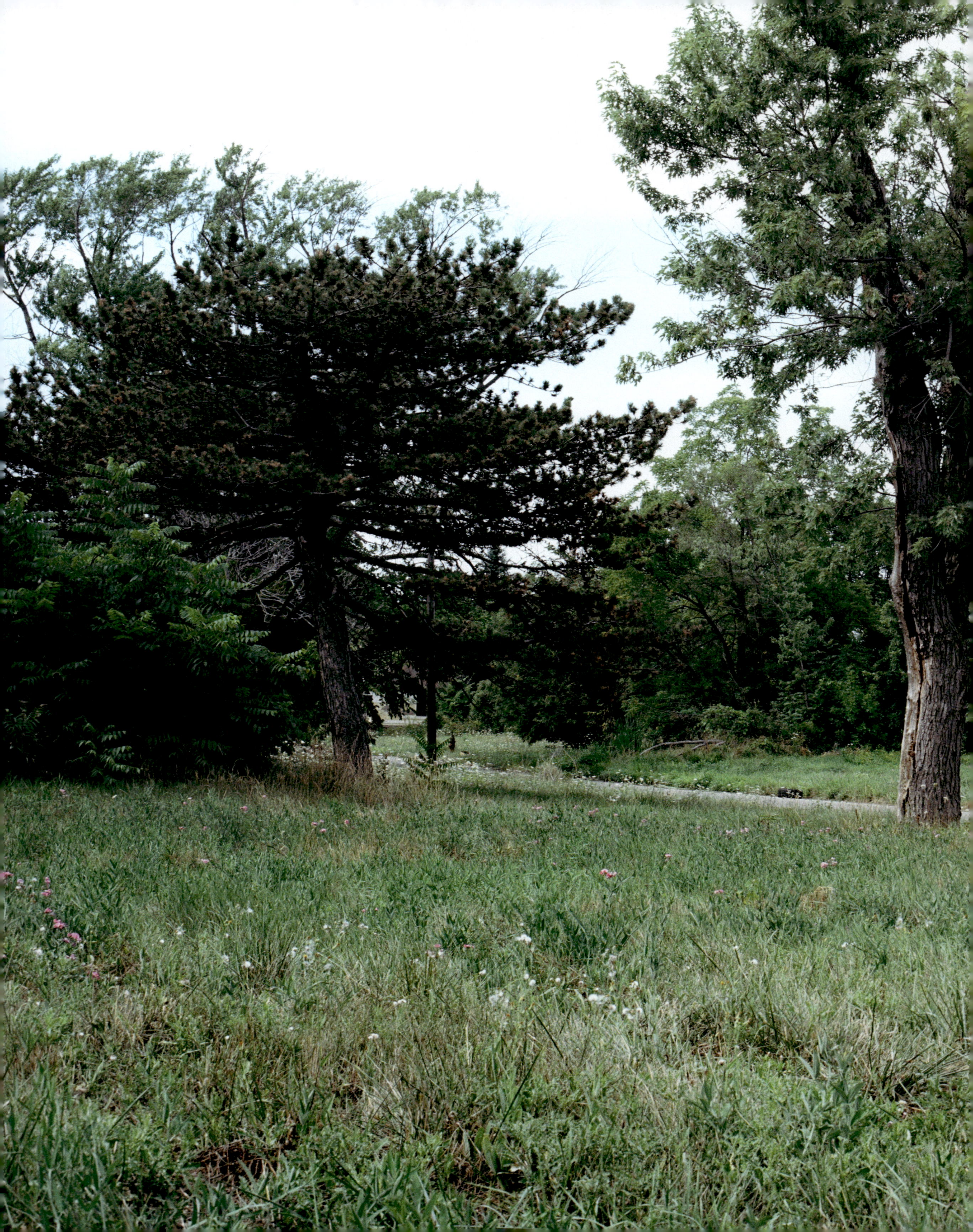

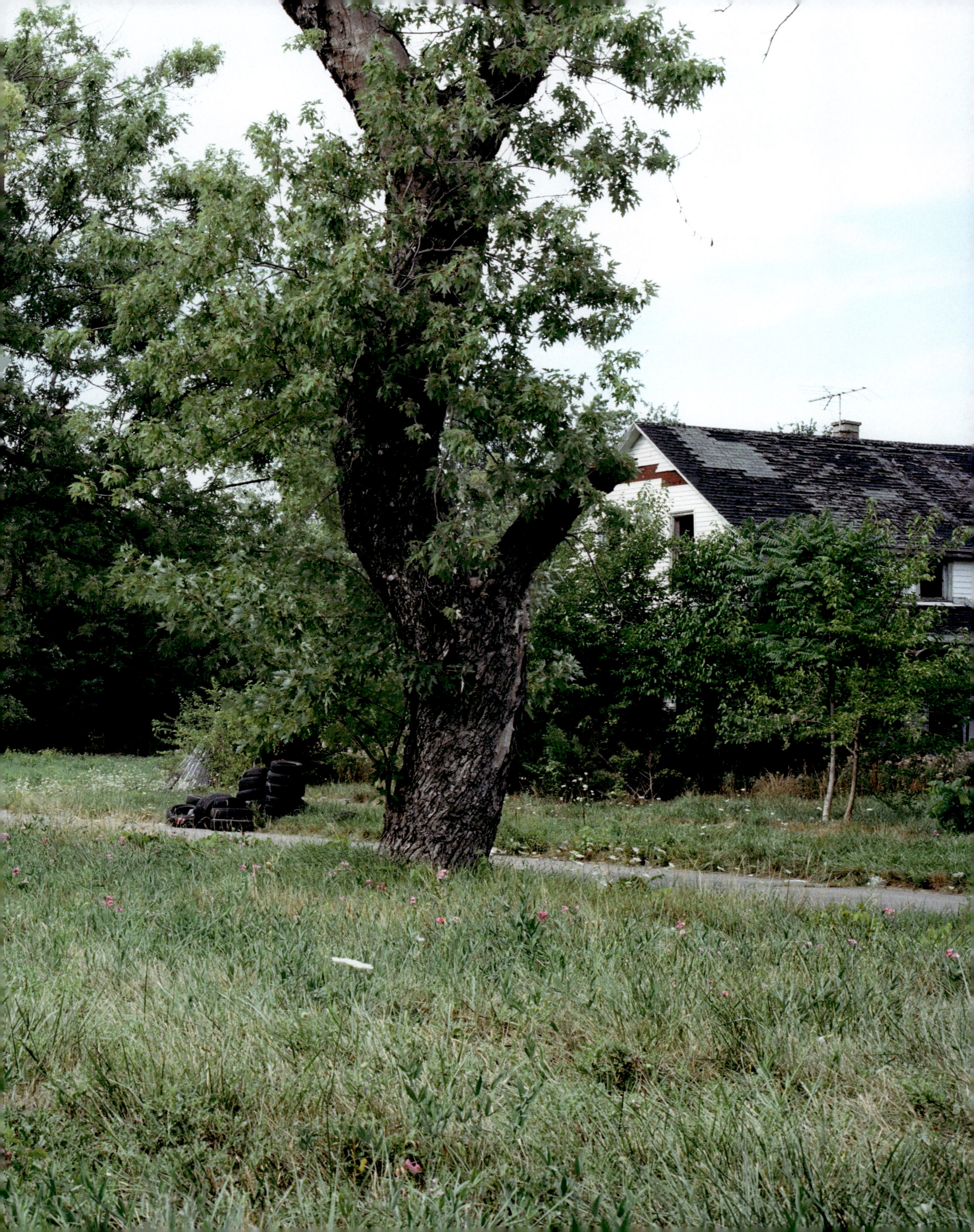

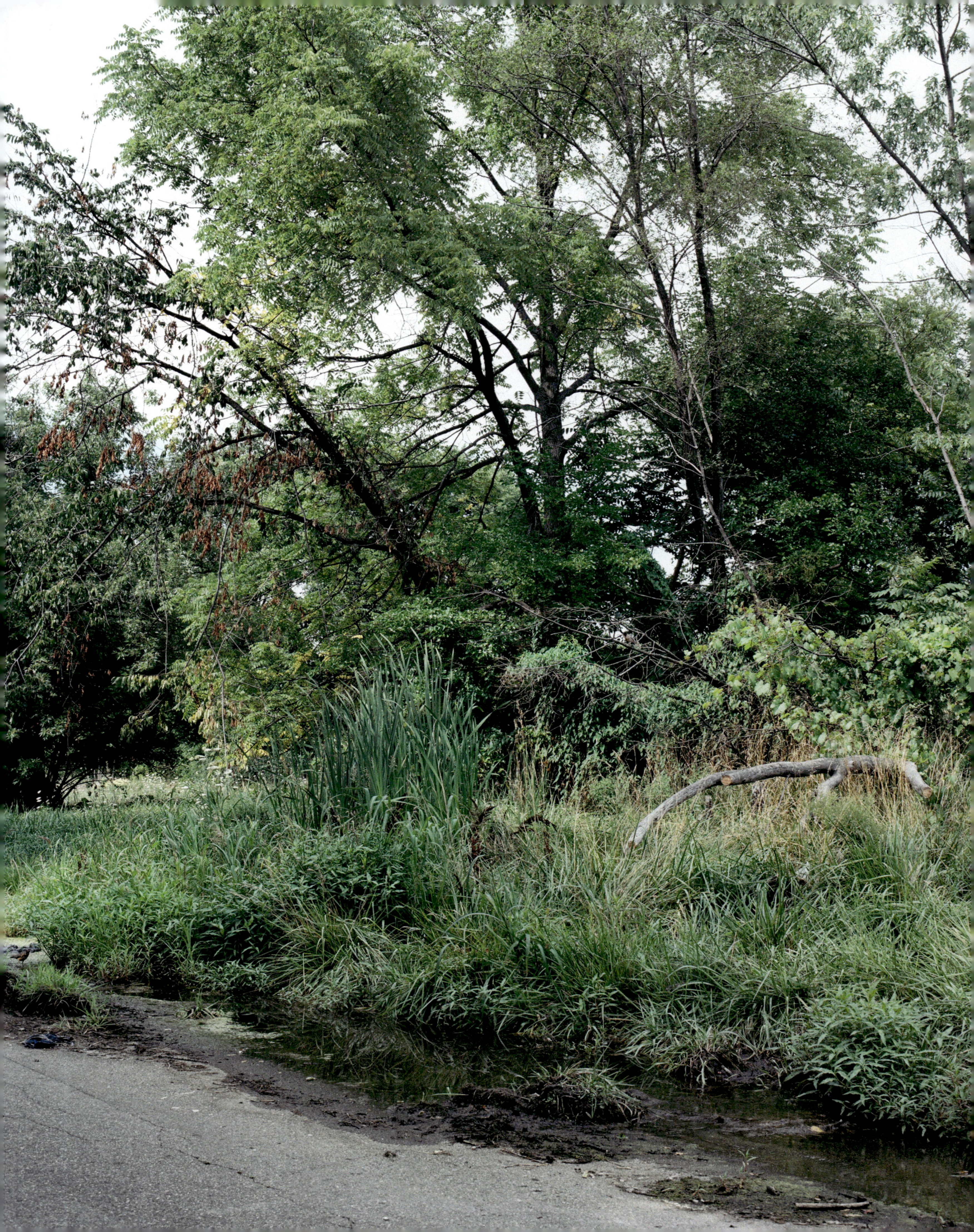

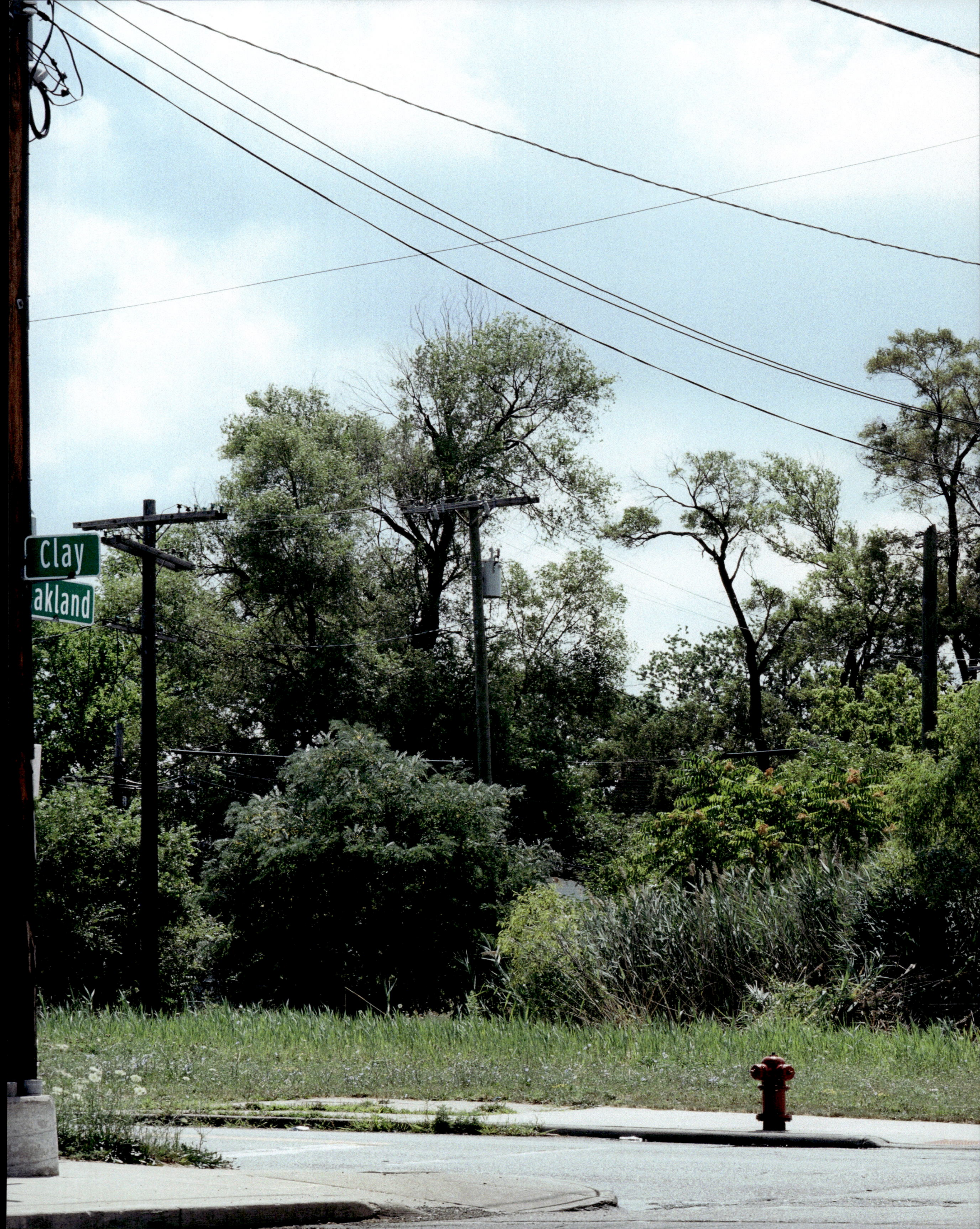
Clay
akland

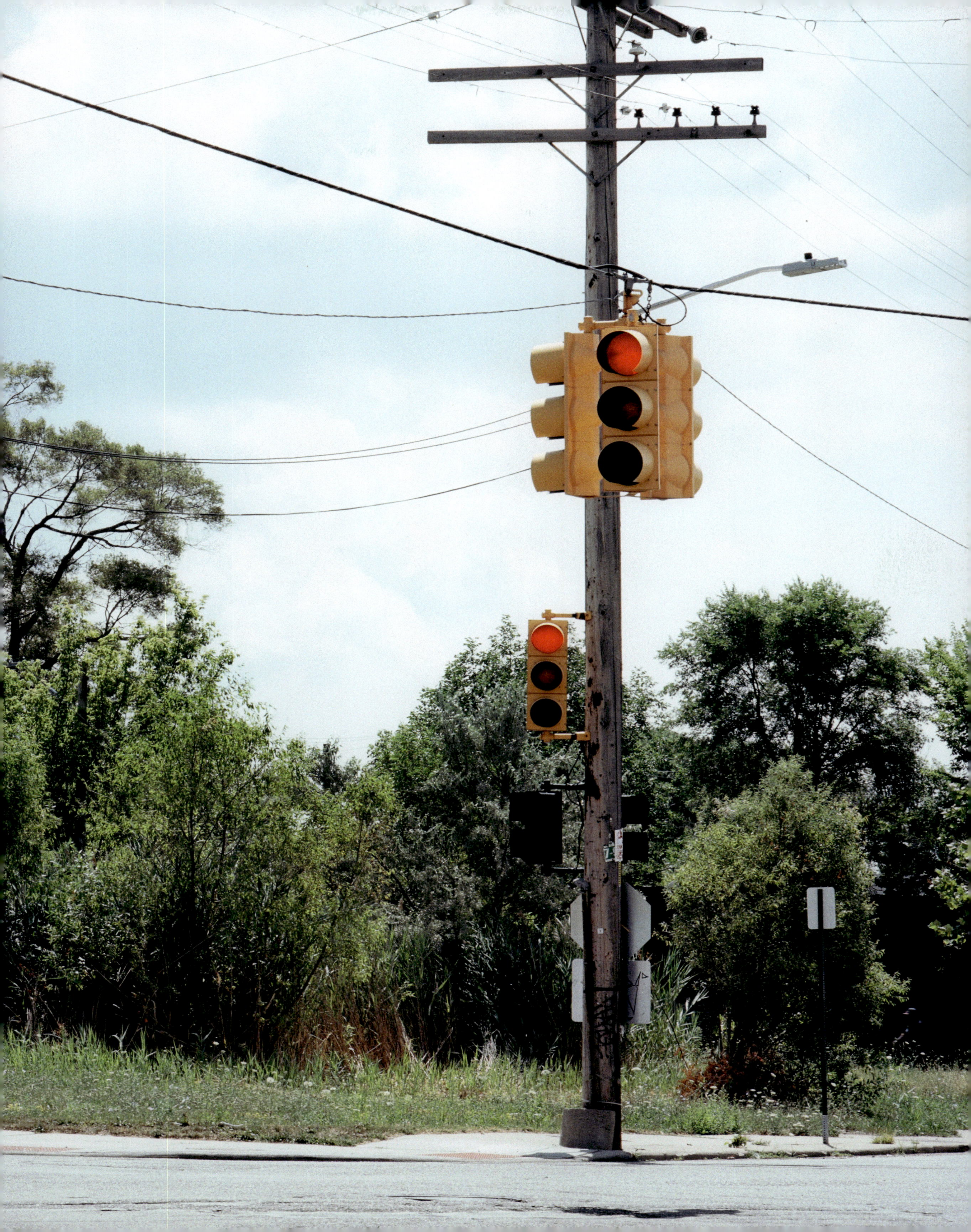

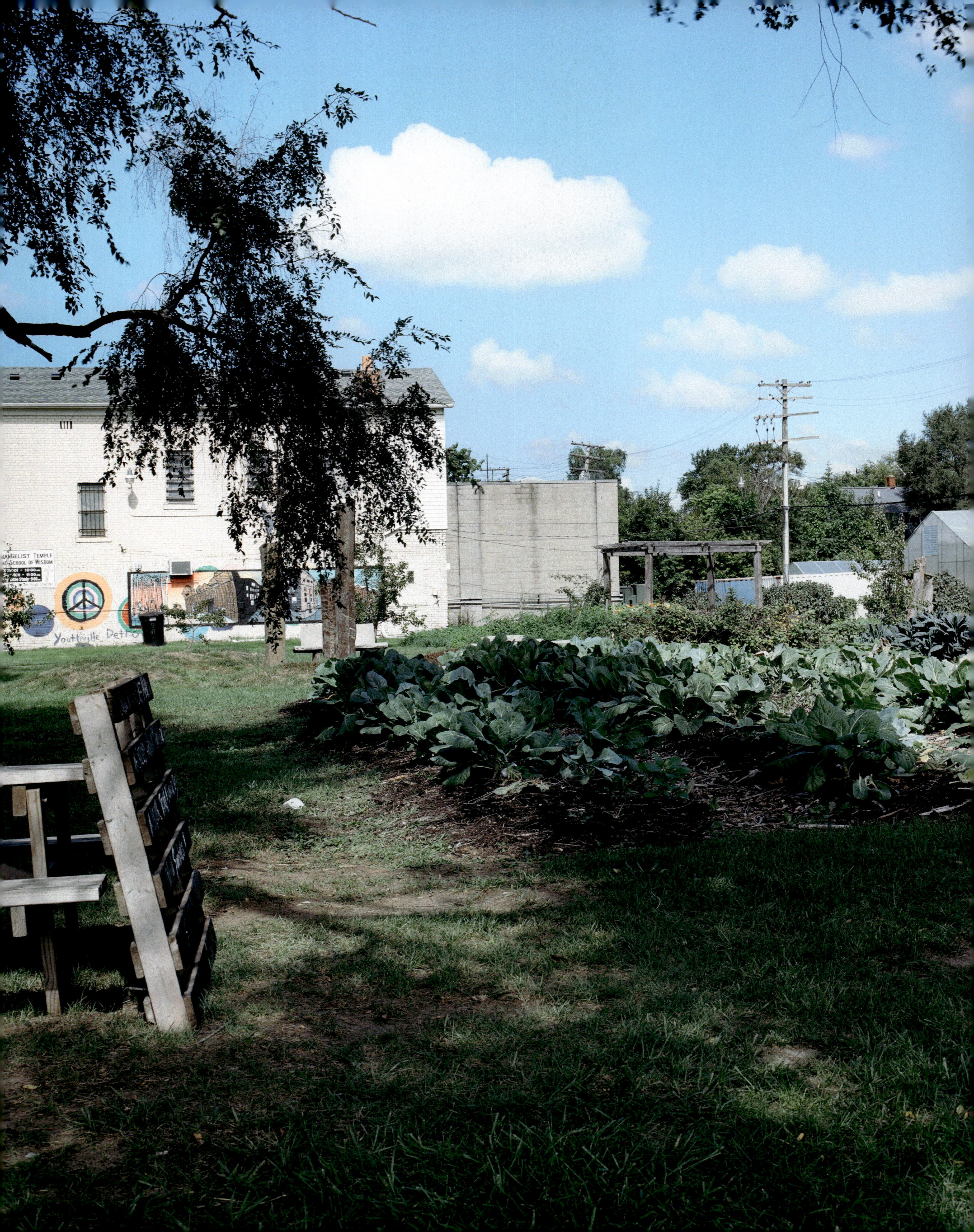
ANGELIST TEMPLE
SCHOOL OF WISDOM
School - 10:00
Service - 11:00
Youthville Detro

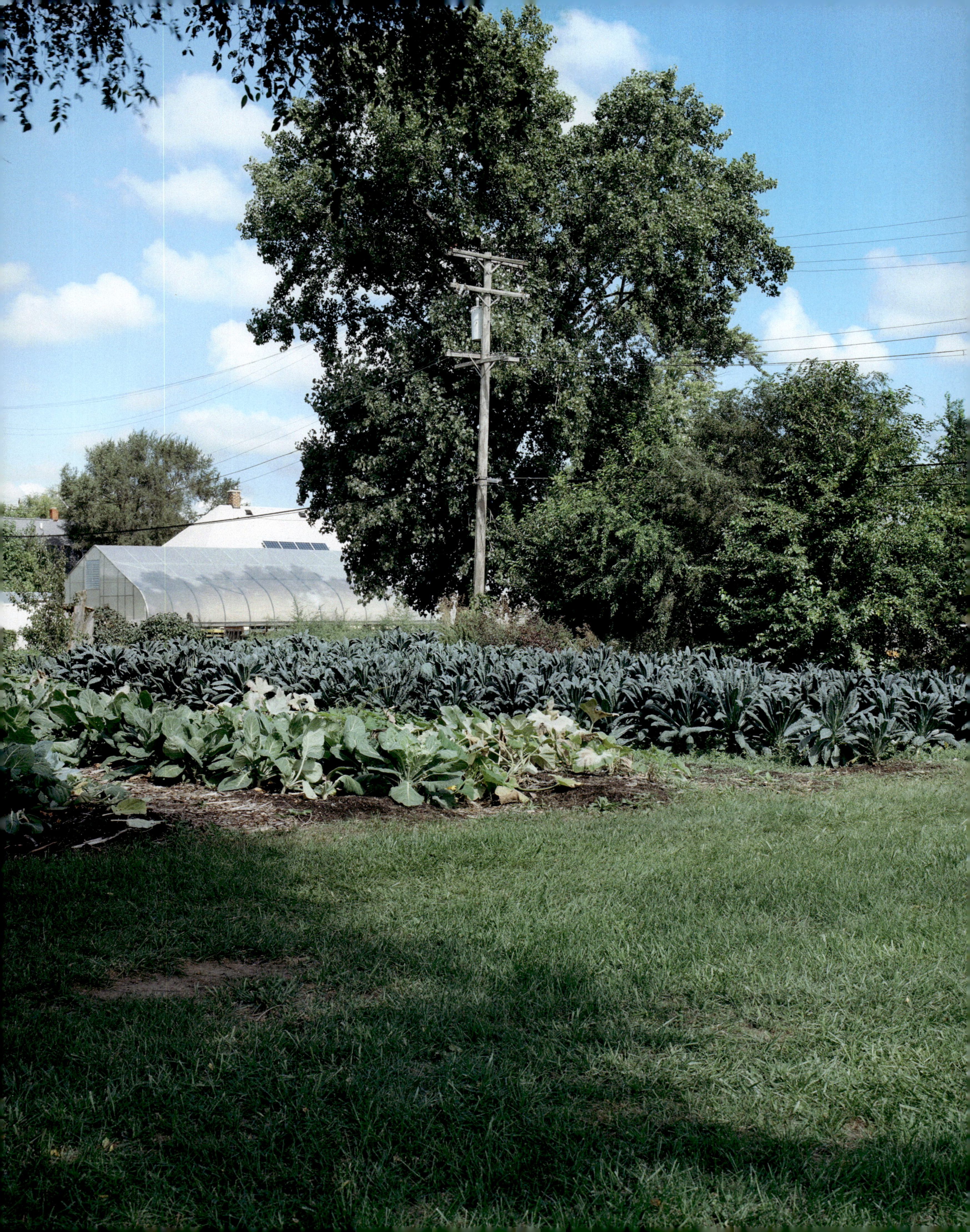

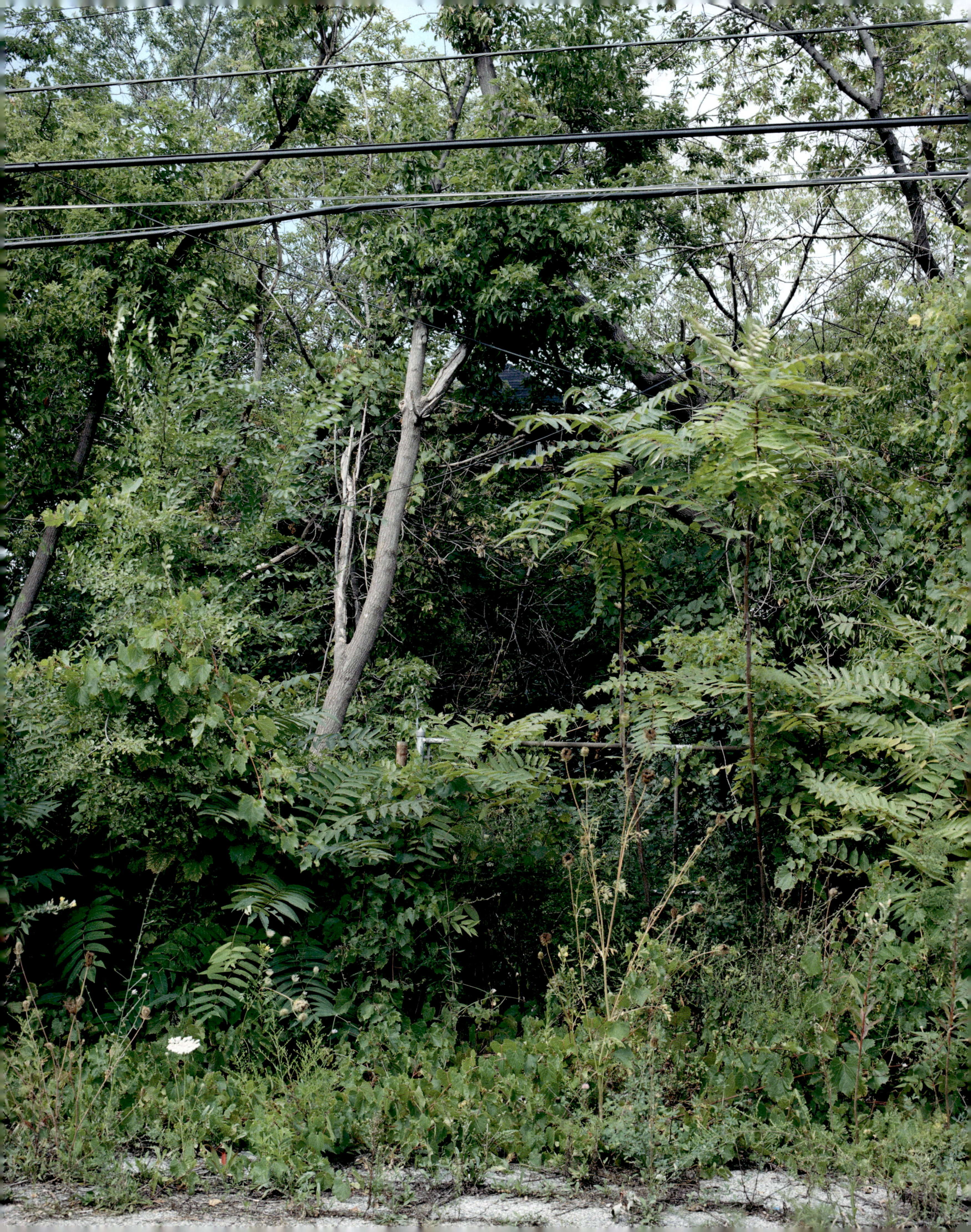

Deindustrialization does not just happen. Conscious decisions have to be made by corporate managers to move a factory from one location to another, to buy up a going concern or to dispose of one, or to shut-down a facility altogether. These things never happen automatically nor are they simply a passive response to mysterious market forces. The planning behind such decisions is usually intricate, often costly, and extensive.

Harry Bluestone / Bennet Harrison (1982). The Deindustrialization of America, 15

13

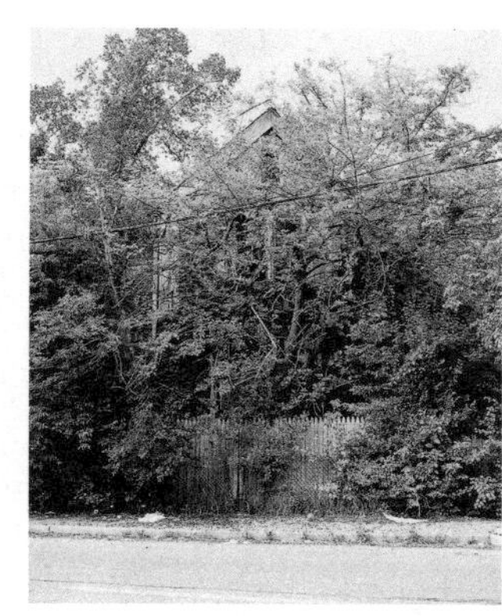

456 Harper Avenue, 2016

Medbury Park Neighborhood

Behind maple ash, Siberian elm, red mulberry, and crabapple trees stands a multi-family home, built in 1903 within sight of Henry Ford's first car work-shop and the Fisher Body Plant 21. The dense mix of factories, work-shops, single-family homes, churches, and diners is very typical of the first industrialized urban districts, and can still be seen in neighborhoods like Medbury Park, Milwaukee Junction, or Gratiot Town / Kettering.

The lot is owned by the Detroit Land Bank Authority. Several real estate websites advertise it as an amazing development opportunity. The property is situated in walking distance from upcoming areas like New Center or North End and the newly build QLine tram, a streetcar line that runs along Woodward Avenue, is nearby. This mostly privately funded tram line is only one mile long and connects New Center, Midtown, and Downtown.

Public streetcars had been intro-duced very early in Detroit—the first one in 1863, which was originally horse drawn. By the 1920s the inner-city railway network was 187 miles long and connected every city district, the downtown area, and such suburbs as Royal Oak. In the 1950s the last line was discontinued when the Motor City became a city of car owners. Today the public transportation system is made up entirely of buses.

14

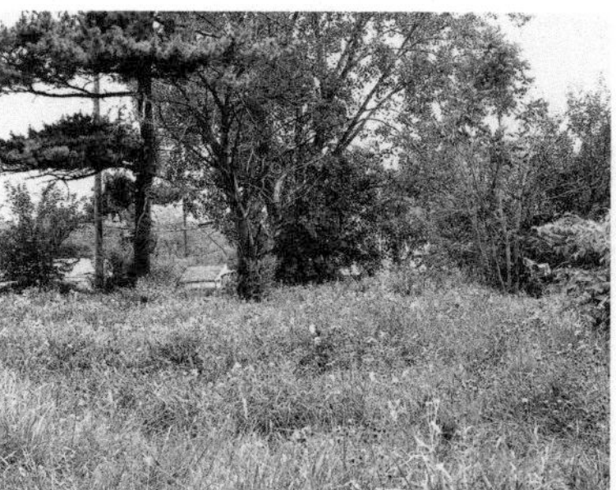

East Ferry Street, 2015

Poletown East Neighborhood

This picture shows two empty lots in the Poletown East neighborhood. Everlasting pea and spotted knapweed bloom in front of a black pine and poplars in the background. While I was taking pictures a neighbor mowed his front lawn.

The Poletown neighborhood was developed from 1870 on farmland, framed between two newly built rail-way lines. By 1900, 48,000 people had already moved here—many of them European immigrants, mostly of Polish descent. Poletown experienced its heyday shortly before the Great De-pression. Numerous factory workers found work at the neighboring auto-mobile plants of Packard, Dodge, Ford, Chrysler, Studebaker, or Fisher. The streets were lined with churches, shops, small restaurants, and the typical two-story framehouses with their small gardens. In 1955, the construction of the Ford Edsel Freeway (part of Inter-state 94) divided the neighborhood in two. The northern half was expropri-ated and demolished in 1981 for a new General Motors plant (see description to pictures 1/2). The southern part is still sparsely populated and resembles an urban prairie in many places.

→ 1/2 2550 East Grand Boulevard, 2015
→ 41 5721 Dubois Street, 2015

15

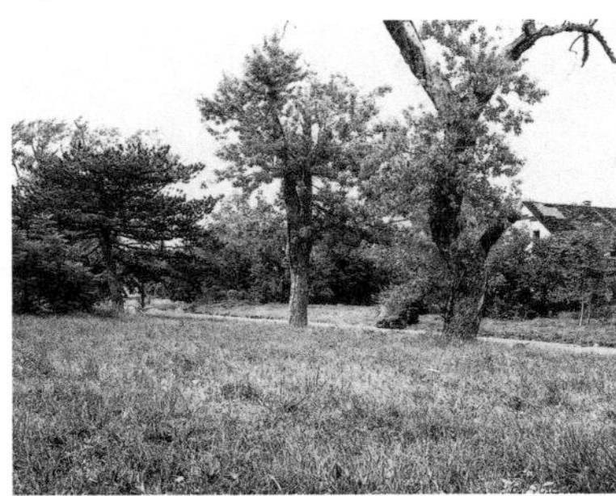

Eastlawn Street (Tires), 2016

Riverbend Neighborhood

Along Eastlawn Street in the Riverbend neighborhood only a few houses remain along a stretch of several blocks, and very few of these are inhabited. The area resembles a rural landscape intersected by streets. The overgrown house in the background was built in 1915. It was re-sided in 2009 but has been empty since 2011. Many vacant lots in Detroit are used to dispose of boats or, as in this case, car tires.

→ 44 Eastlawn and Lakeview Streets (Burned Down House), 2016

16

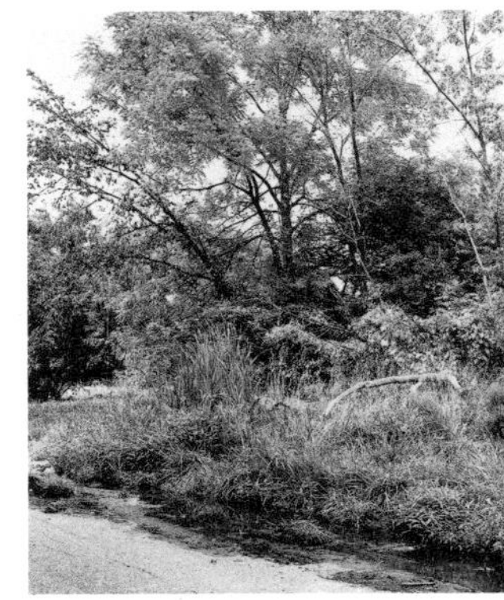

3034 Eastlawn Street (Water Leak), 2016

Riverbend Neighborhood

As described in picture 15, Eastlawn Street resembles a rural setting. Between Jefferson and Warren Avenue most residential houses have already been demolished. The picture shows a runlet on the side of the road. As water-loving plants, water reed, lady's thumb, and various willow herbs have established themselves in this new habitat. Many of the thousands of vacant lots and houses in Detroit still have running water. When pipes burst it leaks out unchecked, at considerable cost to the city.

These leaks are contrasted by so-called water shutoffs. Since Detroit's bankruptcy in 2013, more than 100,000 private households have had their water turned off temporarily, even after short delays in the payment of their water bills. "People were given no warning and had no time to fill bathtubs and buckets, leaving everyone, including sick people, without water to drink, without toilets, without the ability to bathe and cook."° To this day, these measures mainly affect low-income households, single parents, senior citizens, and families with children, as Detroit does not only have high unemployment but also one of the most expensive water rates in the entire United States.

° Apel (2015). Beautiful Terrible Ruins, 31

→ 17 908 Clay Street (Water Leak), 2016

17

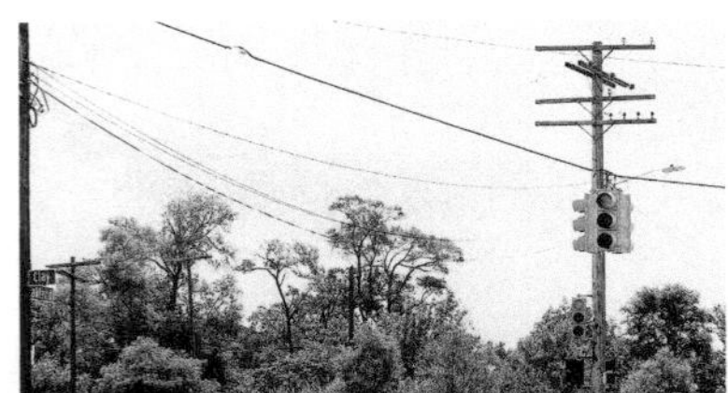

908 Clay Street (Water Leak), 2016

North End Neighborhood

This corner lot is on Oakland Avenue, about a mile from downtown Detroit. A brick building from the 1920s was demolished here in 2009. Ever since, water has been leaking from the sewer system (clearly visible on Google Maps Streetview). Over the years a wetland area with common reed and different willows has developed. As described in picture 16, the unhindered water leakages from uninhabited properties are in stark contrast to the water shutoffs. Since 2015, the Improve Detroit mobile app helps report water leaks on empty properties to the Department of Public Works.

→ 16 3034 Eastlawn Street (Water Leak), 2016

Water Shutoffs
Detroit Bancruptcy

Detroit suffers from the highest poverty levels in the country. At the same time, Detroiters face some of the highest water rates in the country. Detroiters also face the highest property taxes in the state and some of the highest rates in the country. Moreover, the city made little effort to adjust property taxes in the wake of the Great Recession, leading to situations in which back taxes often exceeded the market value of the home. It is expensive to live in a poor city.

Peter Hammer (2017). Detroit 1967 and Today: Spatial Racism and Ongoing Cycles of Oppression, 280

18

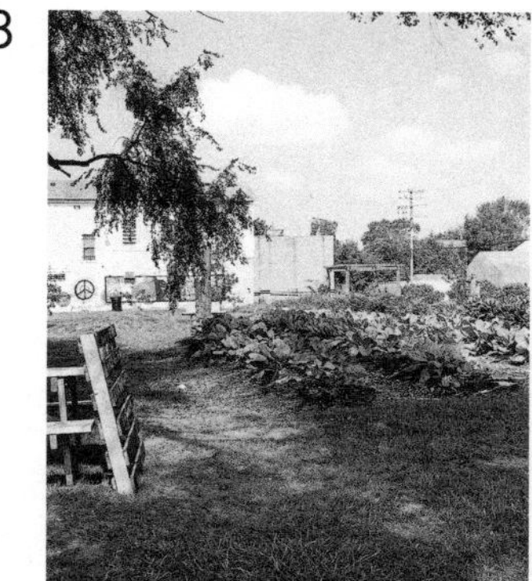

19

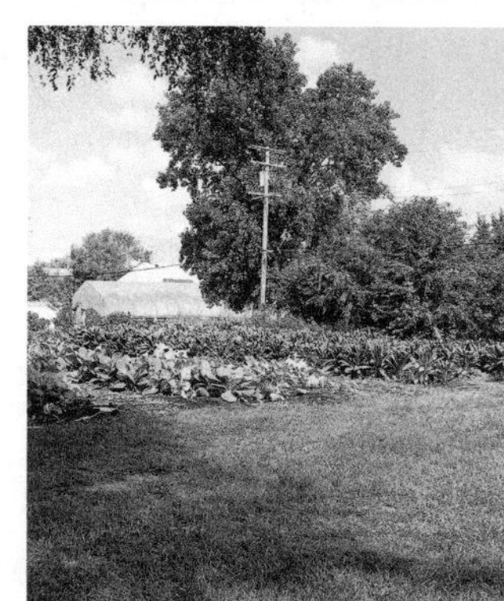

Oakland Avenue Urban Farm, 2016

North End Neighborhood

In 1999, Reverend Bertha L. Carter started to distribute food from the back of her van to homeless people in her neighborhood. In the following year, she founded the North End Christian Community Development Corporation which runs the Oakland Avenue Urban Farm program. Sustainable and self-determined neighborhood development is the farm's mission. The urban agriculture initiative does not only provide the basis for food security, it also serves to create youth education programs and job opportunities for the majority African-American community. The farm grew out of an urban garden planted by Jerry Ann Hebron and the Youth Making a Difference program at the location seen in both pictures. In addition to the production of fresh food, the farm hosts one of the Detroit Community Markets and organizes cultural events like Garden on the Plate dinners or outdoor art shows. It is well connected to several other farming programs and initiatives throughout the city and is part of the Detroit Food Policy Council. When I visited in 2016 and 2018, the farm was managed by Jerry Ann and Bill Hebron, local residents, and volunteers.

The North End neighborhood borders on the now demolished Paradise Valley neighborhood to the north and Oakland Avenue is one of its main thoroughfares.

www.oaklandurbanfarm.org

→ 46 Oakland Avenue Urban Farm (Lacinato Kale), 2016

Detroit has served as a metaphor for much that is wrong in America during the second half of the twentieth century, just as it once served as a metaphor for much that was positive in America. But Detroit is much more than a metaphor. Detroit is a real place where real people live. Throughout this nation, Americans living in numerous cities and regions are facing the same problems that have beset Detroit.

Dan Georgakas / Marvin Surkin (1975). Detroit, I Do Mind Dying, 232

20 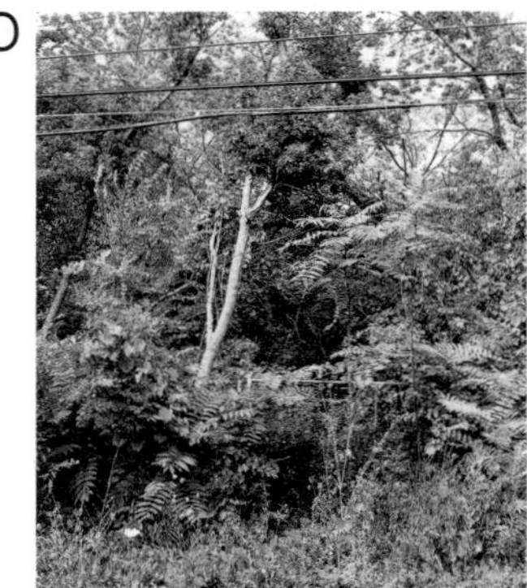

Ford Park (Ferris Street), 2015
Highland Park

"When I first came over, I worked at Fisher Bodies for three months. ... But then I went to Ford's—like everybody else ... Ye get the wages, but ye sell your soul at Ford's—ye're worked like a slave all day, sleep on a car comin' home. ... Ye've never get any security in your job."

English immigrant 1931 in: Wilson (1958), 219

Ford Park is located to the north of the former Ford Highland Park Plant, where Henry Ford revolutionized industrial production. In 1910, Ford had his first large factory built in the Highland Park community, because land was cheaper and taxes were lower there. The factory building was designed by Albert Kahn and commonly referred to as the "Crystal Palace" because of its innovative, large window fronts. It was here that in 1913 Ford introduced the moving Assembly Line — a system that still shapes industrial production and organization today. Skilled personnel could henceforth be replaced by unskilled workers who are cheaper and easily replaceable. Without fixed contracts and not used to the monotony of working on the assembly line, the workers frequently moved from one factory to another, so that in 1913 Ford hired more than 52,400 people to maintain a constant workforce of 14,000. As a consequence, in January 1914 the Five Dollar Day was introduced to great fanfare — a doubling of the daily wage to $5 with the intention of retaining workers. When sales dropped or when the machines were converted for the production of new car models, work was halted and the workers temporarily laid off. During such times Henry Ford recommended that the unemployed work in agriculture. After only 18 years, Ford moved car production to the Ford River Rouge Complex in the neighboring town of Dearborn.

A part of the Crystal Palace still stands today. What was once the site of the power plant and office buildings is now home to the low-price Model T Plaza shopping mall — named after Ford's most successful car model.

Assembly Line
Five Dollar Day
American Dream

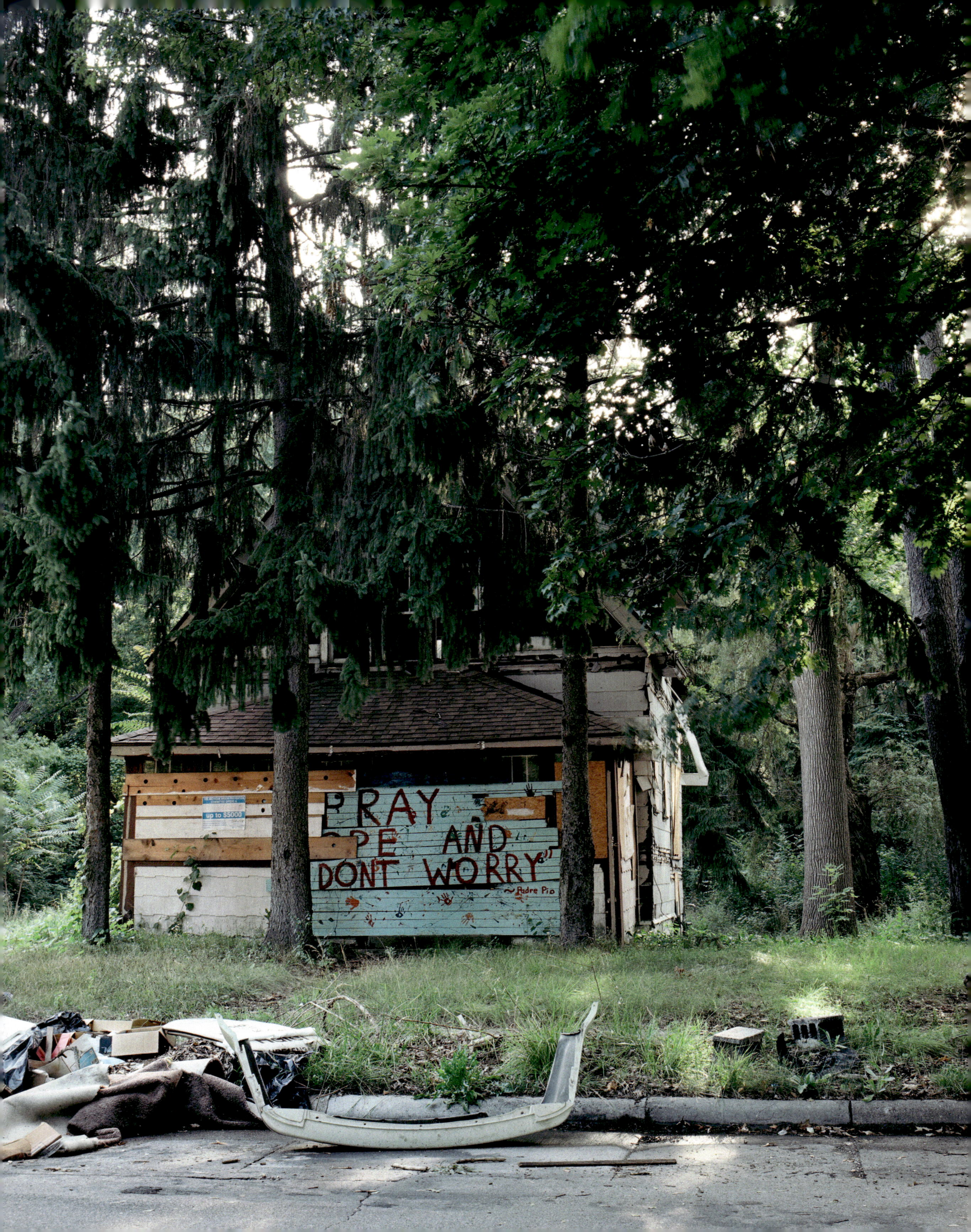
up to $5000
PRAY
PE AND
DONT WORRY"
~Padre Pio

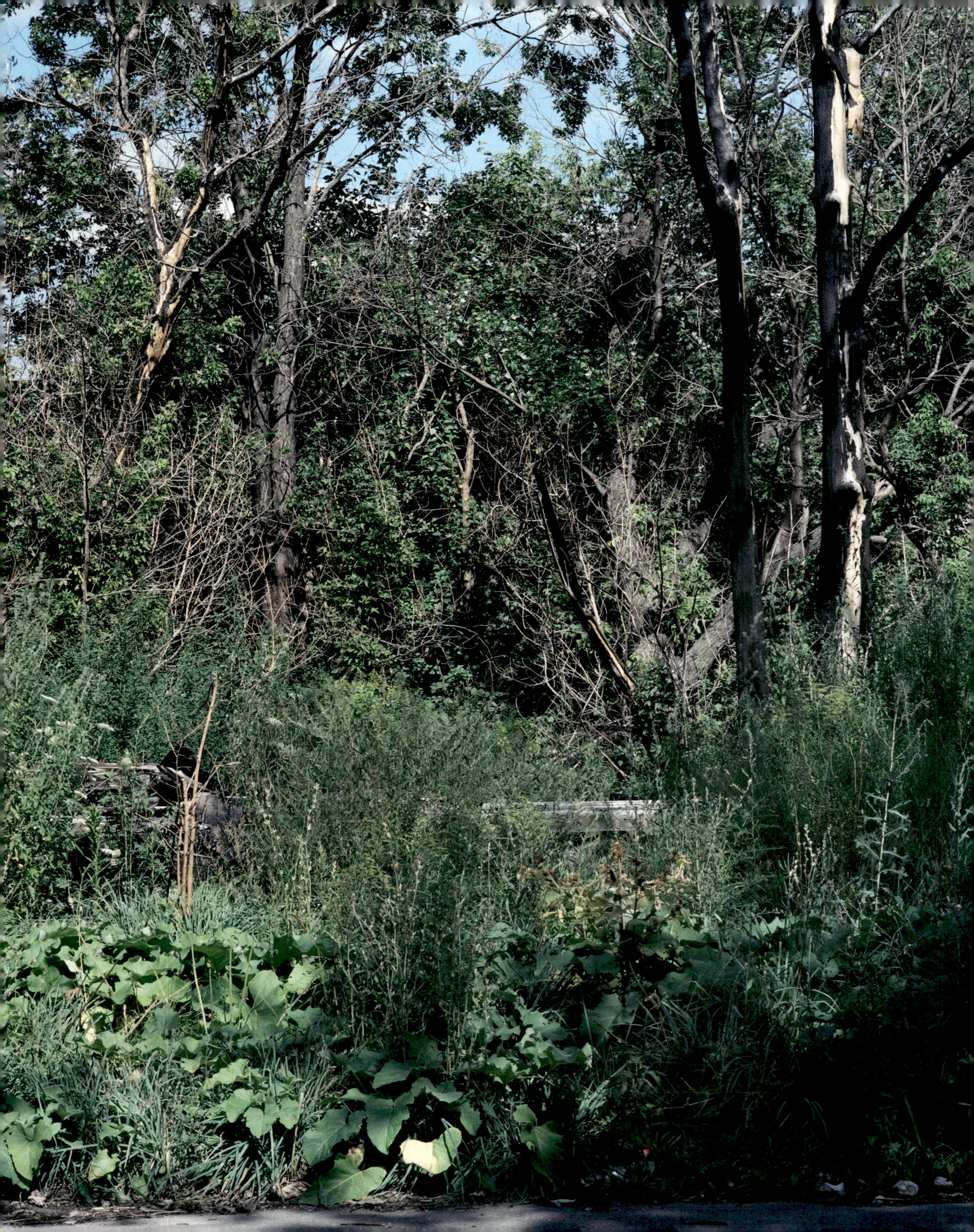

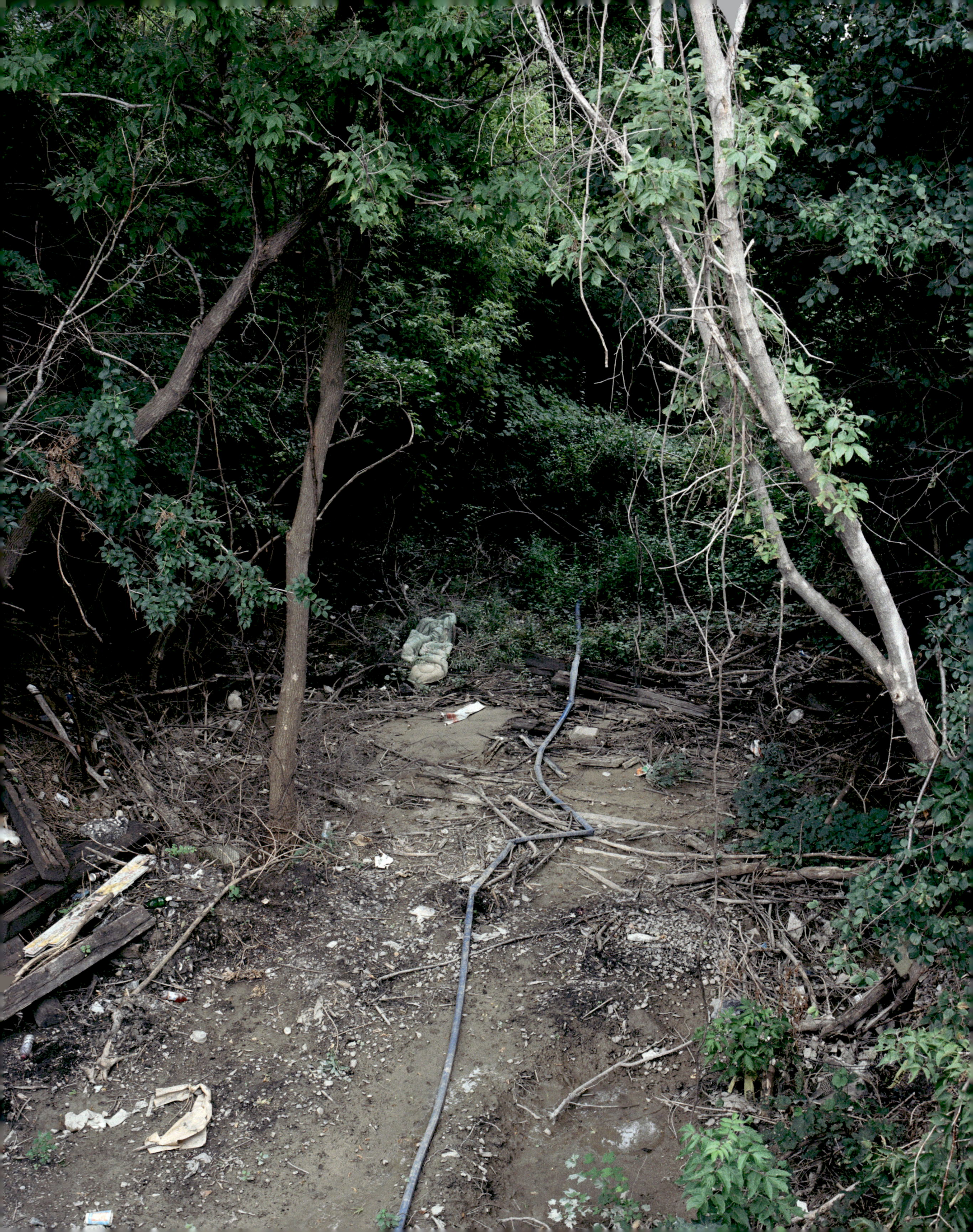

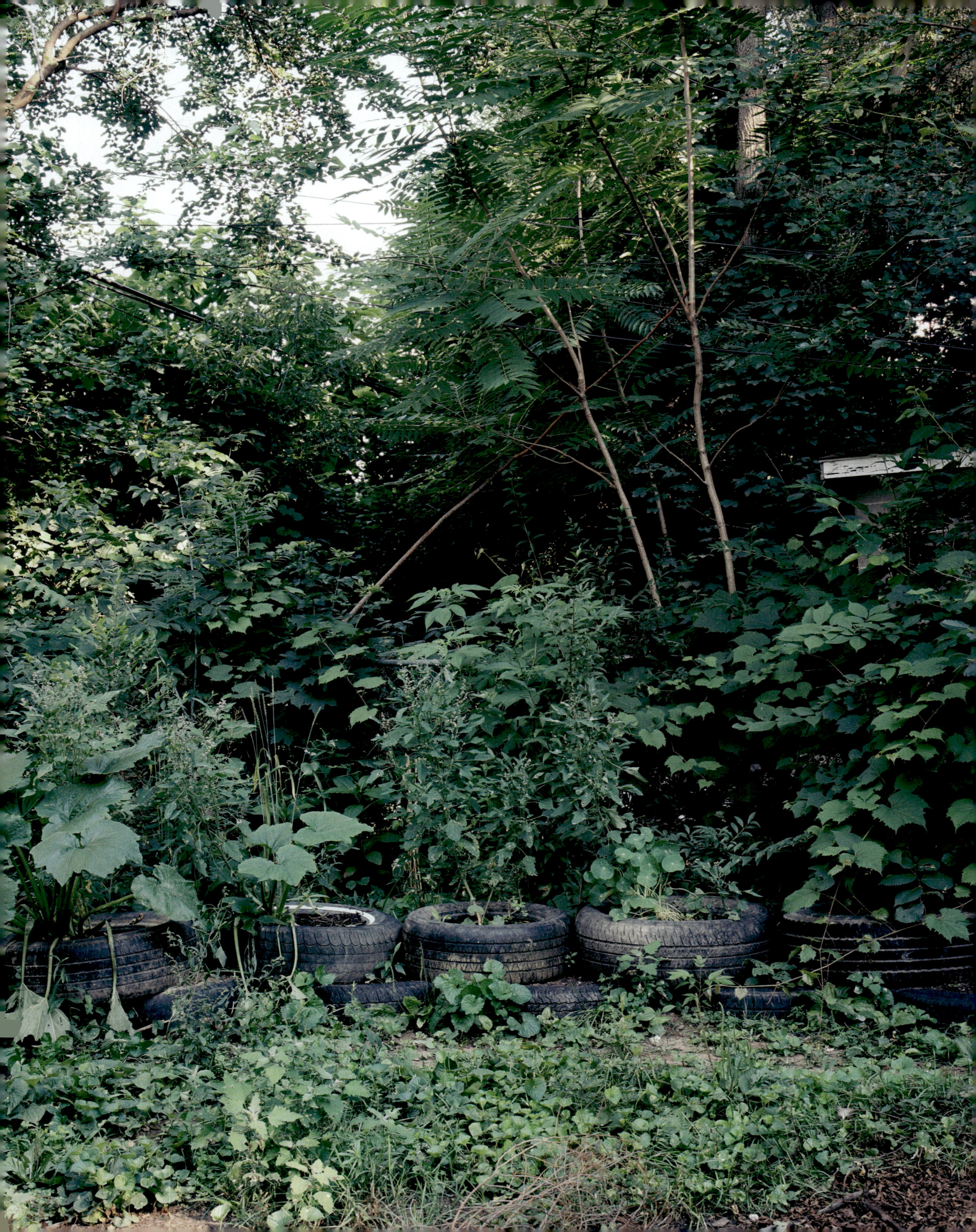

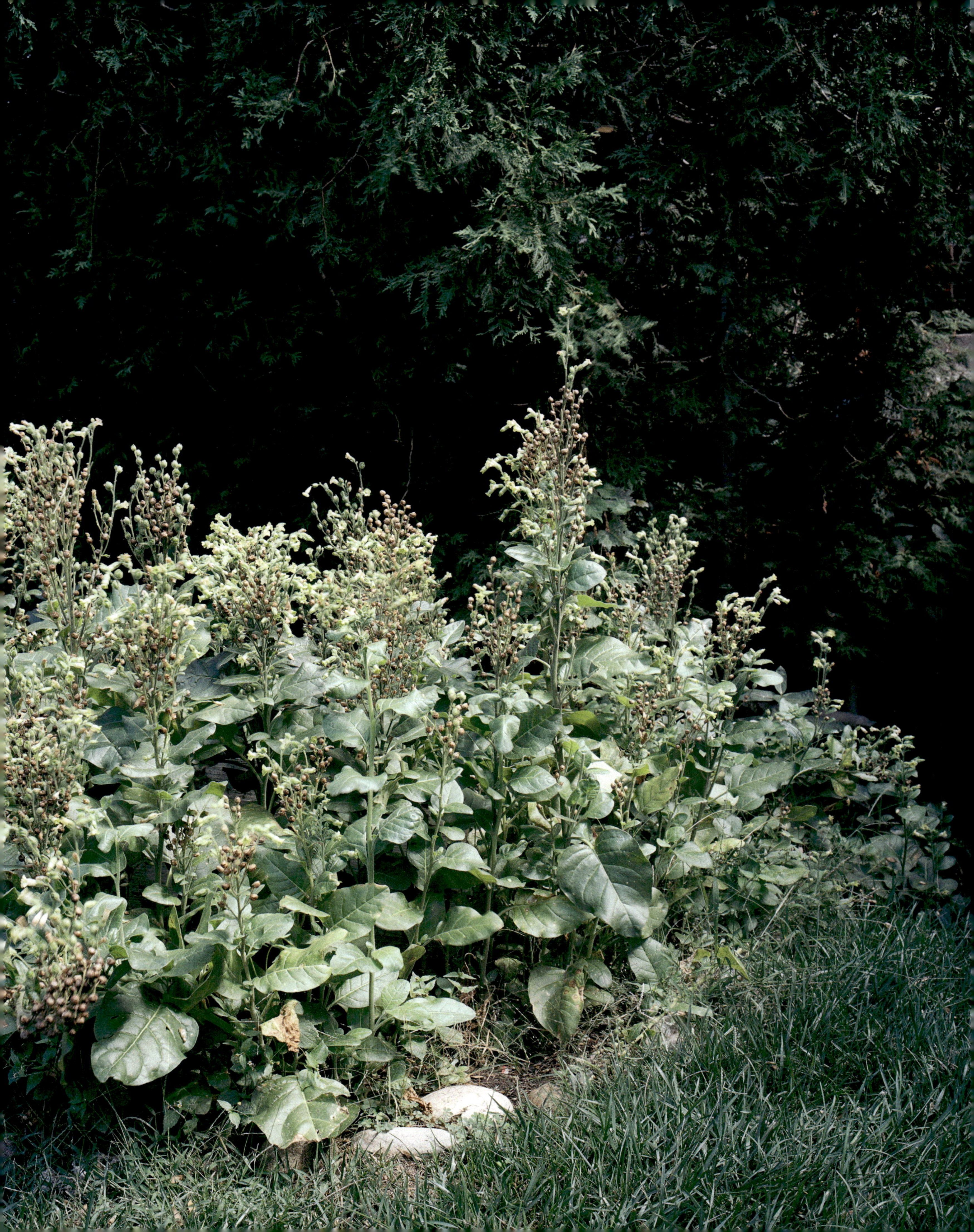

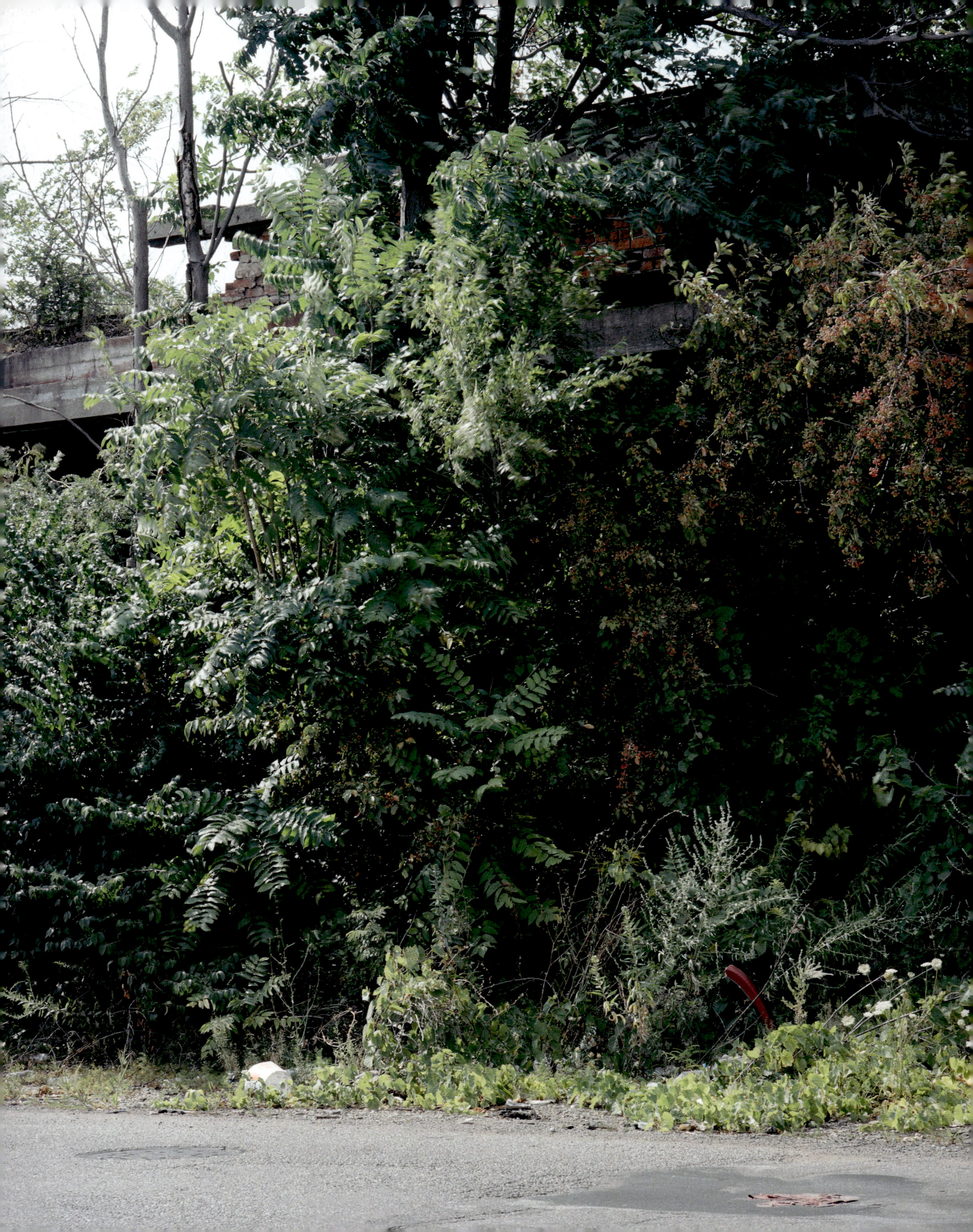

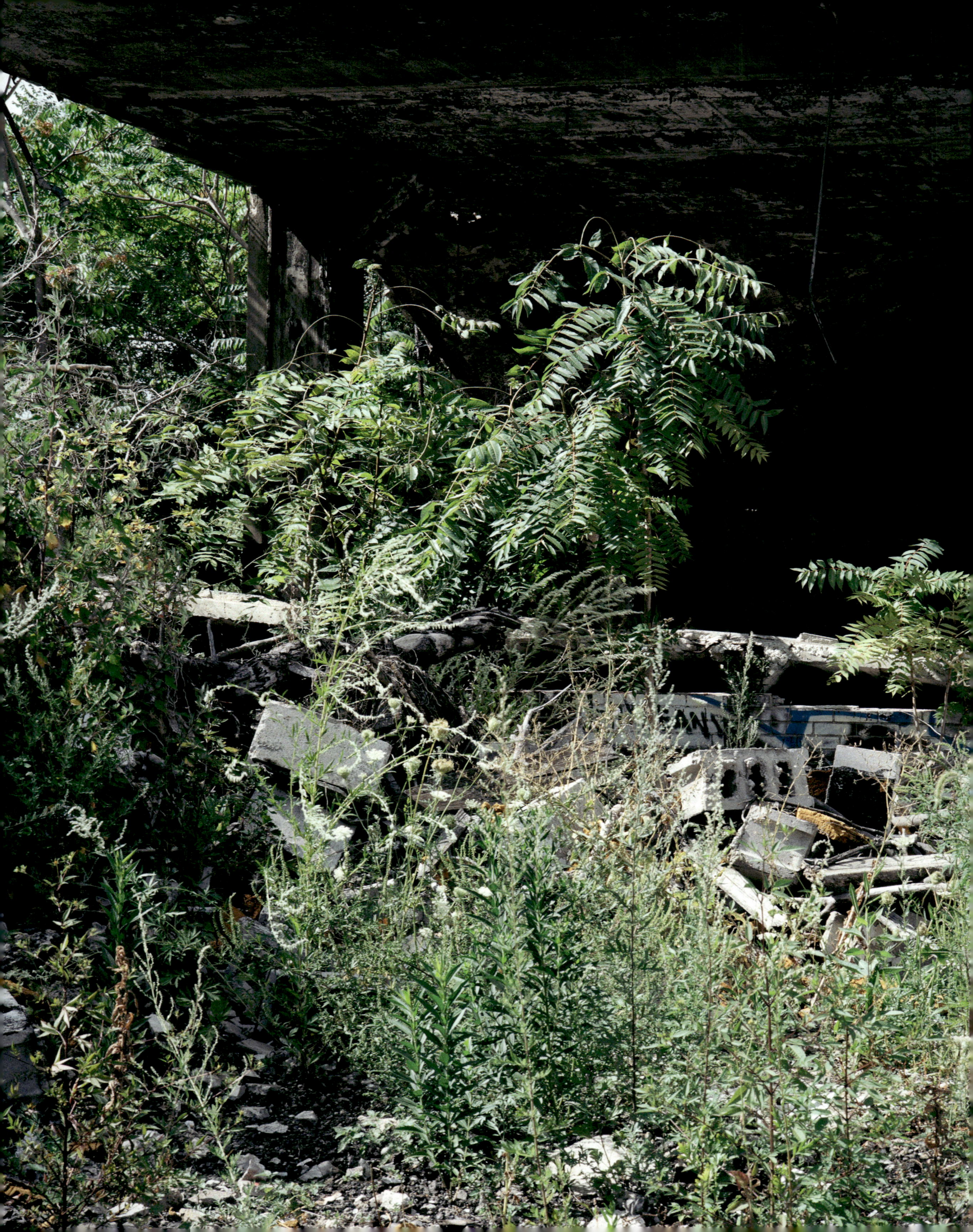

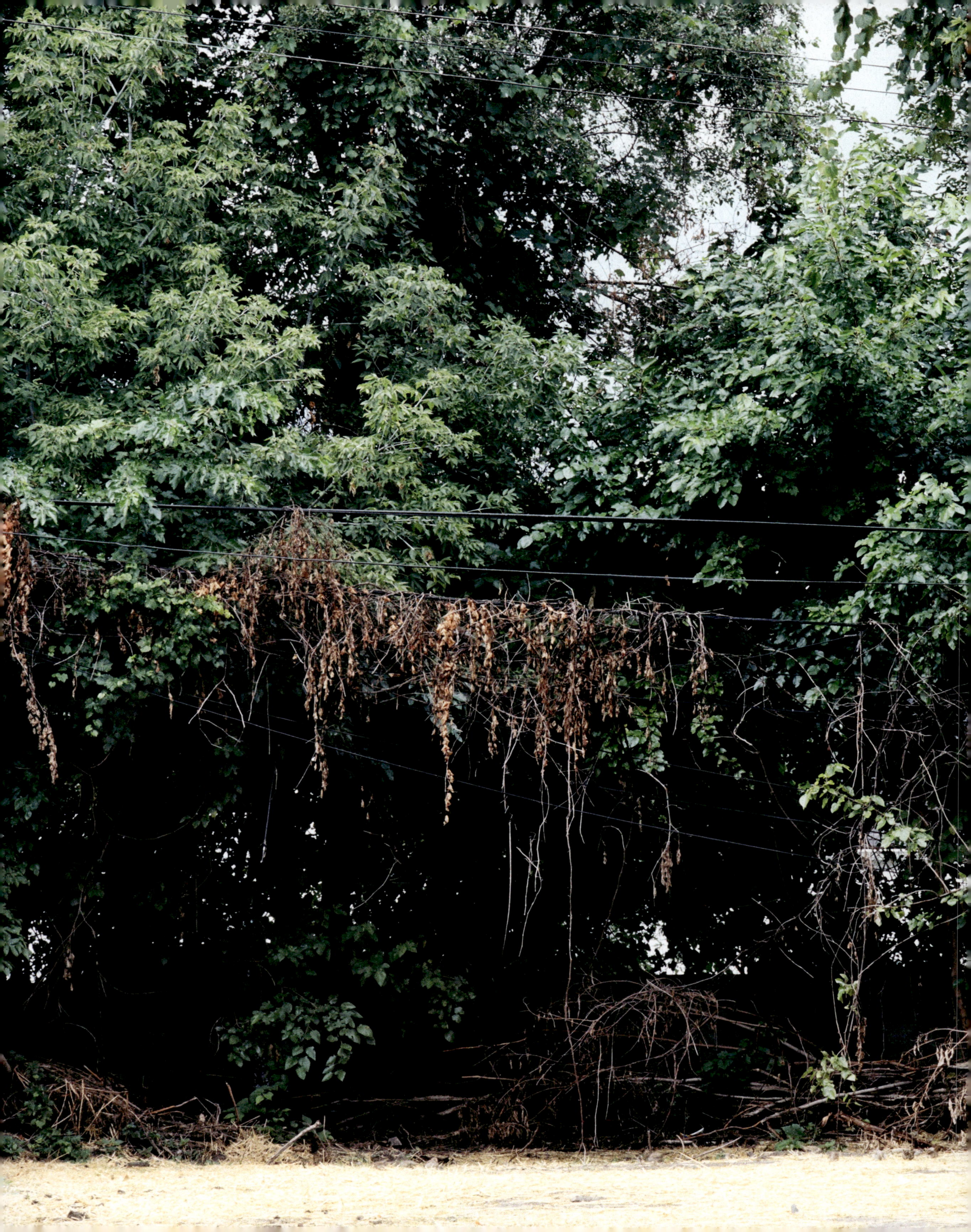

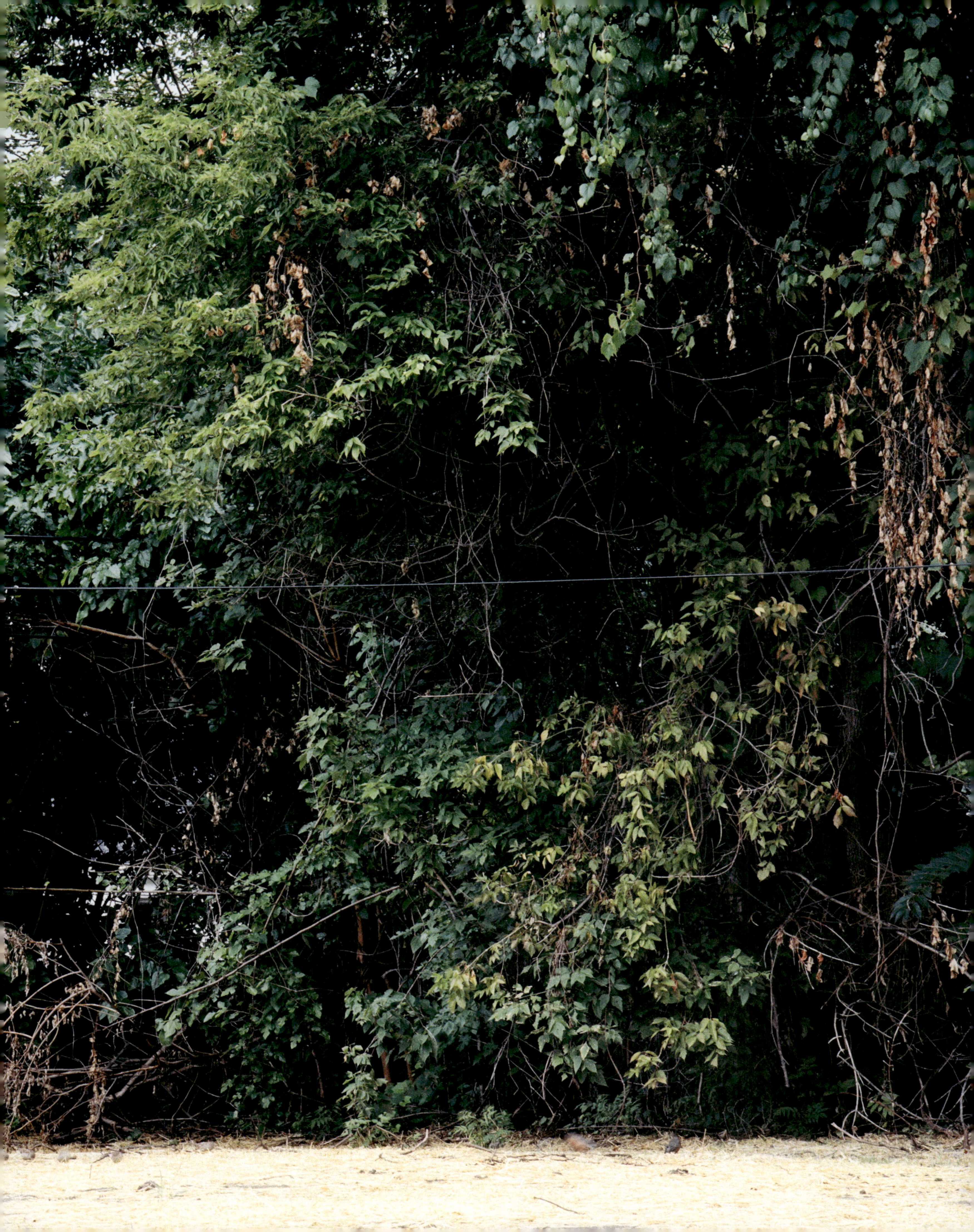

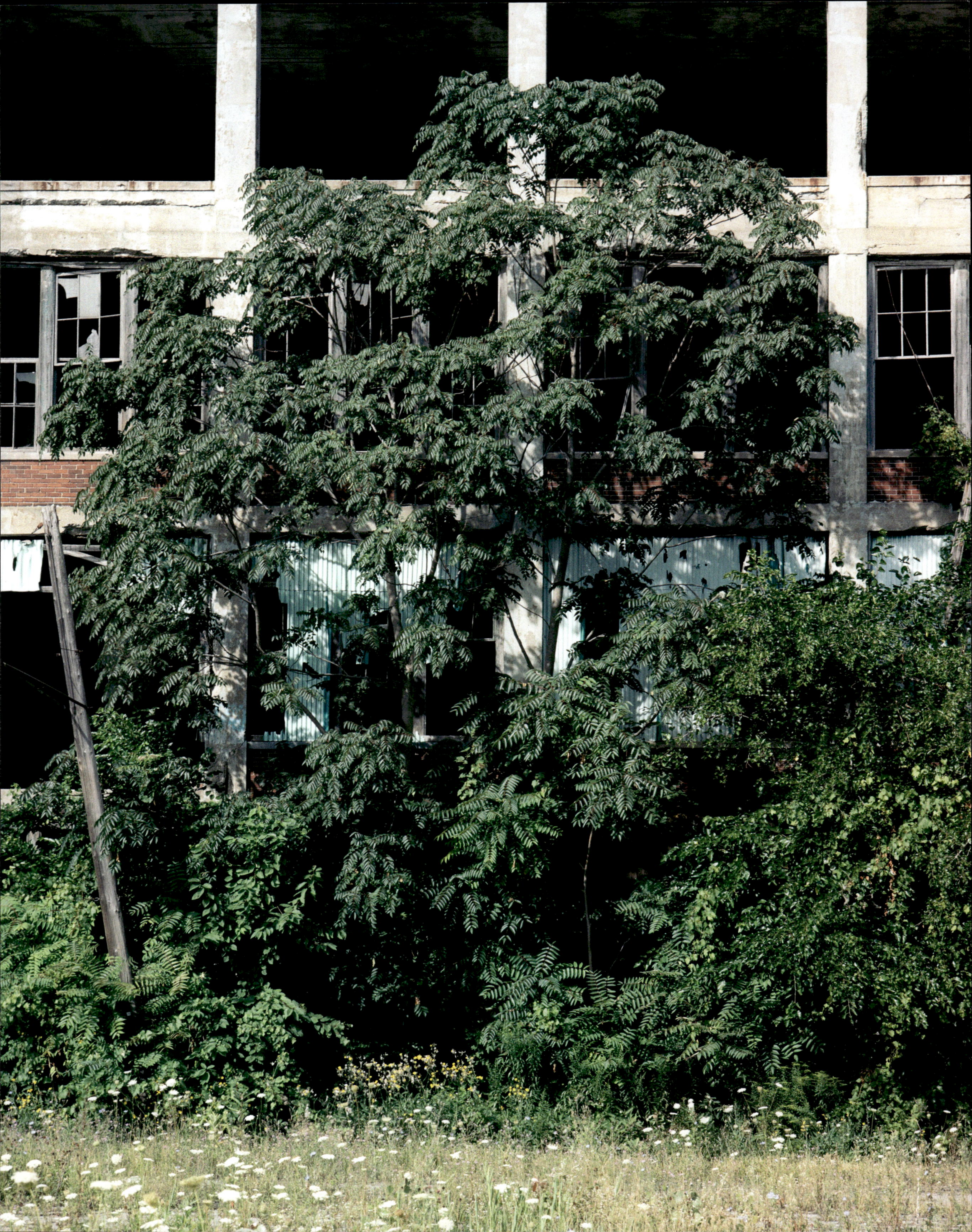

And then the Rouge appeared against the sky, rising out of the smoke it generated. At first all that was visible was the tops of the eight main smoke-stacks. ... It was like a grove of trees, as if the Rouge's eight main smokestacks had sown seeds to the wind, and now ten or twenty or fifty smaller trunks were sprouting up in the infertile soil around the plant.

Jeffrey Eugenides (2003). Middlesex, 94–95

21

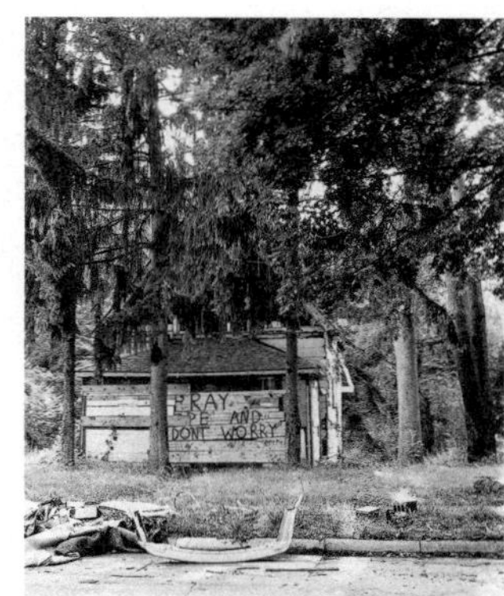

14409 Burgess Street (Pray Hope and Don't Worry), 2016

Brightmoor Neighborhood

"The early days in Brightmoor saw frantic home building on every side. ... Where a row of vacant lots stood one week, you would find people living in houses the next. ... zoning or restrictions were not a part of the planning. (The only restrictions in force were against colored residents)."

John W. Carey (1940). Growth of Brightmoor, 1

The house behind the fir trees was built in 1922, the same year that entrepreneur B. E. Taylor started developing the land. He bought up farms, divided them into lots, and sold them, some with mass-produced houses on them. These developments had no sewers or paved roads. Like many of the working class suburbs that emerged after World War I, Brightmoor was segregated by race—strictly white with an active Ku Klux Klan chapter. Today, Brightmoor is an unevenly populated neighborhood with many open spaces. To combat crime, the Neighbors Building Brightmoor initiative boarded up a number of abandoned houses in 2012 and painted them together with children and young people from the neighborhood.

→ 62 Beaverland Street (Neighbors Building Brightmoor), 2015
→ 65/66 Bentler Street, 2018

22

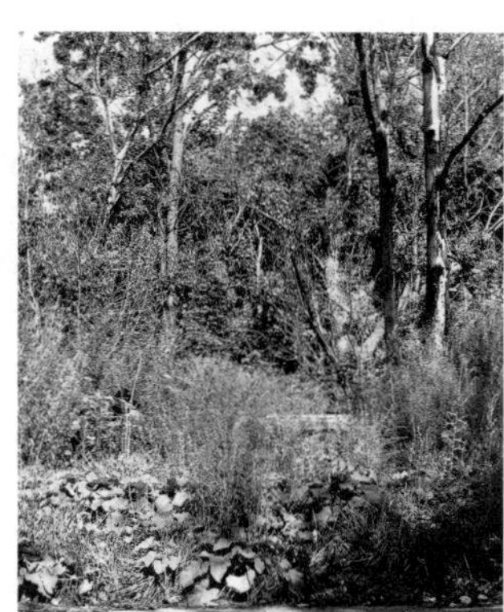

5972 Canton Street (Burned Down House), 2015

Gratiot Town / Kettering Neighborhood

In November 2014, a two-story residential building on this property burned to the ground, as can still be seen from the charred trees in the background. House fires are widespread in Detroit and have various causes. The most common are cable fires and arson. These fires are especially dangerous for the inhabitants of neighboring houses.

23

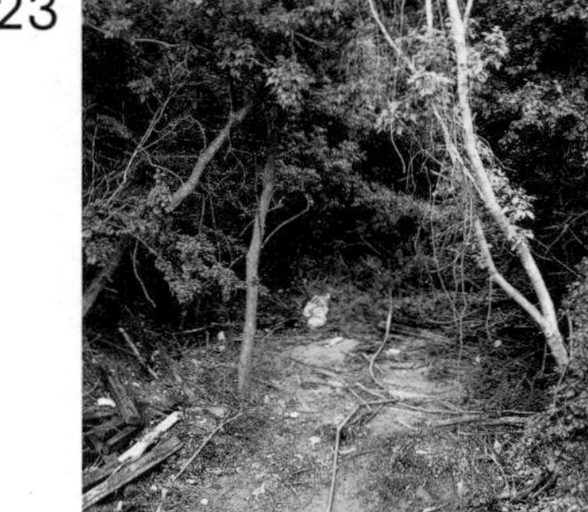

Uniroyal Tire Plant (East Jefferson Avenue), 2015

Rivertown Neighborhood

"Uniroyal has been making steel-belted radials continuously since 1961. A good 10 years longer than any other American tire manufacturer."

Advertisement Life Magazine, October 06, 1972

The Uniroyal Tire Plant shut down in 1980, putting 5,000 people out of work. 100,000 additional workers lost their jobs when auto-related suppliers and

Ford River Rouge Complex
Ku Klux Klan

shops were closes or relocated. The plant had been in operation since 1905 under different names and corporations. The city of Detroit bought the production site in 1981 for $5 million and demolished all the buildings four years later to open a vast stretch of attractive waterfront property. Unfortunately the ground was heavily contaminated with toxic chemicals left over from 70 years of tire production and still remains vacant. Uniroyal now produces in Brazil, Turkey, Spain, and Australia. The photo was taken from a bridge overlooking the river.

24

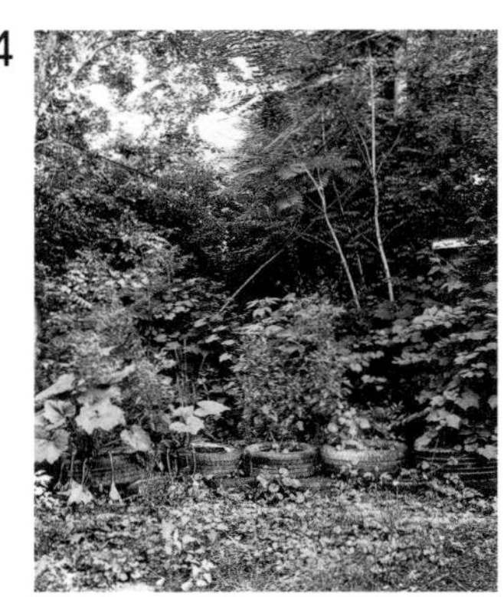

Beaverland Farms (Quinoa), 2016

Brightmoor Neighborhood

→ For a description see 10 Beaverland Farms (Elderberry Trees), 2016

25

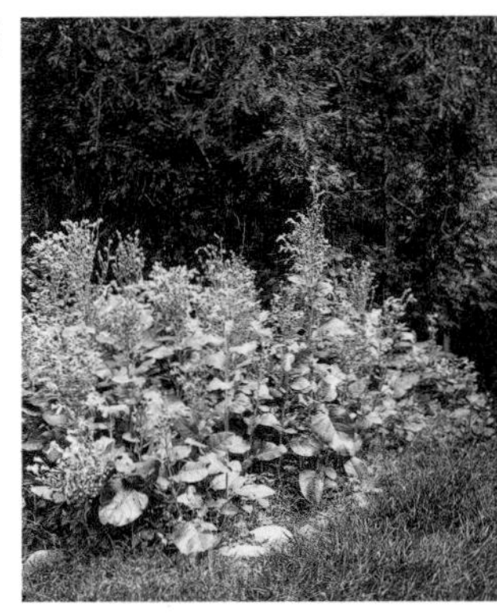

Sacred Roots Garden (Tobacco), 2018

Claytown Neighborhood

The picture shows a bed of tobacco plants in the Sacred Roots Garden—a small, educational garden of the nonprofit health center American Indian Health & Family Services. The garden program teaches about traditional indigenous plants and healthy nutrition and lifestyle.

During the 1970s, Detroit's auto industry recruited workers on Native American reservations. Members of various tribes moved to southeastern Michigan, where new car factories were built. In 1978, the American Indian Health & Family Services was founded to provide medical and psychological care for native communities and other groups who are disadvantaged or excluded from the health care system. In addition to a clinic that also treats uninsured patients, the center provides comprehensive health counseling and organizes culturally integrated services to empower and enhance the physical and mental as well as the spiritual and emotional well-being of Native Americans and other underserved populations. Since 1993, the center has been located on the site of a former Catholic church, in the garden of which the bed of tobacco plants is located. Tobacco is traditionally tended by young men. The plants are dried after harvest and used for various ceremonies.

www.aihfs.org

→ 54/55 Sacred Roots Garden, American Indian Health and Family Services, 2018

26

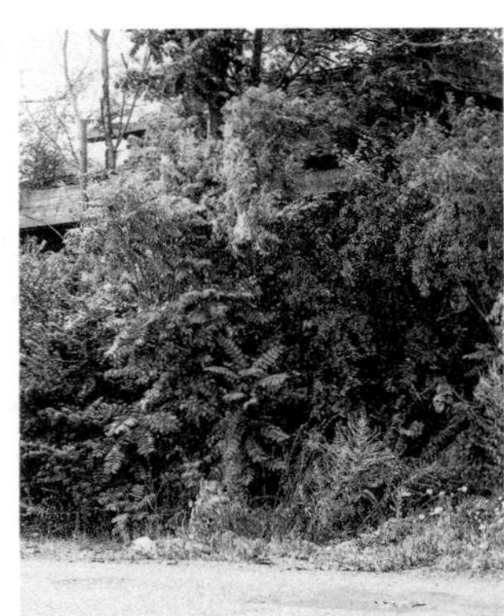

Kelsey-Hayes Wheel Company (McGraw Avenue), 2015

Chadsey Condon Neighborhood

The Kelsey-Hayes Wheel Company was founded in 1927 to manufacture wheels for automobiles (then still made of wood). It became the main supplier to Ford, General Motors, Buick, and other companies. During the Second World War production was shifted to machine guns, armor plates, aircraft tires, and during the Korean War to aircraft components. After the successful 1950s, the company developed brake systems that were installed in 85 percent of all American cars. From 1978 Kelsey-Hayes was bought and sold several times. It ceased to exist as an independent company in 1998. The factory buildings on McGraw Street were built in 1920 and have been empty since the 1990s. In 1936, amidst the Great Depression and in the early days of the United Auto Workers union, the first organized sit-down strike in Detroit took place here for ten days.

We are standing by a window in the great stone castle of the General Motors company. Before our eyes there was a scene of the unspeakable ugliness and chaos. There were mills in the midsts of the city, belching thick smoke, high office buildings side by side with wooden frame residences, grimy garages and desolate parking-spaces for automobiles. Finally our eyes fell upon a small and hideous wooden cottage with drawn blinds, just across the street. "It's a 'blind pig'," said the official. "Yes, this is a terrible city. I wouldn't have my son grow up in the smoke and filth here. We live away in the country. I have a garden."

Matthew Josephson (1929).
Detroit: City of Tomorrow, 166

27

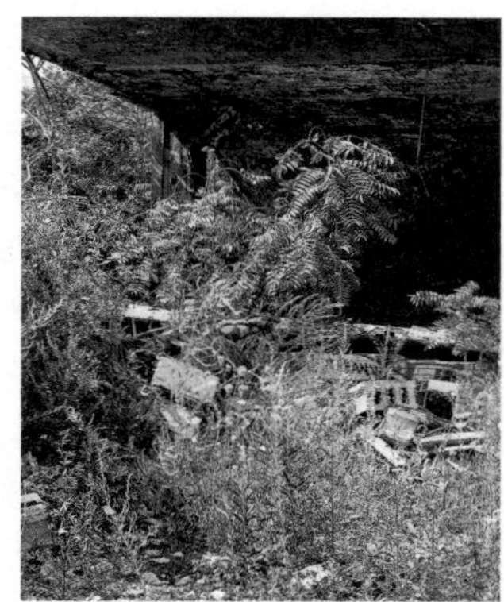

Packard Automotive Plant (Bellevue Street), 2015

Gratiot Town / Kettering Neighborhood

Between 1903 and 1910, the Packard Motor Car Company erected a production complex with 47 buildings over a stretch of 1.5 miles along the Detroit Belt Line. Designed by Albert Kahn, the reinforced concrete structure with large sliding windows was praised at the time by the trade journal Motor Age for the "bright, cleanly, and cheerful aspect of the different departments. It is one of the new style of factories … that are gradually displacing the old prison workshops."° The factory produced high-end Packard automobiles and during World War II supplied engines for bombers and patrol torpedo boats. In 1956, as a result of a recession, the factory closed and 11,000 workers were laid off. After a short period of use by other companies, in the 1980s the empty property was the site of raves and techno parties and used by sprayers and skaters. As Detroit's largest industrial ruin, the steel construction building became an icon of ruin porn. To this day it is the setting for apocalyptic, zombie, and science fiction movies and is featured in international coffee-table books and numerous magazine articles about the city's economic decline. In 2013, a Peru-based developer bought the site at the Wayne County Tax Foreclosure Auction with the intention of historically restoring it. Since then it has been secured with boards and guarded around the clock by a security company. In 2018, you could book a guided tour of the industrial ruin for $40 or rent it as a "crazy and amazing" location for a wedding photo.

During World War II, when Detroit was the Arsenal of Democracy, "the Packard plant had by far the most, the largest, and the longest hate strikes of the war, starting in 1941 and extending through 1944. The circumstances at Packard almost guaranteed racial unrest: the vast majority of the workers were southern whites and Polish Americans, both hostile to African Americans; the U.A.W. local union was allegedly controlled by members of the Ku Klux Klan; and the personnel manager at Packard was openly racist. Following dozens of earlier strikes, Packard workers walked off the job in May and June 1943 to protest the promotion of three black foundry workers to aircraft-engine assembly work."°° 25,000 white workers walked out on a wildcat strike. Later this summer, amid the ongoing war, housing shortages, rising racial tensions, and several hate strikes all over the city, the Detroit Riot of June 1943 broke out.

° Ferry (1970). The Legacy of Albert Kahn, 11
°° Stone (2017). Detroit 1967, 50–51

→ 29 Packard Automotive Plant (Concord Avenue), 2015

Albert Kahn
Arsenal of Democracy
Detroit Riots

28

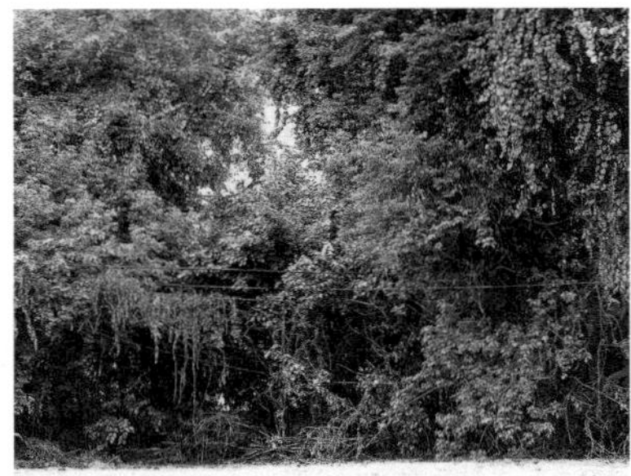

20037 Birwood Avenue (Eight Mile Wall), 2015

McDowell Neighborhood

With the onset of war production in 1940, Detroit's industry boomed and thousands moved into the city, despite housing shortages and extreme racial segregation. The Eight Mile Wall is a relic of this time. It is six feet high and runs for half a mile between the houses on Mendota Street and Birwood Avenue just below Eight Mile Road, Detroit's northern city limits. Built in 1941 by a white developer, the wall was intended to separate the newly developed land for exclusively white buyers from the neighboring "slum." This "slum" was an African-American housing development that had been built 20 years earlier. The Wyoming/Eight Mile Pocket was one of the few enclaves where Black Detroiters could buy land and houses. Many had small gardens to ensure self-sufficiency to supplement the erratic factory work.

From the 1930s, America's real estate market had been characterized by redlining and white homeowners' associations, whose structurally racist practices still have an impact on urban development today. This enduring segregation is still not noticed by many people, precisely because of its everyday occurrence.

In picture 28, the Eight Mile Wall can be seen on an empty lot where a house had just been demolished. It can also be seen in the Alfonso Wells Memorial Playground in picture 30. The 2006 mural shows children from the neighborhood and civil rights activist Rosa Parks.

→ Structural Racism

→ 30 Alfonso Wells Memorial Playground (Eight Mile Wall), 2015

29

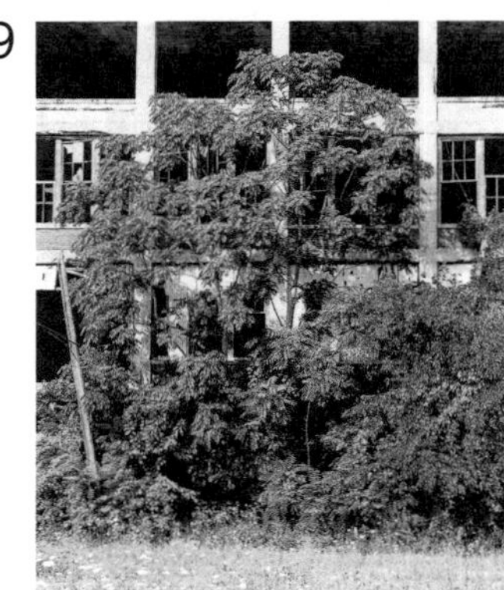

Packard Automotive Plant (Concord Avenue), 2015

Gratiot Town / Kettering Neighborhood

For a description see
→ 27 Packard Automotive Plant (Bellevue Street), 2015

Grab at the chain, put the nut in place, grab at the chain, insert the bolt, grab at the chain, two hits with the hammer, grab at the chain, turn on the automatic drill, sparks pour out, grab at the chain, securing the lead plate, paraffin pasteboard, a fastener, a bundle of candles, a crankshaft and continually without a break, grab at the chain, grab at the chain, movement of your hand and the result, body posture and parts assembly—man and machine, always in harmony.

Egon Erwin Kisch (1929). At Ford's Place in Detroit, 129

Redlining
Homeowners' Associations

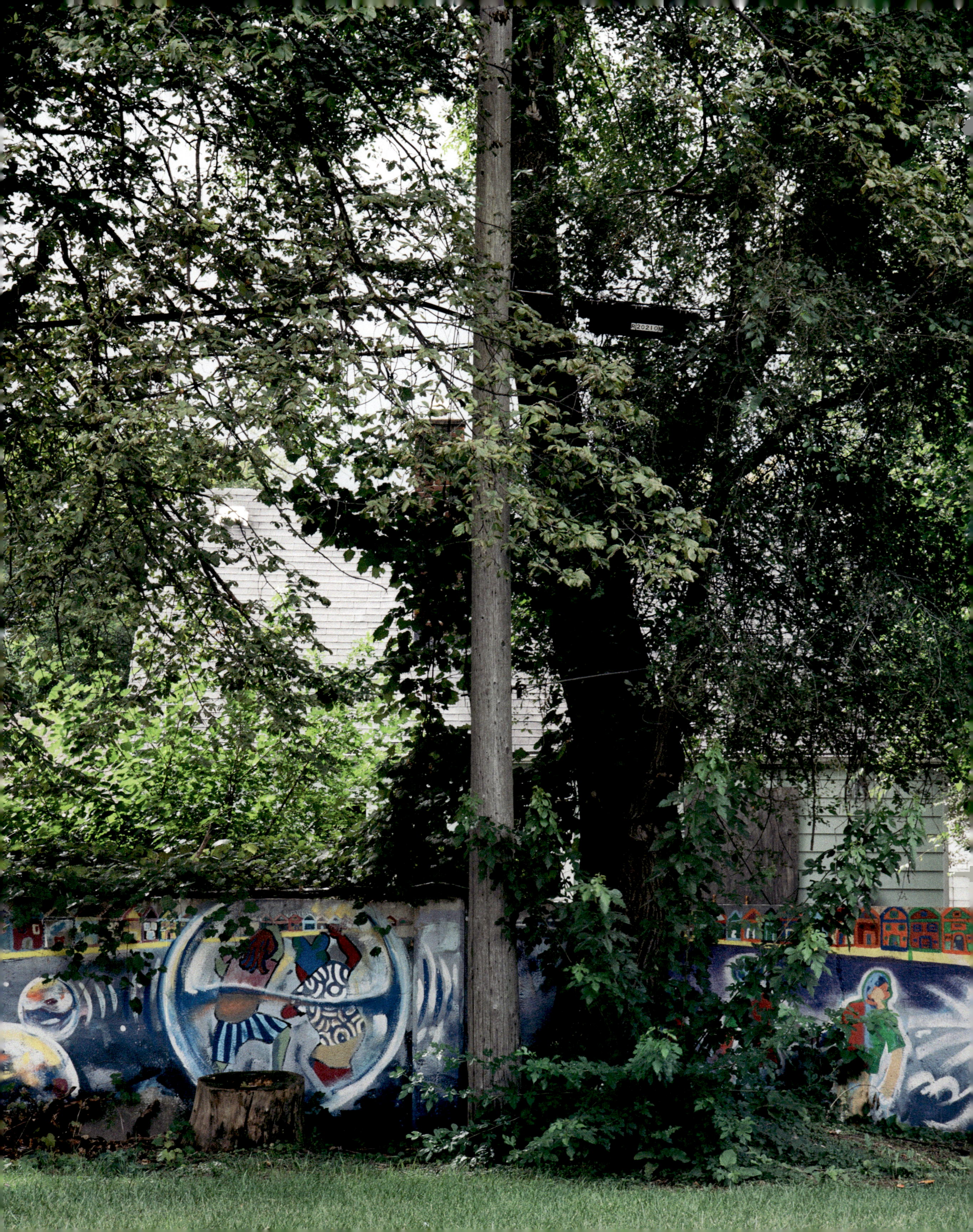
R2021OM

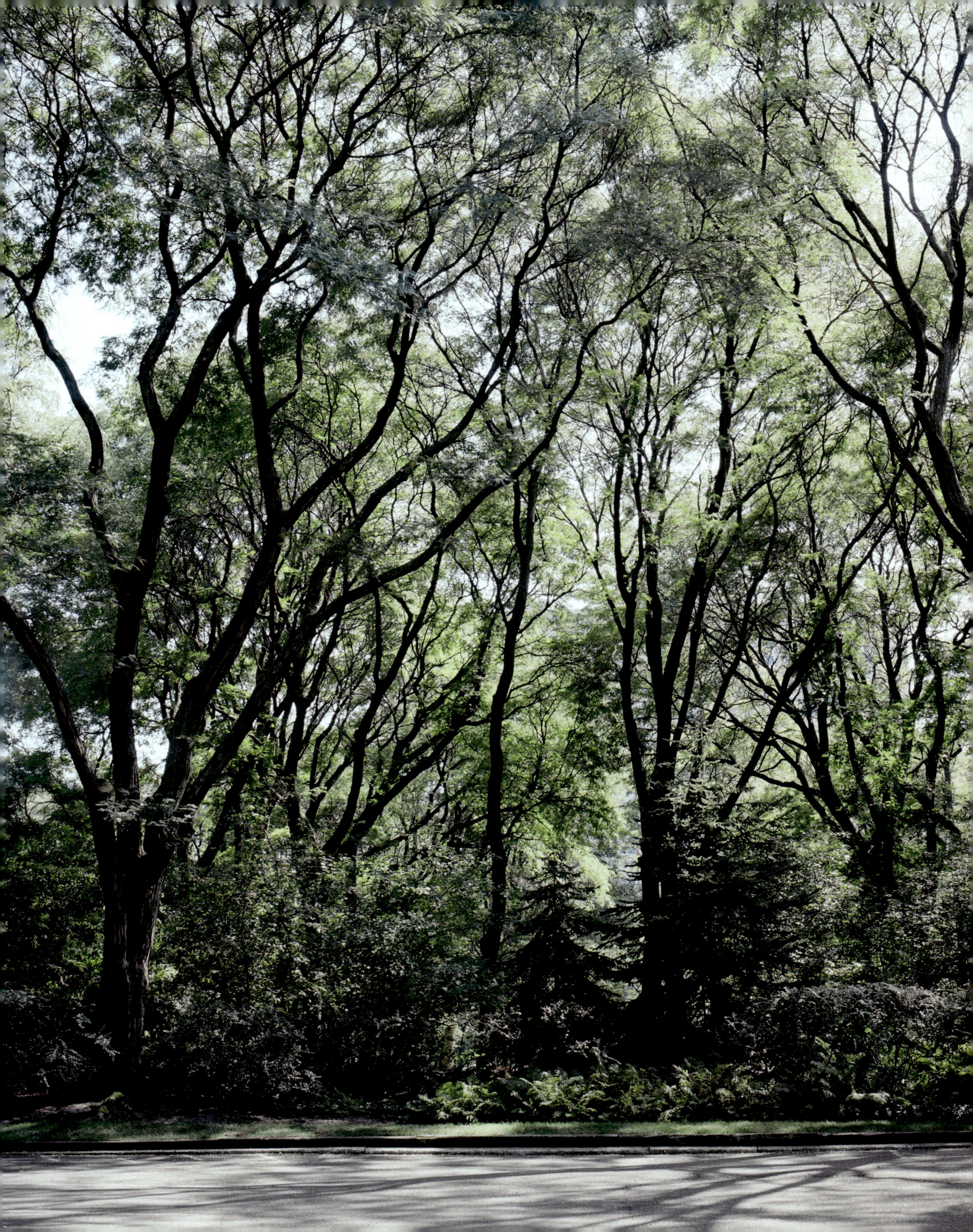

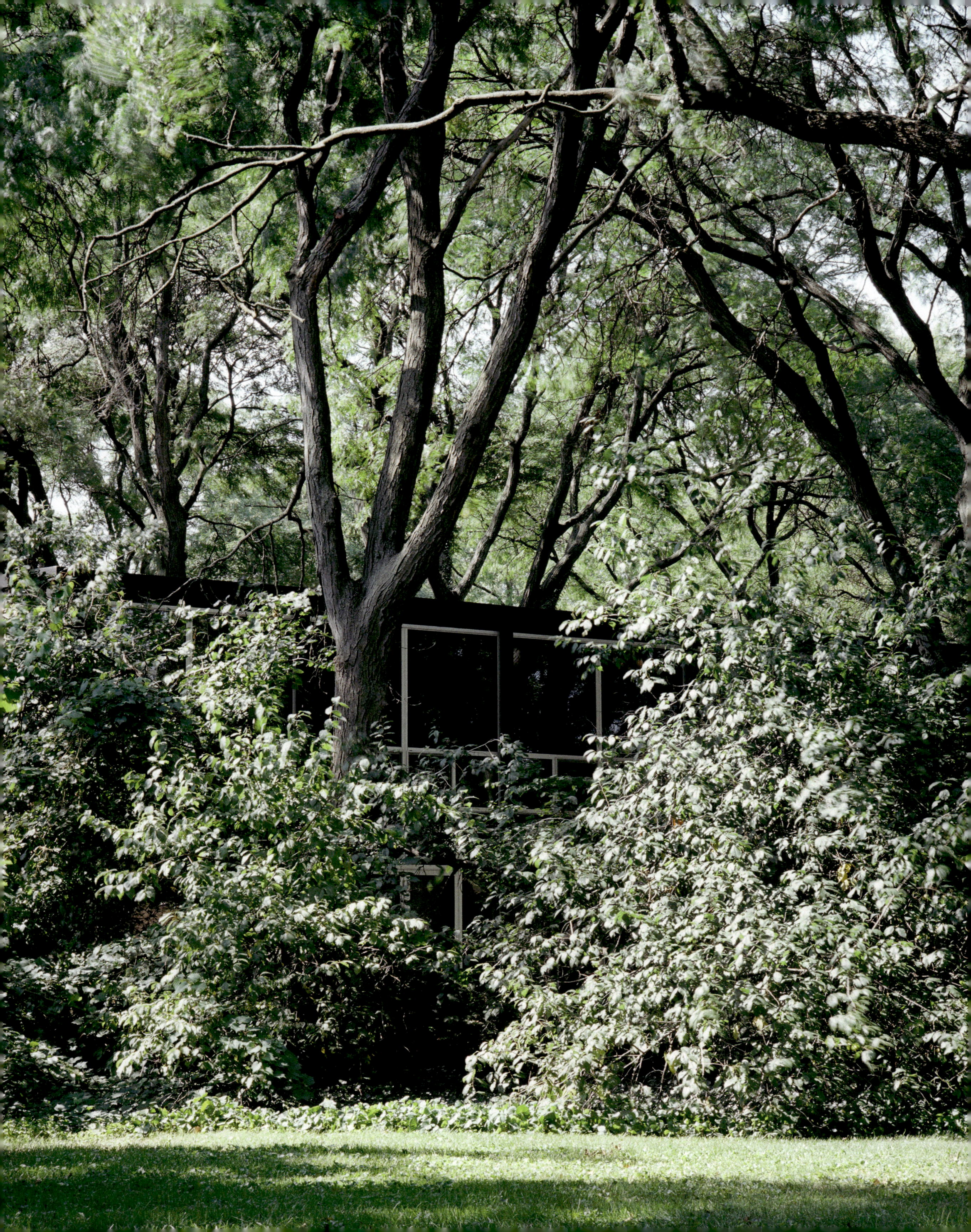

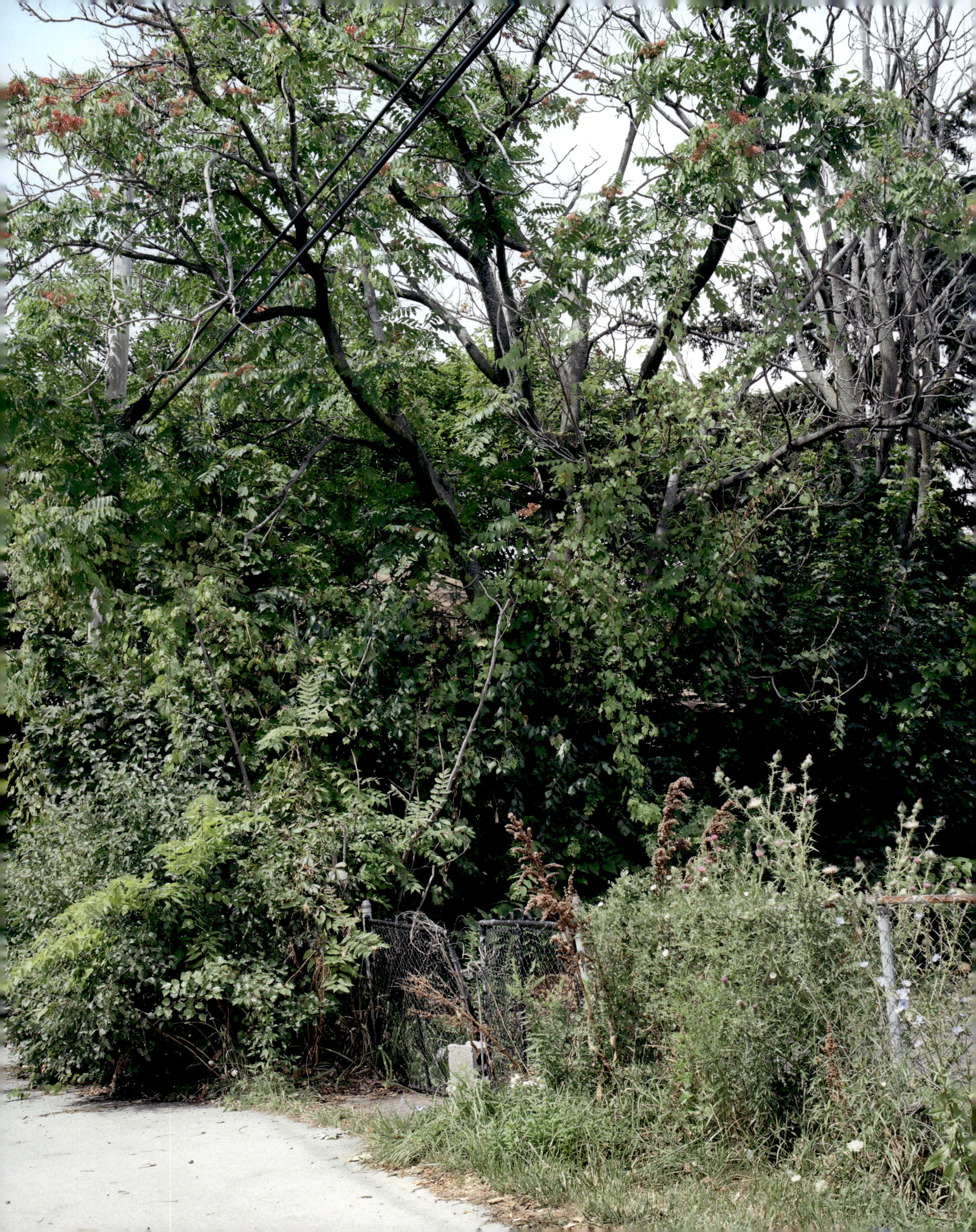

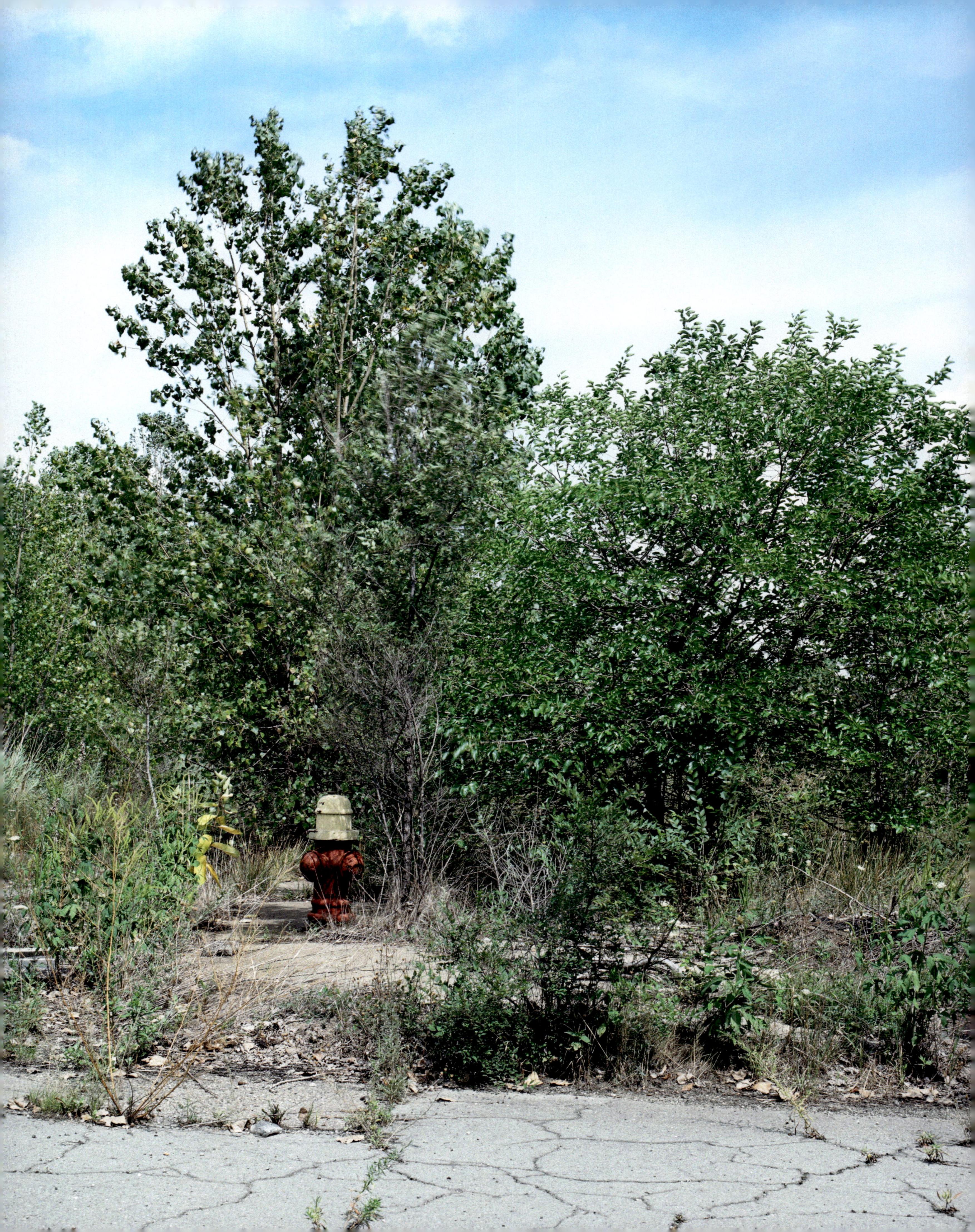

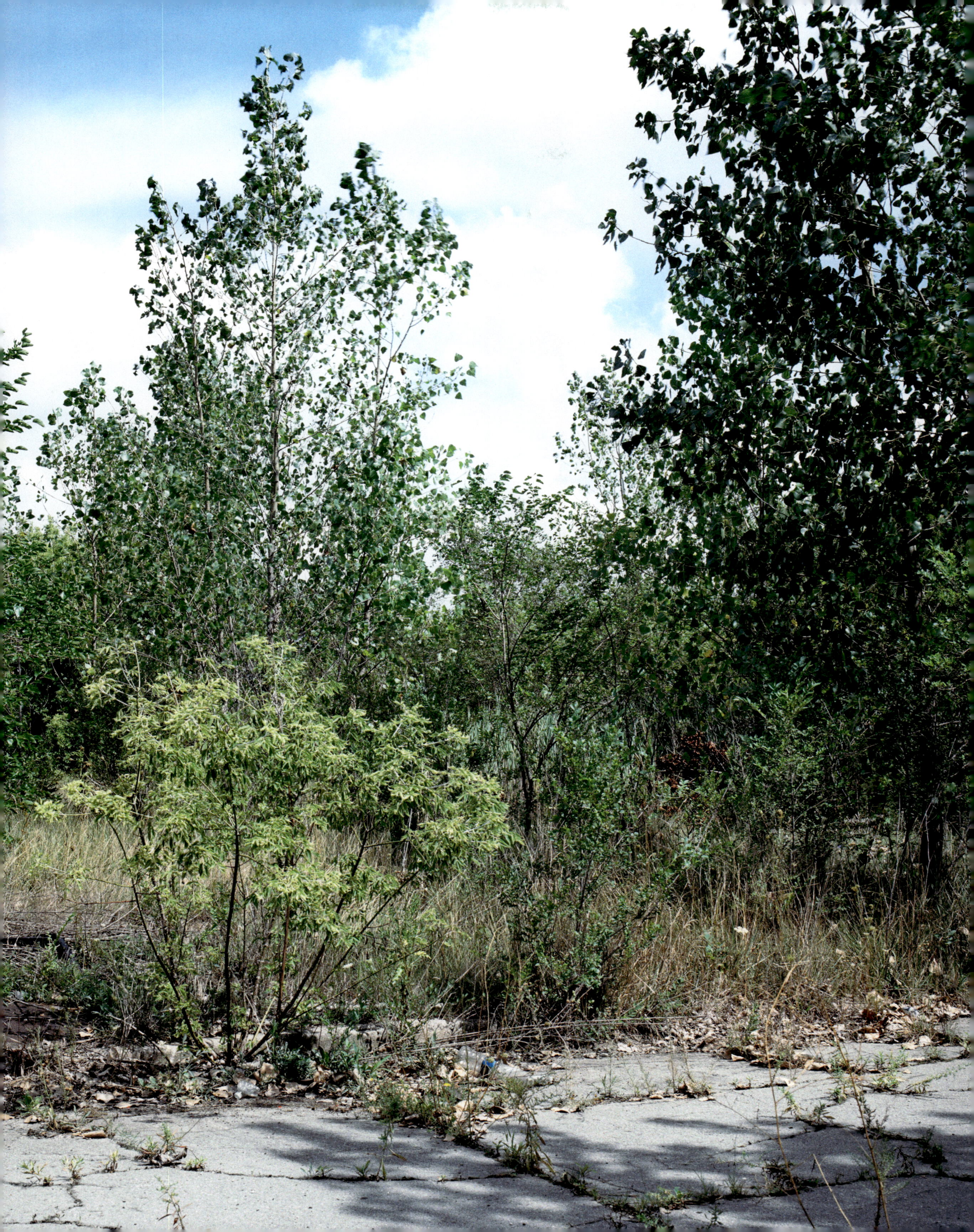

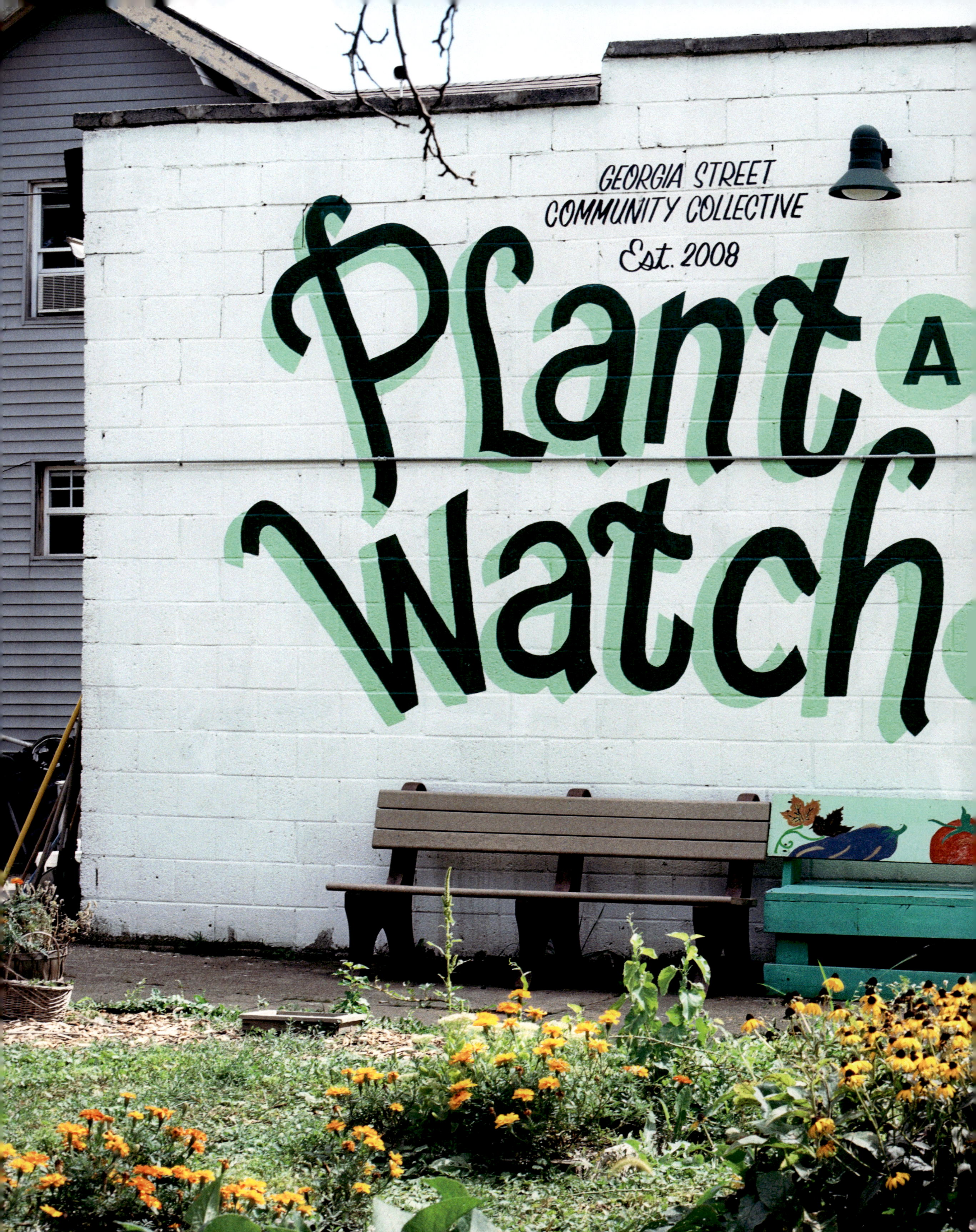
GEORGIA STREET
COMMUNITY COLLECTIVE
Est. 2008
Plant A
Watch

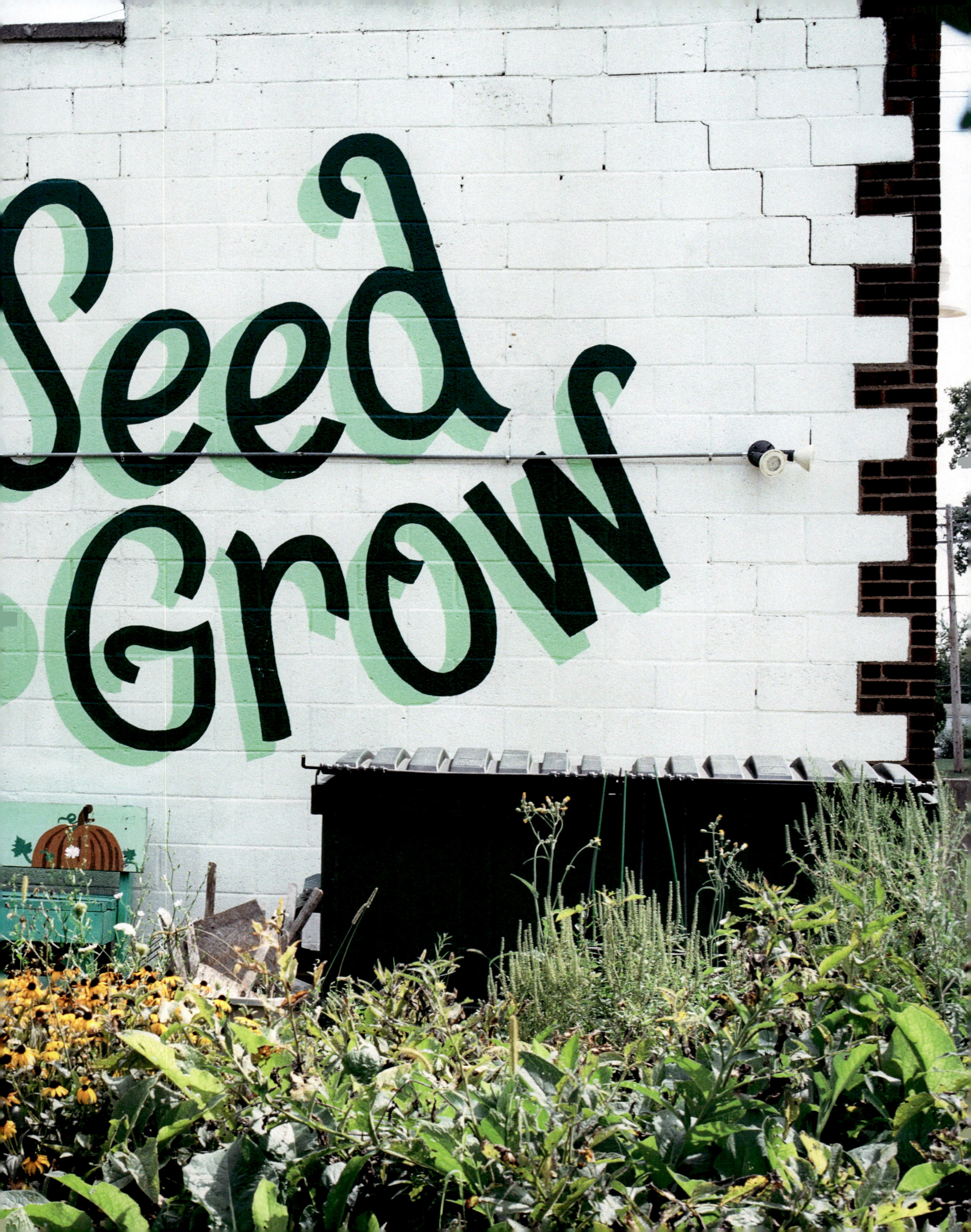
Seed
Grow

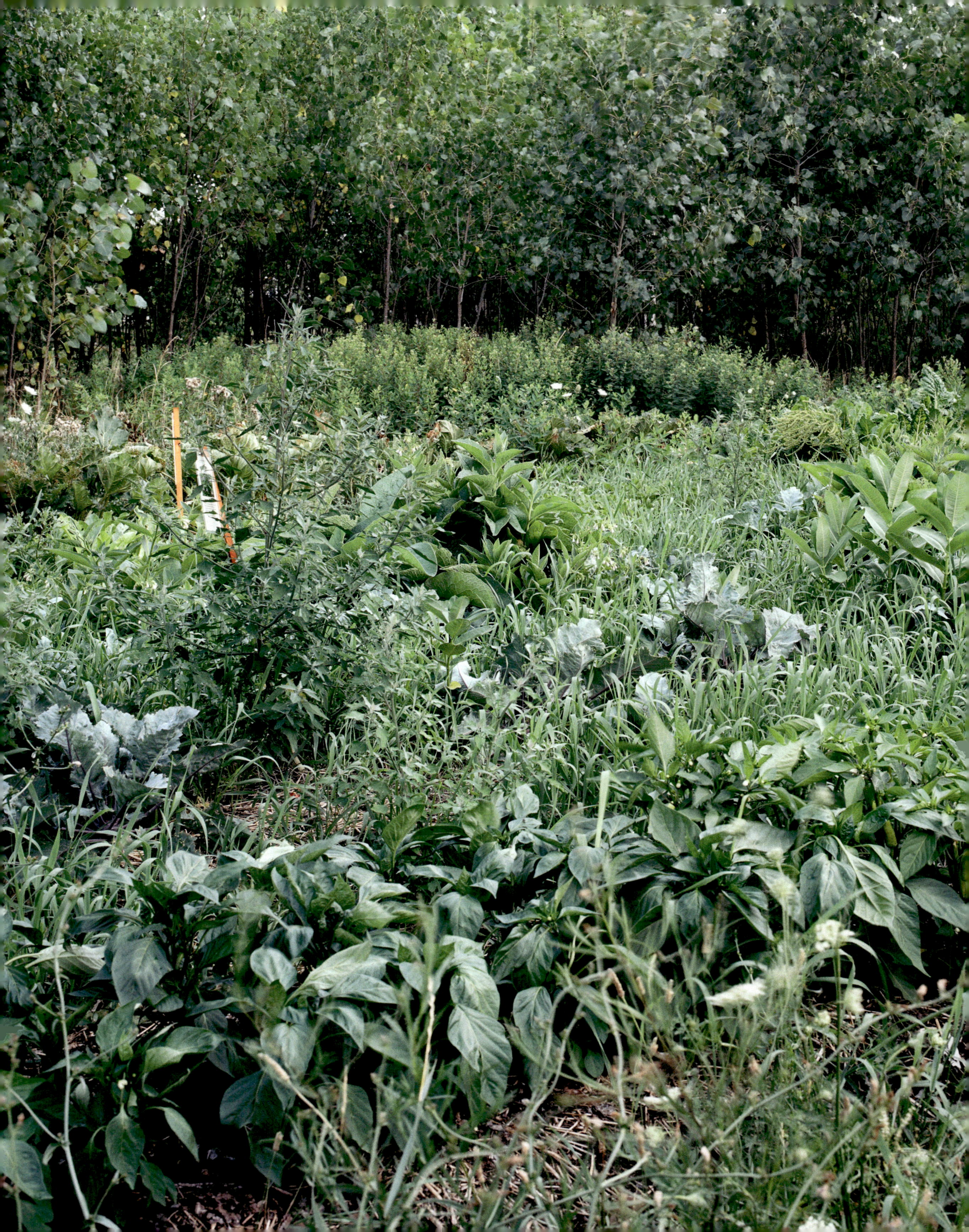

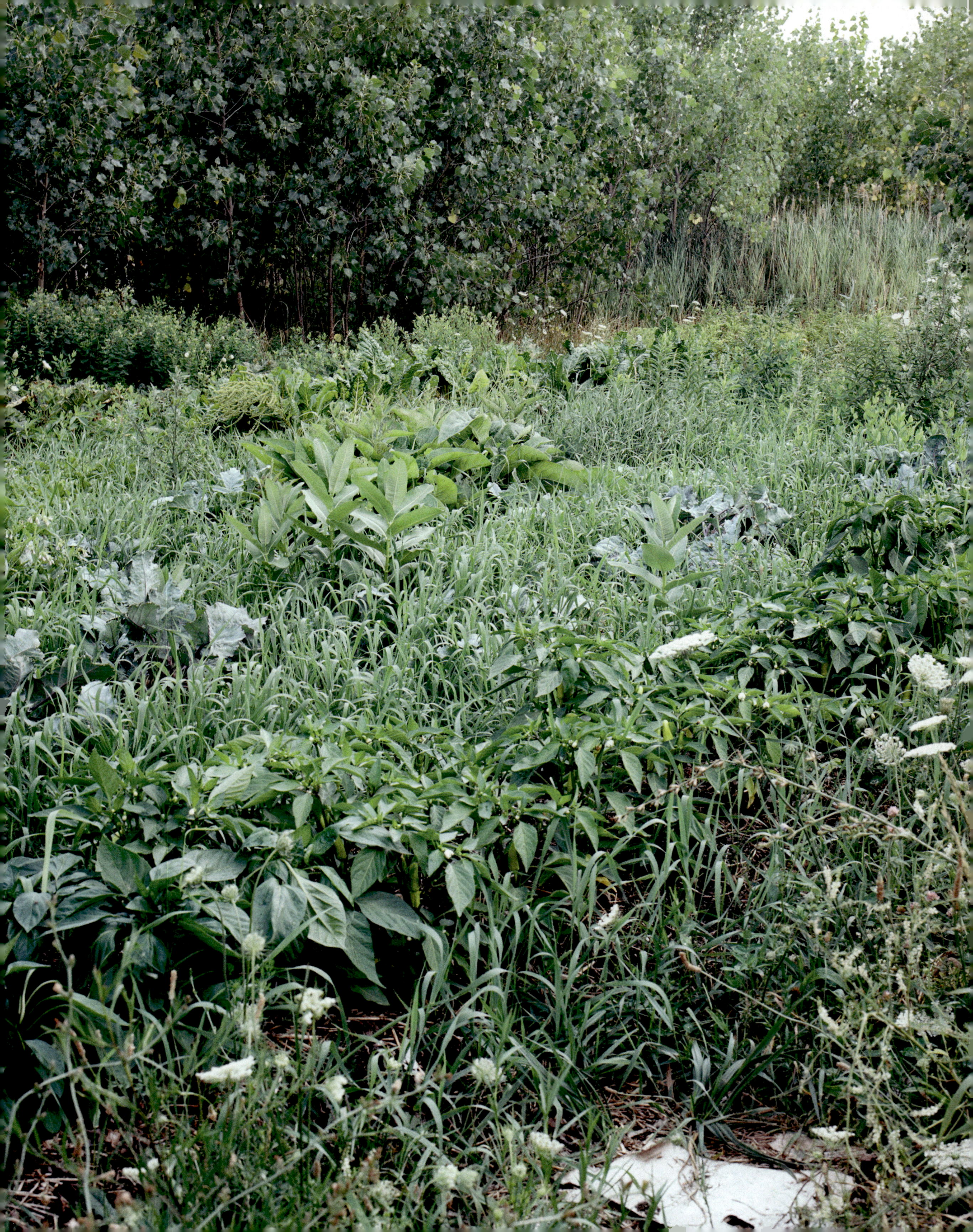

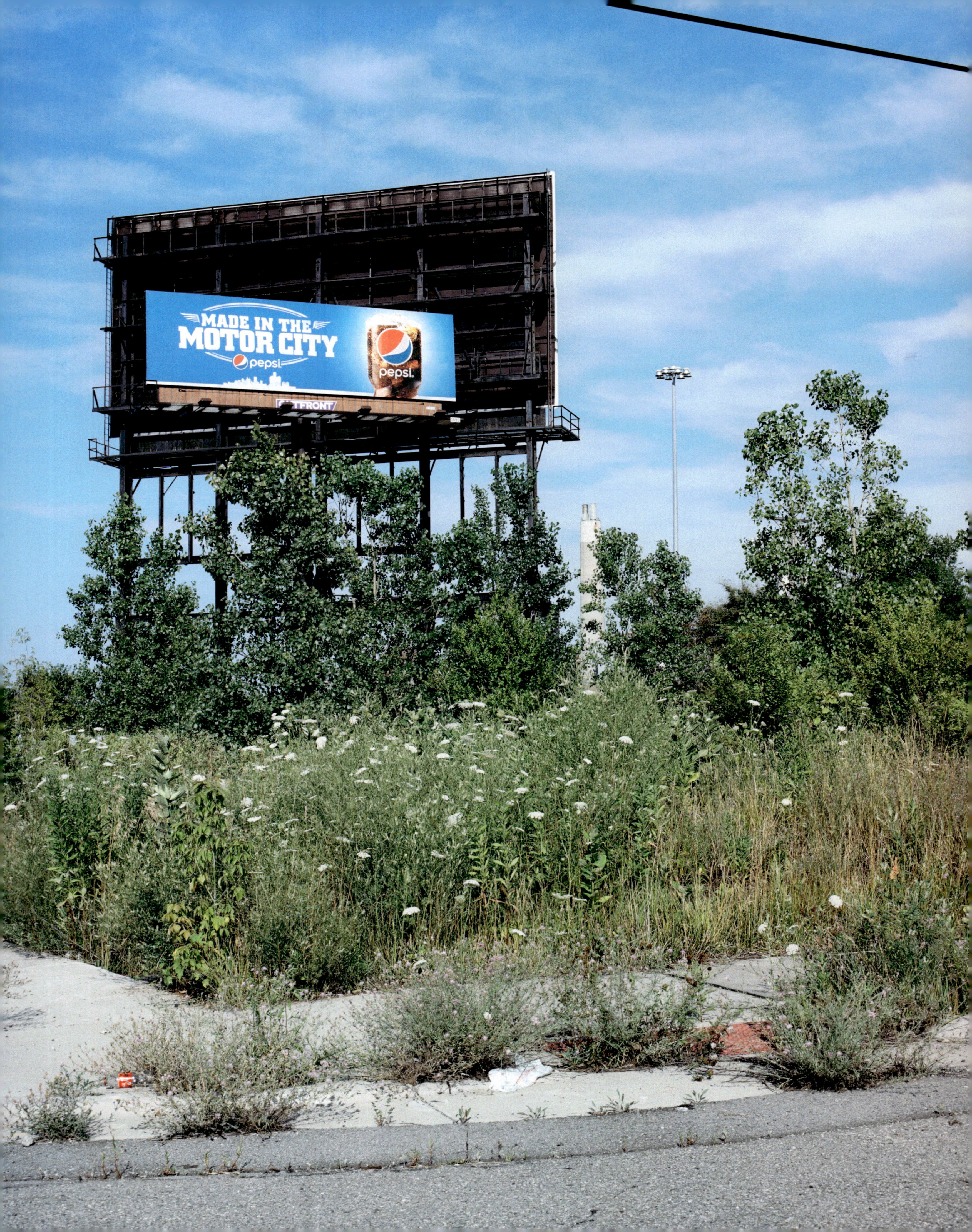
MADE IN THE
MOTOR CITY
pepsi
pepsi

Urban renewal came relatively late to Detroit, but when it arrived there was no stopping the bulldozers. A broad belt encircling the downtown area ... is in a constant state of flux as old buildings are vacated, then demolished, gradually to be replaced by new apartments, town houses, hotels, motels, and small plants and office buildings. Eventually, according to plans that go back a decade or more, the entire blighted core of the city will be a vast panoply of new middle-class housing, hospitals, museums, parks, schools, as well as civic, cultural, and commercial structures.

Stanley H. Brown (1965). Detroit: Slow Healing of a Fractured City

30

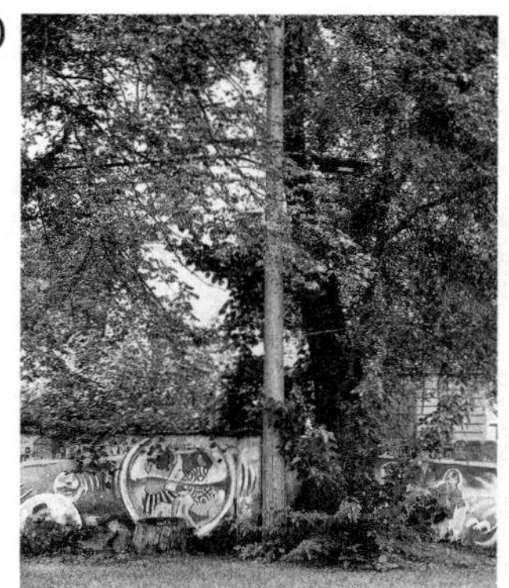

Alfonso Wells Memorial Playground (Eight Mile Wall), 2015

McDowell Neighborhood

For a description see
→ 28 20037 Birwood Avenue (Eight Mile Wall), 2015

31

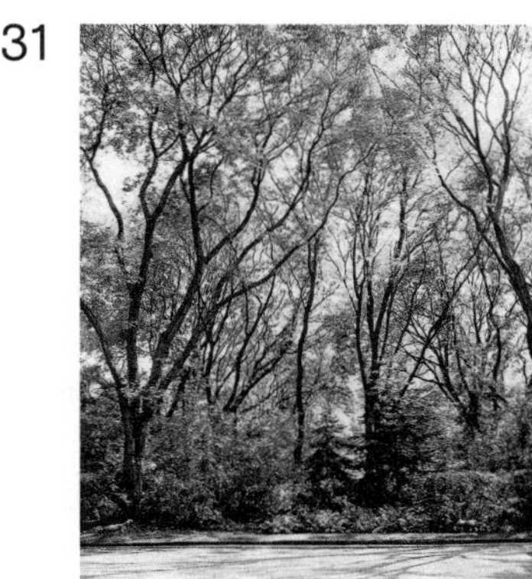

32

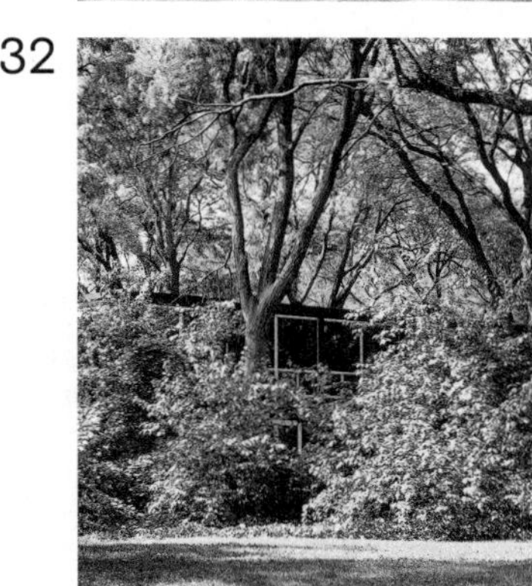

Lafayette Park (Parking Lot and Townhouse), 2015

Lafayette Park Neighborhood

Lafayette Park is a mixed-income residential complex that was designed as a modern garden city by Ludwig Mies van der Rohe, Ludwig Hilberseimer and Alfred Caldwell, as part of the Urban Renewal program from 1955. By 1969, several townhouse units had been built, in addition to the Lafayette Twin Towers, pavilion apartments, a school, a mall, and a park. The complex was erected on the site of Black Bottom, one of Detroit's oldest neighborhoods, which had been demolished five years earlier. Before World War I, it was a typical immigrant neighborhood. Newly arrived immigrants rented their first overpriced apartments here and after they built their own houses elsewhere other newcomers would move in. At the times of the Great Migration and industrialization, formerly ethnically divided neighborhoods were increasingly segregated by class and, above all, race. Black Bottom became a residential area for tens of thousands of African-Americans and people of color. Houses and rooms were rented out, but the landlords provided no maintenance. By World War II, the neighborhood was dominated by old wooden houses with precarious extensions and structural modifications, for the most part only with outdoor toilets. All of this just a few blocks from downtown Detroit.

"The Mies community is at peace, enveloped by the trees and foliage emerging from the fertile, primordial loam of old Black Bottom. ... The peace here may be a reward bequeathed through the ages, for having the commitment and audacity to maintain an integrated community in one of the most segregated cities in the United States. ... We have proven that it is possible to have a neighborhood of mixed colors and incomes, professionals and working class, in a collection of architectural gems, just as was envisioned at its inception."

Marsha Music (2012). Hidden in Plain Sight, 51

"In all honesty, at first I felt really weird with so many African-American people around me. Don't get me wrong, but where I grew up there were mainly white people—mainly rich, very manicured people. I didn't know what to expect. A situation like this was all new to me. But little by little I got more comfortable with this community. I got to know my neighbors and I no longer have those thoughts. I learned that they are just people living their lives, like I am. I like it a lot now."

A Lafayette Park Pavilion resident, in: Aubert (2012), 220

The gentrification in this neighborhood started about ten, twelve years ago. And it is almost complete. Low income and working people have just been displaced. We are approaching the most expensive condominium and townhouses conglomerates anywhere in the world. There are these groups of homes that are right here on my left and the homeless veterans here on the other side of the streets begging people to come into their parking lots. I mean, what a dichotomy.

Maureen Taylor from the Michigan Welfare Rights Organization (2013) in: Collapsing Auto Industry in Detroit

33

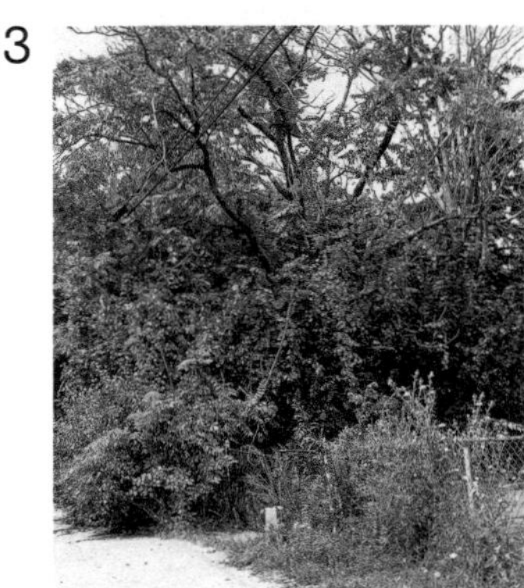

Alley in Midtown, 2015

Brush Park Neighborhood

Brush Park is one of the few neighborhoods in Detroit experiencing a development boom today. Since 2016, the neighborhood has been radically transformed by urban development investors. Comfortable condominiums are being built on vacant lots between the expensively renovated villas. While some neighborhoods around the downtown area benefit from the millions invested by private developers, in other less densely populated areas there is a tendency to reduce infrastructure and massively demolish unused and vacant properties.

Brush Park was built from 1850 on the site of a former ribbon farm. Elijah Brush and later his son Edmund Askin divided their property, named the streets after family members, and sold the land to Detroit's upper class. The new Victorian villas were already abandoned around 1900 by its affluent residents, who left for the quieter fringes of the city. The rapidly growing working class moved into the neighborhood until the 1970s, when people began to follow their relocated jobs. For some decades Brush Park was characterized by boarded up houses, empty lots, petty crime, and urban wilderness.

The photo was taken in a small alley and shows a blossoming tree of heaven.

34

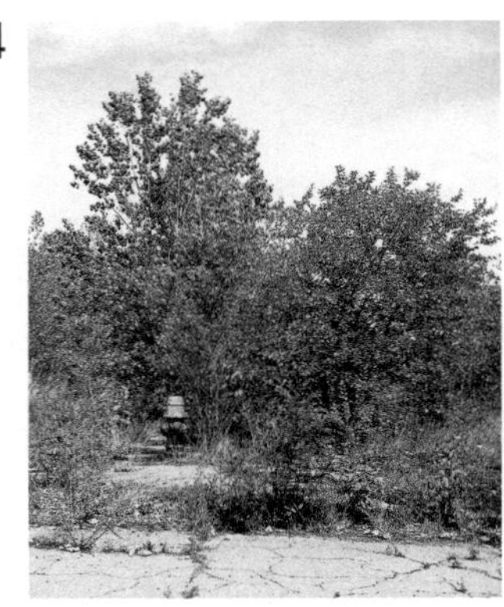

35

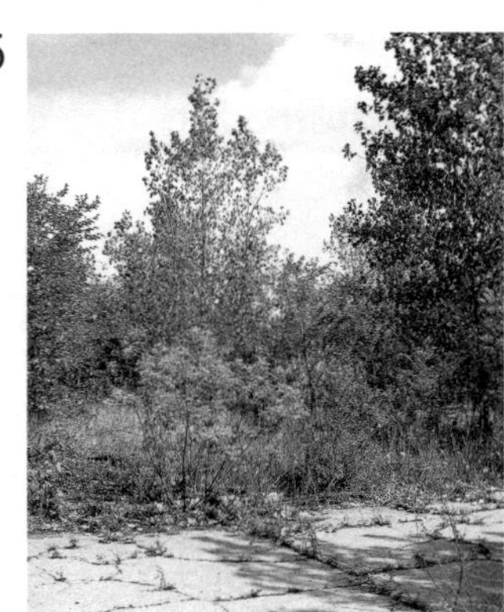

I-94 Renaissance Park, 2016

Airport Sub Neighborhood

"Since the late 1990s, I've watched this neighborhood become abandoned, torn down, and blocked off by concrete barricades. The last residents moved out, their houses and the burnt ones surrounding them were demolished; the haunted church of St. Cyril's village was scrapped to the point of collapse; ... the trees were torn out, to appease potential builders; .... But the sale of the land never happened. Aside from the massive complexes along Huber, The Zone still sits vacant. Large uprooted trees lay in piles. Random mounds of earth and demolished debris have overgrown with grasses and wildflowers. Flooded streets have become marshlands and swamps. Wildlife abounds: pheasants, rabbits, snakes, frogs, hawks, numerous birds, along with stray cats or dogs, can all be found here. The I-94 Industrial Park Renaissance Zone has inadvertently become one of the most natural topographies of Detroit."

Scott Hocking (2017). The Zone

Gentrification
Tree of Heaven
Detroit Renaissance

Some of Detroit's wide-open spaces were created by the ambitious demolition of vacant structures and neighborhoods in expectation of new investors. The strategy was to buy out blighted neighborhoods, demolish the houses and offer strong tax incentives. In 1997, the city of Detroit established six industrial renaissance zones to lure companies back into the city. One was the I-94 Renaissance Park near the former City Airport. By 2009, the Detroit Economic Development Corporation had spent around $ 19 million to purchase 189 acres and demolish buildings like the Jane Cooper Elementary School. When investors did not materialize, the wilderness found its way to the former neighborhoods. I counted over 30 different plants: pioneer shrubs, flowers, and herbs like red clover, mulberry, and grape vines. To be seen is the junction of Helen and Marcus Streets.

36

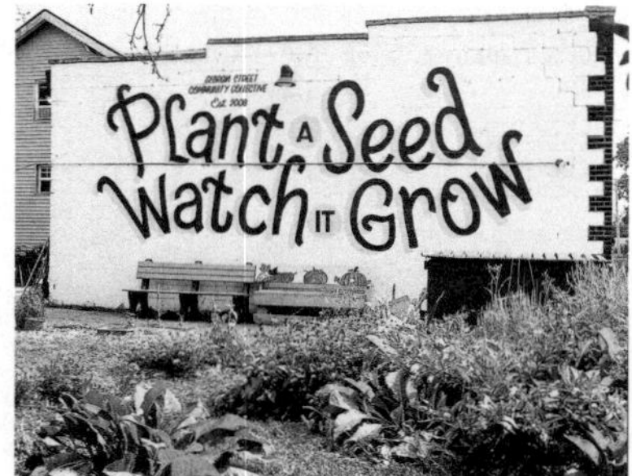

Georgia Street Community Collective, 2018

Airport Sub Neighborhood

In 2008, Mark Covington planted some flowers and vegetables at a corner near his grandmother's house to stop people from dumping garbage on these lots. Soon, senior neighbors as well as neighborhood kids embraced these gardening efforts as a resource for fresh food, thus offsetting their living costs. People from outside the neighborhood started to donate school supplies for kids, so that a few months later the non-profit organization Georgia Street Community Collective was founded with the goal of empowering and revitalizing the neighborhood. Within the last ten years a community center has grown around the first garden beds: an educational garden, a fruit orchard, and a free picking field as well as a library with a computer lab. Donations spawned annual Giveaway Days — in summer for school backpacks and in winter for coats or turkeys. Other plans include rehab houses and a donation center in an old corner warehouse. Unfortunately that warehouse together with two other buildings were set on fire in 2018. The city of Detroit demolished it only a few weeks later. The numerous arsons, the city's practice of a two-year reconveyance on acquired farming lots, and rumors the neighborhood might be turned into an industrial area illustrate well that grassroots development in Detroit seems to grow on thin soil.

As Laura Lawson and Abbilyn Miller put it in their 2013 essay about community gardens: "How city officials approach community gardens says a lot about how they value citizen-led initiatives. Quick to invoke the virtues of gardening in times of crisis, when the crisis lessens, the state (in most cases, city government) often changes the story of the garden — it becomes land to be used as a resource for the 'public good,' defined narrowly as a site for private development." °

www.georgiastreetcc.com

° Laura Lawson; Abbilyn Miller (2013). Community Gardens and Urban Agriculture as Antithesis to Abandonment, 39

→ 43 Georgia Street Community Collective (Free Picking Field), 2018

37

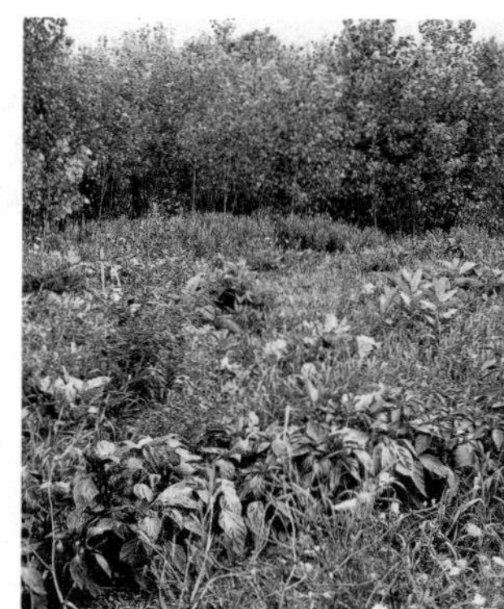

38

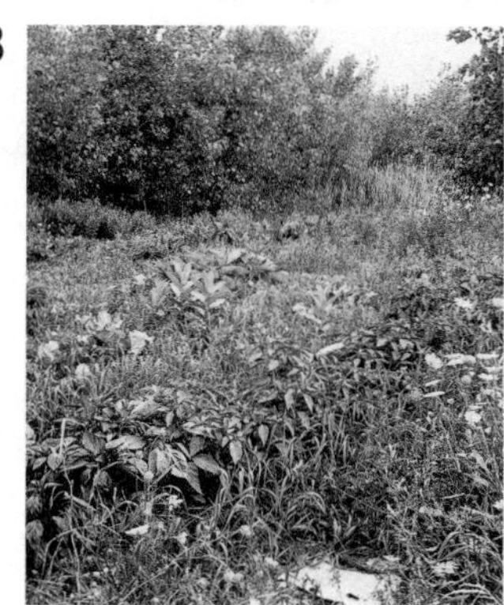

Guerilla Gardening, 2016

To buy land for a garden in Detroit in the year 2016 you usually had to own a house. The city then permitted the purchase of one or more adjoining lots. Exceptions seem to be large-scale private investors, some of whom can purchase up to 2,000 lots (see picture 59). In areas of the city that are deemed to be food deserts, small gardens are often established illegally by people growing their own food. They are tolerated by the city as long as their location is not attractive for urban development and real estate investment. This means that low-income residents in particular and smaller garden projects have no guarantee that they can continue to grow their crops the following year (in a city with a poverty rate of 36.4 percent in 2018).

Some food activists therefore occupy land with gardens and make the case that the city should allow vacant lots to be legally used as gardens and even to be purchased at low cost — in order to promote self-sufficiency and as a sustainable economic and employment measure for the city's residents. The pictures show such a field with kohlrabi, basil and chili, which grow between clover, common milkweed, wild carrot, grasses, and thistles. This property was previously occupied by residential buildings, which were demolished in 2004. Next to it a new gated community has already been built.

→ Food Desert, Food Security, Detroit Food Policy Council

→ 59 Charlevoix Street (Dr. Sweet's House/ Hantz Woodlands), 2018

39

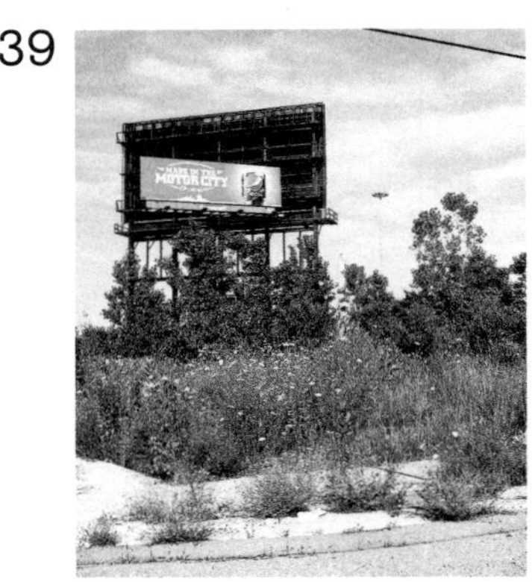

Hastings Street, 2015

Milwaukee Junction Neighborhood

The picture shows the remnants of Hastings Street, once a bustling street in Detroit's African-American community with bars, nightclubs, restaurants, barber shops, and stores. It has been immortalized in songs by Blind Blake and John Lee Hooker, among others. In the name of Urban Renewal, Hastings Street was torn down, along with the entire Black Bottom and Paradise Valley neighborhoods. Today it is buried under the Chrysler Freeway that is part of I-75. Marsha Music, whose father owned a record store on Hastings Street, remembers the street's demolition: "My first memory of Hastings was that my father took me to a place near where his record shop had been. I was a little girl, about three or four. He walked me across the street from the place where we were standing over to this gigantic dirt pit that was in the ground. It looked like a canyon to me. He looked at me and said ... 'This is where Hastings used to be.' ... As I get older I realized that it was the initial diggings for the I-75 freeway. What my father so graphically understood and expressed with that sentence was that a way of life had been totally destroyed by the Chrysler Freeway. The street of Hastings just no longer existed." °

° Latzman Moon (1994). Untold Tales, Unsung Heroes, 361

Detroit is the end result of decisions we made, laws we passed, economic policies, and cultural attitudes we supported, on our way to the suburbanized, mall-bound, racially and economically segregated world we live in today. ... When America happens to a place, Detroit is the result, all of it, hard-scrabble urban core and suburban millionaire enclaves and everything in between.

Jerry Herron (2013). Motor City Breakdown

Suburbanization
Black Bottom & Paradise Valley
Freeways / Interstates

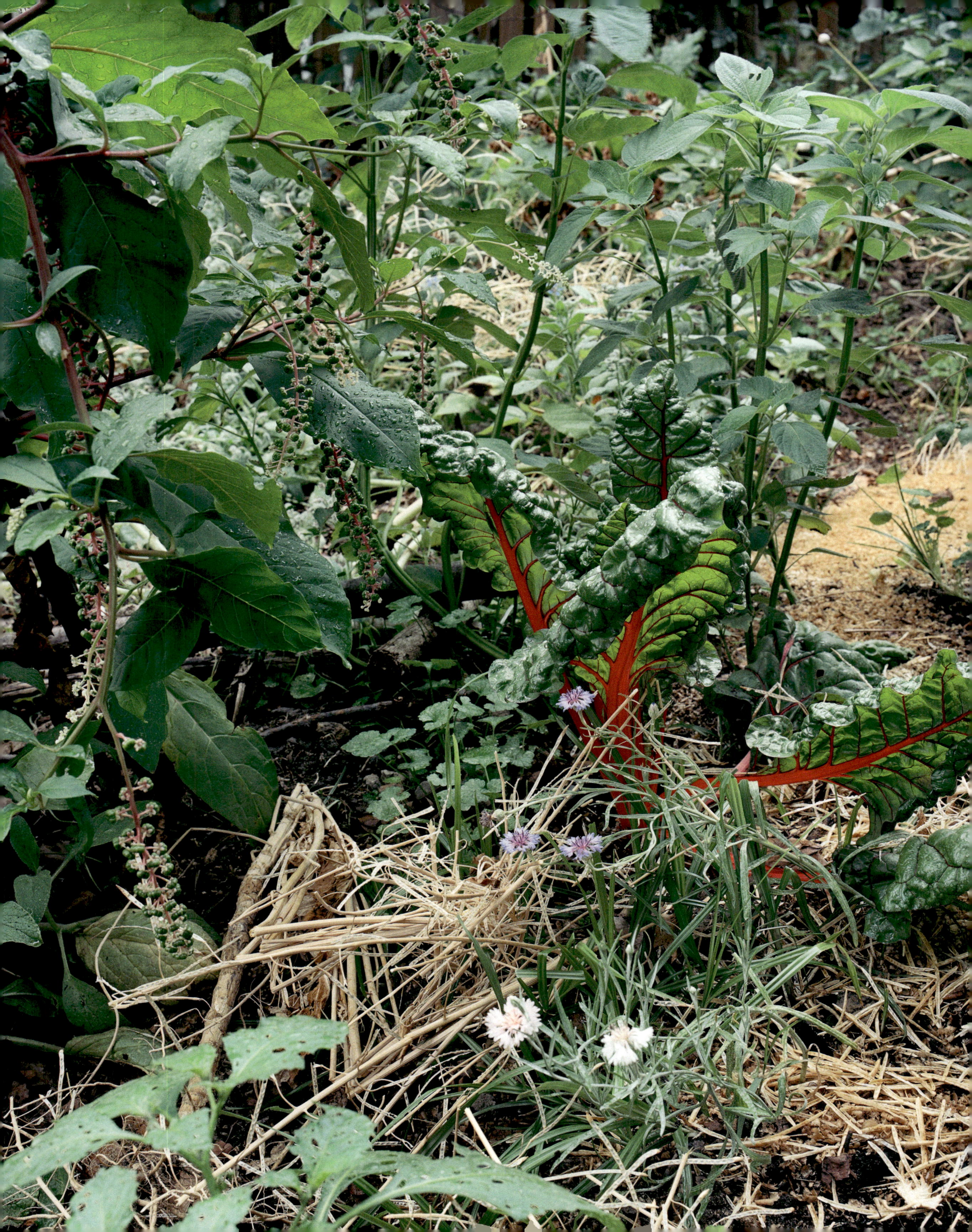

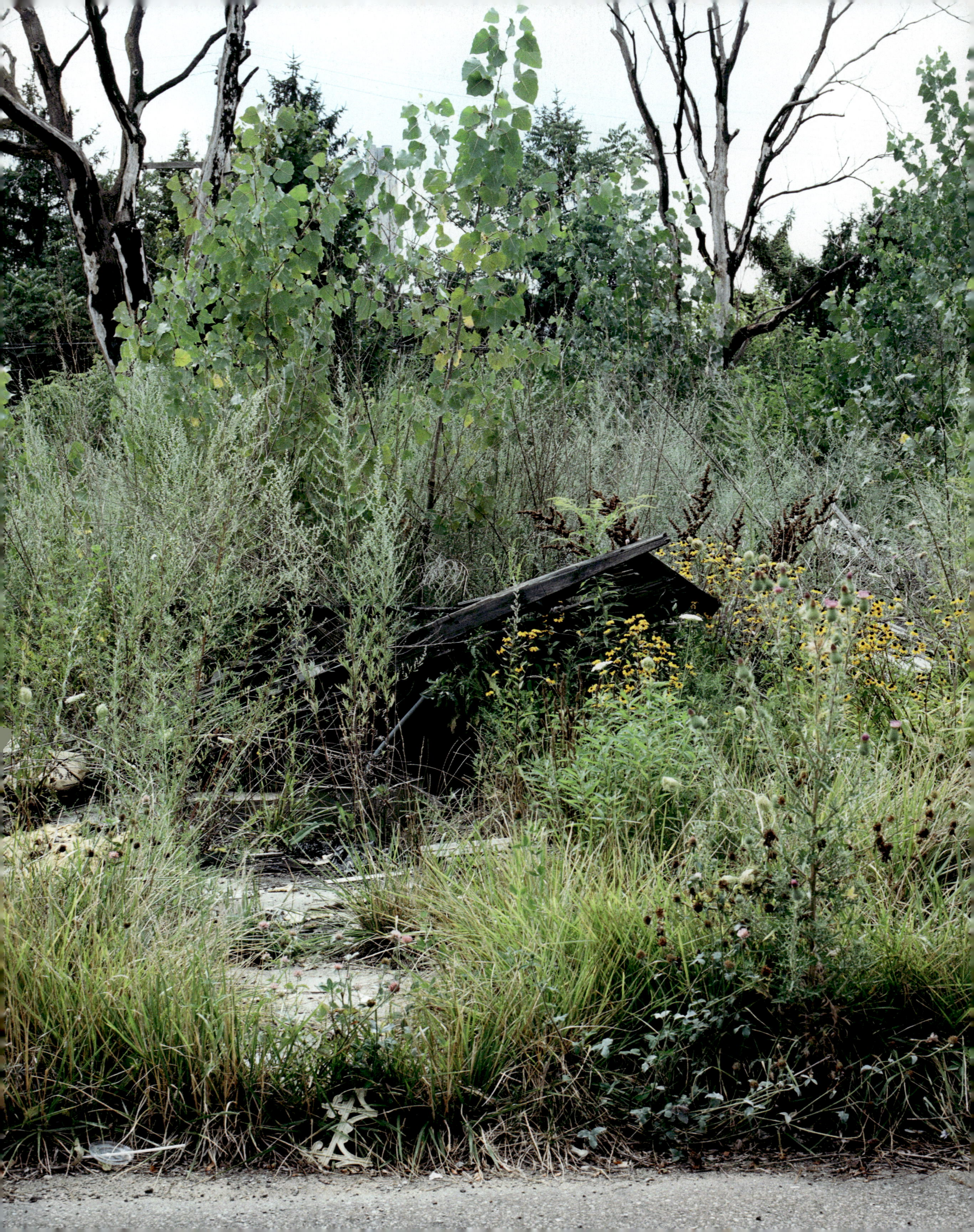

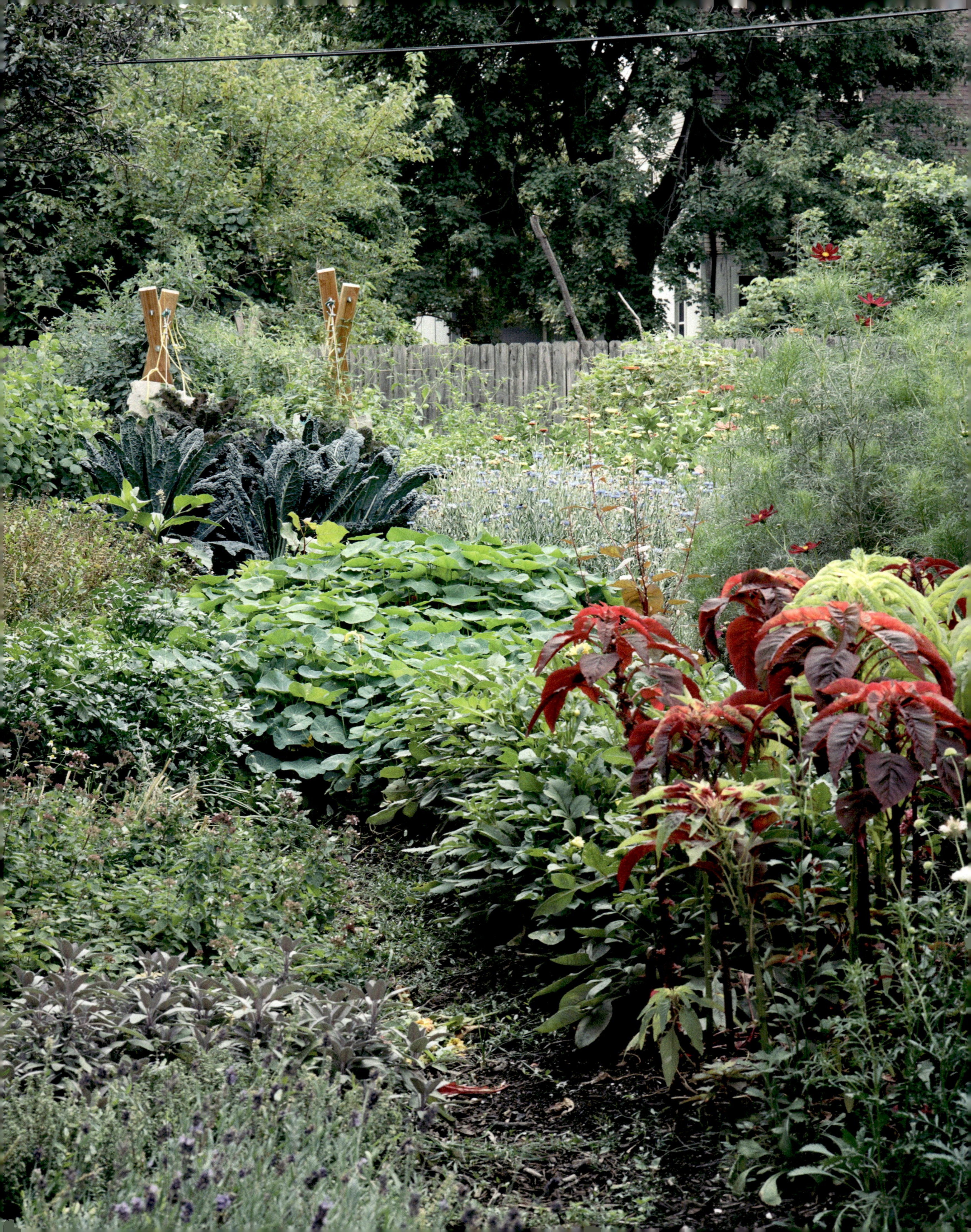

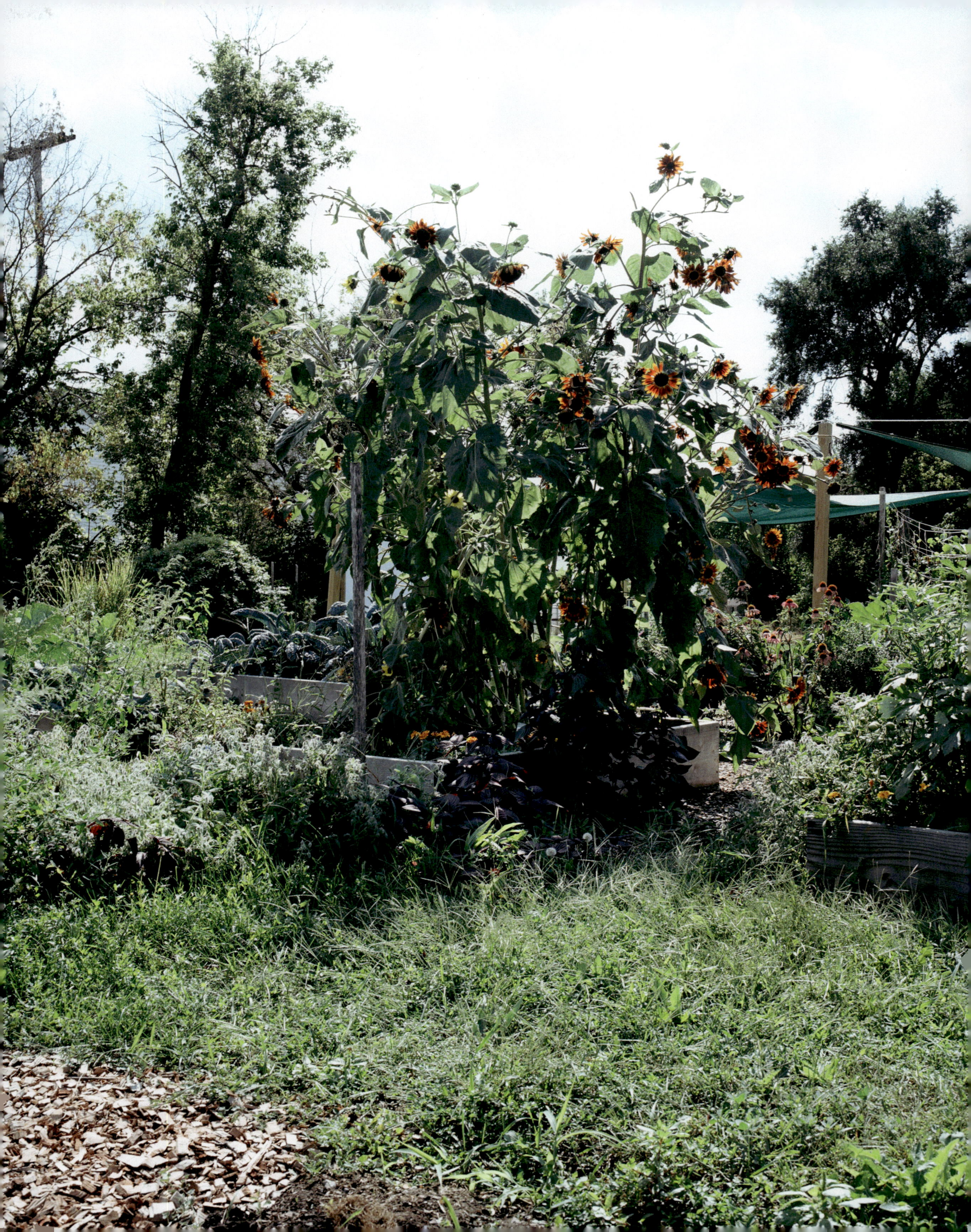

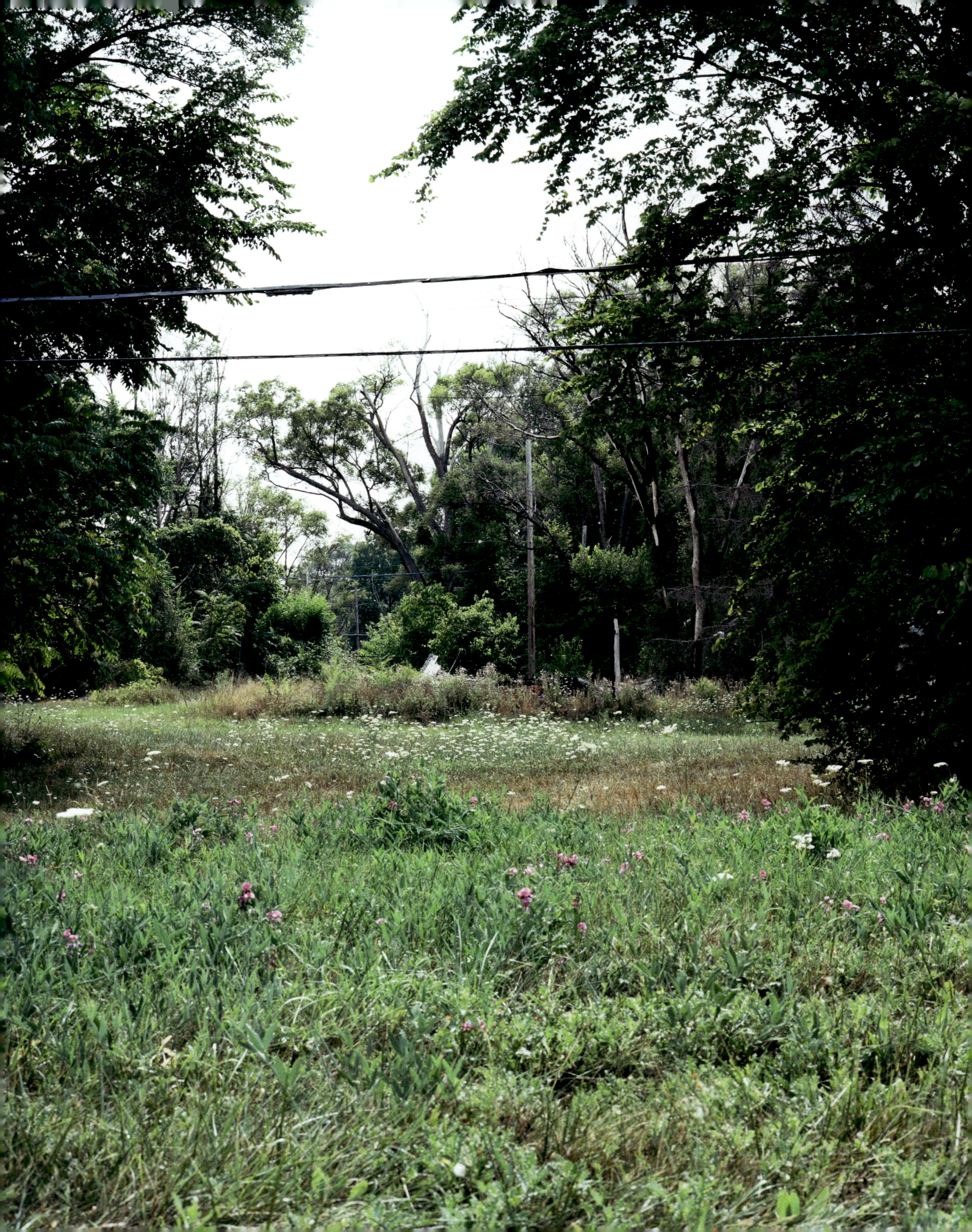

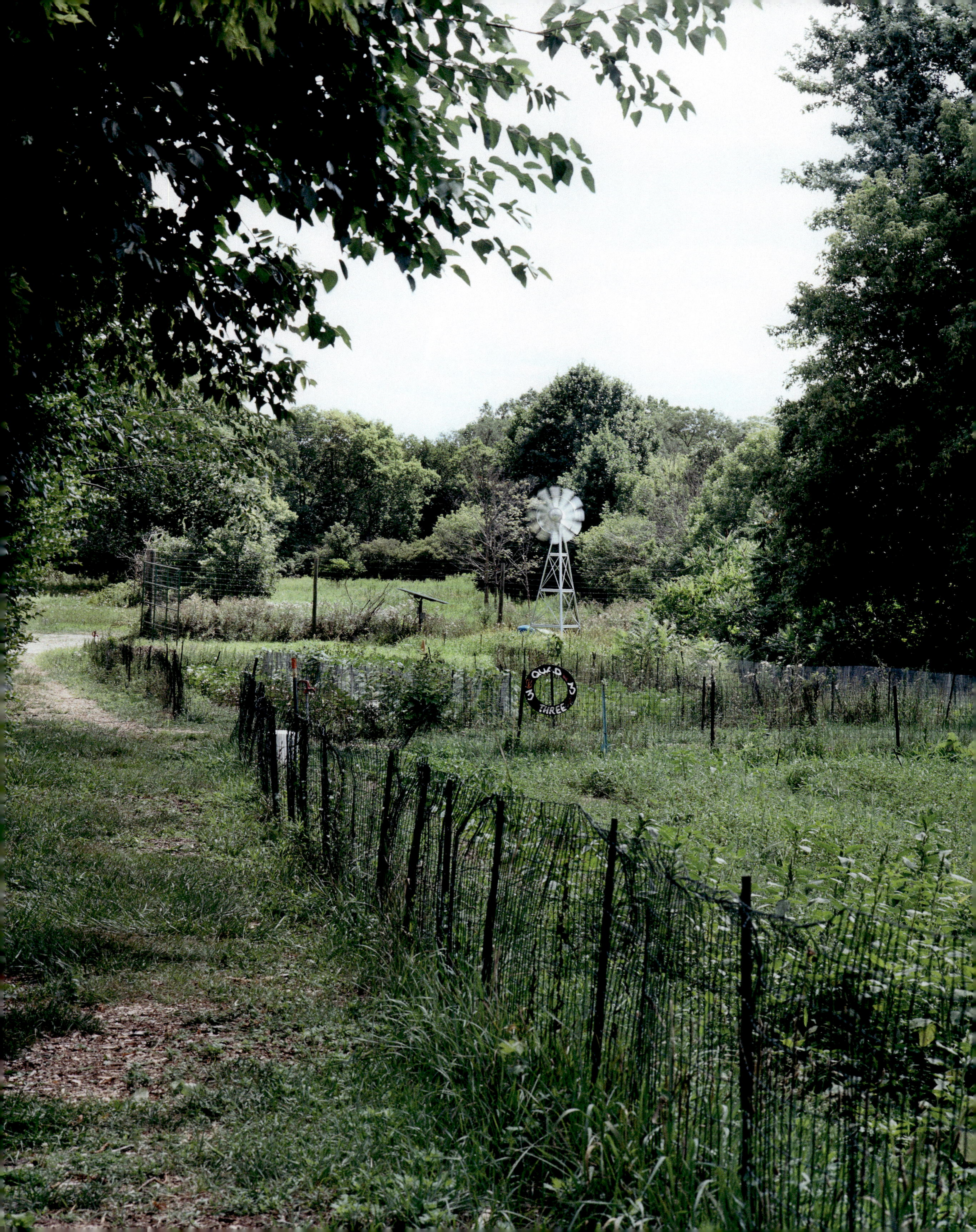
3
3
THREE

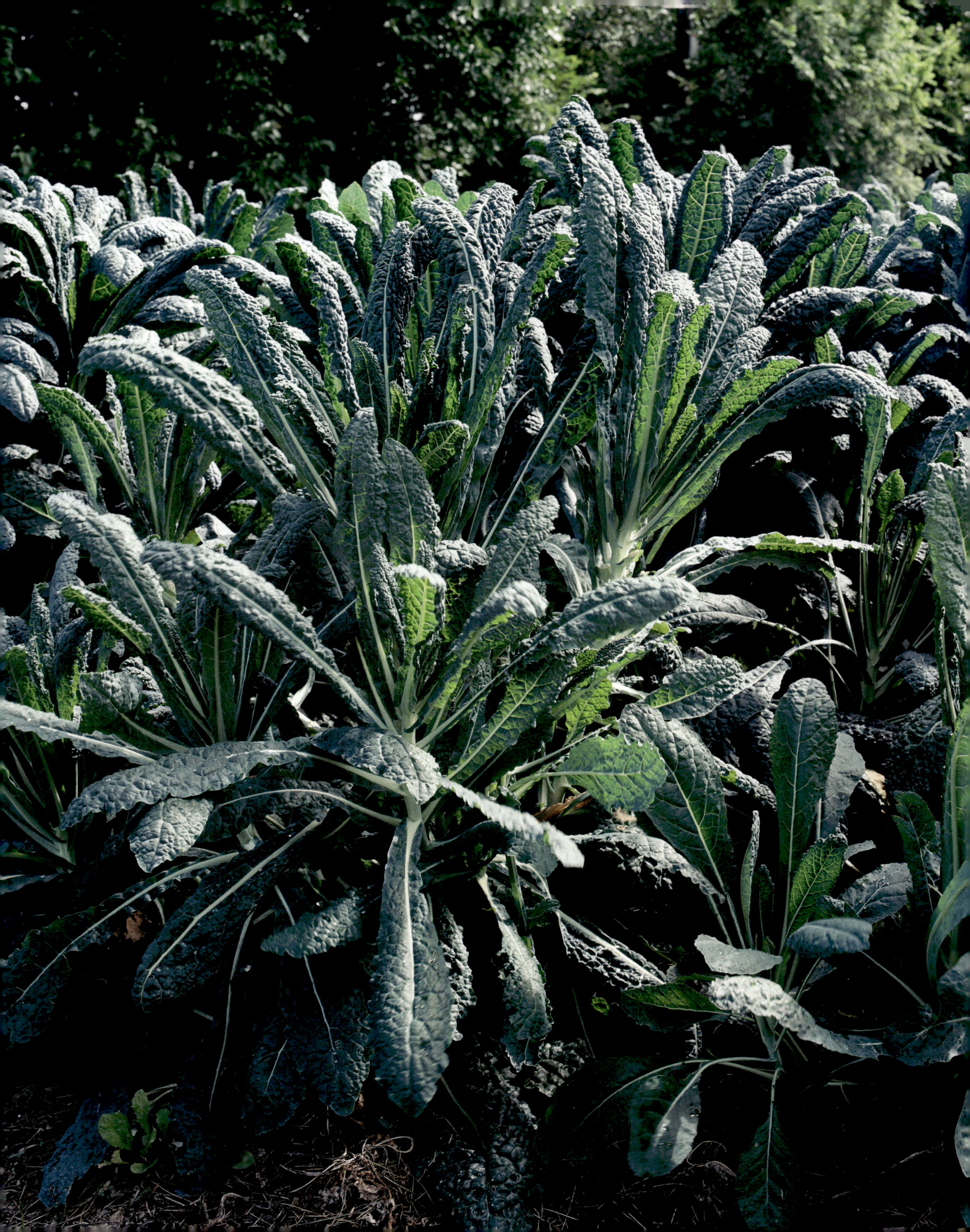

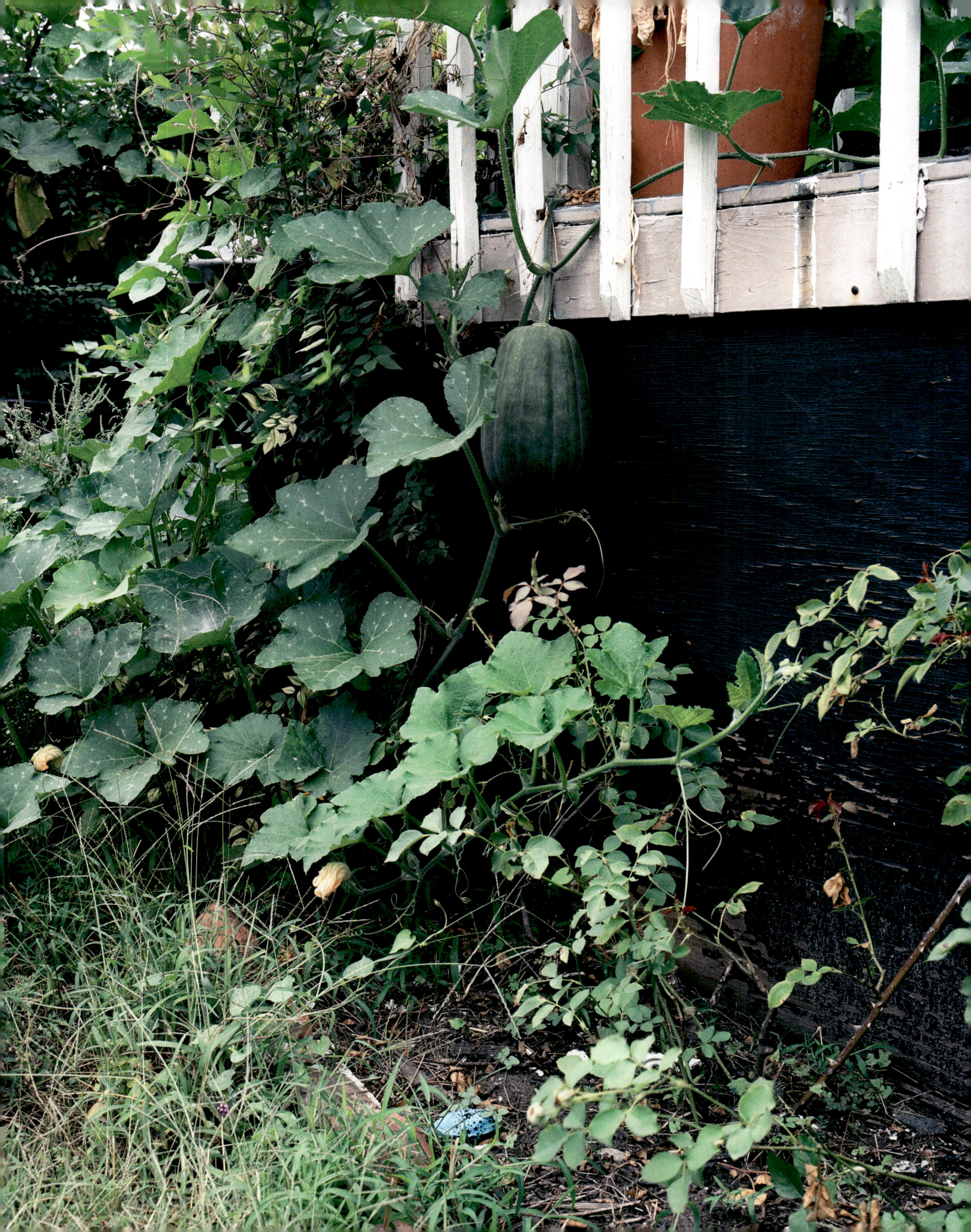

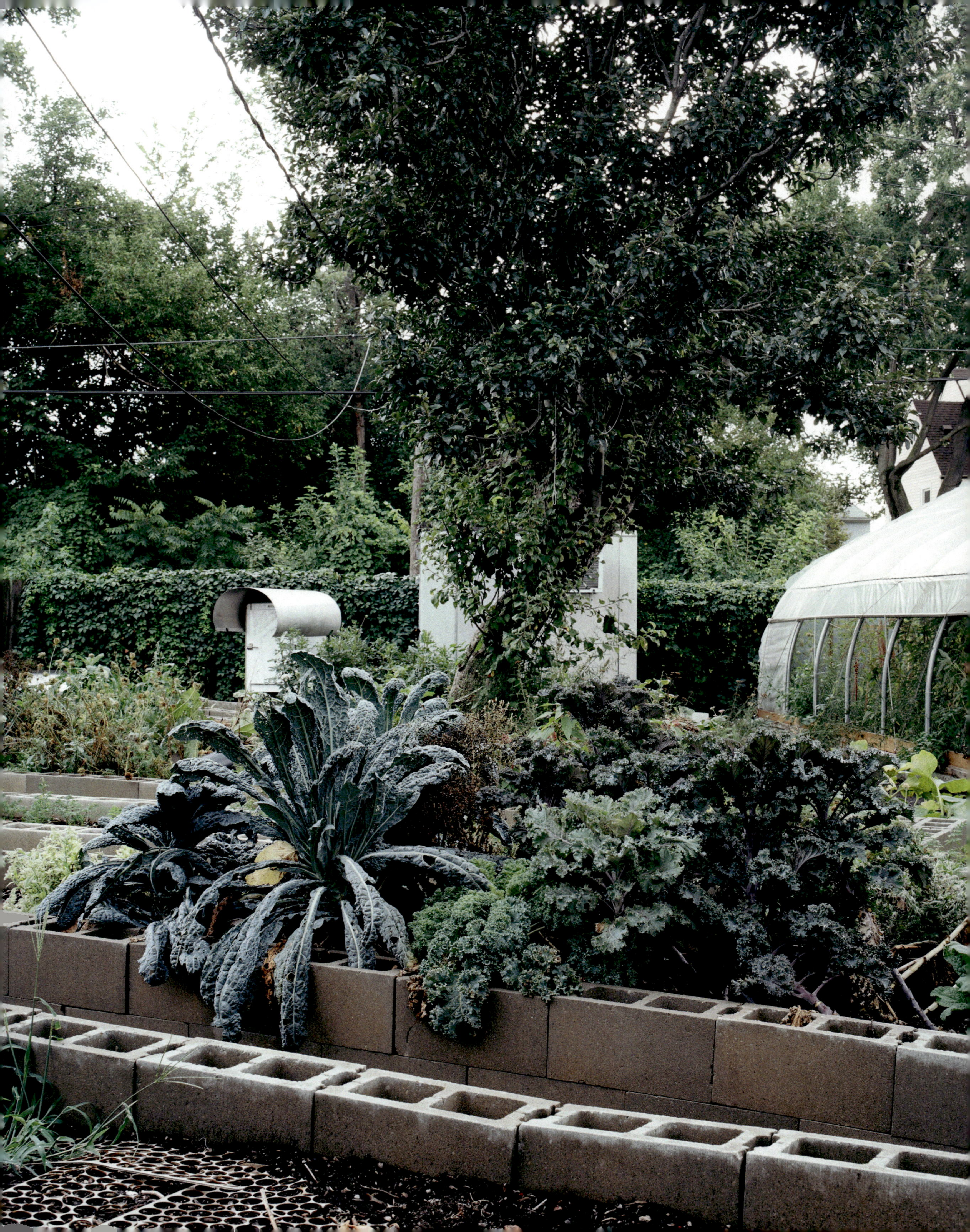

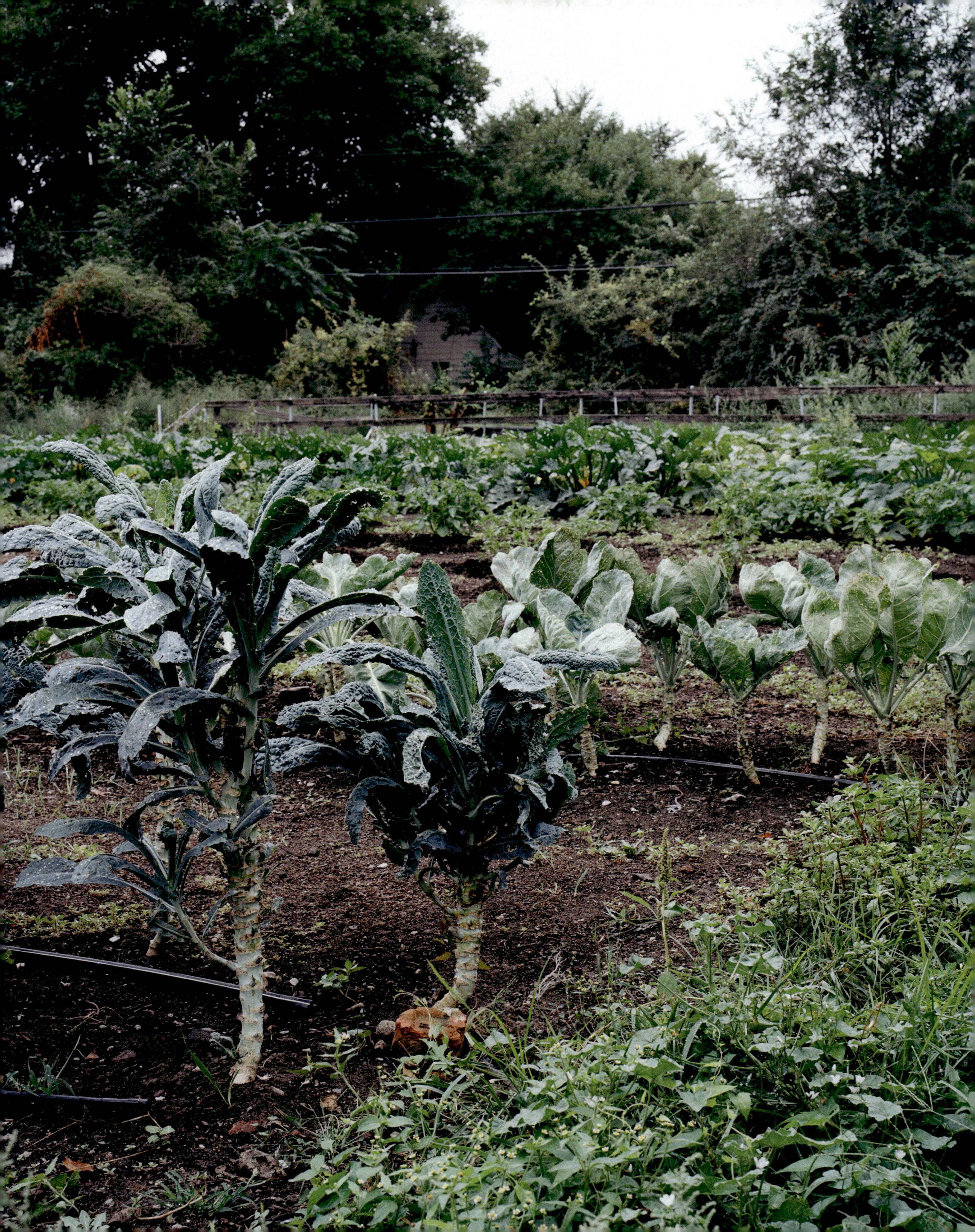

When urban farming gets talked about it gets presented as a new thing. But people have been farming here for a long time. ... when we bring it up as a new thing, we invisibalize the struggles of the people that were here prior to us: The Ribbon Farms, Victory Gardens, Liberty Gardens, the Farm-A-Lot Program in the 1970s, the Gardening Angels, Gerald Hairston. But even before them, the original people of this land, the Native Americans, the Anishinaabe people, they also grew food here, too. So in that sense, agriculture in this area is not new. What is new is the city.

Shane Bernardo, then manager at Earthworks Urban Farm in our interview 2016

→ Anishinaabe, Farm-A-Lot Program, Gardening Angels, Ribbon Farms, Victory Gardens / Liberty Gardens

40 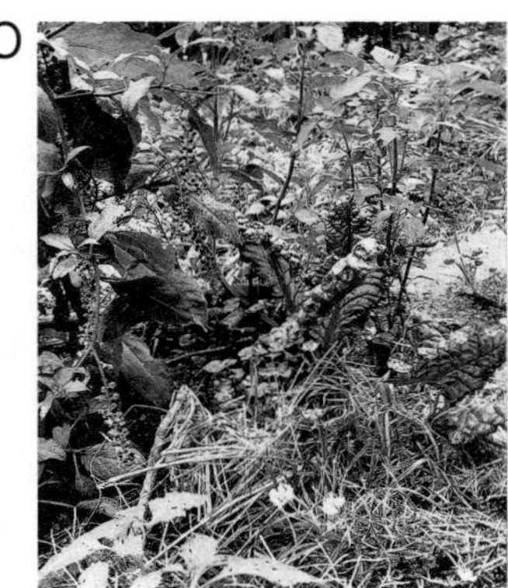

Ile Oko Farm (Swiss Chard), 2016

Jefferson Chalmers Neighborhood

Ile Oko Farm was founded in 2012 by Atieno Nyarkasagam and Lorenzo Herron on their home property. The name Ile Oko is taken from the Yoruba language and loosely translates as House of Agriculture. Lorenzo grew up in the neighborhood and Atieno grew up in Nairobi, Kenya. Both have been engaged in urban agriculture since 2002, growing vegetables, fruit trees, and medicinal plants. In addition to providing a sustainable food source, for them farming is also a political act that touches on issues of food security, land distribution, social justice as well as their African cultural roots. They see urban agriculture as a way to guarantee access to adequate, nourishing, sustainable, and culturally relevant food. Together with other initiatives and urban farmers, they campaign for the city of Detroit to provide its citizens with empty lots for the cultivation of fresh food, or to make it possible for everyone to buy land.

The picture shows the garden bed in front of their house, with Swiss chard, peppers, American pokeweed, creeping charly, and small clove pinks.

41 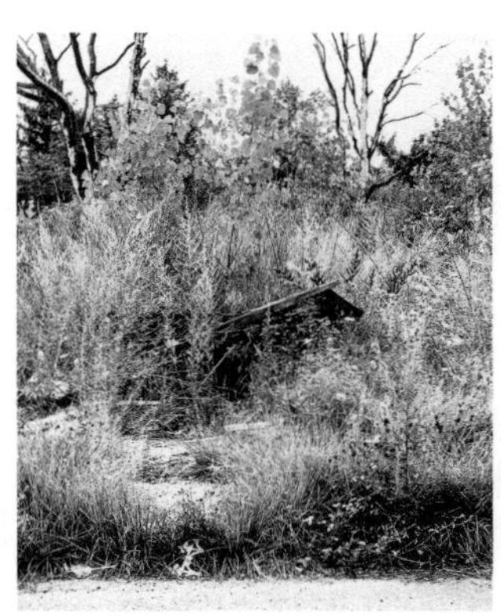

5721 Dubois Street, 2015

Poletown East Neighborhood

“Owning a home in a ‘Polish’ neighborhood was of prime importance. ... There had to be a garden with carrots, parsley, onions, beets, and tomatoes, to be eaten in season and canned and stored for the winter. There had to be a lawn, neatly trimmed and weeded. There had to be flowers — many different varieties for continuous bloom and for trading with the neighbors. Seeds were gathered and stored for the next spring — one could not afford to buy flower seeds every year! During the spring and summer, to keep this vegetables, flowers, and lawn thriving, there was the daily ritual of watering, even on the days it rained.”

Regina Kóscielski. Portrait of a Polish-American, in: Hartmann (1974), 115

Until 2013, a simple framehouse from 1908 stood on this property. It probably burned down, the charred remains of the roof are still visible. Brown-eyed susans are still flowering in the front garden. The property is located in the Poletown East neighborhood, where until 1900 many Polish migrants had settled on former ribbon farms.

→ 1/2 2550 East Grand Boulevard, 2015
→ 14 East Ferry Street, 2015

You can look at a vacant lot and instead of seeing devastation, see hope. See the opportunity to grow your own food ... A vacant lot represents the possibilities for cultural revolution.

Grace Lee Boggs (2011) in an interview with Democracy Now!

42

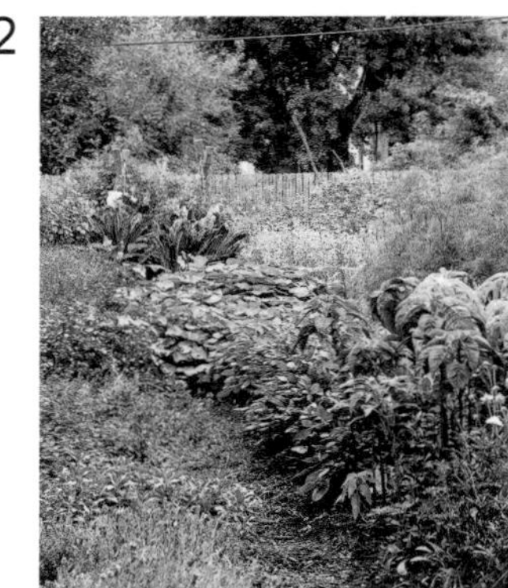

Molly and Mike's Garden, 2015

North End Neighborhood

Molly Hubbell and Mike Zuzolo run a garden behind their house. Both came to Detroit in 2014. While Mike is working on an aquaponics system — a self-contained cycle of aquaculture fish farming and hydroponic plant cultivation — Molly grows flowers and vegetables using traditional methods. Due to high lead levels in the soil on their site, the plants grow in organic compost inside raised beds that are sealed off from the contaminated subsoil. Many properties in Detroit are contaminated with heavy metals or oil because house paints used to contain lead and there exist insufficient environmental regulations for industry. Before they start growing anything, gardens and farms therefore have their soil tested.

Besides her own garden, Molly works at Keep Growing Detroit. Through its Garden Resource Program, the organization provides urban farmers and gardeners with seeds and seedlings. It also helps them network with one another to cultivate a food sovereign city where the majority of fruits and vegetables consumed by Detroiters are grown by residents within the city's limits.

→ 48 Molly and Mike's Garden, 2018

43

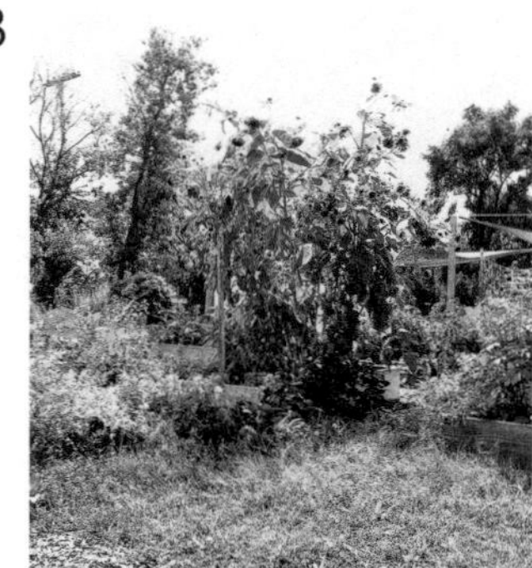

Georgia Street Community Collective (Free Picking Field), 2018

Airport Sub Neighborhood

→ For a description see 36 Georgia Street Community Collective, 2018

44

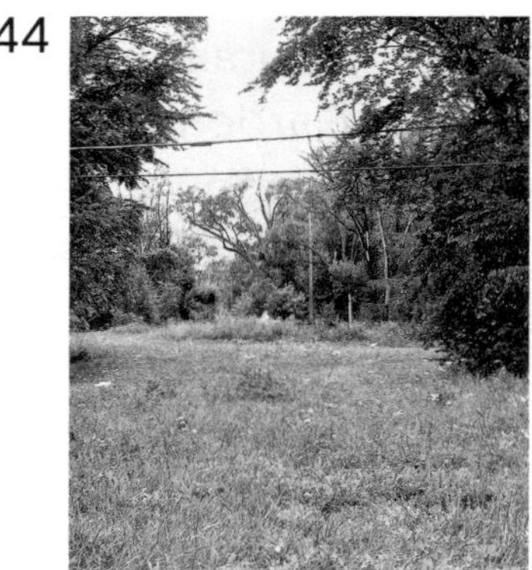

Eastlawn and Lakeview Streets (Burned Down House), 2016

Riverbend Neighborhood

This photo was taken on Eastlawn Street and shows a view of Lakeview Street, which runs parallel. Behind everlasting pea and wild carrot in flower, you can see the remnants of a burned down house. It was built in 1924 and was one of the last occupied houses in the neighborhood until 2009. As activist Grace Lee Boggs points out in an interview, Detroit's many open spaces may appear to be a disadvantage, but at the same time they offer the opportunity to rethink the entire city. Detroit's vacant land can be the starting point for an urban agriculture that could not only feed the entire city, but also create meaningful, autonomous jobs.

45 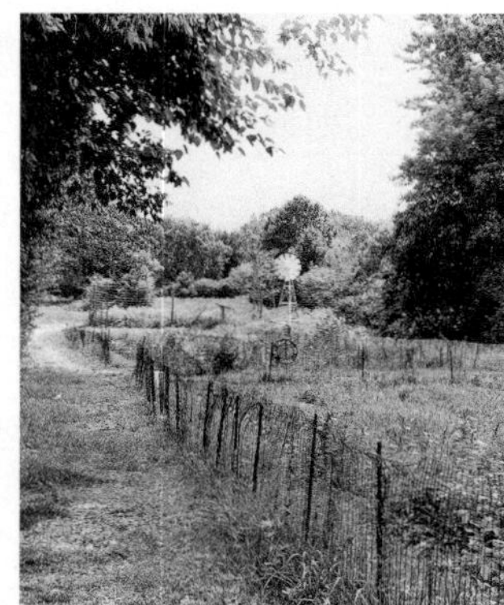

D-Town Farm, Detroit Black Community Food Security Network, 2016

Franklin Park Neighborhood

Since 1950, Detroit's population has shrunk by two thirds. Yet the surface area of the city has remained the same, which has radical consequences for its infrastructure. Large sections of the city are so-called food deserts, areas where there are no grocery stores or supermarkets for miles. The Detroit Black Community Food Security Network (DBCFSN) was formed in 2006 to address this food insecurity. The network organizes African-American Detroiters to play a self-determinate and active leadership role in the local food security movement. This means creating wealth, ownership, and prosperity for and in the community as well as raising questions about the role of racism and injustice in relation to the food system and urban development. In a city that is predominantly African-American, mostly white developers have privileged access to land and predominantly white, well educated newcomers benefit from the current redevelopment. At the suggestion of the DBCFSN the Detroit Food Policy Council was founded in 2009 to represent urban growers dealing with the city administration. Its demands include that: "Vacant land should be available for agricultural use. ... Priority should be given to city residents for the purchase of vacant land. ... The City should acknowledge the importance of community gardens and protect them as resources that will not be taken over for other types of development." °

The main project of the DBCFSN is D-Town Farm, one of the largest urban farms in Detroit. Besides the cultivation of organic fresh food and a Detroit Community Market there are child and youth training programs. A cooperative supermarket is currently in planning. Since 2008, the farm has been located in the Meyers Tree Nursery in Rouge Park. The use of the land is regulated by long-term license agreements with the city of Detroit, as there is still no legal basis for a purchase.

The wind turbine in the picture, behind the beds of amaranth, okra, and jalapeño pepper, is part of the rainwater supply system.

www.dbcfsn.org

° Detroit Food Policy Council (2012). Public Land Sale Process in Detroit: A Community Perspective

46 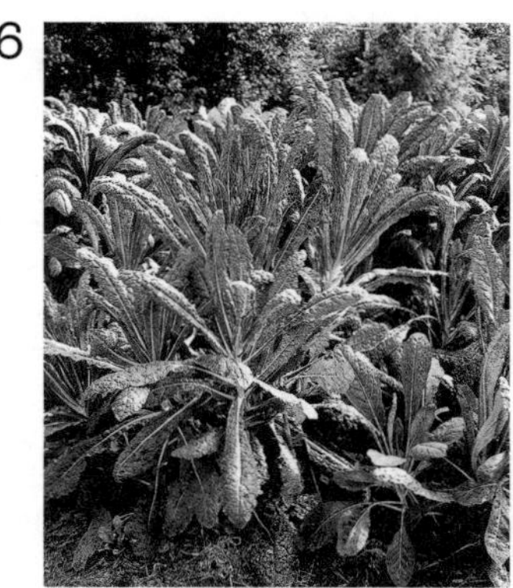

Oakland Avenue Urban Farm (Lacinato Kale), 2016

North End Neighborhood

The picture shows lacinato kale, which is very popular in Detroit and can be seen in almost every garden. This type of cabbage originates from Tuscany in Italy and has been grown there for centuries. It is also known as Tuscan kale or cavolo nero, which means black cabbage.

The picture was taken in a field on the Oakland Avenue Urban Farm in North End Detroit, which is described in detail in pictures 18 and 19.

→ 18/19 Oakland Avenue Urban Farm, 2016

47 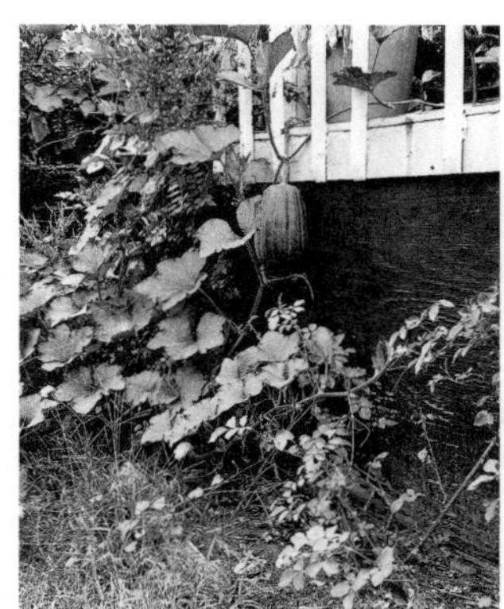

Bandhu Garden (Water Squash), 2018

Campau / Banglatown Neighborhood

Bandhu Gardens was founded in 2015 by Emily Staugaitis and Minara Begum when both became neighbors and friends despite not speaking a word of each other's languages. They live in Banglatown, a neighborhood that is home to over five thousand Bangladeshi Americans. Women and families grow dense and vibrant vegetable gardens in their backyards, on their verandas, or close to their homes, planting such South Asian vegetables as bitter melon, long beans, sweet and water squashes, and a wild variety of peppers.

Bandhu Gardens is a small business network for gardens managed by Bangladeshi women, allowing them to manage their households as well as to earn some money. As neighbors they work together to sell vegetables, provide catering services, do pop-up events, and teach cooking classes. A community house was in preparation when I visited the gardens in 2018. "Bandhu Gardens" is half Bangla, half English and means Friend's Garden. The photograph shows a sweet squash growing on Emily's veranda.

www.bandhugardens.com

48 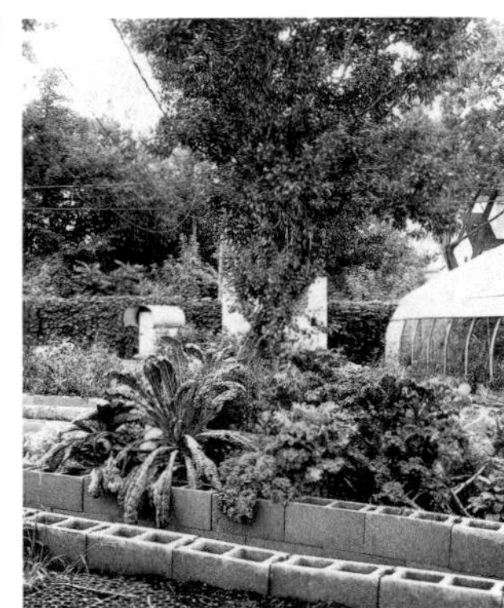

Molly and Mike's Garden, 2018

North End Neighborhood

For a description see
→ 42 Molly and Mike's Garden, 2015

49 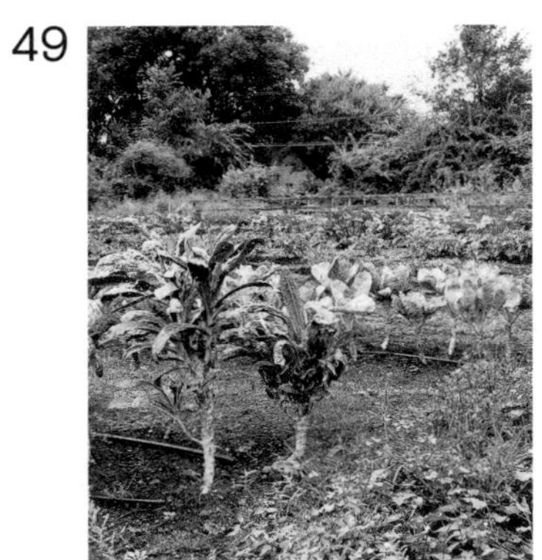

Earthworks Urban Farm, The Capuchin Soup Kitchen, 2018

Islandview Neighborhood

Earthworks Urban Farm is part of the Capuchin Soup Kitchen in Detroit. It was founded in 1929 during the Great Depression in the Capuchin Monastery of St. Bonaventure and served around 2,000 food rations per day at the time. It still serves the same amount of meals. Over time, activities have been expanded to include donations of clothing, household appliances, and pantries, as well as various facilities and programs to support people after incarceration or substance abuse.

In 1997, the Capuchin friar Rick Samyn started a small garden after noticing that children in the neighborhood were buying their food at the gas station (see Register for Food Desert). Over time, the garden grew into the Earthworks Urban Farm. Today, it supplies the soup kitchen with vegetables and many neighborhood gardens with seedlings. It runs garden training programs that qualify Detroit residents to start their own business or find jobs in urban agriculture. Earthworks' mission is to develop, educate, and inspire the community and to restore the connection to the environment through urban agriculture. It is rooted in the awareness that injustice and racism are manifested in the current food system.

Pictures 49 and 52 both show a field with yellow summer squash, a variety of kale, potatoes, peppers, and asparagus. In picture 52 the monastery is also visible in the background.

www.cskdetroit.org/earthworks

→ 52 Earthworks Urban Farm (Church), 2018

Behind the garage ... there was a vegetable garden—rows of tomatoes held up ... with yard sticks and metal rods, yellow summer squash, cucumbers, peppers, and a fig tree sent from Lebanon years ago as a seedling. Mint leaves and oregano lined the edge of the garage, and at the fence separating the house from a neighbor no one in the family knew, bunches of onions.

Hayan Charara. Becoming the Center of Mystery, in: Abraham / Shryock (2000), 407

Great Depression
Food Desert

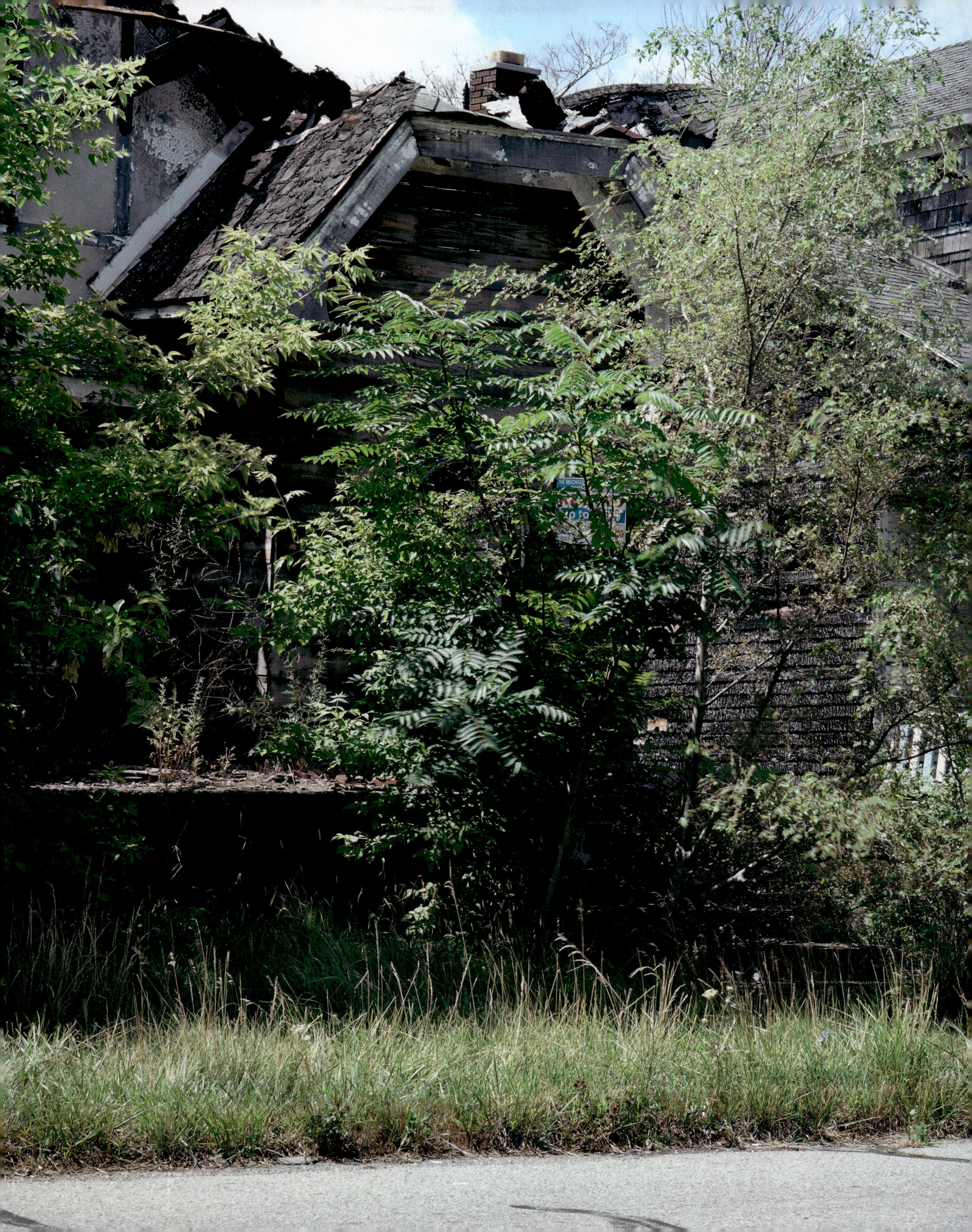

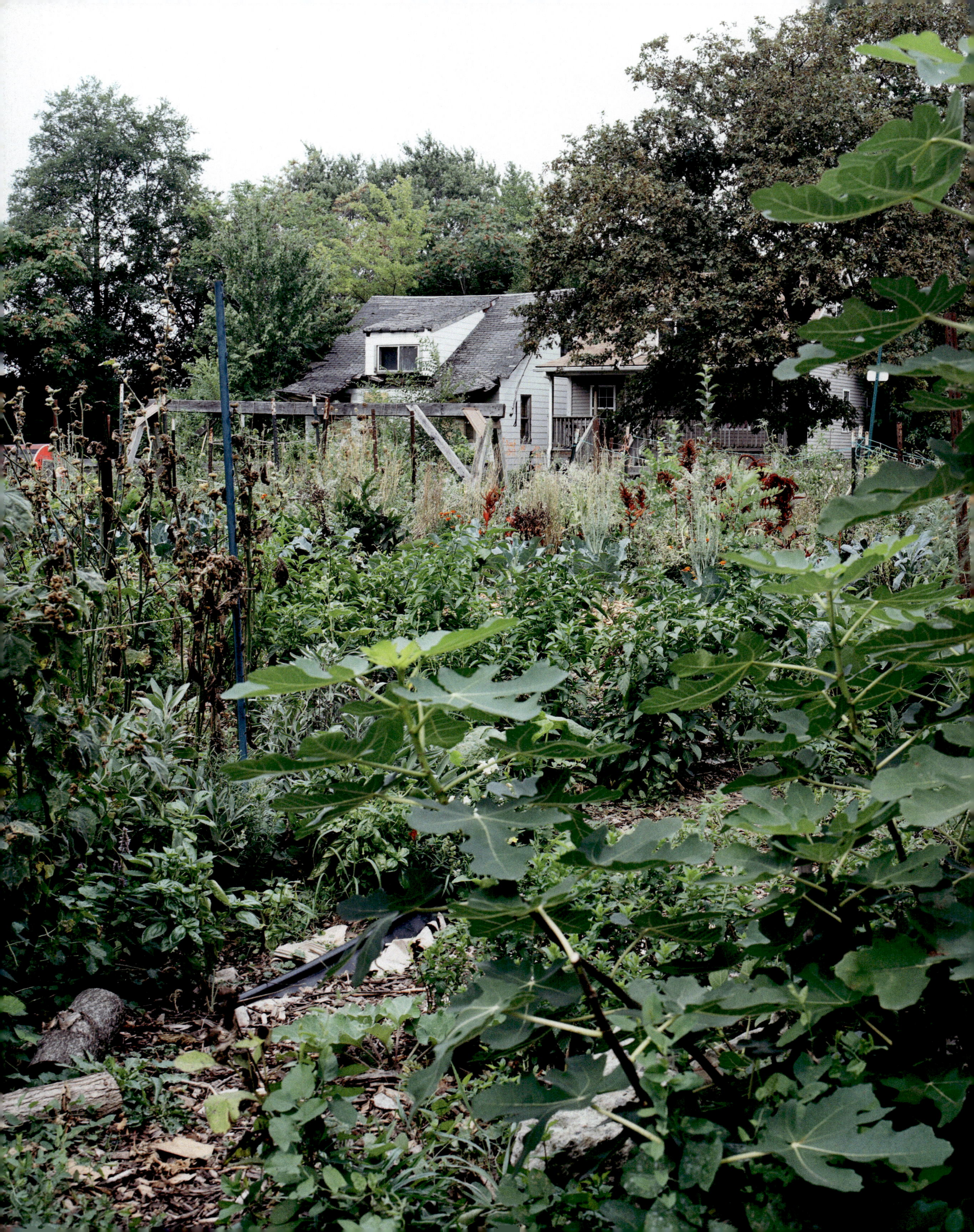

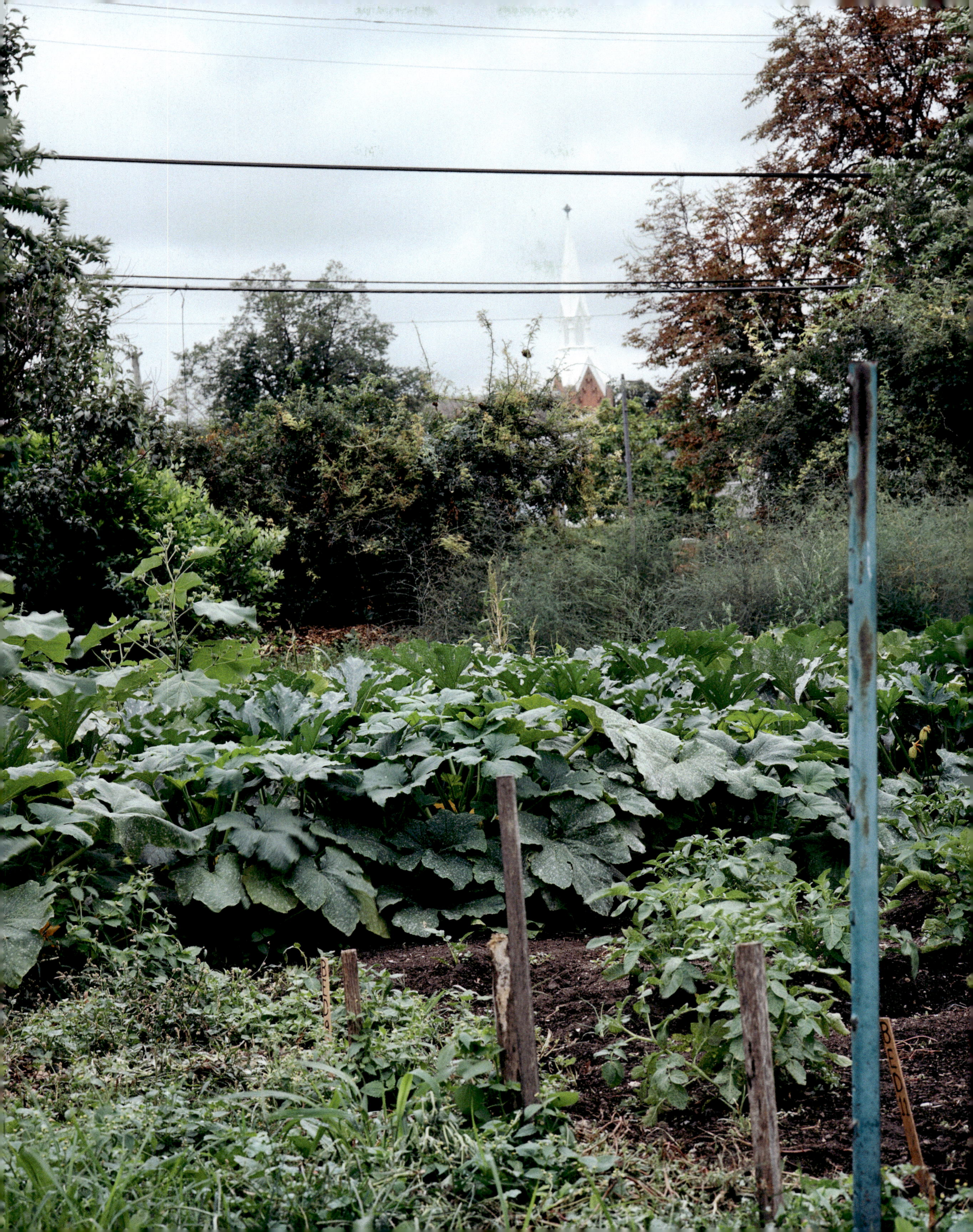

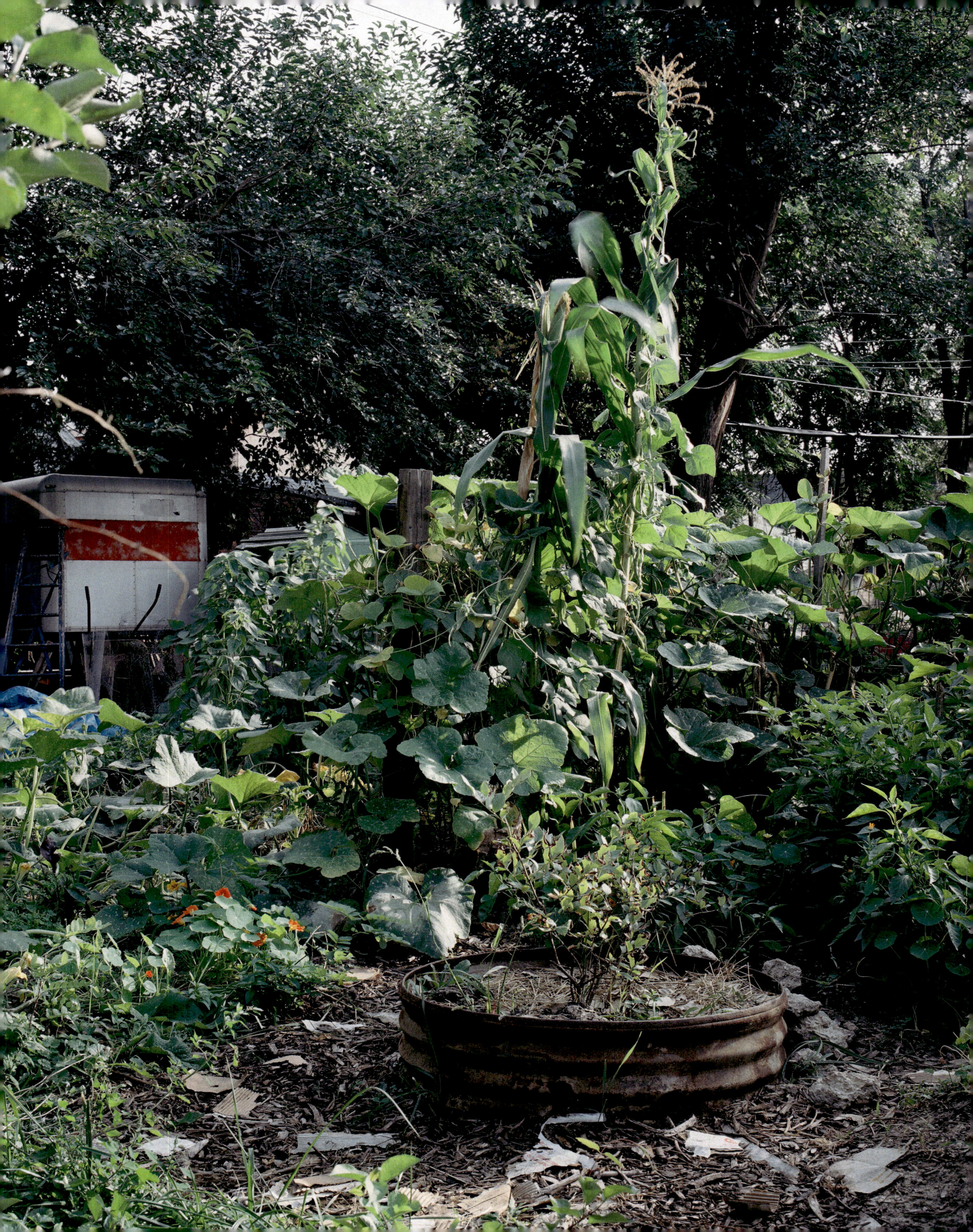

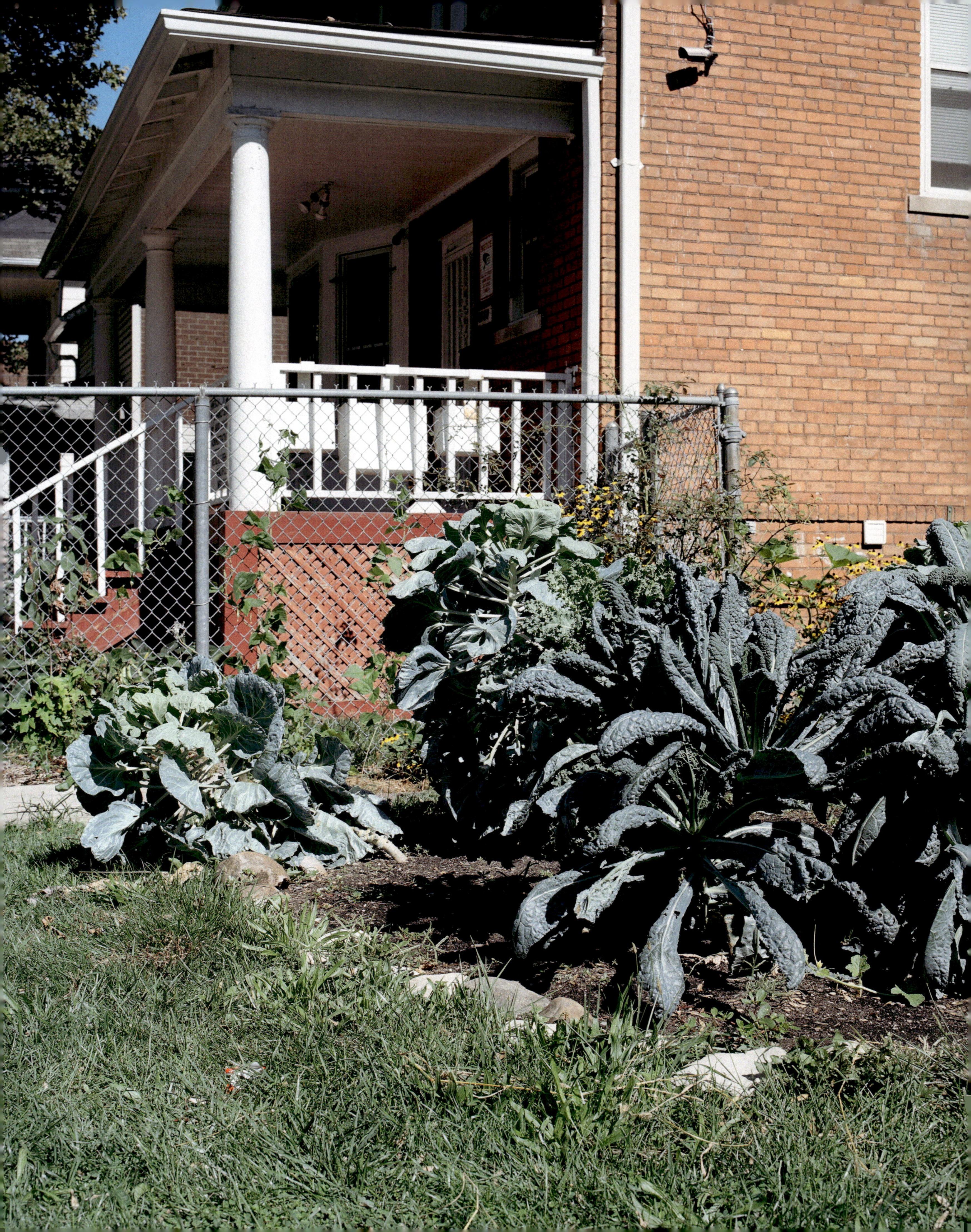

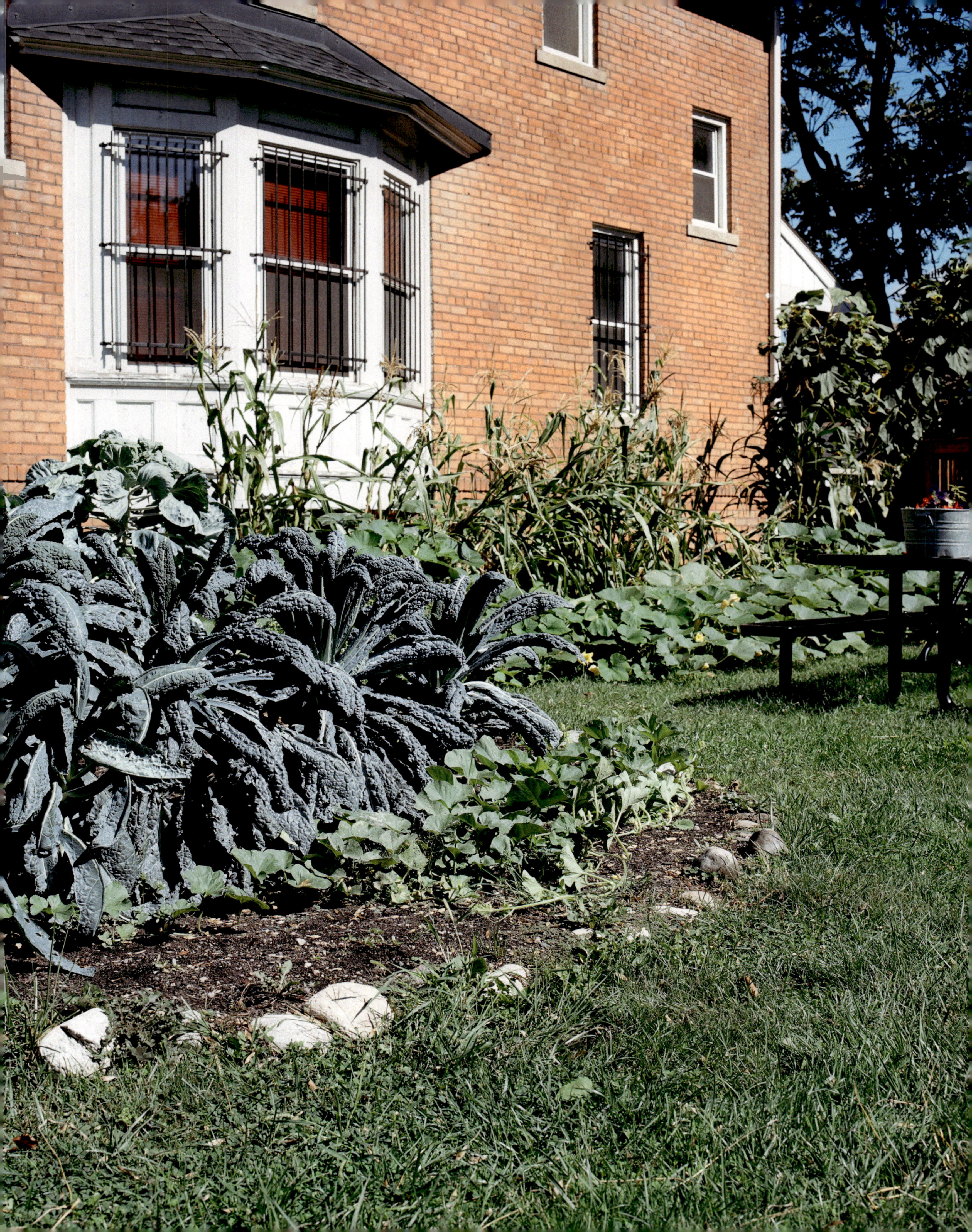

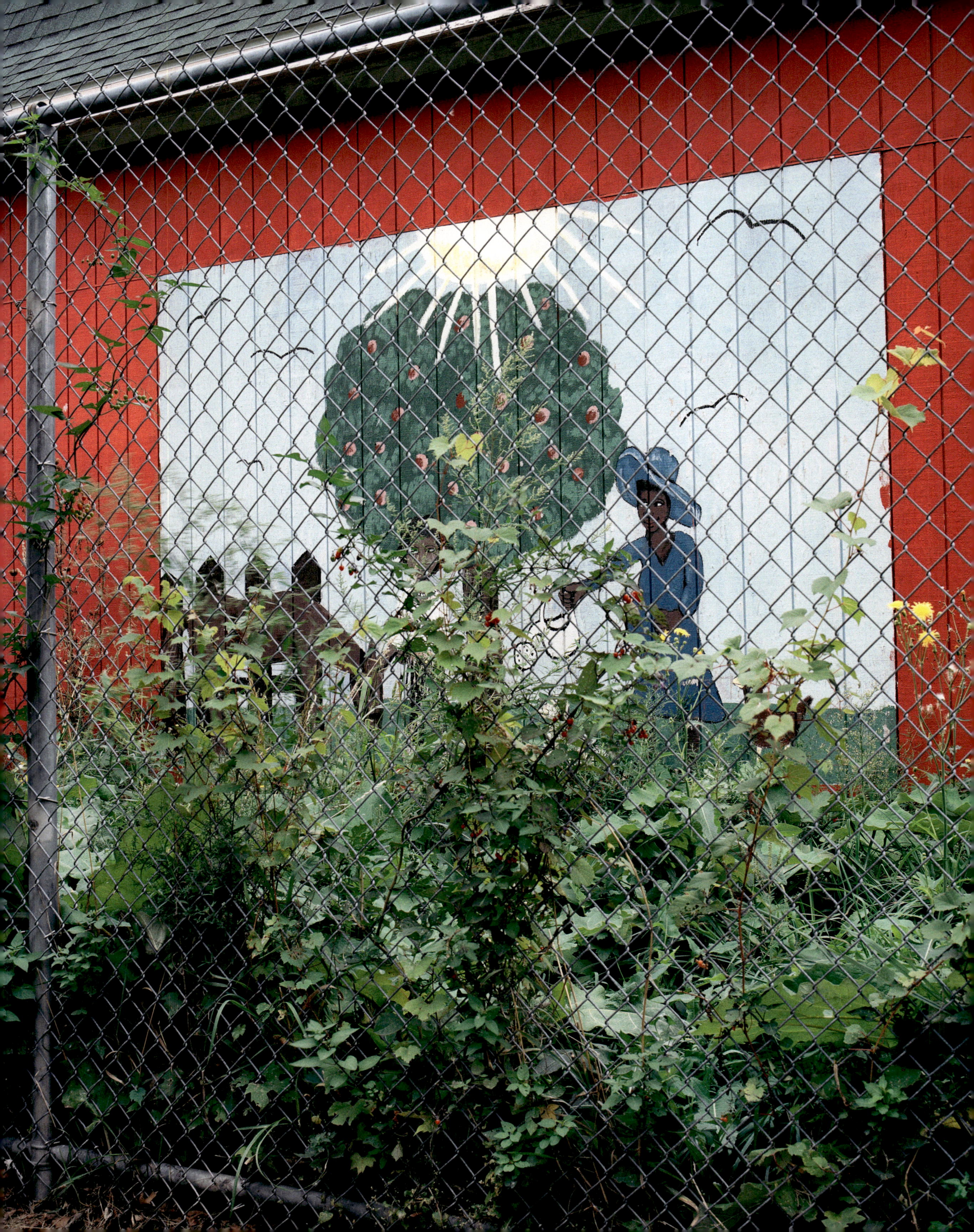

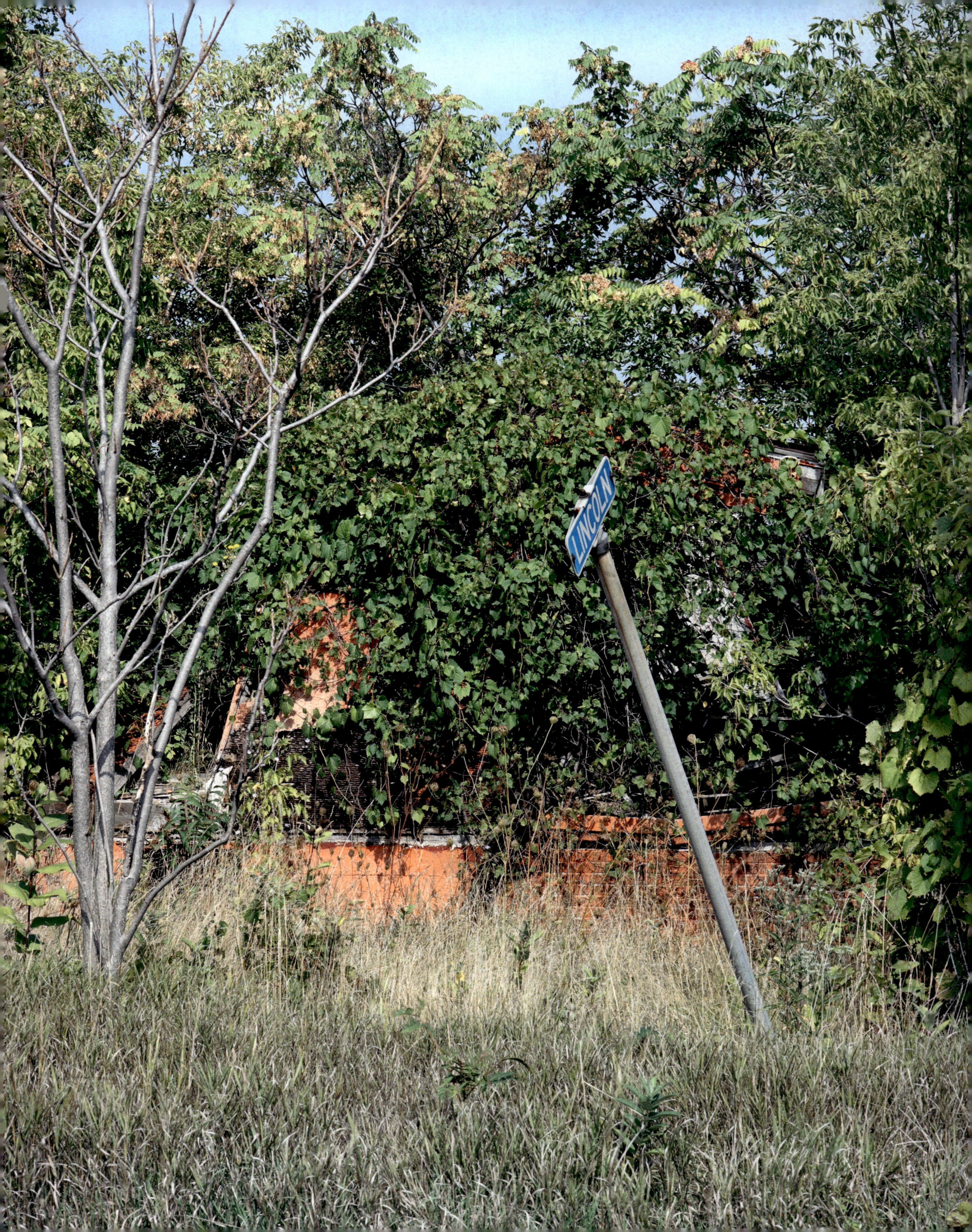
LINCOLN

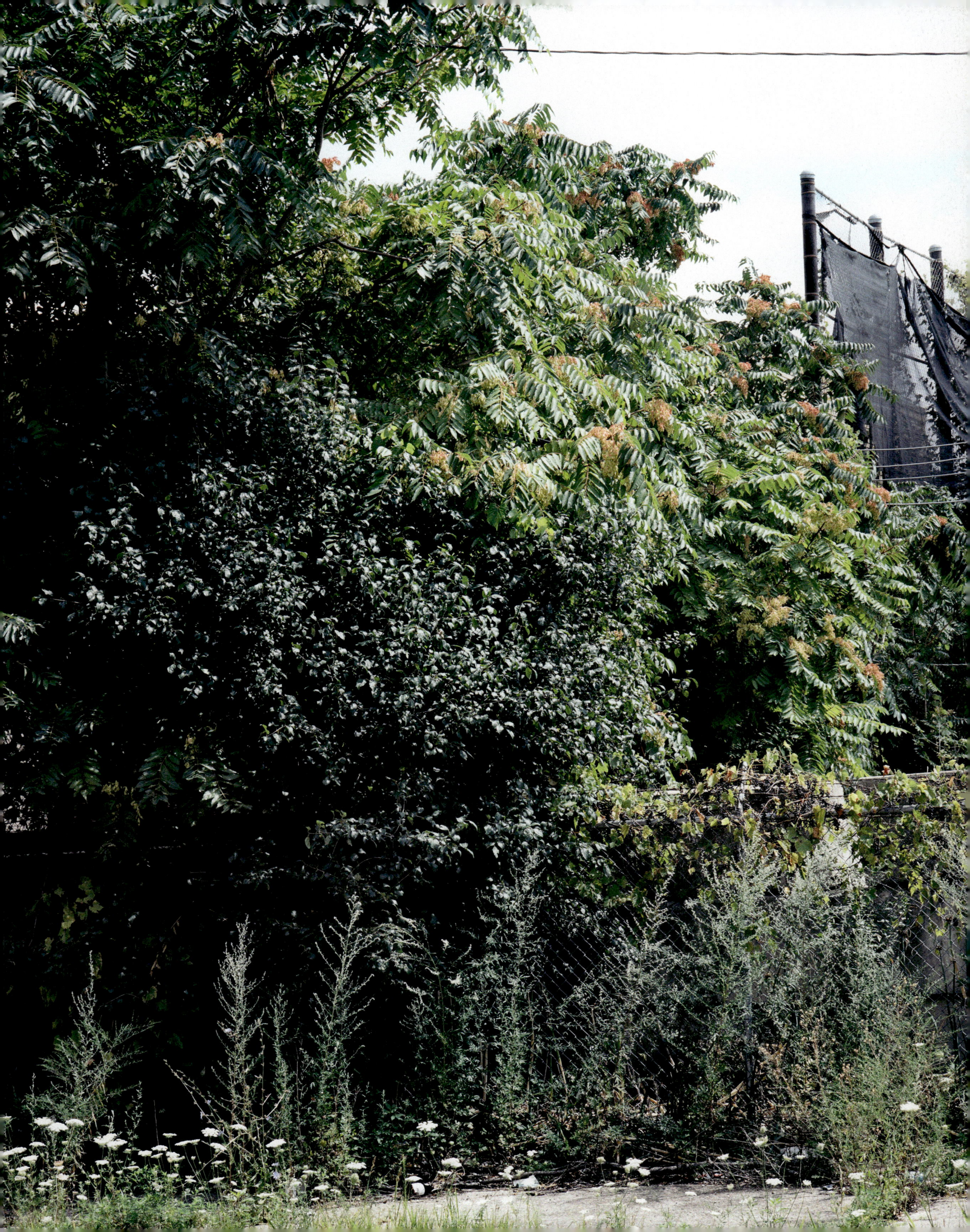

Growing your own food is self-determination, food that you put in the ground, you grew, and you then prepared … It nourishes you and detaches you from the need to go and pay a food bill. Growing food should be a life skill. If you know how to brush your teeth, you should know how to grow squash.

Bianca Danzy, a student farmer at Earthworks Farm, in: Guzmán (2016)

50

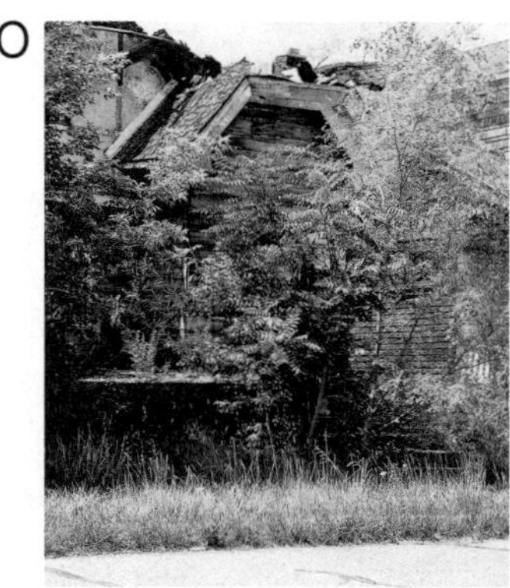

8120 Georgia Street, 2016

Airport Sub Neighborhood

This single-family home dating from 1927 was overgrown with trees of heaven, maple ash, and mulberry trees. Orange day-lily and rose mallow, planted by the former residents, still grew wild in the front lawn. The house was demolished in October 2018. The empty property now belongs to the Detroit Land Bank Authority.

Before I took the photograph in 2016, the house must have been set on fire several times. Behind the little tree of heaven you can make out an "Arson Reward" sign. It promises a reward of $ 5,000 for information leading to an arrest of the arsonists. These rewards were offered by the nonprofit Michigan Arson Prevention Committee for more than 40 years. In 2017, the insurance company that was its sole funder stopped its payments and the committee ceased operation. That year there were 3,400 house fires.

51

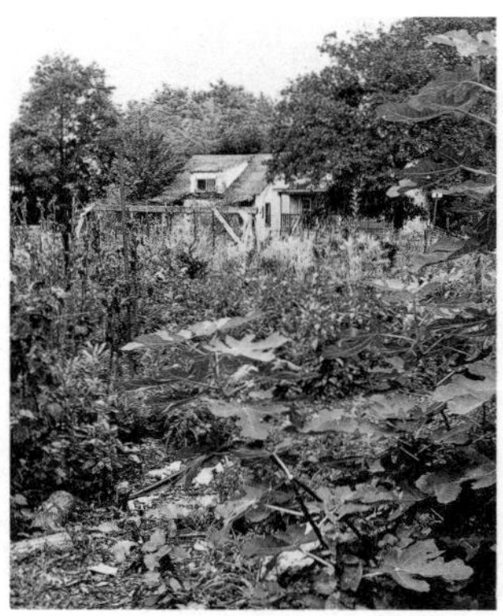

Faina and Graem's Garden (Popps Packing), 2018

Campau / Banglatown Neighborhood

In 2009, Faina Lerman and Graem Whyte founded their artist-run, neighborhood-based non-profit organization Popps Packing in a former meat packing plant. It is their mission to create impactful arts programming and foster cultural exchange between local and international artist communities, while leveraging the unique features of their neighborhood and personal practices. Popps Packing is located on the border of Banglatown and Hamtramck, in an exceptionally multicultural part of Detroit. This is where Polish Catholic, various Muslim, Bangladeshi, and American cultures meet. Both in 2015 and 2016, I lived for one month at Popps Packing, in addition to my residency at Fortress Studios in the North End.

Popps' garden is situated on a vacant lot next to their new adventure playground Camp Carpenter Kids Playland. It had been used for different purposes each year: for installations, mushroom-workshops, or planted by neighbors. In 2018, a small fig tree was growing beside the vegetables, flowers, and pears.

www.poppspacking.org

→ 53 Dean's Garden, (Three Sisters), 2016

Maple Ash
Detroit Land Bank Authority
Hamtramck

In this neighborhood there is no specific plan, but there are thoughts of turning it industrial. Like tear down all the houses and making it a big industrial park. … When I was a little kid, the speculation was that the airport was going to expand. So that's how our housing crisis came here. People started leaving, and it wasn't because of jobs or anything, it was because they went to other neighborhoods, because they thought the city was coming through. And it never happened. So it's kind of like we're having the same issue 30 years later.

Mark Covington, Airport Sub resident and founder of the Georgia Street Community Collective in our interview 2018

52

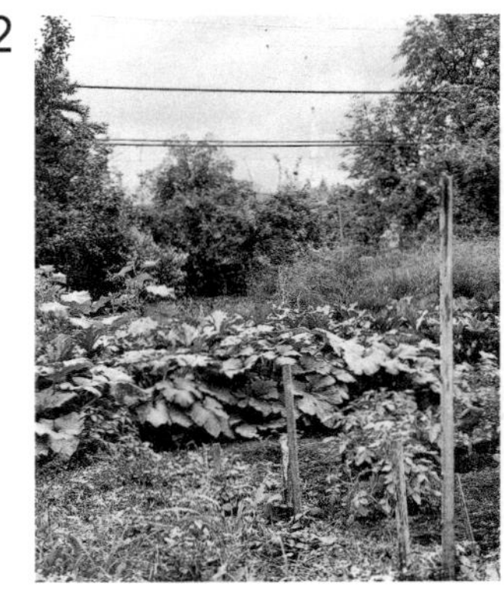

Earthworks Urban Farm, (Church), 2018

Islandview Neighborhood

→ For a description see 49 Earthworks Urban Farm, The Capuchin Soup Kitchen, 2018

53

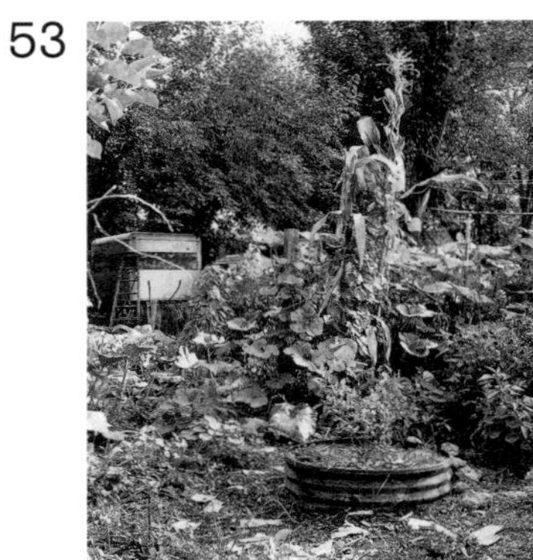

Dean's Garden, (Three Sisters), 2016

Campau / Banglatown Neighborhood

In 2016, Dean Simionescu cultivated the lot next to the Popps Packing Residency. He brought most of the seeds for vegetables and medicinal plants back with him from trips to South America. The picture shows garden nasturtium, peppers, and calendula as well as the Three Sisters: corn, beans, and squash, which are planted together and support each other symbiotically in their growth. This cultivation method originates from Mexico and is about 6000 years old.

One week before I took the photograph, we planted edible mushrooms in a Radical Mycology workshop with Marion Neumann and Geoffroy Grignon to compost garden waste, coffee grounds, and cigarette butts.

→ 51 Faina and Graem's Garden (Popps Packing), 2018

54

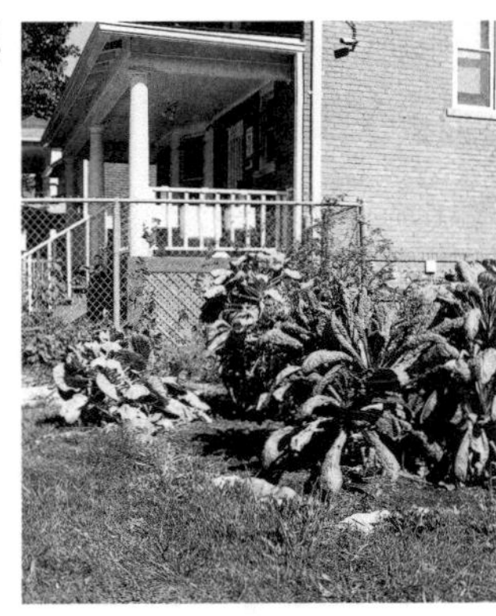

55

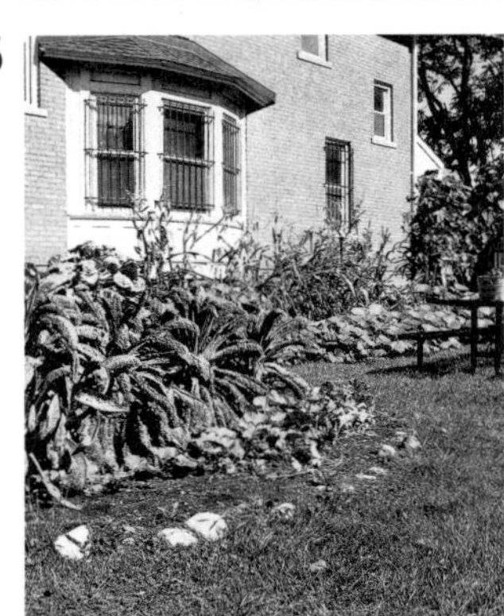

Sacred Roots Garden, American Indian Health and Family Services, 2018

Claytown Neighborhood

The Sacred Roots Garden is part of the American Indian Health and Family Services Center in southwest Detroit. In addition to vegetables and flowers, traditional medicinal plants such as tobacco, sweet grass, and yew are grown and Three Sisters cultivation is practiced. It can be seen in the background on the house wall. Corn, beans, and squash are planted together and support each other in their growth. The philosophy of nourishing coexistence as well as cultivation and eating as a healing activity is something I encountered on other farms in Detroit as well. It is easy to understand when one acknowledges the wounds that uprooting, forced relocation, enslavement, discrimination, racism, murder, and violence have inflicted on indigenous and non-white "minorities" throughout American history. The legacy of these traumas continues to be felt today in the form of inequality, poverty, and their negative effects on health.

In the summer of 2017, the Sacred Roots Garden was extended by a two-hectare plot of land in a public

Gardening—it's like being a producer of culture and not just a consumer of culture, being an active participant, it's like food as a civic engagement. … It's thinking about progress as cyclical rather than linear, so the garden has been a very good teacher for me.

Emily Staugaitis from Bandhu Gardens in our Interview 2018

park to further expand food sovereignity. The garden program was managed by Shilo Maples and Rosebud Schneider.

→ 25 Sacred Roots Garden (Tobacco), 2018

56

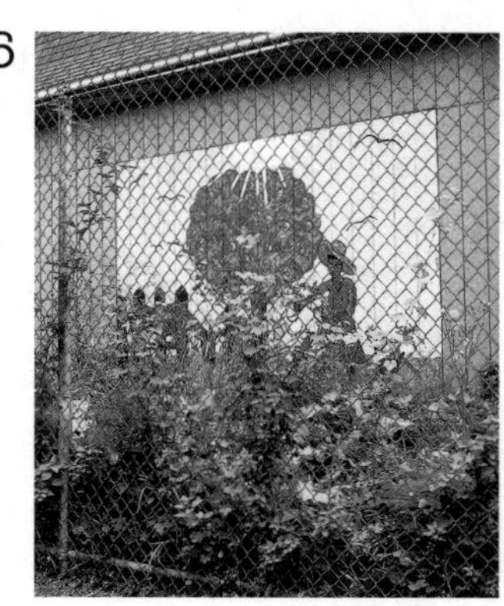

Catherine Ferguson Academy (Barn), 2018

Core City Neighborhood

"We've planted seeds all over that playground, we were growing every kind of vegetable that grows in Michigan, we even grew sweet potatoes. But what was more important was that we've planted the seed of being in our girls. We've planted confidence, we've planted strength, we've built a barn. And if you can build a barn … you know, it's like I'm my own woman, I can do what I wanna do! … Do I miss my school? I miss my school every day. But I have girls everywhere. I have artists and musicians and business owners and doctors and nurses and lawyers, one politician … I have all kinds of girls everywhere. Every girl who went to Catherine Ferguson Academy is obligated to leave a trail. Because Catherine Ferguson was a place."

Asenath Andrews (2017), Catherine Ferguson Academy's former school principle in a "School Days" Talk at the Charles H. Wright Museum Detroit

Catherine Ferguson Academy was one of the very few public high schools for pregnant girls and teen mothers in the United States. Founded in 1986, the school provided day care and preschool education for the students' newborns and toddlers. Urban farming was taught as well as economic skills for self-sufficiency. Every woman that graduated in 2010 was accepted to a two or four year college program. Most of them were African-American and came from lower income backgrounds. Only one year later, in 2011, the unique school project was scheduled to be shut down by an emergency manager as part of a system-wide deficit reduction plan for Detroit public schools. As a private school it was able to be run for another three years, before finally closing its doors in 2014.

The photograph shows the mural on the barn that was built by the young student mothers.

57 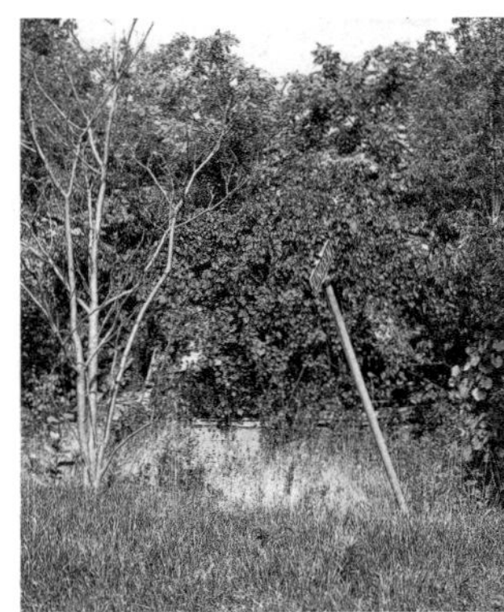

13603 Lincoln Street, 2015

Highland Park

Highland Park was founded in 1889 as a small residential village with well-built medium-sized houses, shaded lawns, and quiet streets. In 1910, Ford opened its first factory here, the Ford Highland Park Plant. Within the space of a few years, the population exploded from 400 to 46,000. During this time, the housing shortage was so great that landlords of jerry-built boarding houses rented out individual beds in three to four shifts around the clock to workers of all ages and nationalities. In the course of the 1920s, Highland Park was transformed into one of the world's most densely populated areas. As early as 1927, Ford outsourced its production to the new Ford River Rouge Complex. "Thousands of staff personnel and manual workers have made their homes in the neighborhood of the factory—now one morning they will wake up ten miles away from it." °
In the meantime, Highland Park had been completely surrounded by Detroit. It continued to provide housing for workers at the Chrysler and Dodge plants until the 1990s. After these factories were relocated as well, the community lost 35,000 inhabitants and practically its entire commercial tax revenue. Insolvency followed in 2001, secondary schools were closed and much of the street lighting was dismantled. The city advised residents to keep porch lights on in order to deter crime.

The photograph was taken on Labor Day on the edge of the Davidson Freeway, on a block that is closed down completely. The orange color is a remnant of the art project Detroit Demolition Disneyland, which sought to draw the attention of passers-by to the desolate state of the city by painting dilapidated houses orange. The derelict house can only be seen from the Freeway—on the way to the suburbs.

° Egon Erwin Kisch (1929). At Ford's Place in Detroit, 126

58 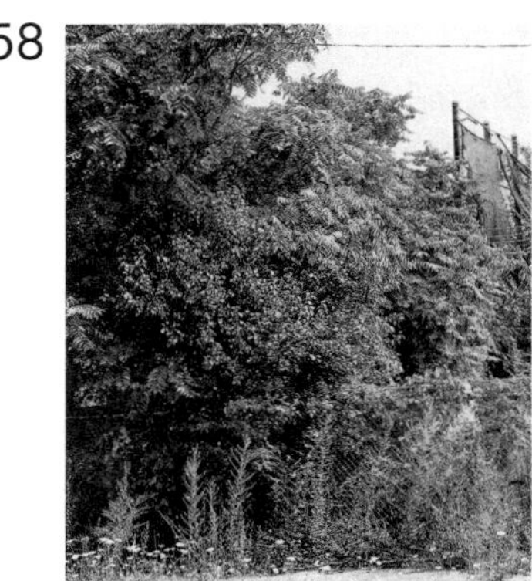

Trombly Street, 2015

Milwaukee Junction Neighborhood

Trombly Street is located in the Milwaukee Junction district, where small businesses, storage areas, and derelict land alternate with railway bridges and large scale murals. The area is one of Detroit's new opportunity zones—the city offers tax breaks for private investment and start-ups. The proximity to gentrified Midtown, New Center, and Tech Town have led newspapers to refer to it as the "next hot neighborhood." °

Trees of heaven and common dogwood grow on a vacant lot next to a mechanical engineering company.

° Detroit Future City (2019), 4

→ 1/2 2550 East Grand Boulevard, 2015
→ 3 Fisher Body Plant 21 (Bucket), 2015

Even though we have a tremendous amount of vacant land in the city of Detroit, there is inequity in terms of who gets access to that land. ... Right now the city leaders seem to have the perspective that land should go to people who are very wealthy developers. We have the perspective that land should be distributed to people so we can build power in our communities.

Malik Yakini from the Detroit Black Community Food Security Network in a talk at OuiShareFest, 2017

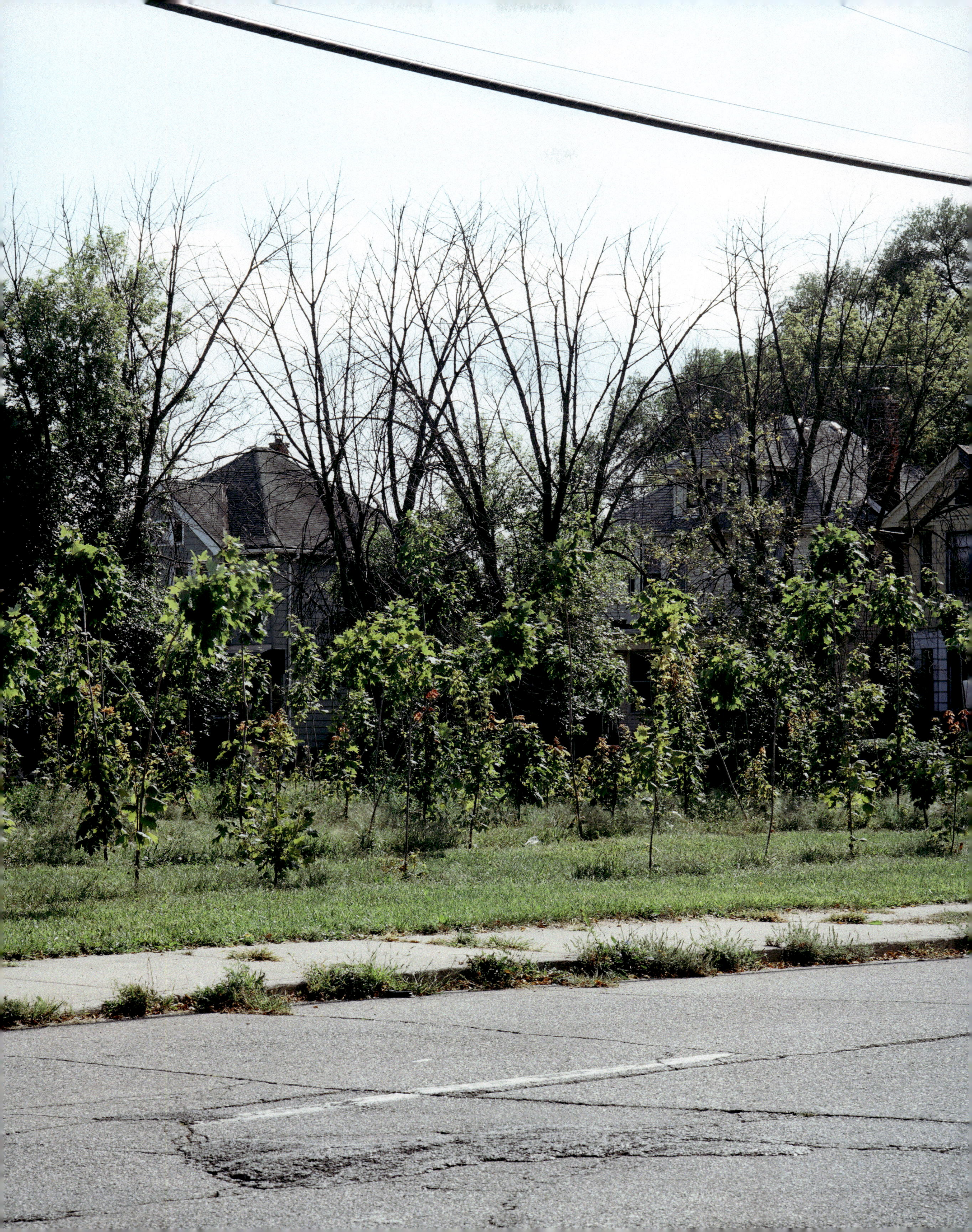

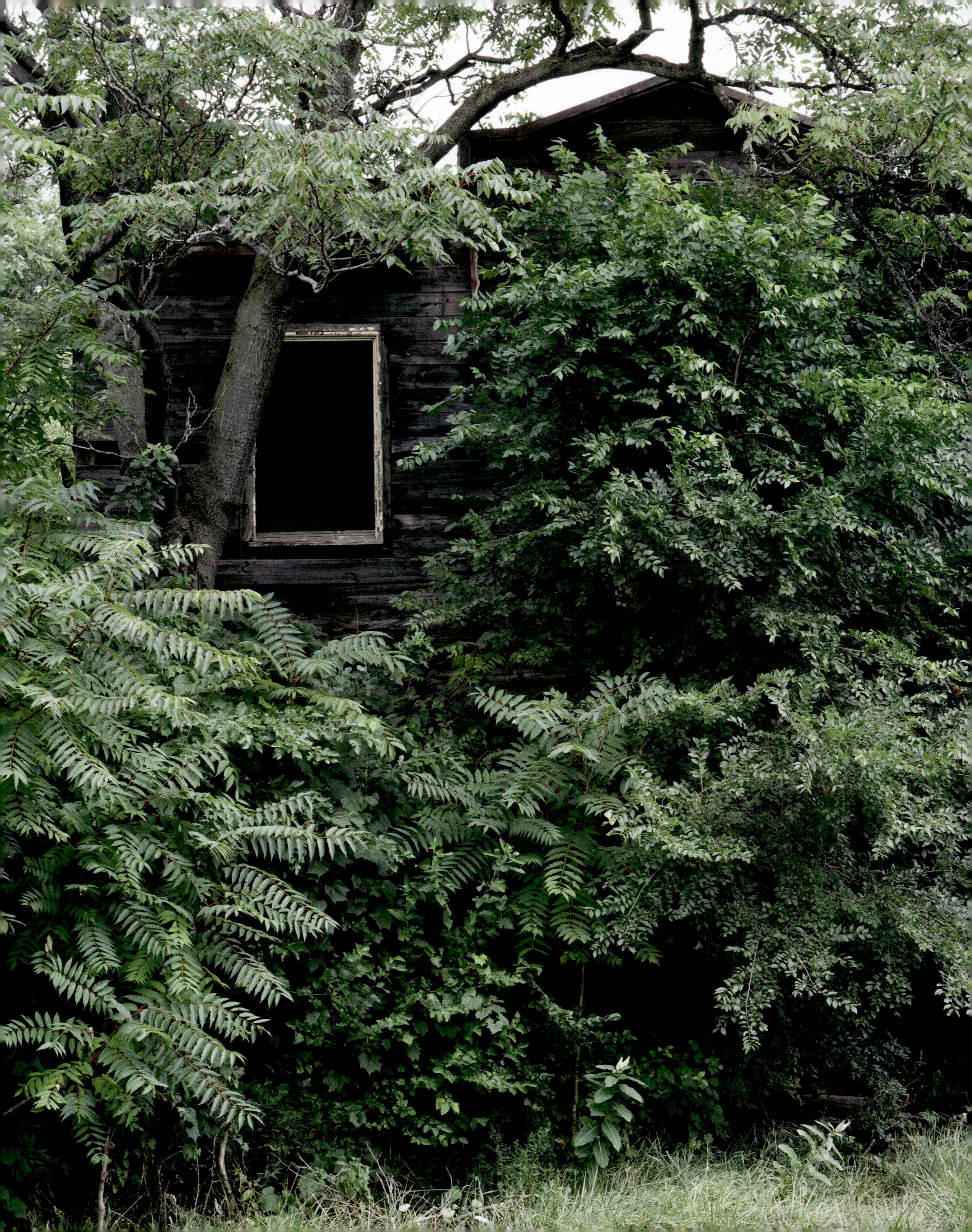

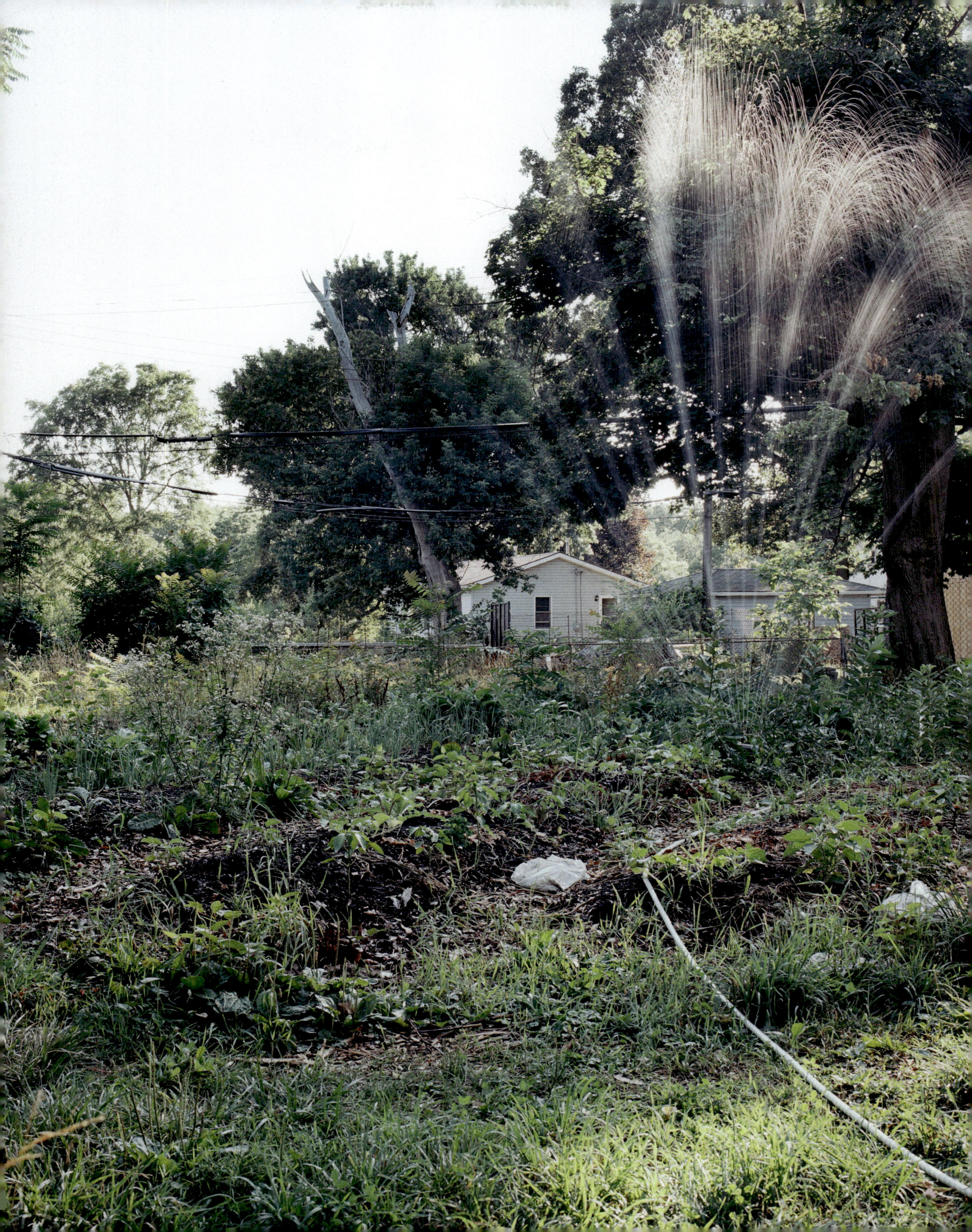

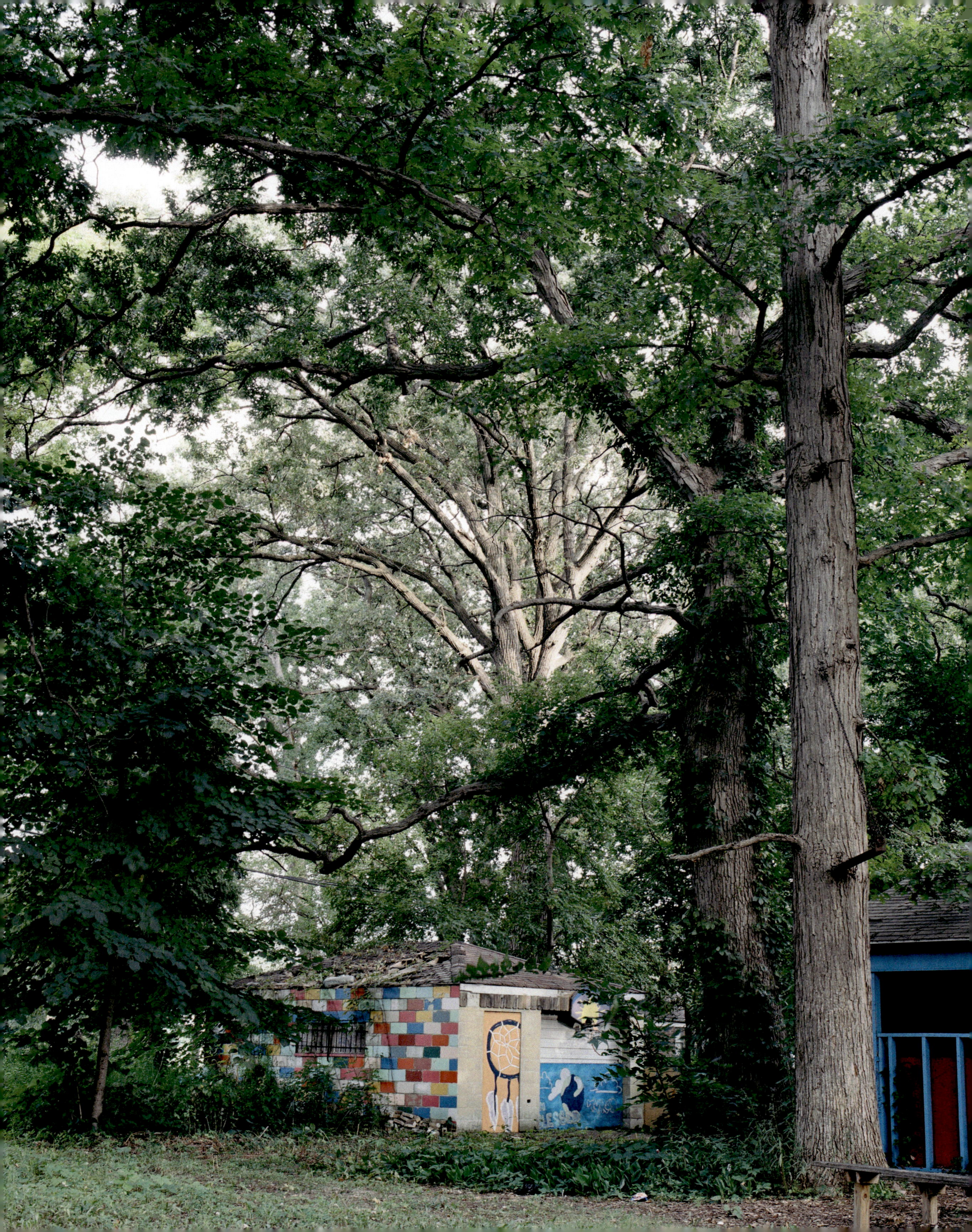

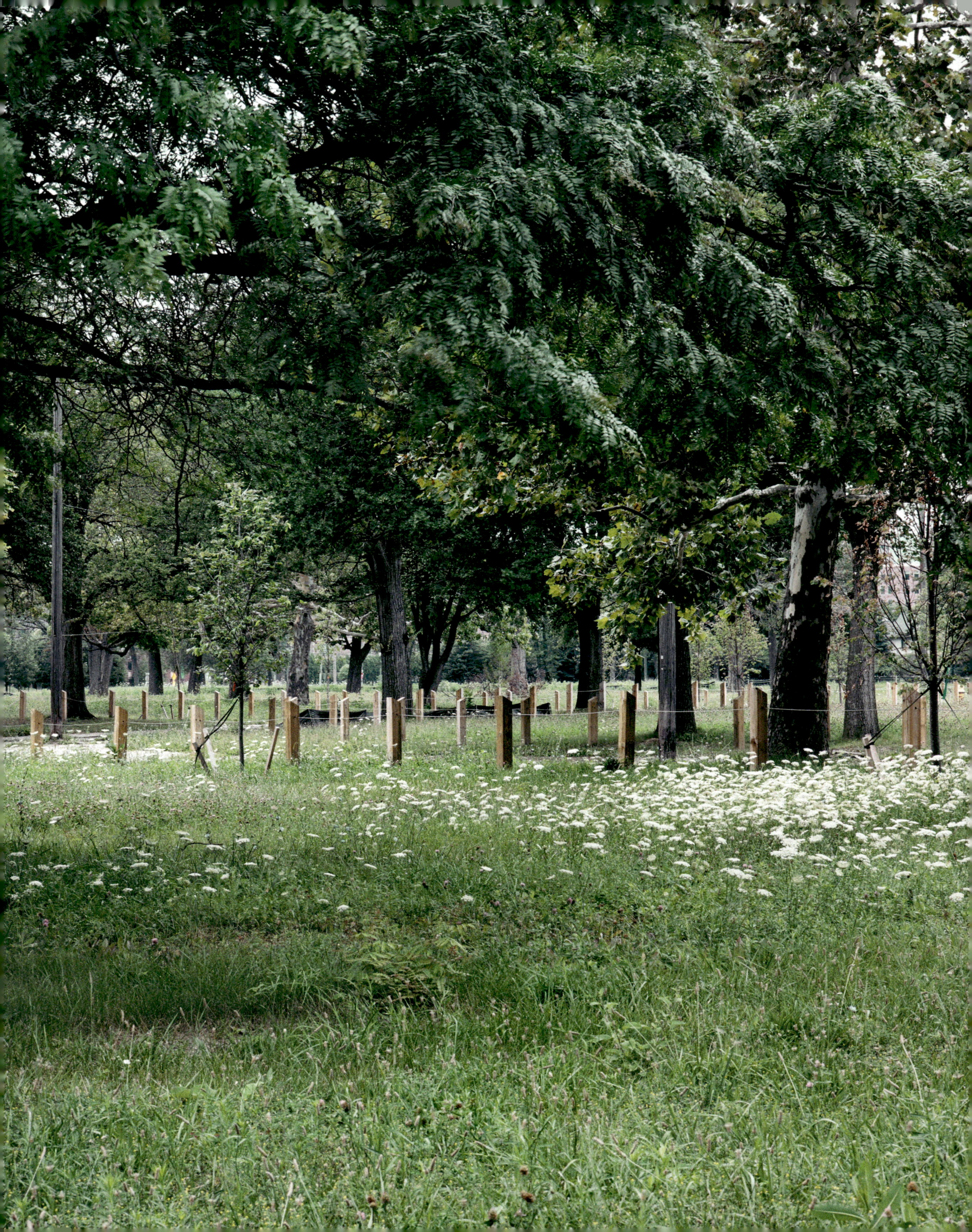

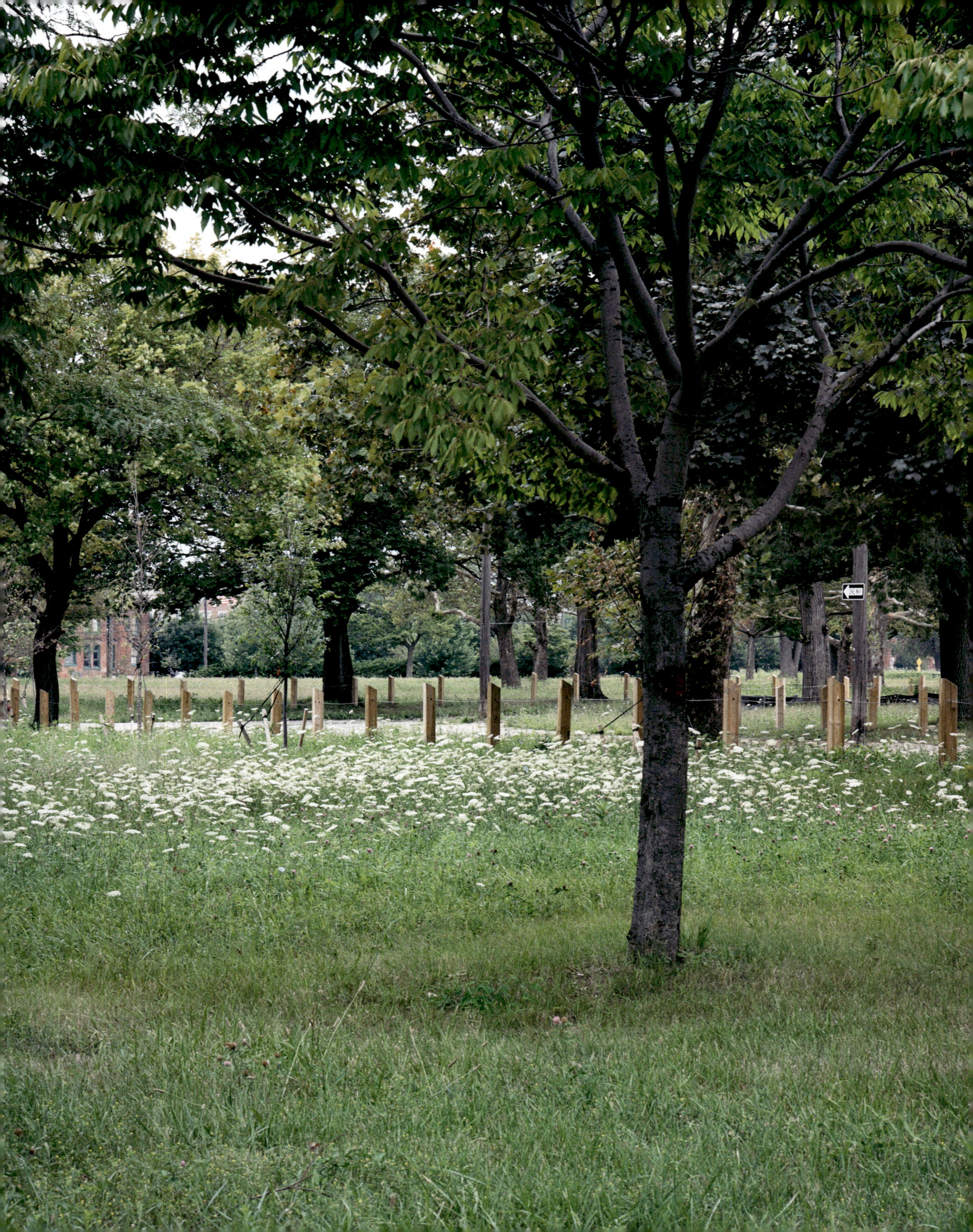

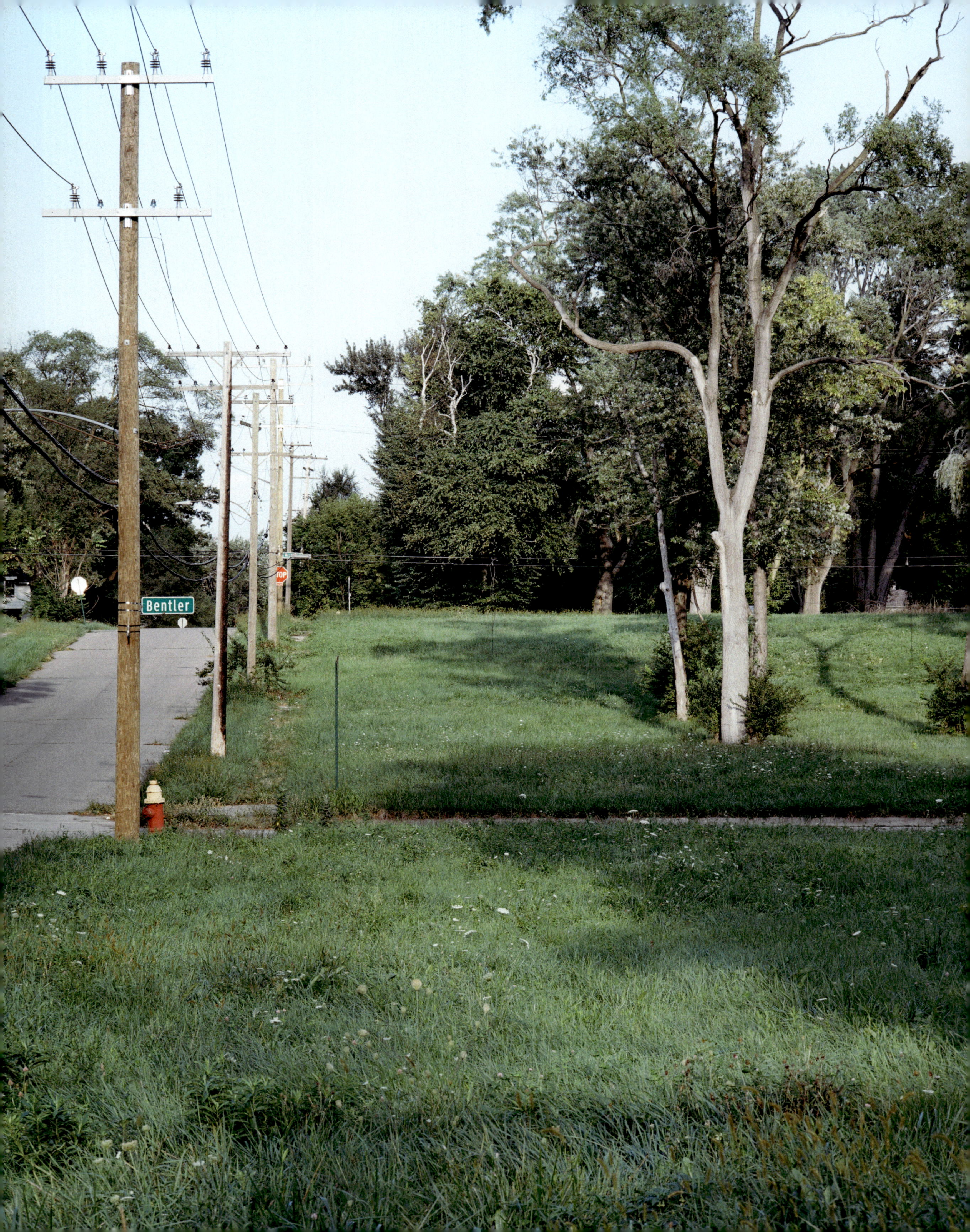
Bentler

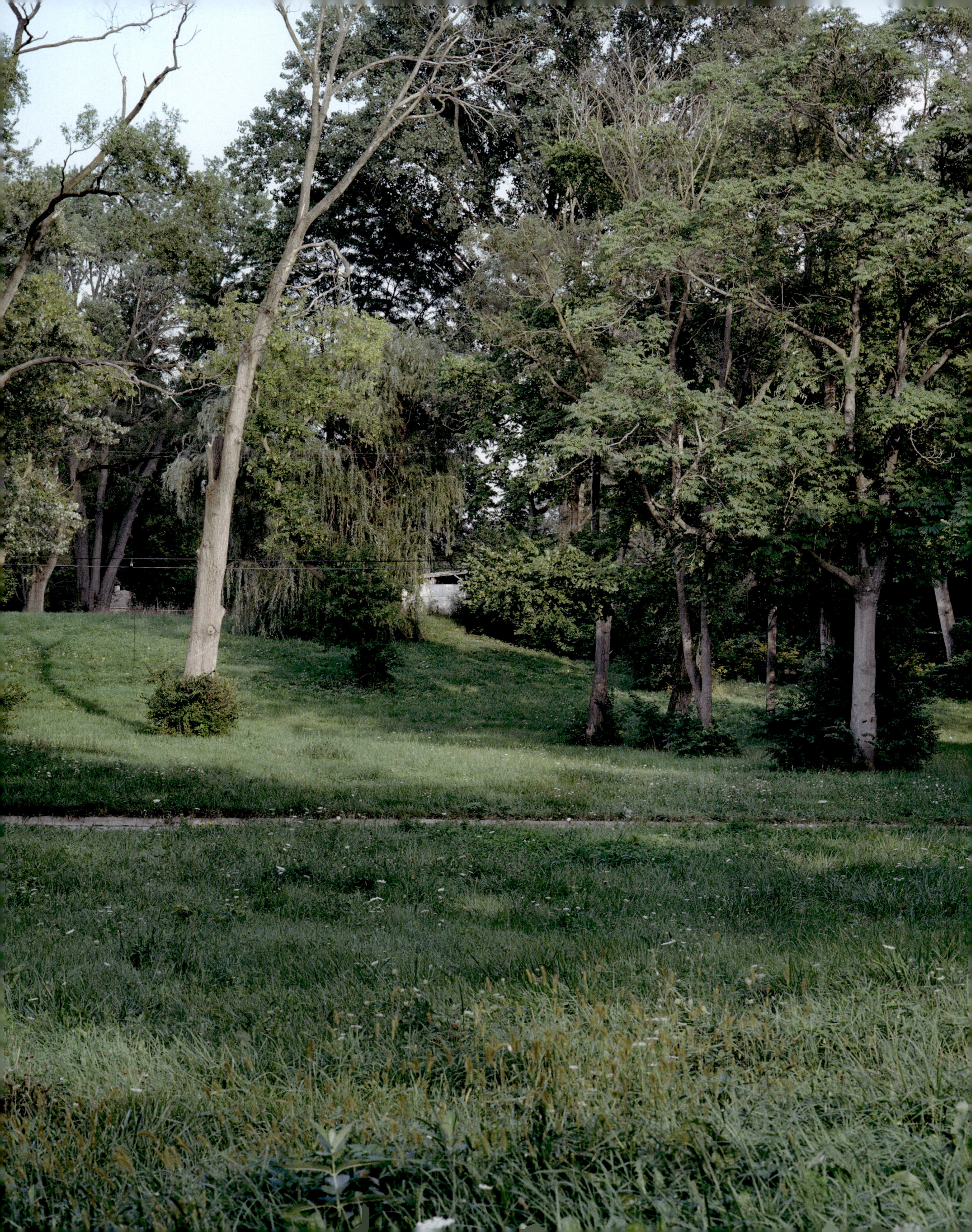

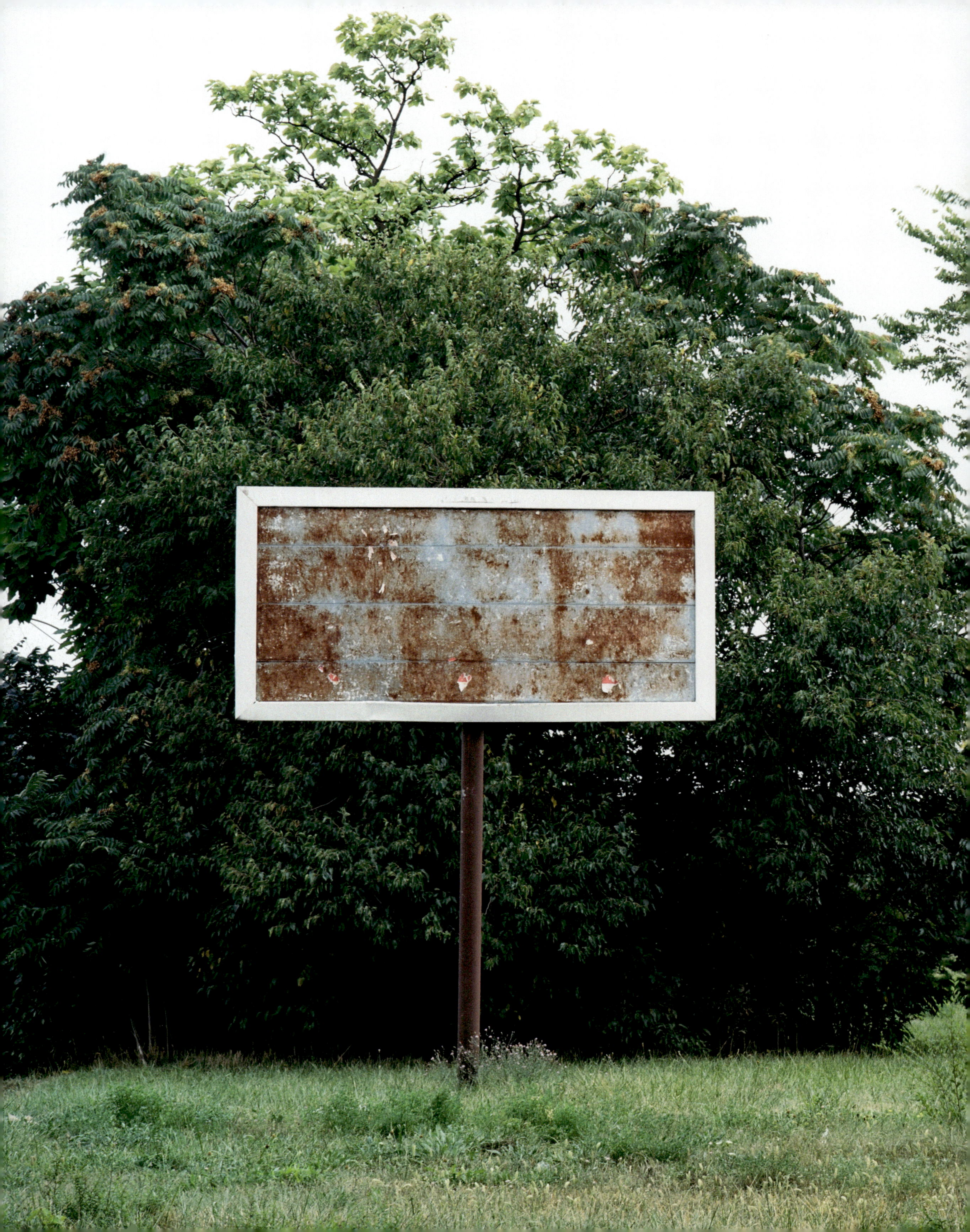

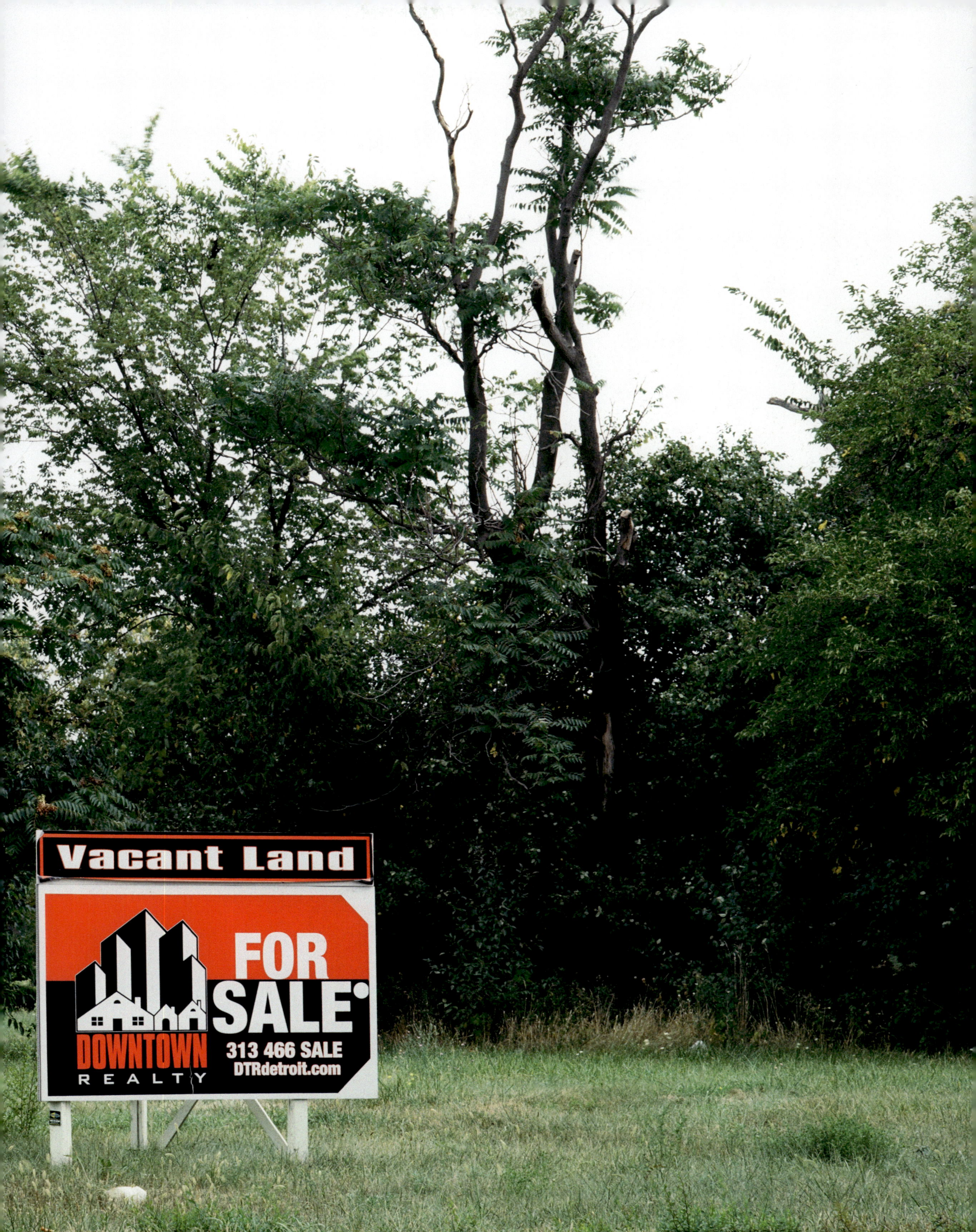

Vacant Land
FOR
SALE
DOWNTOWN
REALTY
313 466 SALE
DTRdetroit.com

Detroit's decay is now its engine: nowhere else in urban America can you do so much with so little money.

Susan Ager (2015). Tough, Cheap, and Real, Detroit Is Cool Again

59

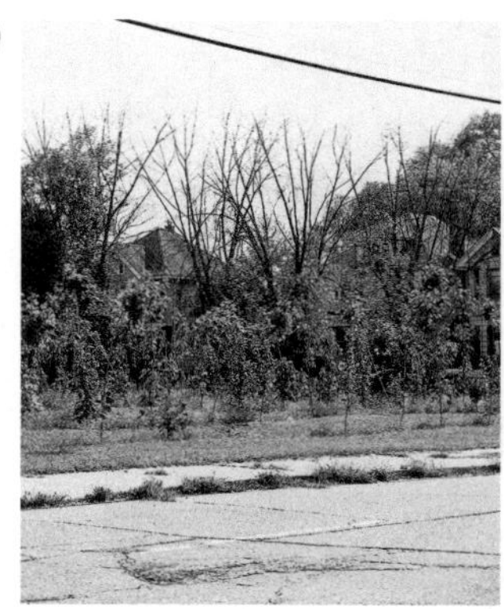

Charlevoix Street (Dr. Sweet's House / Hantz Woodlands), 2018

East Village Neighborhood

The picture shows the view from the former house of the physician Dr. Ossian Sweet onto the trees of Hantz Woodlands.

In 1925, the physician Dr. Sweet and his wife Gladys moved into their new house at the corner of Garland and Charlevoix Street. They were the first African Americans to move into this all-white neighborhood. The following night they were attacked by a mob of hundreds of white people, who surrounded the house, threw rocks, and tried to break in. In self-defense the Sweet family fired shots from inside the house. The police answered with shots from outside. One white man was killed and another was wounded. All eleven people in the Sweet home were arrested and charged with murder. The trial prosecutor described the night as "a warm summer evening in a quiet, neighborly community," when, "suddenly, unexpectedly and without provocation, a fusillade of shots rang out from the rear, sides and front of the house." ° Yet the defendant, Otis Sweet, stated "The street was a sea of humanity. The crowd was so thick you couldn't see the street or the sidewalk. Just getting to the front door was like running the gauntlet. I was hit by a rock before I got inside. ..." °° With the support of the National Association for the Advancement of Colored People, and after two hearings in which police officers and witnesses repeatedly contradicted each other, all the defendants were acquitted. Today the house is part of the National Register of Historic Places.

Opposite the house, also visible in the picture, are newly planted rows of trees belonging to Hantz Woodlands, a hardwood tree farm. Its founder, John Hantz, has purchased over 2,000 plots of land from the city of Detroit since 2012 through the foundation associated with his financial services company at an average price of just $350 per lot. This made him the largest property owner in Detroit after the city itself and the Detroit Land Bank Authority. After derelict houses and garbage were removed, trees such as oak, maple, birch, and poplar were planted on the vacant lots. Several initiatives criticize the fact that the city of Detroit has granted a single private investor the right of first refusal for thousands of discounted plots of land without a typical development agreement, while Detroit residents and urban growers struggle to gain long-term access to and ownership of land.

° Arthur Garfield Hays (1929) in: Widick (1989), 7

°° Widick (1989). Detroit: City of Race and Class Violence, 10–11

→ Redlining, Structural Racism

Wayne County Tax Foreclosure Auction
Detroit Land Bank Authority

Despite the narratives of a resurgent Detroit, it is a city in which one third of all residential properties were in foreclosure in the last decade. The pockets of condo development and small-plate restaurants and the luring of suburban companies for remodeled downtown offices account for just over seven square miles of a 139-square mile city. The most active forces in the city's housing market remain displacement and dispossession.

Joshua Akers (2017). Contesting Economies of Displacement and Dispossession, 1

60

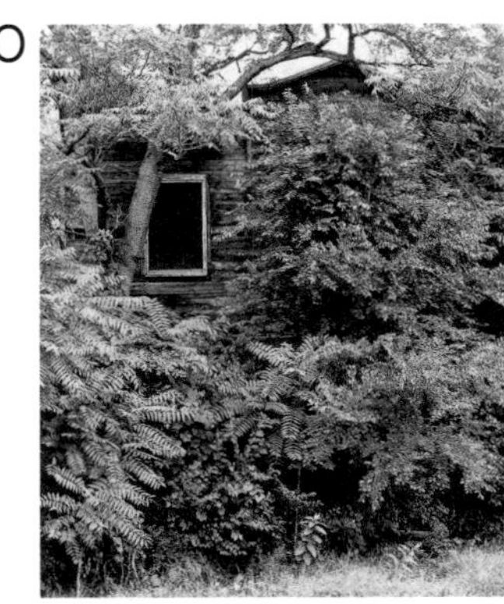

6000 16th Street, 2015

Northwest Goldberg Neighborhood

This two-story family home stood empty for about ten years before it was demolished in August 2018 as part of the Detroit Demolition Program. It stood in an area that otherwise resembles an urban prairie. The house is surrounded by tree of heaven, American elm, mulberry, and dogwood, as well as wild carrot, English plantain, stinging nettle, riverbank vine, dandelion, and common milkweed. Adjacent are the apple trees of the former residents.

61

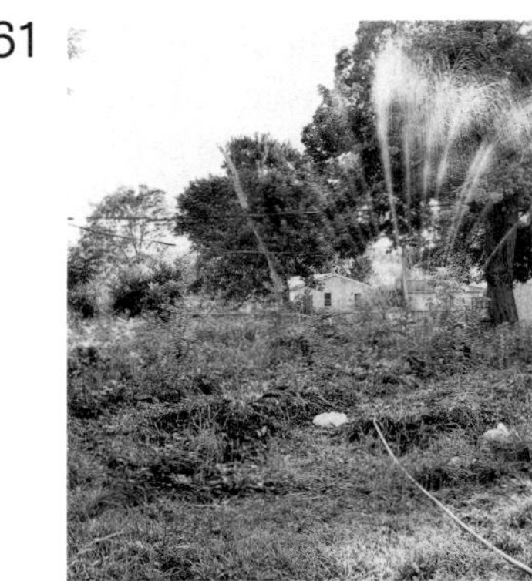

Beaverland Farms, 2016

Brightmoor Neighborhood

For a description see
→ 10 Beaverland Farms (Elderberry Trees), 2016

62

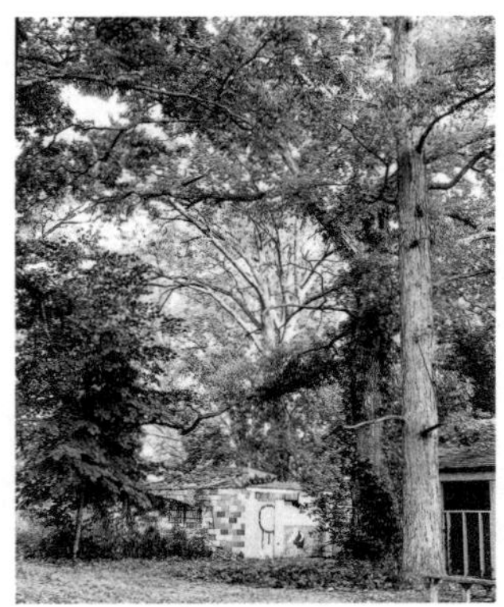

Beaverland Street (Neighbors Building Brightmoor), 2015

Brightmoor Neighborhood

Like many others in Brightmoor, the small house in the picture was painted by youth, children, and other neighbors in 2012. In 2009, local residents founded Neighbors Building Brightmoor and established a Youth Market Garden. Neighborhood kids own the garden, grow all the vegetables, sell them at the market, and keep the profits. Founders and neighbors Riet Schumack and Gwendolyn Shivers said in an interview in 2015: Riet: "Our one little garden has resulted in hundreds of little gardens. And more important is that it has become community. ... On the 15 blocks where we have Neighbors Building Brightmoor, where everybody knows us, there is virtually no more crime ..." Gwendolyn: "We have a diversity now, it's no longer about race. And the greatest part about it is that we all work together." °

Since then, a Detroit Community Market and the Community Center Brightmoor Artisans Collective have emerged, which "serves as a safe community space, café, food business incubator, and classroom where neighbors can gather to purchase affordable products, eat healthy food together, and share ideas." °°

www.neighborsbuildingbrightmoor.org

° Healing Detroit One Garden at a Time (2015)
°° www.brightmoorartisans.org

→ 21 14409 Burgess Street (Pray Hope and Don't Worry), 2016
→ 65/66 Bentler Street, 2018

63

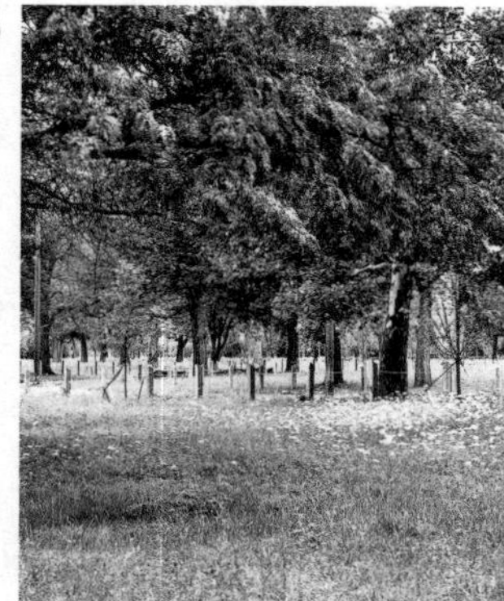

64

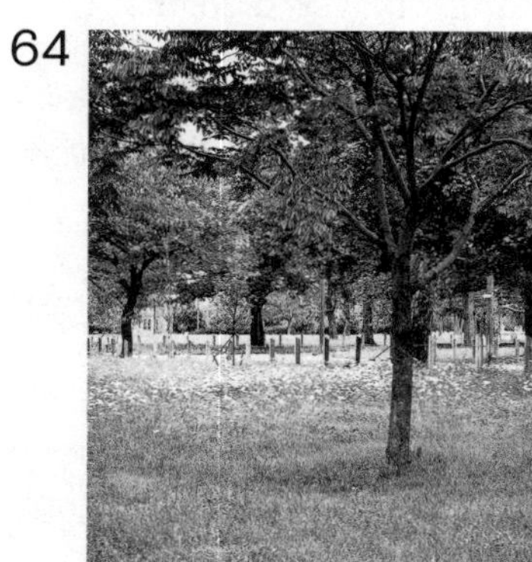

Brewster-Douglass Housing Projects, 2015

Brush Park Neighborhood

"Moving to the Brewster Projects in 1956 was a turning point in my life. ... Many people would have considered a move to the Projects as a step down. But for me, having already stepped down from a middle-class neighborhood to various apartments in the inner city, this was a step back up. I felt like I just moved into a Park Avenue skyscraper."

Mary Wilson, singer of The Supremes
in: Smith (1999), 157

The Brewster-Douglass Homes were one of the nation's first public housing projects and the largest owned by the city of Detroit. It was named after Frederick Douglass, an African-American abolitionist, author, and reformer. The development was built just south of Hastings Street between 1935 and 1955. At that time, Detroit's housing market was highly racially segregated. The Brewster-Douglas Homes opened in 1938 for African-American workers "in the lower middle-income bracket. ... Applicants must be employed occupants of substandard quarters, who have lived in Detroit for more than one year. The minimum family income must be slightly more than four times, but not more than five times, the rent." ° At its peak capacity up to 10,000 residents lived in the apartment rows, low and high rise buildings with a recreation center and playgrounds. During Detroit's hard times in the 1970s and 1980s the houses began to deteriorate, crime increased, and the neighborhood fell into disrepair. The first low-rise apartments were demolished in 1991. As only 280 families remained in the complex by 2008, the housing was closed down entirely and stood vacant for another ten years. During 2013 and 2014 all remaining residential buildings were demolished and the site was turned into a park-like area, monitored by security. The pictures show the spot where the high-rises used to stand and there was once a basketball court.

The Brewster-Douglass site is directly opposite the Ford Field Stadium that was built in 2002 and is adjacent to Downtown and Brush Park, the two areas of Detroit currently undergoing the most intensive redevelopment. In December 2019, the complex was purchased by Douglass Acquisition Community for $23 million. A few months later, their affiliate, Bedrock Detroit LLC, presented initial architectural renderings. Bedrock is a property management company and part of Dan Gilbert's Rock Ventures LLC, the largest developer, employer and taxpayer in the city.

° Michigan (1949). A Guide to the Wolverine State, 273

65

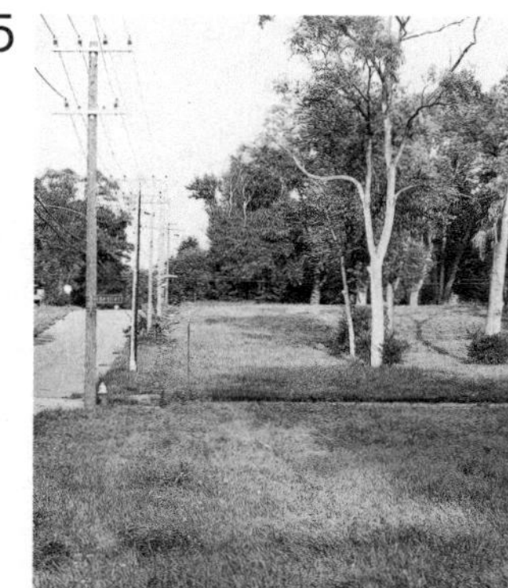

66

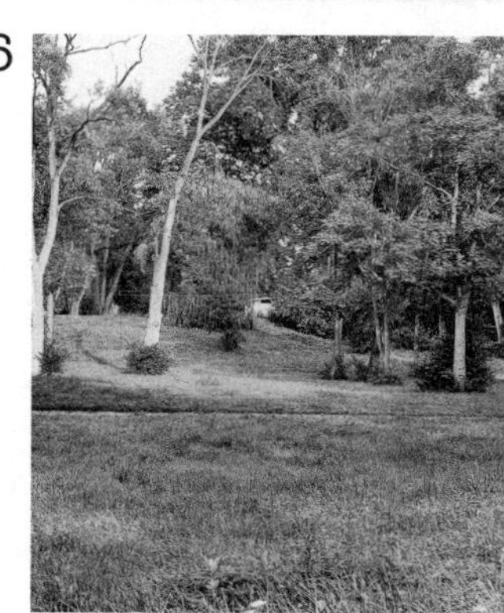

Bentler Street, 2018

Brightmoor Neighborhood

The once highly segregated Brightmoor neighborhood is today home of reams of small gardens, farms, and neighborhood networks. The pictures show a small hilly road that suggests how the landscape looked before it was developed in 1922.

→ 21 14409 Burgess Street (Pray Hope and Don't Worry), 2016
→ 62 Beaverland Street (Neighbors Building Brightmoor), 2015

... we need to embrace the idea that we are the leaders we've been looking for.

Grace Lee Boggs (2011). The Next American Revolution, 159

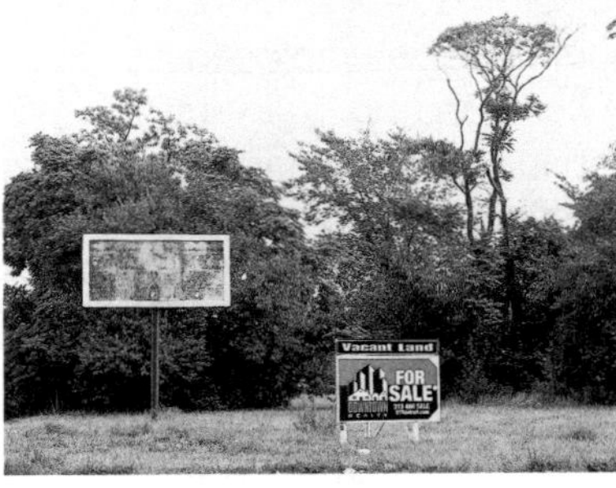

Oakland Avenue (For Sale Sign), 2018

North End Neighborhood

Detroit is changing fast. When I visited the city again in 2018, many neighborhoods had changed their appearance. As was the case earlier in Brush Park, sales signs were clustered on empty lots. Since 2014, the Detroit Demolition Program has been demolishing thousands of empty houses and creating new open spaces. This land offers the potential for an urban, self-managed agriculture that could make Detroit the first major city in the United States to be self-sufficient and allows for civil self-determination. However, these vacant plots are still first and foremost real estate, speculation objects, or financial investments for private capital, especially in times of low land prices. As far back as 1890, an author described Detroit as follows: "What is extraordinary is that the city's vacant areas accounted for almost half the available space. ... One cannot avoid being struck by the large quantity of open space, some of it still in farmland but most of it unused and held for speculative purposes ... ." °

Yet every cyclical recession, crisis, and eagerly awaited comeback of Detroit leads to new approaches that can make it possible for its diverse communities to actively participate in the city's development. This continuous development of new ideas paired with the commitment of Detroit residents to actively shape their city, seems to me to be a constant in all this change. It is to be hoped that the city administration will also recognize this potential. As James Boggs put it as early as 1988: "We have to begin thinking of creating small enterprises which produce food, goods, and services for the local market, that is, for our communities and for our city ... In order to create these new enterprises, we need a view of our city which takes into consideration both the natural resources of our area and the existing and potential skills and talents of Detroiters." °°

° Unknown author (1890) in: Zunz (1982), 30
°° Guyette (2001). Down a green path

→ 33 Alley in Midtown, 2015
→ Gentrification, Speculation and Eviction

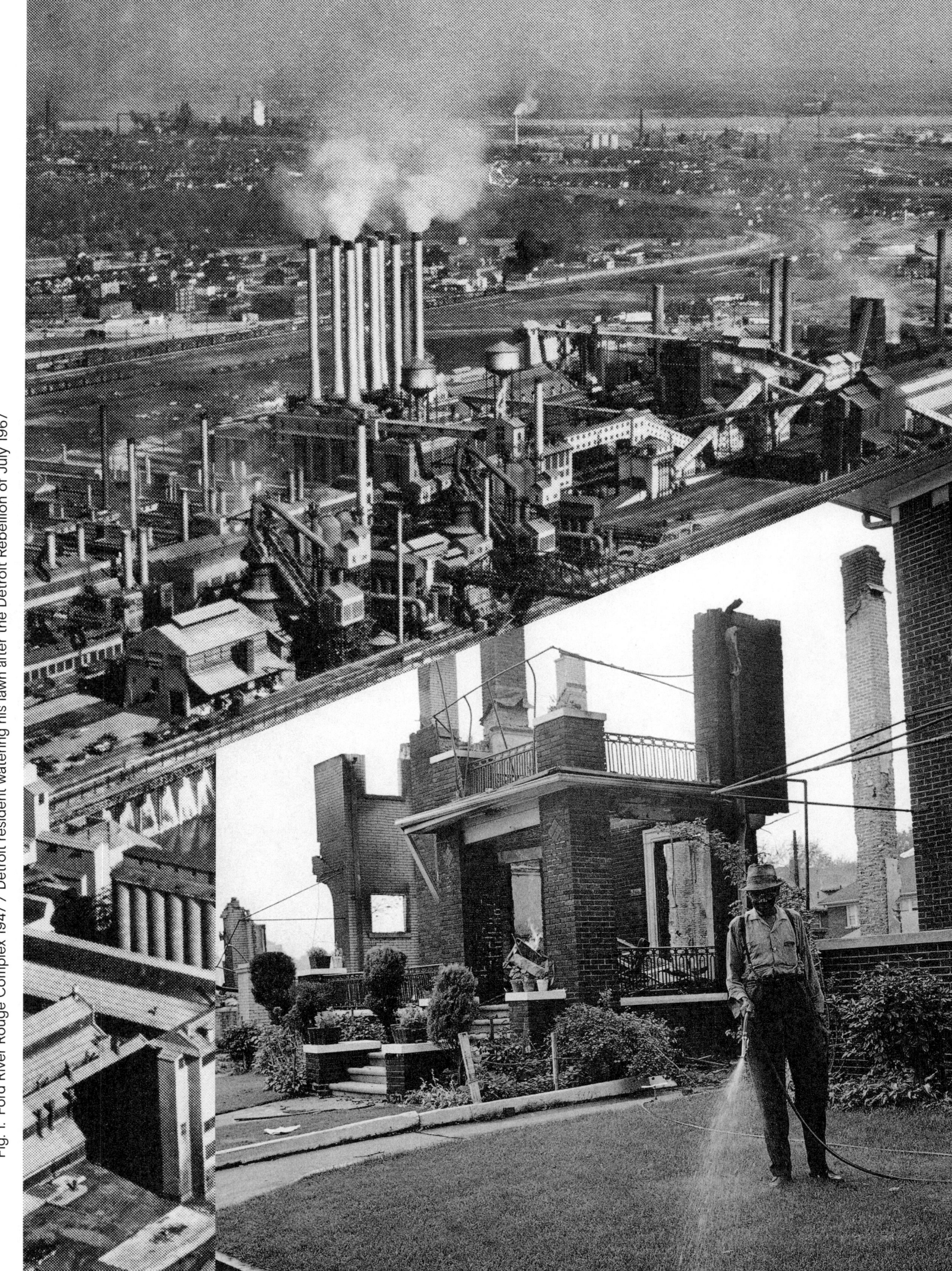

Fig. 1: Ford River Rouge Complex 1947 / Detroit resident watering his lawn after the Detroit Rebellion of July 1967

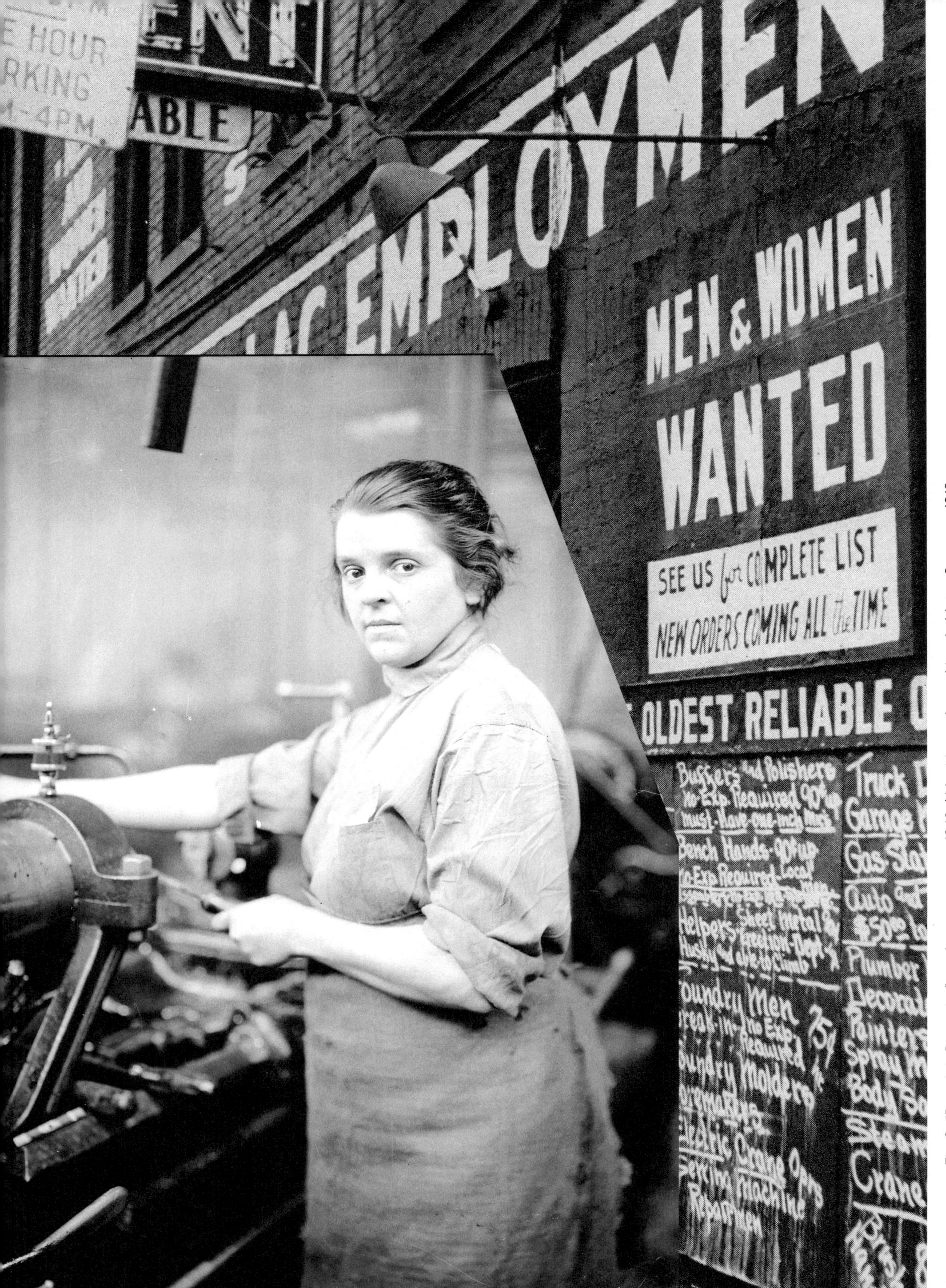

Fig. 2: "Detroit is Dynamite," employment agency 1942 / Munition maker at Lincoln Motor Company 1918

REGISTER

Albert Kahn
(1869–1942) was one of the most important industrial architects of his time. Together with his brother Julius, he developed innovative reinforced concrete structures in Detroit, which were first used in the construction of the → Packard Automotive Plant in 1903. Kahn designed so many industrial buildings and architectural landmarks in the city that he is often referred to as Detroit's architect.

Algonquian
is the name of the most widespread indigenous language family in North America and at the same time the name of a tribe of Native Americans consisting of several different branches. The Algonquian belong to the eastern branch of the → Anishinaabe people.

Alien Plants
are plant species that are newly established in an area. They are mostly introduced by humans as ornamental or agricultural plants or imported accidentally. Since plants spread globally over millions of years, nature conservationists consider the time limit for distinguishing between "old" and "new" species to be 1492—the year of Christopher Columbus' arrival in America.

American Dream
is "the idea of individual upward mobility based on merit instead of class, available to all if only they work hard enough." (Apel (2015), 8). This notion ignores the statistical fact that a child's place of birth and social background determine its life course more than its actual attitude or work performance.

Anishinaabe
is one of the largest indigenous peoples in North America today. It includes the → Algonquian, Mississauga, Nipissing, Odawa, Ojibwe, Oji-Cree, Potawatomi, and Saulteaux tribes. The Anishinaabe peoples come from the Great Lakes region.

Arsenal of Democracy
is the epithet Detroit was given during the wartime production efforts of World War II. The automakers switched their production to tanks and bombers. All new factories were built in the urban hinterland. Half a million migrants from Europe, the Southern States, and rural America poured into the city. At times, the newly arrived workers lived in tents. After the U.S. entered the war, women and ethnic "minorities" moved into jobs previously reserved for white men. Detroit was in full employment with all the discomfort that went along with it: housing shortages, racist resentments, and hate strikes. See also → Detroit Riot of June 1943.

Assembly Line
An assembly line is an industrial production line based on the conveyor belt principle. It was already in use in slaughterhouses and by the car manufacturer Ransom E. Old when Henry Ford made it famous by introducing it in his → Ford Highland Park Plant in 1913. The assembly line enables profitable mass production by breaking down complex assembly operations into a series of simple operations that can be performed by unskilled, cheap, and easily replaceable workers. Today's assembly lines are mostly fully automated.

Big Three
stands for the three largest American car manufacturers → Ford, → General Motors, and Chrysler (Fiat Chrysler Automobiles). They are usually closely associated with the Motor City, although only General Motors still has its headquarters in Detroit.

Black Bottom and
Paradise Valley
were among Detroit's oldest neighborhoods. They were demolished in the course of the city's → Urban Renewal program during the 1950s. Black Bottom got its name from the fertile black soil of the flood plain or river bottom. During industrialization and the first wave of the → Great Migration, tens of thousands of African-Americans flocked to the city from the South to seek their fortune. Neighborhoods that were once divided by ethnic affililation were now segregated by class and above all by race, and in both neighborhoods an African-American ghetto emerged. Paradise Valley was the cultural entertainment district with fancy diners at Hastings and St. Aubin Streets. Black Bottom in the south became the residential and business neighborhood. During World War II the already overcrowded area became highly over-populated. The then old, dilapidated houses had only substandard living conditions to offer. Detroit's → Urban Renewal program resulted in the demolition of Black Bottom and a large part of Paradise Valley in the 1950s in order to build new → Freeways, the Lafayette Park Complex, the Brewster Douglas Homes (→ pictures 31/32 and 63/64), and others. Tens of thousands of people were displaced and moved to the 12th Street area on the west side, forgotten until it became the center of the → Detroit Rebellion of July 1967.

Detroit
is the largest city in the state of Michigan and county seat of Wayne County. 82.7 percent of the population of Detroit are African-Americans. This makes Detroit one of the largest Black communities in the United States. Detroit was founded in 1701 by Antoine de la Mothe Cadillac as Ville d'Etroit (city on the strait) on the Detroit River, which connects Lake St. Clair and Lake Erie. The Motor City became famous after 1900 for its rapidly growing car industry. After 50 years of prosperity, most of the factories and 60 percent of the inhabitants left the city.

Detroit Bankruptcy
In July 2013 the city of Detroit filed for Chapter 9 bankruptcy with a debt of $18–20 billion. Until December 2014 the city's finances were administered by

the State of Michigan. The appointed emergency manager, Kevin Orr, hired various lawyers and consulting firms in addition to his former law firm Jones Day. Consulting services have cost the city a total of $170.2 million. The city was advised to cut the pensions of municipal employees, sell off public land, municipal companies, and valuable artwork of the Detroit Institute of Art to private investors. In preparation for the sale of the Detroit Water Sewerage Department, the city started the → water shutoffs. Private households were temporarily cut off from the drinking water supply if they owed even modest sums in water charges. In the so-called "Great Bargain," private and public interventions, as well as donations, helped to secure municipal pensions, save artworks, and facilitated an agreement on debt cuts to end the insolvency.

Detroit Community Markets
are neighborhood markets, farm stands, or food box programs where Detroit local growers sell their produce directly to their neighborhood community.

www.detroitmarkets.org

Detroit Demolition Program
is a federal and state funded demolition program. Since its inception in 2014, with a budget of $250 million, 18,000 buildings have been demolished that had stood empty or fallen into disrepair due to out-migration, fire damage, foreclosure, or → speculation on land. Another 40,000 buildings are scheduled to follow. Parallel to this profitable business for demolition companies, new vacant properties are being created throughout the city.

Detroit Food Policy Council
was founded in 2009 by the Detroit City Council on the initiative of the Detroit Black Community Food Security Network (→ picture 45). Led by Detroiters, the organization is committed to creating a sustainable, local food system, → food security, food justice, and food sovereignty in the city of Detroit. It represents the interests of urban growers and warns, among other things, of the lack of protection of and access to agricultural land for the local population, while significant suburban investors can buy large areas of land for development purposes.

www.detroitfoodpolicycouncil.net

Detroit Future City
is a non-profit organization of architects and city planners founded in 2012. After a two-year research phase they published a 50-year vision plan of a post-shrinking New Detroit. The concept envisages the concentration of individual commercial and residential corridors, while other regions of the city are to be used as parks, gardens, innovative farms, or woodlands. The current urban development with mass demolitions, tax breaks for private investors in → opportunity zones, neighborhood branding, and → gentrification seems to follow these concepts. On the other hand it is striking that there is no specific planning for low-income housing—in a city with a current poverty rate of 36.4 percent.

www.detroitfuturecity.com

Detroit Land Bank Authority
is the largest landowner in Detroit in the year 2019. The state-owned enterprise was created in 2008 to reduce the number of properties that are in public ownership. Its inventory consists of vacant lots, abandoned houses, and structures forced into tax foreclosure, which are resold through the → Wayne County Tax Foreclosure Auction and several other programs. For example the Side Lot Program allows home-owners to purchase vacant lots adjacent to their property, a foundation for many Detroiters to purchase land for private farms and gardens.

Detroit Renaissance
(Renaissance, French for rebirth) This phrase emerges regularly in times of economic crisis, conjuring up the return to previous prosperity, which demonstrably never existed for all inhabitants. The city's "comebacks" mostly consist of privately financed building projects, which are accompanied by tax breaks and are mostly concentrated in Downtown or Midtown.

Detroit Riots
A riot is a form of civil disorder, a violent public disturbance against authority, property, or people. Most of the riots in Detroit were preceded by small-scale clashes between sections of the population or with the police. They all occurred at times of enormous population growth, economic and social tensions, or during a war. Most riots in Detroit had a racist background and were related to the mixture of ethnic groups in housing and unemployment. After the Race Riot of 1863, the Detroit Police was founded. In 1929 the house of Dr. Ossian Sweets was attacked (→ picture 59). Among the largest riots were:

Detroit Riot of June 1943
In the midst of war production (→ Arsenal of Democracy), racial unrest escalated on June 20, 1943 into a riot that lasted two days and was ended by the deployment of federal troops. 34 people were killed. White and Black mobs of people turned on each other, randomly attacking innocent civilians and destroying homes. The events were preceded by various hate strikes in factories (→ picture 27) and protests the previous year against the African-American social housing project Sojourner Truth Housing Project.

Detroit Rebellion of July 1967
Following the raid of a blind pig bar on July 23, 1967, there was mass unrest that lasted for five days and claimed 43 lives. Thousands of people were injured, more than 7,000 were arrested, and 1,000 buildings burned down. Looting, arson, and sniping occurred. The uprising was ended by the National Guard, which fired over 150,000 rounds of ammunition in four days. It started in one of Detroit's most dense neighborhoods, to which displaced Black residents from → Black Bottom and Paradise Valley had flocked after these were leveled by the → Urban Renewal Program. This rebellion was one of the uprisings in over 265 American cities between 1963 and 1968 against racism and police brutality for civil and racial equal rights during the Vietnam War.

Detroit Summer
was founded in 1992 by Detroit activists → Grace Lee and James Boggs, amongst others. It is a multi-racial, intergenerational collective with the goal of empowering local youth to improve

and transform their communities. Planting gardens, painting murals, recycling waste, and repairing homes are the tools to create ownership of the neighborhoods and youth leadership.

www.detroitsummer.wordpress.com

Farm-A-Lot Program
was instituted by Detroit Mayor Coleman Young in 1975. Similar to Mayor → Pingree's Potato Patches in 1894, gardens were allowed to be planted on vacant areas during an economic recession. The city supplied seeds and technical aid to Detroit families and encouraged them to grow food on vacant lots to cut their living costs. By 1979 nearly 7,000 Detroiters were cultivating small gardens across the city. After the support from the city began to wane other gardening efforts like the → Gardening Angels or → Detroit Summer continued community gardening and are still doing so.

Five Dollar Day
refers to the daily wage introduced by the → Ford Motor Company on January 4, 1914 as part of the "Profit Sharing Plan." This plan included a doubling of the previous standard wage and the introduction of an eight-hour working day (with six working days a week). The plan benefited 10,000 workers who had worked for Ford for more than six months and met the company's criteria (fluent English, a clean home, punctuality, and flawless work performance). The Five Dollar Day made headlines worldwide. For days tens of thousands of job seekers flocked to the → Ford Highland Park Plant. Turmoils arose and water hoses were deployed to control the crowds.

Food Desert
is the term for residential areas with limited access to affordable and healthy food. More than 75 percent of all United States food deserts are located in cities, often in low-income districts. Without healthy food, the risk of illness increases for children, families, and the elderly. In Detroit there are sometimes so few grocery stores that people without a car (about 20 percent of the inhabitants) can only shop at liquor stores or gas stations.

Food Security
means the condition in which all members of a community have local access to adequate amounts of nutritious, culturally appropriate food at all times, from sources that are environmentally benign and just.

Ford Motor Company
was founded in 1903 by Henry Ford (1863–1947) as a car manufacturer in → Milwaukee Junction. In 1908, Ford employed about 450 workers, in 1939 almost 90,000. The company introduced the → Assembly Line and → Five Dollar Day, maintained a Ford English School, the Ford Sociological Department to control the living conditions of its employees, and the Ford Service Department, an internal security department inspect of ex-policemen, informers, and prizefighters. Ford was one of the last companies to resist labor unions until 1941. The company shaped the city like no other, although no Ford model had been produced in Detroit since 1910. All factories were built outside the city limits. The Ford Motor Company is part of the → Big Three.

Ford Highland Park Plant
was Henry Ford's first automobile factory. Designed by → Albert Kahn it opened in 1910 in → Highland Park, back then one of Detroit's suburbs. The complex included offices, factories, a power plant, and a foundry. Here, Ford produced the Model T, introduced the moving → Assembly Line and the → Five Dollar Day. By 1928, the automobile assembly has been moved to the → Ford River Rouge Complex and production was closed down by the 1970s. Today the factory hosts storage units and a shopping center.

Ford River Rouge Complex
was Henry Ford's second car factory. It was built southwest of Detroit in the town of Dearborn, and when it opened in 1927, it was the largest integrated factory complex in the world. Designed by → Albert Kahn, it is now a National Historic Landmark. The Ford Rouge Center Industrial Park still consists of six Ford factories and two steelmaking operations.

Freeways / Interstates
During the Second World War, new roads were built around armament factories and military bases, which became the basis of the country's Interstate Highway System. Detroit built the first city and interstate highways from the 1950s onwards as part of → Urban Renewal. By 1958, over 5,000 buildings in Poletown and → Black Bottom had been destroyed in the process. The new highways acted as a funnel to the new suburbs and thus promoted → suburbanization.

Gardening Angels
was an informal network of mainly African-American elders raised in the South, who had seized the opportunity of vacant lots and the city's → Farm-A-Lot free seeds to plant small gardens all over the city. The network emerged in the 1990s when Gerald Hairston (1947–2001), a former autoworker and passionate environmentalist, started to create community gardens in vacant lots, at schools, and on playgrounds.

Garden Resource Program
supports around 1,500 family, neighborhood, and school gardens as well as commercial market gardens in Detroit, → Hamtramck, and → Highland Park with seeds and seedlings. Workshops, training courses, and meetings are also offered to promote home growers and urban agriculture. Founded in 2003, it has been part of Keep Growing Detroit since 2013.

http://detroitagriculture.net

General Motors Company
was founded in 1908 as a holding company in order to retain the capital of other companies. In the year of its foundation General Motors acquired the automanufacturers Buick and Oldsmobile and later took over Cadillac, Fisher Body, Chevrolet, and many others, which continue to be managed as independent brands. The General Motors Company is one of the largest car manufacturers in the world and is the only one of the → Big Three to maintain its headquarters in Detroit. In 2009, the company filed for bankruptcy with $90 billion in debt and was briefly nationalized in order to be saved.

Gentrification
is the process of increasing the economic value of an urban district through redevelopment or conversion. As one consequence, long-time residents are displaced by more affluent segments of the population. This process often begins with the interim use and upgrading of vacant space either by the local community itself or by the so-called creative class, a mostly well-educated middle class that establishes cultural projects or enterprise start-ups.

Ghost Landlords
are landlords who act as shell companies and buy up houses at the → Wayne County Tax Foreclosure Auctions. They continue to rent them out, but do not pay property taxes or necessary repairs until the houses revert to the city as tax liens, only to go to auction once again. The defrauded residents have almost no chance of recovering their rent or escaping eviction.

G. I. Bill
is the common term for the Servicemen's Readjustment Act of 1944, a law that provided benefits for returning World War II veterans, including low-cost mortgages. These mortgages led to the construction of thousands of homes in new suburbs around the cities. The granting of the loans continued the → redlining established at that time so that people of color were systematically disadvantaged. Today this results in a predominantly Black inner city of Detroit surrounded by white → suburbs.

Grace Lee and James Boggs
Philosopher Grace Lee (1915–2015) and autoworker James Boggs (1919–1993) were Detroit activists who stood up for an equal and self-determined civil society. Together with others, they founded several projects, including the → Detroit Summer Youth Program and the Boggs Center, from which new institutions such as the Boggs School emerged.

www.boggscenter.org

Grassroots
refers to political or civil society initiatives that originate from small, locally organized groups.

Great Depression
was the longest and most severe economic downturn in modern history. It began in the United States in 1929, spread worldwide after the stock market crash the same year, and lasted ten years. It was marked by banking panics, steep deflation, mass unemployment, and sharp increases in poverty and homelessness. In 1939, the Great Depression ended in the United States with the New Deal—increased government spending on jobs and social welfare programs and increased military spending in preparation for the country's entry into World War II.

Great Migration
was the mass-migration of six million African-Americans from the rural South to the industrial Northeast, Midwest, and West with a first wave from 1910 to 1940 and a second one from 1940 to 1970. Both waves were associated with the war production efforts of World War I and II. Their main reasons were the severe poverty and racism in the South.

Hamtramck
is an independent municipality, which like → Highland Park is surrounded by Detroit. After the original settlement of 1798, the city was founded in 1910 by German and Polish immigrants and, like Detroit, grew with the car industry. The building boom at that time can still be seen in the uniformity of the houses. Today Yemeni, Bangladeshi, Polish, and American communities live here side by side. Since 2015, Hamtramck has been the first community in the U.S. with a majority of Muslim city councilors.

Hastings Street
was often called the heart of → Paradise Valley. Between the 1920s and 1950s, it was the African-American business and entertainment strip in segregated Detroit, most known for its bars and music clubs. During the → Urban Renewal Program, the street and all its shops and businesses were demolished to make way for the Chrysler → Freeway.

Highland Park
is an independent municipality which, like → Hamtramck, is surrounded by Detroit. Founded in 1889 as a quiet suburb of Detroit, during the construction of the → Ford Motor Company's Highland Park Plant about 400 people lived in Highland Park. Only one year later, in 1910, there were already 4,125 and in 1920 the population stood at more than 46,000. The boom lasted only briefly. Ford moved car production to Dearborn as early as 1927. Since then, the city has constantly shed inhabitants and tax revenue. Today about 11,000 people live in the city, which has been under emergency financial management since 2010.

Homeowners' Associations
In 1940 Detroit was one of the fastest-growing cities in the world. Within eight years, half a million people moved here. Officially, there was no segregation, but in reality, neighborhoods were segregated strictly by color. Fearing that the newly arrived African-Americans, Jews, or Eastern Europeans might move into their neighborhoods and "endanger stability," white homeowners' associations were formed to "protect their investments" (→ Redlining). In addition to illegal arrangements for sales, there were also pickets, complaints, and violence. In 1956, there were 143 such associations. In the course of → suburbanization, they took their racist practices to the suburbs.

Industrial Flight
As early as 1910, Detroit's car manufacturers relocated and built new factories outside the city in order to cut costs. The last new factory built within Detroit was Chrysler's Plymouth Plant in 1929. Starting in the 1950s, production was outsourced to Michigan, the Southern States and other countries. An exception is the → General Motors Hamtramck Assembly Plant, which was built in 1981 with tax breaks after a part of Poletown had been cleared and demolished, also with tax money. (→ pictures 1/2).

Ku Klux Klan
is a white supremacist hate group, which seeks to enforce racial purity and professes the superiority of the white race. Since its founding in Tennessee in 1865 it has committed countless arson attacks, violent crimes, and murders against African-Americans, members of

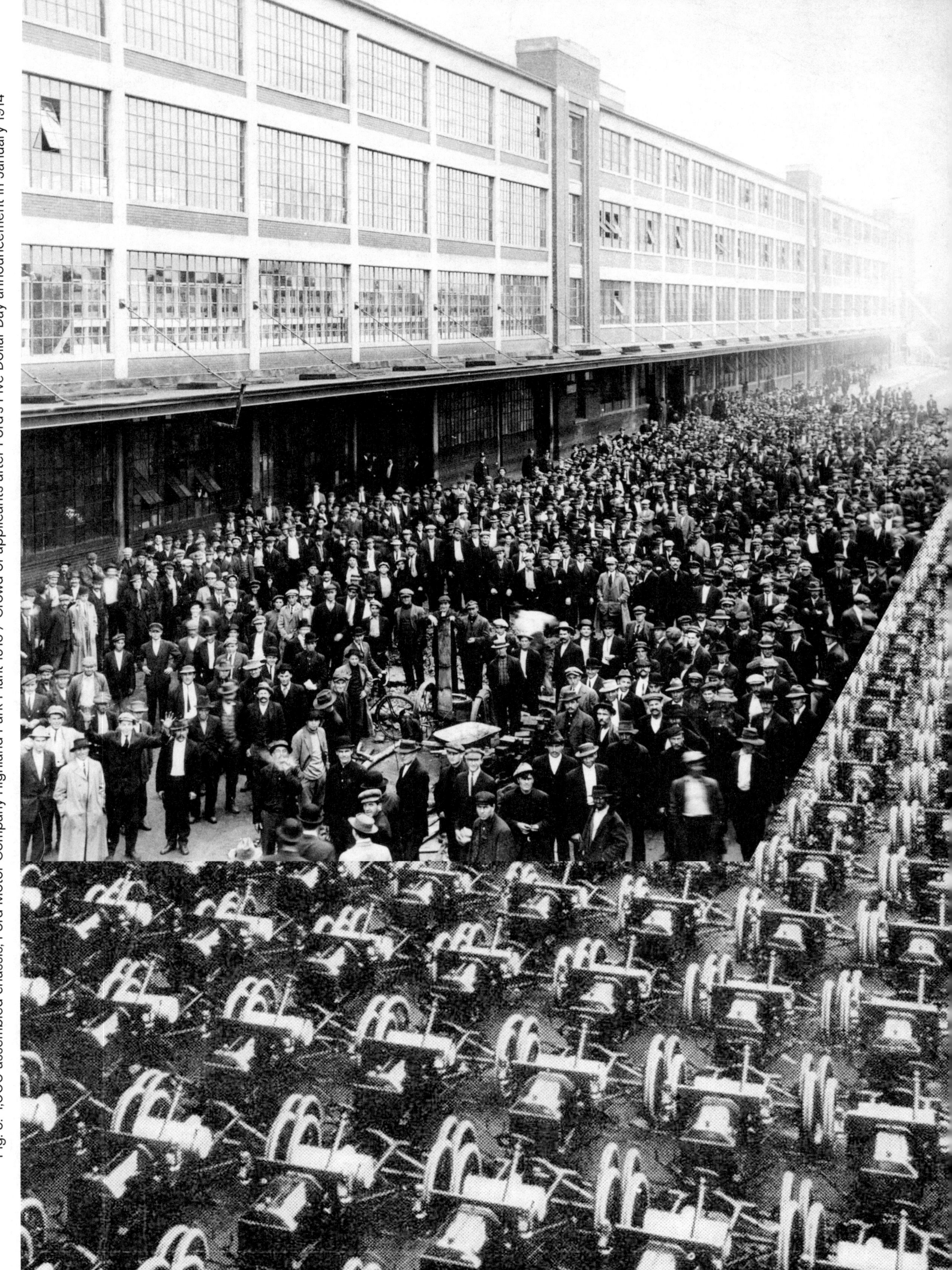

Fig. 3: 1,000 assembled chassis, Ford Motor Company Highland Park Plant 1913 / Crowd of applicants after Ford's Five Dollar Day announcement in January 1914

the civil rights movement, colored, Catholic, and Jewish people. In Detroit, the Ku Klux Klan groups were particularly active during the → Great Migration and the → Great Depression.

Maple Ash (Acer negundo)

is a tree native to North America. It is also known as Manitoba Maple. Various indigenous societies used maple ash as a medicinal plant, in ceremonies, to extract sugar, or to make plates and bowls, drums, or pipe stems. The fast-growing tree only lives for about 100 years and can now be found all over the world. It is also very common in Detroit.

Milwaukee Junction

named after a railway junction, it was in this district that the cradle of the automobile industry emerged around 1900. Almost all of the first manufacturers such as Anderson Electric, Brush Motor, Cadillac, Dodge, Hupp, Packard, Studebaker, and Ford had their first headquarters here. In the immediate vicinity, commercial and residential areas were established, along with diners and churches. Only one mile away from the city center, the district was long home to some of Detroit's poorest households. It is now one of the new → opportunity zones.

Opportunity Zones

are economically distressed areas in which financial incentives and favorable tax conditions are offered to encourage private and long-term capital investment. They were authorized by the Tax Cuts and Jobs Act of 2017 and are designated by individual states. In Detroit, these zones are concentrated in Downtown, Midtown, and around the City Airport. Though referred to as a new economic tool, Detroit has been offering tax breaks to business enterprises on a regular basis since at least the 1980s. Critics argue that urban social citizenship and empowering people to invest in their communities would be far more successful than tax breaks for investors.

Packard Automotive Plant

was one of the first major car factory complexes in Detroit. It was built between 1903 and 1910 in reinforced concrete according to designs by → Albert Kahn and his brother Julius and spans a length of 1.5 miles. In 1953 production of the high-end Packard car models was discontinued. The deserted factory is an icon of so-called → ruin porn. (For a more detailed description → picture 27).

Pingree's Potato Patches

During the economic crisis of 1893, Mayor Hazen Pingree encouraged impoverished residents to cultivate land that had previously been used for speculative purposes. The program, criticized as socialist, was very successful and reduced the city's social spending for several years.

Poplar Trees (Populus)

are widespread in temperate zones of the northern hemisphere. The trees can live up to 200 years. Their leaves are preserved as fossils that date back around 58 million years. Due to their rapid growth, poplars are typical pioneer plants on derelict land. Besides the → maple ash (Acer negundo) and → tree of heaven (Ailanthus altissima), poplars are the most common trees in Detroit.

Redlining

stands for discriminatory demarcation and exclusion of residential areas. From 1935 "Residential Security Maps" were drawn up to prevent home foreclosures as part of the New Deal after the → Great Depression. To this end, the security of mortgages was assessed in 239 U.S. American cities and marked on city maps, which then served as a guide for lenders such as banks and the Federal Housing Administration (→ G.I. Bill). The residential areas that were deemed the "safest" for property investment were marked in green and usually purely white, Protestant neighborhoods. Less profitable were neighborhoods with Jewish, Catholic, Eastern European, or Asian homeowners, while African-American neighborhoods were outlined in red. This gave rise to the term redlining.

Ribbon Farms

is the name given to the farms of the first French settlers in the area of Detroit after 1701. These stretched inland from the river in the form of ribbons so that all farmers could benefit from the river water.

Ruin Porn

The term refers to a voyeuristic, contemporary depiction of ruins, which focuses exclusively on the aesthetics of decaying cities, buildings, or industrial sites without describing their context in detail. The places are stylized as zones that hold a certain thrill for visitors without consideration for their inhabitants.

Speculation and Evictions

The effects of the 2007–2008 financial crisis led to a wave of foreclosures in Detroit. Many families lost their homes, because they could no longer afford to pay the rising installments of their mortgages, and as a result of a lack of poverty exemptions for low-income workers, many homeowners became renters. At the same time, falling land prices and the → Wayne County Tax Foreclosure Auction increasingly attracted speculators or bulk buyers who purchased large volumes of residential property to rent or sell to low-income residents. They often use predatory contracts that are meant to fail (→ Ghost Landlords and → Water Shutoff) resulting in the eviction of renters. This cycle is repeated several times and once the house deteriorates it is abandoned to tax foreclosure and demolished at the cost of the public. Since 2014, more than 2,000 homes have moved from foreclosure to speculative ownership to demolition at a cost of nearly $34 million. The evictions increased fivefold between 2010 and 2016 and mostly affect African-Americans. The speculation has been proven to destabilize and erode the property values of entire neighborhoods. (See Akers/Seymour (2019). www.urbanpraxis.org; The Eviction Machine.)

Structural Racism

is the institutional discrimination of people because of the color of their skin or ethnic background that is embedded in policies and practiced by public organizations. It leads to disparity in income, class, health, housing, education, and to legal injustice and limits civic participation. Structural racism and white supremacy (the structural privileging of white people) are the inverse reality to the vision of the → American Dream.

Suburbanization
is a population shift from central urban areas into suburbs, resulting in the formation of so-called sprawl. In Detroit, it began in the 1950s with construction of inner city → freeways, the heyday of the automobile, → G.I. Bill mortgages, and the ongoing relocation of plants and jobs outside the city. The practice of → redlining was adopted in the suburbs, so that today Detroit is 83 percent African-American and surrounded by suburbs that are 90 percent white.

Three Sisters
is an approximately 6000-year-old agricultural cultivation method, which has its origin in indigenous Mexican cultures. Corn, beans, and squash are grown in such a way that the beans climb up the corn, providing it with nutrients and natural pesticides. The squash forms a protective ring around both, providing shade and preventing desiccation. Each plant species is referred to as a sister, from which the term Three Sisters is derived.

Tree of Heaven
(Ailanthus altissima)
originates from China, Vietnam, and Taiwan. The tree was introduced as an ornamental plant in Europe and America in 1740 and is now common all over the world. The Chinese name "chouchun" means foul-smelling tree. It is used in Traditional Chinese Medicine and for silk production. In the United States it is also called ghetto palm because the trees spread quickly on wasteland. Trees of heaven grow to a height of 50 to 100 feet. They rarely live longer than 50 years. Outside of Asia, they are considered an → alien plant. In Detroit, they grow almost everywhere.

United Auto Workers (U.A.W.)
With its full name, The International Union, United Automobile, Aerospace, and Agricultural Implement Workers of America, the U.A.W. is one of the main labor unions in the automobile industry of the U.S. It was founded in 1935 in Detroit, where it still has its headquarters today. After numerous labor disputes, it was recognized by GM and Chrysler in 1937 (by Ford only in 1941). Collective bargaining with the companies regulated the working hours, wages, retirement provisions, and health insurance of the workers. In the 1950s and 1960s, its members were considered to be the highest-paid in the United States.

Urban Renewal
was a program by the City of Detroit in the 1950s and 1960s, with its mission to clear out blighted areas in inner cities and create new opportunities for housing and business. One consequence of the initiative is that the poorest and oldest neighborhoods, → Black Bottom and Paradise Valley, were demolished for the construction of city highways and the Lafayette Park residential complex (→ pictures 31/32). In addition Poletown was divided in two by Ford Edsel → Freeway, while half of the district and its established infrastructure were destroyed. Other neighborhoods were replaced by the Lodge Freeway, the Medical Center, and Wayne State University. The city's urban renewal projects of that period demolished more than 10,000 structures and led to the displacement of 43,000 people, 70 percent of them African-American.

Victory Gardens/
Liberty Gardens
were vegetable, fruit, and herb gardens planted on private and public property during World War I and World War II throughout the U.S. and Europe. They helped reduce pressure on public food supply and were also considered a civil morale booster for daily life on the home front.

Water Shutoff
The Detroit City Water and Sewerage Department was to be privatized during → Detroit's Bankruptcy in 2013. The outstanding invoices of about $5 million were to be collected in preparation for the sale. To this end, the demolition firm Homrich Wrecking Inc. was hired for $5.6 million to shut off water to delinquent customers until they paid their bills. According to the Michigan Welfare Rights Organization, over 100,000 private households had their drinking water turned off by 2019, two-thirds of them families with children. They or their landlords were either more than six weeks behind on their payments or more than $150 in arrears. In October 2014, the United Nations accused the City of Detroit of human rights violations. Those affected receive help from self-organized groups such as the Detroit Water Collections Project or the Detroit Water Brigade, which deliver water financed by donations or set up water stations. Not affected by the shutoffs were the Red Wings' Hockey Arena, the Ford Football Stadium, and the Detroit Golf Course, though they all had outstanding debts of around $1 million. In addition, thousands of empty houses still have running water that often leaks from burst pipes. Despite a poverty rate of over 36 percent, Detroit residents pay some of the most expensive water rates anywhere in the United States.

Wayne County Tax
Foreclosure Auction
has been an annual auction for previously foreclosed houses and land since 2002. Foreclosure happens when property taxes have not been paid or debts have not been settled for more than two years. In addition to vacant buildings, evictions also affect homeowners or tenants who have been defrauded by → Ghost Landlords; in 2019, the number was around 3,000. A report by the University of Michigan from 2019 shows that since the financial crisis of 2007–2008, the auction has been increasingly used by bulk buyers and ghost landlords for real estate → speculation on housing, leading to more evictions, vacancies, and demolitions and thus contributing to the destabilization of entire neighborhoods in Detroit. (→ Detroit Demolition Program; see Akers/Seymour (2019). The Eviction Machine)

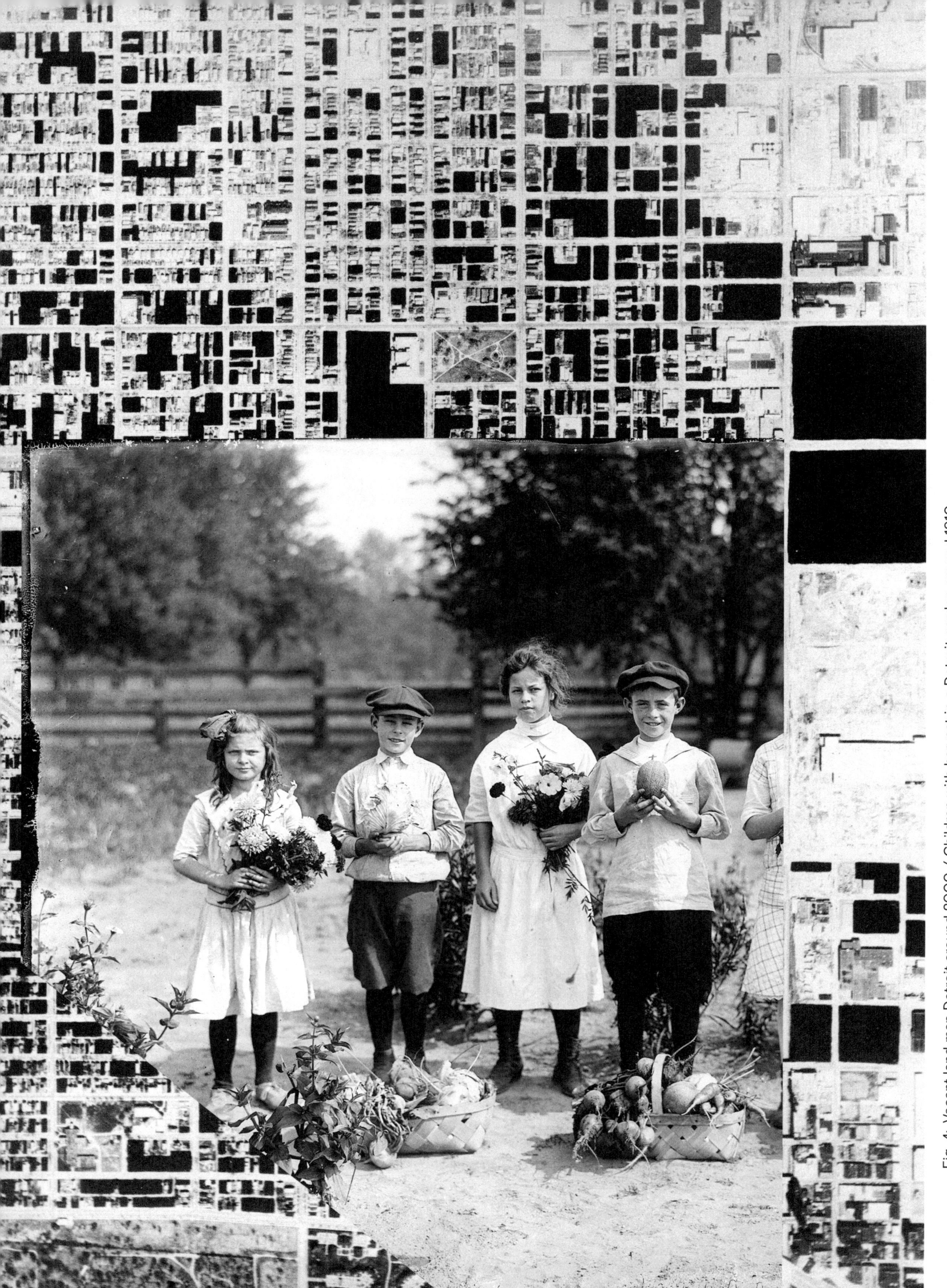

Fig. 4: Vacant land map Detroit around 2000 / Children with harvest in a Detroit garden around 1910

REFERENCES

Interviews

Shane Bernardo, Earthworks Urban Farm, The Capuchin Soup Kitchen, August 15, 2016.

Marc Convington, Georgia Street Community Collective, August 30, 2018.

Bill Hebron, Oakland Avenue Urban Farm, September 04, 2018.

Lorenzo Herron, Ile Oko Farm, July 29, 2016.

Molly Hubbel and **Mike Zuzolo**, Gardeners at North End, September 11, 2015.

Faina Lerman, Popps Packing's Garden, September 07, 2018.

Kieran Neal, Beaverland Farms, July 18, 2016.

Rosebud Schneider, Sacred Roots Garden, American Indian Health and Family Services, September 11, 2018.

Dean Tomel Simionescu, Popps Packing's Garden, September 16, 2016.

Emily Staugaitis, Bandhu Gardens, Banglatown, September 08, 2018.

Malik Yakini, D-Town Farm, Detroit Black Community Food Security Network, August 06, 2016.

Literature

Abraham, Nabeel; Shryock, Andrew (Ed.). **Arab Detroit: From Margin to Mainstream.** Detroit: Wayne State University Press, 2000.

Ager, Susan. **"Tough, Cheap, and Real, Detroit Is Cool Again,"** National Geographic, Issue May 2015.

Akers, Joshua; Seymour, Eric. **"The Eviction Machine: Neighborhood Instability and Blight in Detroit's Neighborhoods,"** Poverty Solutions, the University of Michigan Working Paper Series, # 5–19, University of Michigan, July 2019 (https://poverty.umich.edu/files/2019/08/Akers-et-al-Eviction-Machine-Revised-August-12.pdf) 01-20-2020.

Akers, Joshua. **"Contesting Economies of Displacement and Dispossession,"** Metropolitics, Jan. 13 January 2017.

Albrecht, Donald (Ed.). **World War II and the American dream: how wartime building changed a nation.** Cambridge / London: MIT Press, 1995.

Apel, Dora. **Beautiful Terrible Ruins: Detroit and the Anxiety of Decline.** New Brunswick / New Jersey: Rutgers University Press, 2015.

Aubert, Danielle; Cavar, Lana; Chandani, Natasha (Ed.). **Thanks For the View, Mr. Mies: Lafayette Park Detroit.** New York: Metropolis Books, 2012.

Babson, Steve. **Working Detroit: Making of a Union Town.** New York: Adama Books, 1984.

Bluestone, Barry; Harrison, Bennett. **The Deindustrialization of America: Plant Closings, Community Abandonment, and the Dismantling of Basic Industry.** New York, NY: Basic Books, 1982.

Boggs, Grace Lee; Kurashige, Scott. **The Next American Revolution: Sustainable Activism for the Twenty-first Century.** Berkeley / London: University of California Press, 2011.

Boggs, James. **Pages from a Black Radical's Notebook: a James Boggs Reader.** Detroit: Wayne State University Press, 2011.

Bossen, Howard; Beck, John P. (Ed.). **Detroit Resurgent.** East Lansing: Michigan State University Press, 2014.

Boyle, Kevin; Getis, Victoria. **Muddy Boots and Ragged Aprons.** Detroit: Wayne State University Press, 1997.

Brown, Stanley H. **"Detroit: Slow Healing of a Fractured City,"** Fortune, Vol. LXXI, No. 6, 1965, pp. 142–262.

Carey, John W. **"The Growth of Brightmoor,"** Brightmoor Community Center. **Brightmoor: A community in action,** Detroit: Brightmoor community center, inc., 1940.

Chinoy, Ely. **Automobile Workers and the American Dream.** Garden City, NY: Doubleday & Company, 1955.

City of Detroit. **Detroit Demolition Program Website** (https://detroitmi.gov/departments/detroit-building-authority/detroit-demolition-program) 01-11-2018.

Daniels, Serena Maria. **"History in Photos: Detroit's 'Farm-A-Lot' program set the stage for urban gardening movement,"** Tostada Magazine, February 28, 2018.

Davis, Donald Finlay. **Conspicuous production: Automobiles and elites in Detroit, 1899–1933.** Philadelphia: Temple University Press, 1988.

Detroit Food Policy Council. **Public Land Sale Process in Detroit: A Community Perspective,** Council Paper, Detroit: 2012 (http://detroitfoodpolicycouncil.net/sites/default/files/pdfs/DFPC%20Report-Public%20Land%20Sale%20Process%20in%20Detroit.pdf) 08-28-2019.

Detroit Future City. **The Land Use Element: The Image of the City,** Detroit, 2012.

Detroit Future City. **Milwaukee Junction District Framework Study: A Framework Study for Industrial Adaptive Reuse and Workforce Development in the Milwaukee Junction area in Detroit,** Detroit: May 2019.

Detroit Historical Museum. **Detroit '67: Perspectives.** Exhibition Texts, 2018.

Doucet, Brian (Ed.). **Why Detroit Matters: Decline, Renewal, and Hope in a Divided City.** Bristol: Policy Press, 2017.

Dunnigan, Brian Leigh. **"Detroit's Ribbon Farms,"** Michigan History, vol. March / April 2013, pp. 54–59.

Eugenides, Jeffrey. **Middlesex.** Hamburg: Rowohlt, 2003.

Eugenides, Jeffrey. **Middlesex.** London: Bloomsbury Publishing Plc, 2003.

Feldman, Richard (Ed.). **End of the Line: Autoworkers and the American Dream.** New York: Weidenfeld & Nicolson, 1988.

Feloni, Richard; Lee, Samantha. **"Billionaire Dan Gilbert has invested $5.6 billion in nearly 100 properties in Detroit — see the full map of exactly what he owns,"** Business Insider, August 30, 2018.

Ferretti, Christine; LeBlanc, Beth. **"Mayor Duggan pledges blight-free Detroit neighborhoods by 2024,"** The Detroit News, May 30, 2019.

Ferry, W. Hawkins (Ed.). **The Legacy of Albert Kahn.** Detroit: Wayne State University Press, 1970.

Ford, Henry; Crowther, Samuel. **Mein Leben und Werk,** Leipzig: Paul List Verlag, 1934.

Ford, Henry; Crowther, Samuel. **My Life and Work.** London: William Heinemann Ltd., 1924.

Galster, George. **Driving Detroit: The Quest for Respect in the Motor City.** Philadelphia: University of Pennsylvania Press, 2012.

Georgakas, Dan; Surkin, Marvin. **Detroit: I Do Mind Dying, a Study in Urban Revolution.** London: Redwords, 1998 (first published 1975).

Gross, Allie. **"How new Detroit historic district impacts the Ilitch family,"** Detroit Free Press, Dec 17, 2019.

Guyette, Curt. **"Down a green path,"** Detroit Metro Times, October 31, 2001.

Guzmán, Martina. **"Black farmers in Detroit are growing their own food. But they're having trouble owning the land,"** PRI's The World, March 30, 2016.

Hall, Kalea. **"GM's Detroit Hamtramck Assembly poised to begin electric transformation,"** The Detroit News, February 19, 2020.

Hall, Jacob Dean. **The Myth of the Motor City: Urban Politics, Public Policy, and the Suburbanization of Detroit's Automobile Industry, 1878–1937.** PhD Thesis, University of Iowa, 2013 (http://ir.uiowa.edu/etd/2219) 01-22-2018.

Hammer, Peter. **"Detroit 1967 and Today: Spatial Racism and Ongoing Cycles of Oppression,"** Stone, Joel (Ed.). **Detroit 1967: Origins, Impact, Legacies.** Detroit: Wayne State University Press, 2017, pp. 273–282.

Harrington, Michael. **The Other America: Poverty in the United States.** Baltimore: Penguin Books, 1981 (first published in 1962).

Hartmann, David W. (Ed.). **Immigrants and Migrants: The Detroit Ethnic Experience.** Detroit: Wayne State University, 1974.

Hays, Arthur Garfield. **Lasst Freiheitsglocken läuten! Zeitbilder aus dem heutigen Amerika.** Leipzig / Zürich: Grethlein & Co, 1929.

Henrickson, Wilma Wood (Ed.). **Detroit Perspectives: Crossroads and Turning Points.** Detroit: Wayne State University Press, 1991.

Herman, Max Arthur. **Summer of Rage: An Oral History of the 1967 Newark and Detroit Riots.** New York et al.: Peter Lang, 2013.

Herron, Jerry. **"Motor City Breakdown: Detroit in Literature and Film,"** Places: The Journal of Public Scholarship on Architecture, Landscape, and Urbanism, April 2013 (https://placesjournal.org/article/motor-city-breakdown) 11-15-2016.

Herron, Jerry. **AfterCulture: Detroit and the Humiliation of History.** Detroit: Wayne State University Press, 1993.

Hocking, Scott. **"The Zone,"** 1999–present (www.scotthocking.com/zone.html) 05-31-2019.

Holli, Melvin G. (Ed.). **Detroit.** New York / London: New Viewpoints, 1976.

Hooker, Clarence. **Life in the Shadows of the Crystal Palace, 1910–1927: Ford Workers in the Model T Era.** Bowling Green: Bowling Green State University Popular Press, 1997.

Ikonomova, Violet. **"Higher rents, 'massive displacement': The unknown cost of Detroit's landlord crackdown."** Detroit Metro Times, August 29 – September 04, 2018.

Josephson, Matthew. **"Detroit: City of Tomorrow"** (1929), Holli, Melvin G. (Ed.). **Detroit.** New York / London: New Viewpoints, 1976.

Kaffer, Nancy. **"3,000 Detroiters could lose their homes, treasurer says he's not doing enough,"** Detroit Free Press, August 14, 2019.

Kisch, Egon Erwin. **"At Ford's Place in Detroit,"** Skaff, Sheila. **"Ambivalence and Cigarettes: Egon Erwin Kisch's 'At Ford's Place in Detroit' with a Translation of the Text,"** Michigan Historical Review, Vol. 29, No. 1 Spring, 2003, pp. 119–131.

Kisch, Egon Erwin. **„Bei Ford in Detroit,"** id. **Paradies Amerika,** Berlin: Erich Reiss Verlag, 1930, pp. 299–308.

LaReau, Jamie L. **"General Motors to close Detroit, Ohio, Canada plants,"** Detroit Free Press, November 2nd, 2018.

Latzman Moon, Elaine. **Untold Tales, Unsung Heroes: An Oral History of Detroit's African American Community, 1918–1967.** Detroit: Wayne State University Press, 1994.

Lawson, Laura; Miller, Abbilyn. **"Community Gardens and Urban Agriculture as Antithesis to Abandonment: Exploring a Citizenship-Land Model,"** Dewar, Margaret; Manning Thomas, June (Ed.). **The City After Abandonment.** Pennsylvania: University of Pennsylvania Press, 2013.

Leary, John Patrick. **"Detroitism. What does "ruin porn" tell us about the motor city?,"** Guernica. A magazine of global arts and politics, January 15, 2011 (www.guernicamag.com/leary_1_15_11/) 07-25-2017.

Levine, Philip. **They Feed They Lion.** New York: Atheneum, 1972.

Lewis, David Lanier. **The Public Image of Henry Ford: An American Folk Hero and his Company.** Detroit: Wayne State University Press, 1976.

Mast, Robert H. **Detroit Lives.** Philadelphia: Temple University Press, 1994.

Meyer, Steven. **The Five Dollar Day: Labor, Management, and Social Control in the Ford Motor Company, 1908–1921.** Albany: State University of New York Press, 1981.

Michigan State Administrative Board. **Michigan: A Guide to the Wolverine State.** American Guide Series Illustrated. New York: Oxford University Press, 1949 (first published 1941).

Millington, Nate. **Post-Industrial Imageries: Nature, Representation, and Ruin in Detroit, Michigan.** Thesis for the degree of Master of Science (Geography). Madison: University of Wisconsin-Madison, 2010.

Music, Marsha. **"Hidden in Plain Sight: The 'Invisibilty' of Mies van der Rohe in Detroit,"** Aubert, Danielle; Cavar, Lana; Chandani, Natasha (Ed.). **Thanks For the View, Mr. Mies: Lafayette Park Detroit.** New York: Metropolis Books, 2012, pp. 45–51.

Office of the United Nations High Commissioner for Human Rights United. **The Right to Adequate Food.** Fact Sheet No. 34, Nations Office at Geneva 2010 (www.ohchr.org/Documents/Publications/FactSheet34en.pdf) 05-20-2019.

Oswalt, Philipp (Ed.). **Schrumpfende Städte: Internationale Untersuchungen.** Hatje-Cantz, Ostfilden-Ruit, 2004.

Perkins, Tom. **"Billionaire Dan Gilbert grabs $ 618M in taxpayer money for new projects,"** Detroit Metro Times, May 22, 2018.

Peterson, Roger Tory; McKenny, Margaret. **A Field Guide to Wildflowers of Northeastern and Northcentral North America.** Boston: Mifflin, 1968.

Petrides, George A. **A Field Guide to Eastern Trees: Eastern United States and Canada.** Boston: Mifflin, 1988.

Pothukuchi, Kameshwari. **"Five Decades of Community Food Planning in Detroit: City and Grassroots, Growth and Equity,"** Journal of Planning Education and Research, Vol. 35, No. 4 (December, 2015), pp. 419-434 (DOI: 10.1177/0739456X15586630jpe.sgaepub.com) 01-16-2016.

Pothukuchi, Kameshwari. **"'To allow farming is to give up on the city': Political anxieties related to the disposition of vacant land for urban agriculture in Detroit."** Journal of Urban Affairs, Vol. 39, No. 8 (2017), pp. 1169-1189 (DOI: 10.1080/ 0735 2166.2017.1319239) 09-03-2019.

Shogan, Robert; Craig, Tom. **The Detroit Race Riot: a Study in Violence.** New York, NY: Da Capo Press, 1976.

Smith, Suzanne E. **Dancing in the Street: Motown and the Cultural Politics of Detroit.** Cambridge: Harvard University Press, 1999.

Solnit, Rebecca. **"Detroit Arcadia. Exploring the post-American Landscape,"** Harper's Magazine, July 2007.

Stone, Joel (Ed.). **Detroit 1967: Origins, Impact, Legacies.** Detroit: Wayne State University Press, 2017.

Sugrue, Thomas J. **The Origins of the Urban Crisis. Race and Inequality in Postwar Detroit.** Princeton: Princeton University Press 1996.

Terkel, Studs. **American Dreams: Lost and Found.** New York: Pantheon Books, 1980.

Thomas, June Manning. **Redevelopment and Race: Planning a Finer City in Postwar Detroit.** Detroit: Wayne State University Press, 2013.

Wacquant, Loïc. **"The Penalization of Poverty in the Hyperghetto,"** Hignett, Jimini. **The Detroit Diary.** Arnheim: Dutch Art Institute / ArtEZ, 2010.

Walter P. Reuther Library, Wayne State University. **12th Street Detroit.** Digital Exhibition about the Civil Unrest 1967 in Detroit (http://projects.lib.wayne.edu/12thstreetdetroit/) 06-08-2017.

Ward, Jim. **"Early Days of the Union: The Kelsey-Hayes Sit-Down Strike,"** Looking Back, Moving Forward Newsletter, Detroit 2011 (www.motorcities.org/story-of-the-week/2016/early-days-of-the-union-the-kelsey-hayes-sit-down-strike) 09-05-2019.

We the People of Detroit Community Research Collective. **Mapping the Water Crisis: The Dismantling of African-American Neighborhoods in Detroit: Volume One.** Detroit, 2016.

"When Packard Workers Went On Strike," The Michigan Chronicle, June 5, 1943.

White, Monica M. Freedom Farmers: **Agricultural Resistance and the Black Freedom Movement.** Chapel Hill: University of North Carolina Press, 2019.

Widick, Branko J. **Detroit: City of Race and Class Violence.** Detroit: Wayne State University Press, 1989.

Williams, Candice. **"'I haven't had my day in court': Packard Plant's resident leaves after eviction,"** The Detroit News, October 01, 2019.

Williams, Candice. **"HUD OKs sale of former Brewster-Douglass site to Bedrock affiliate for $ 23M",** The Detroit News, December 16, 2019.

Williams, Jeremy. **Detroit: The Black Bottom Community.** Series Images of America, Chicago/Portmouth/San Francisco: Arcadia Publishing, 2009.

Wilson, Edmund. **The American Earthquake: A Documentary of the Twenties and Thirties.** Garden City: Doubleday, 1958.

Wylie, Jeanie. **Poletown: Community Betrayed.** Urbana / Chicago: University of Illinois Press, 1989.

Zunz, Olivier: **The Changing Face of Inequality: Urbanization, Industrial Development, and Immigrants in Detroit, 1880–1920.** Chicago: University of Chicago Press, 1982.

Films / Documentaries / Videos /

Bredow, Gary. **High Tech Soul: The Creation of Techno Music.** documentary film, 2006 (www.youtube.com/watch?v=gElNoedRj5Q) 09-10-2016.

Collapsing Auto Industry in Detroit. Fault Lines, program of Al Jazeera English, 2013 (www.youtube.com/watch?v=9TSITlsK4eQ) 01-28-2019.

Grace Lee Boggs in an interview with Democracy Now!, 2011 (www.youtube.com/watch?v=cEI8FDAlgoE) 11-25-2015.

Healing Detroit One Garden at a Time. Oprah Steep Your Soul, June 2015 (www.oprah.com/steepyoursoul/steep-your-soul-revitalizing-detroit-one-garden-at-a-time-video) 09-03-2019.

Lee, Grace. **American Revolutionary: The Evolution of Grace Lee Boggs.** documentary film, produced by LeeLee Films, 2013.

Metropolitan Detroit Convention and Visitors Bureau. **Greater Detroit: Super City USA.** Commercial video, produced by Metropolitan Detroit Convention and Visitors Bureau, Sony 15 U-Matic videotape, 1983 (http://detroithistorical.pastperfectonline.com/archive/BFE1BF7D-4C8D-4036-A32D-526037233936) 07-12-2018.

One of Us Films. **Ms. Gwen's Edible Garden.** Detroit, 2013 (https://vimeo.com/73421629) 09-03-2019.

Park, Kyong. **Detroit: Making It Better for You.** Artist video, 2000 (https://vimeo.com/11457098) 12-05-2017.

School Days: Asenath Andrews. An event co-presented by Chalkbeat and The Secret Society of Twisted Storytellers at The Charles H. Wright Museum in Detroit, March 2017 (https://vimeo.com/209584121) 11-23-2018.

Yakini, Malik. **From 'Motor City' to Food Resilience: How Detroit has risen from the Ashes.** Talk at OuiSharefest in Paris, July 2017 (www.youtube.com/watch?v=yXb1zBszJpM) 06-28-2019.

Collage sources

Fig. 1 / Abb. 1

Ford River Rouge Complex 1947; Photo: E.S. Purrington / Ford Motor Company, in: Lewis, David Lanier. The Public Image of Henry Ford: An American Folk Hero and his Company. Detroit: Wayne State University Press, 1976, p. 172.

Detroit resident watering his lawn after the Detroit Rebellion of July 1967; unknown photographer, Credit: picture alliance / Associated Press.

Fig. 2 / Abb. 2

"Detroit is Dynamite," employment agency 1942; unknown photographer, in: "Detroit is Dynamite," Life Magazine, August 17, 1942, p. 15.

Munition maker at Lincoln Motor Company 1918; unknown photographer, Credit: Walter P. Reuther Library, Archives of Labor and Urban Affairs, Wayne State University.

Fig. 3 / Abb. 3

1,000 assembled chassis, Ford Motor Company Highland Park Plant 1913; Photo: Ford Motor Company, in: Ford Motor Company. Ford Factory Facts. Detroit, 1915, p. 58 / Credit: From the Collections of The Henry Ford. Gift of Ford Motor Company.

Crowd of applicants after Ford's Five Dollar Day announcement in January 1914; unknown photographer, Credit: From the Collections of The Henry Ford. Gift of Ford Motor Company.

Fig. 4 / Abb. 4

Vacant land map Detroit around 2000; unknown photographer, in: Daskalakis, Georgia; Waldheim, Charles; Young, Jason (Ed.). Stalking Detroit. Barcelona: Actar, 2001, p. 100.

Children with harvest in a Detroit garden around 1910; unknown photographer, Credit: Burton Historical Collection, Detroit Public Library.

IMPRINT

Franziska Klose
Detroit –
Field Notes from a Wild City

Photographs, Collages, Texts:
Franziska Klose
Book concept: Franziska Klose, Ina Kwon
Graphic design: Ina Kwon
Translation: Jan Caspers
Copy-editing:
Florian Henrich (German),
Chris Michalski (English),
Kerstin Niemann
Lithography: Carsten Humme
Printing and binding:
DZA Druckerei zu Altenburg

Spector Books
Harkortstraße 10
D-04107 Leipzig

Distribution:
Germany, Austria: GVA, Gemeinsame Verlagsauslieferung Göttingen GmbH&Co. KG, www.gva-verlage.de
Switzerland: AVA Verlagsauslieferung AG, www.ava.ch
France, Belgium: Interart Paris, www.interart.fr
UK: Central Books Ltd, www.centralbooks.com
USA, Canada, Central and South America, Africa: ARTBOOK | D.A.P. www.artbook.com
Japan: twelvebooks, www.twelve-books.com
South Korea: The Book Society, www.thebooksociety.org
Australia, New Zealand: Perimeter Distribution, www.perimeterdistribution.com

www.franziskaklose.de
www.spectorbooks.com

First Edition
Printed in the EU

ISBN 978-3-95905-468-3

Funded by:
Kulturstiftung des Freistaates Sachsen (diese Maßnahme wird mitfinanziert durch Steuermittel auf der Grundlage des von den Abgeordneten des Sächsischen Landtags beschlossenen Haushaltes),
Frankfurter Stiftung maecenia für Frauen in Wissenschaft und Kunst

Supported by:
Museum für Kunst und Kulturgeschichte der Philipps-Universität Marburg,
Deutsches Dokumentationszentrum für Kunstgeschichte – Bildarchiv Foto Marburg

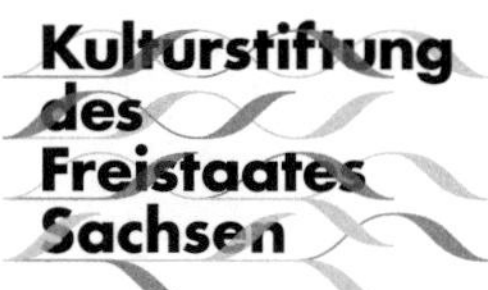

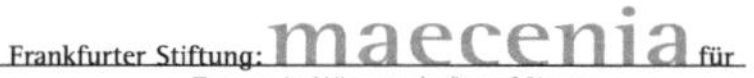

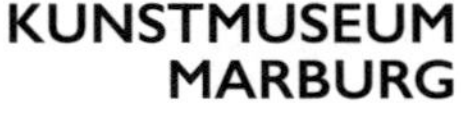

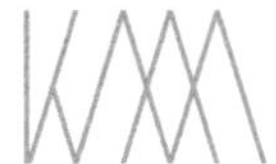

Thank You:
Jennifer Bennet, Blandine Blachère, Benjamin Brandt, Burton Historical Collection–Detroit Public Library, Bill Ciesliga, all crowdfunders, Markus Dreßen, Fortress Studios (Steve Kuypers, Kevin McCoy, Steve McShane), Walter Fruge and Marisa Benzle, Scott Hocking, Anna Jander and Klaus Jordan, Marianne and Matthias Klose, Ina Kwon, Elise Martin, Chris Michalski, Kerstin Niemann, Lucy Owen, Popps Packing (Faina Lerman, Graem Whyte), Julia Schäfer, Thomas Scheidt, Paul Szewczyk, Helmut Völter, and Florian Henrich

Molly Hubbel for introducing me to Detroit's urban agriculture.
All farmers and gardeners for their generosity and patience:
Shane Bernardo (Earthworks Urban Farm, Capuchin Soup Kitchen and Food as Healing), Marc Covington (Georgia Street Community Collective), Bill and Jerry Hebron (Oakland Avenue Urban Farm), Lorenzo Herron (Ile Oko Farm), Molly Hubbel and Mike Zuzolo (Ambassador Fridge), Brittney Rooney and Kieran Neal (Beaverland Farms), Rosebud Schneider (Sacred Roots Garden, American Indian Health and Family Services), Dean Tomel Simionescu, Emily Staugaitis (Bandhu Gardens), Malik Yankini (Detroit Black Community Food Security Network's D-Town Farm)

Detroit for being Detroit: open hearted, radical, and vital.

Wenn mich jemand fragt: „Wird die Stadt jemals ein Comeback erleben?“ Dann antworte ich: „Sie ist zurück, sie ist ja nie weg gewesen. Ihr seid vielleicht fortgegangen, aber die Stadt war immer hier.“

Jerry Herron, in: Bredow (2006): High Tech Soul

PFLANZEN

L

M

N

O

P

Q

R

S

Eines Tages nach einem kurzen Gewitter, als es aufgehört hatte zu regnen und dicke weiße Wolken den Himmel bedeckten, spazierte ich durch ein Stadtviertel oder besser gesagt durch ein ehemaliges Stadtviertel mit mindestens einem Dutzend Straßenblöcke, an denen Götterbäume ihre Äste in den Himmel streckten. In jedem Block stand meist nur noch ein verfallenes, verkohltes Haus. Ich konnte das Summen von Grillen oder Zikaden hören, und ich fühlte mich, als wäre ich tausend Jahre in die Zukunft gereist.

Rebecca Solnit (2007): Detroit Arcadia

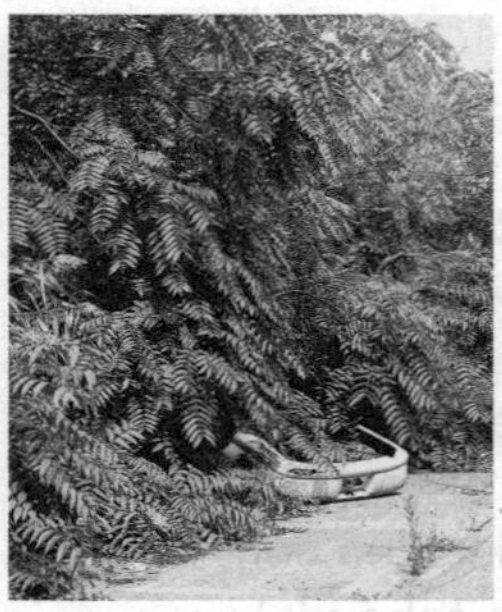

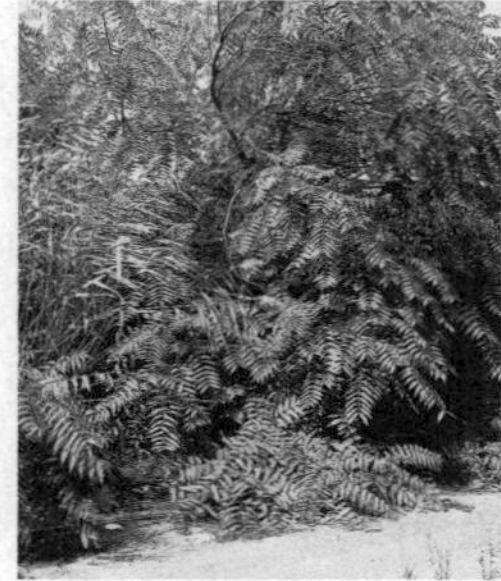

1/2

2550 East Grand Boulevard, 2015

Milwaukee Junction

Das Grundstück 2550 East Grand Boulevard liegt im Stadtteil Milwaukee Junction, der Wiege der Detroiter Autoindustrie. Fast alle der ersten Automanufakturen gründeten sich hier. Die beiden Fotos entstanden in Sichtweite zur General Motors Hamtramck Assembly Plant Fabrik. Sie wurde 1985 eröffnet. Während einer der wirtschaftlichen Flauten Detroits hatte die Stadt General Motors Steuervergünstigungen für den Bau der neuen Fabrik gewährt und gleichzeitig bewohnte Haus- und Kirchengrundstücke im Stadtteil Poletown East enteignet, auf denen die Fabrik heute steht. Der Abriss dieser Häuser fand unter Protest der Bewohner*innen und auf Steuerkosten statt. Die Enteignung von Privatbesitz zugunsten wirtschaftlicher Stadtentwicklung wurde kurz zuvor durch eine Gesetzesänderung des Bundesstaates Michigan ermöglicht. Während Francis James McDonald, der Präsident von General Motors, 1981 in einem Interview äußerte: „Die Achtzigerjahre werden ein sehr aufregendes Jahrzehnt werden. Ich bin der Meinung, dass Regierung, Arbeitnehmer sowie Industrie und Management sich wirklich zusammentun müssen, um die Herausforderungen zu bewältigen, die vor uns liegen. Und ich sehe, dass dies auch geschieht.“°, kritisierte der Priester der St. Hyacinth's Church, Francis Skalski: „... es war eine Schande, dass Leute wie General Motors hierher gekommen sind und die Gegend von den armen Leuten einfach übernommen haben. Es erinnert mich an einen mittelalterlichen König – es gibt ein riesiges Areal, einen schönen hohen Zaun vor dem Grundstück, schöne Landschaftsgestaltung, und dahinter haben sie ihr Schloss – ihre Fabrik.“°°

Im November 2018 kündigte General Motors die Schließung der Hamtramck Assembly Plant an, um „proaktive Schritte zu unternehmen, die Geschäftsentwicklung insgesamt zu verbessern, was eine Neuordnung der globalen Entwicklungsabteilung, die Neuausrichtung der Fertigungskapazitäten und eine Reduzierung der fest-angestellten Arbeitnehmer beinhaltet.“°°°

Zwei Jahre, einen 40-tägigen Streik und 800 Entlassungen später wird die Fabrik im Jahr 2020 auf die Herstellung von Elektro-Trucks umgerüstet.

° Wylie (1989): Poletown, 29
°° Wylie (1989): Poletown, 72
°°° GM Pressemitteilung, in: LaReau (2018)

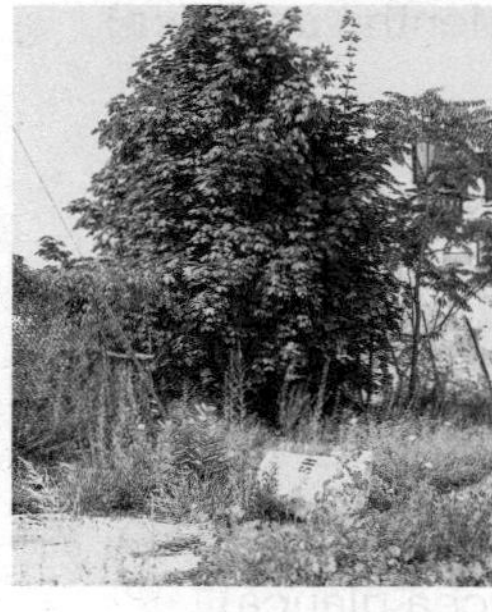

3

Fisher Body Plant 21 (Bucket), 2015

Milwaukee Junction Neighborhood

Die ehemalige Fabrik Fisher Body Plant 21 liegt im Stadtteil Milwaukee Junction, in dem um 1900 die ersten Automanufakturen entstanden. Von den anfangs 43 Herstellern waren 1926 nur noch acht übrig. Fisher Body wurde wie viele andere von einem der sogenannten Big Three aufgekauft.

Das Fabrikgebäude wurde 1919 nach einem Entwurf von Albert Kahn gebaut. Mit Ausnahme der Weltwirtschaftskrise, als die Fabrik als Suppenküche und Obdachlosenheim diente, wurden hier 80 Jahre lang Autoteile produziert: Karosserien (anfänglich noch aus Holz), Teile für Limousinen, Krankenwagen und Busse sowie in Kriegszeiten Komponenten für Flugzeuge, Flugabwehrgeschütze und Panzer. 1983 schloss General Motors die Fabrik und lagerte die Produktion nach Flint aus. Seit 1993 steht das Gebäude leer. Neben der Packard Automotive Plant ist das Gebäude von Fisher Body eine Ikone des Ruin Porn in Detroit.

Die Fotografien entstanden auf dem Grundstück gegenüber des Fabrikgeländes, das früher zur Lagerung diente.

→ 8 Fisher Body Plant 21 (Poplar Tree), 2015
→ 9 Fisher Body Plant 21 (Rugs), 2015

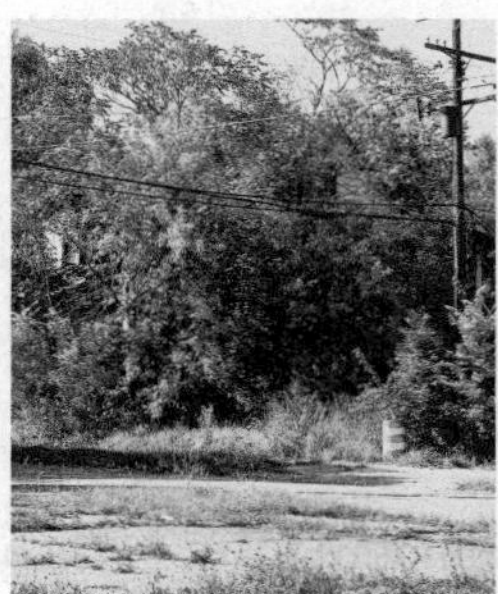

4

6203 Marcus Street, 2015

Airport Sub Neighborhood

Hinter Götterbäumen und Eschen-Ahorn verbirgt sich ein Einfamilienhaus von 1926. Im Dezember 2015 wurde es im Zuge des Detroit Demolition Program abgerissen. Das leer stehende Grundstück ist nun im Besitz der Detroit Land Bank Authority.

Während das Detroit der 1920er Jahre oft als „totale Industrielandschaft“° beschrieben wird, in der Fabriken, Werkstätten und Wohnviertel dicht an dicht miteinander verschmelzen, ist der Anblick nur wenige Jahrzehnte später ein ganz anderer. Leere Industriekomplexe, verlassene Häuser und weite Grasflächen sind überall zu sehen – wie eine von der Industrie verbrauchte Stadtlandschaft.

° Zunz (1982): The Changing Face of Inequality, 3

Ein Winterdienstag, die Stadt gießt Feuer aus, / Ford Rouge schwefelt die Sonne, Cadillac, Lincoln / Chevy grau. Die fetten Schornsteine / der Brauereien halten ihre Zunge im Zaum. Lumpen / Papiere, Hände, die Stämme der Birken / beschmutzt mit Worten. ... Ein braunes Kind / starrt und starrt in deine gefrorenen Augen / bis die Ampel umschaltet und du gehst / vorwärts zur Arbeit. Die verkohlten Gesichter, die Augen / mit Brettern vernagelt, die Trümmer der Eingeweide, der Schrei / von nassem Rauch, der in deiner Kehle hängt, / der verschlungene Fluss blieb in der Farbe des Eisens stehen. / Wir verbrennen diese Stadt jeden Tag.

Philip Levine: Coming Home, Detroit 1968

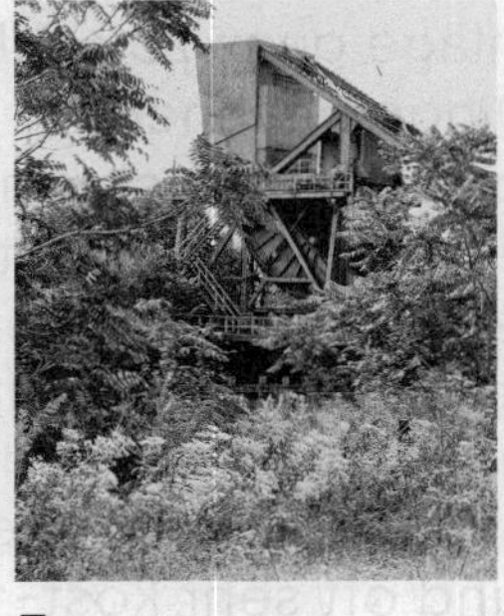

5

Zug Island (Steel Mill), 2015

River Rouge

Zug Island ist eine künstliche Insel, die zur Stadt River Rouge gehört. Sie liegt im Zusammenfluss der Flüsse River Rouge und Detroit River. Seit 1901 wird hier von der Schwerindustrie Stahl geschmolzen und Koks produziert. Der blaue Turm im Bild ist Teil einer Stahlmühle von United States Steel. Die Insel ist dem Ford River Rouge-Komplex vorgelagert und nicht öffentlich zugänglich. Auch heute geben der rege Schiffsverkehr, Rauchfahnen und Stahlhämmer hier noch den Eindruck eines industriellen Detroits. Trotz braunen Flusswassers, bleibelasteten Bodens und lösungsmittelhaltiger Luft sind die Ufer um Zug Island beliebte Angelplätze. Sie sind gesäumt mit „Chemicals in the Food Chain"-Schildern, die darauf hinweisen, welche Fische man besser nicht essen sollte.

Benannt ist die Insel nach dem Möbelunternehmer Samuel Zug, der das sumpfige Stück Land 1879 kaufte. Ein Kanal zur Umschiffung von Stromschnellen ließ die Insel 1891 entstehen. Weit vor der Besiedlung durch Europäer diente das Marschland den indigenen Stämmen als Gräberfeld.

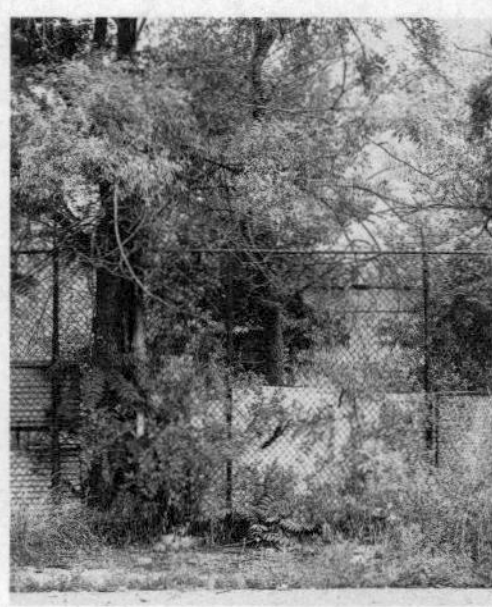

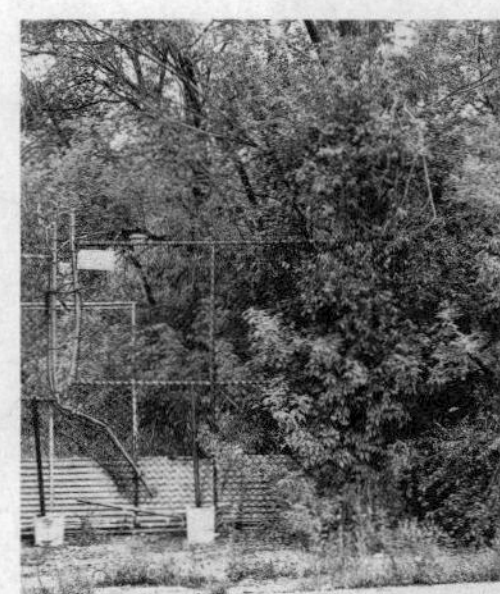

6 / 7

6437 East Palmer Street, 2015

Gratiot Town / Kettering Neighborhood

Die beiden Bilder zeigen den Zaun eines Werkstattgeländes, das benachbart zum Friedhof Trinity Cementary, der Packard Automotive Plant und den Eisenbahngleisen der Detroit Belt Line gelegen ist. Ganz in der Nähe traf ich 2015 Allan Hill, einen älteren Mann mit Jesus-Baseballkappe. Der ehemalige Autoworker lebte seit elf Jahren neben der Packard-Fabrik in einer Werkhalle und reparierte dort Fahrräder und Autos. Im Einverständnis mit dem Besitzer war er eine Art Hauswart der Ruine und führte gelegentlich Leute herum. In den letzten Jahren hatte er durch Zeitungsartikel und einen kleinen Dokumentarfilm einige Berühmtheit erlangt. 2019 schloss Detroits Building Safety Engineering and Environmental Department seine Werkstatt wegen „zahlreicher Verletzungen von Instandhaltungsvorschriften" °. Allan Hill wurde im Alter von 74 Jahren hinausgeworfen.

° Williams (2019): "I haven't had my day in court"

→ 11 / 12 East Palmer Street (Balsam Poplar), 2015
→ 27 / 29 Packard Automotive Plant, 2015

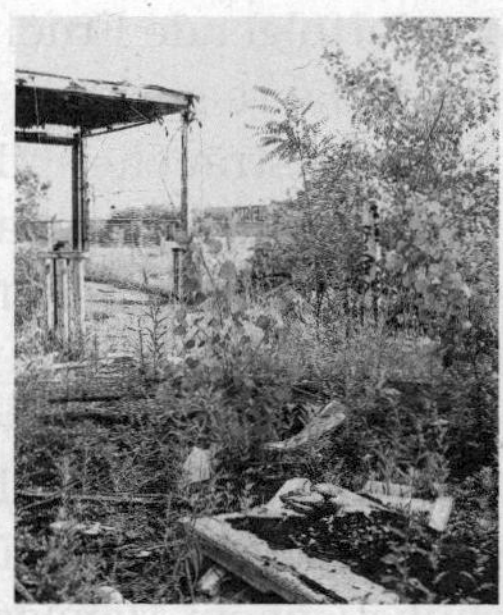

8

Fisher Body Plant 21 (Poplar Tree), 2015

Milwaukee Junction Neighborhood

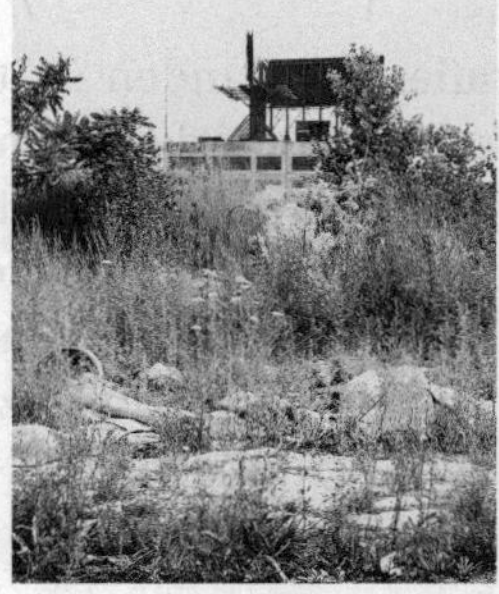

9

Fisher Body Plant 21 (Rugs), 2015

Milwaukee Junction Neighborhood

Zur Beschreibung siehe
→ 3 Fisher Body Plant 21 (Bucket), 2015

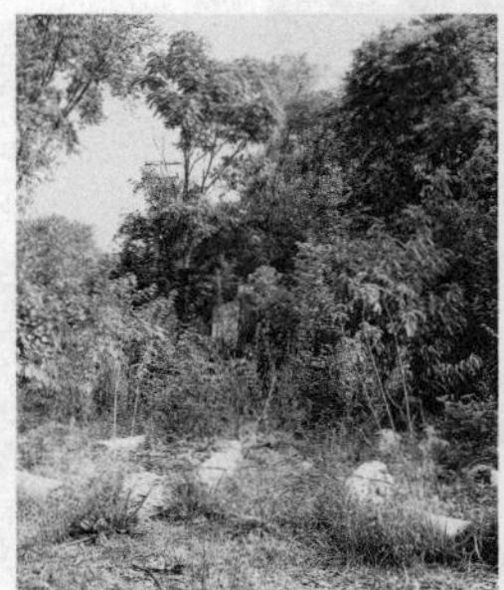

10

Beaverland Farms (Elderberry Trees), 2016

Brightmoor Neighborhood

Beaverland Farms ist eine kleine Waldfeldbau-Farm im Stadtteil Brightmoor. Sie wurde 2015 von Brittney Rooney und Kieran Neal zur Selbstversorgung und als Experimentierfeld gegründet. Im Unterschied zu vielen anderen urbanen Gärten, in denen oft Palmkohl, Kürbis und anderes Sommergemüse angebaut wird, bauen sie ausdauernde Pflanzen an, die jedes Jahr wieder wachsen, sowie Kartoffeln, Mais und Getreide, deren Früchte viele Kohlenhydrate enthalten und die man über den Winter gut lagern kann. Die Beete waren so bepflanzt, dass mit sehr wenig

Aufwand aufeinanderfolgende Fruchtstände über mehrere Jahre geerntet werden können. Beerensträucher bilden lebende Zäune, der Obst- und Nussbaumgarten wird in wenigen Jahren Schatten spenden und Wasser sparen. Als ich die Farm 2018 erneut besuchte, war das Experimentierfeld einer kommerzielleren Nutzung gewichen. Beide hatten eine GmbH mit holistischem Management gegründet, in dem Wirtschaftlichkeit, Lebensqualität und nachhaltige Schonung des Bodens gleichwertige Bestandteile sind. Neben ihrem eigenen Marktstand belieferten sie auch Restaurants mit Gemüse.

Die Fotografien entstanden 2016. In Bild 10 sind kleine Holunderbäume zu sehen, die in recycelten Papierrohren gepflanzt sind, in Bild 24 wachsen Quinoapflanzen in Autoreifen, die in der Nachbarschaft herumlagen. Bild 61 zeigt ein neu angelegtes Gemüsefeld.

www.beaverlandfarms.com

Für Beaverland Farms und Brightmoor siehe auch

→ 24 Beaverland Farms (Quinoa), 2016
→ 61 Beaverland Farms, 2016
→ 21 14409 Burgess Street (Pray Hope and Don't Worry), 2016
→ 62 Beaverland Street (Neighbors Building Brightmoor), 2015

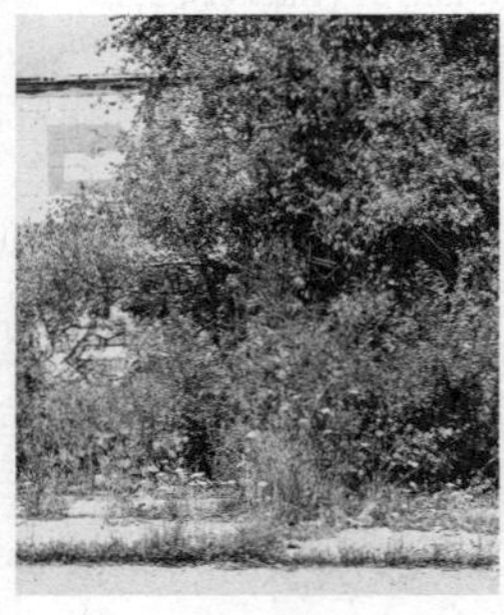

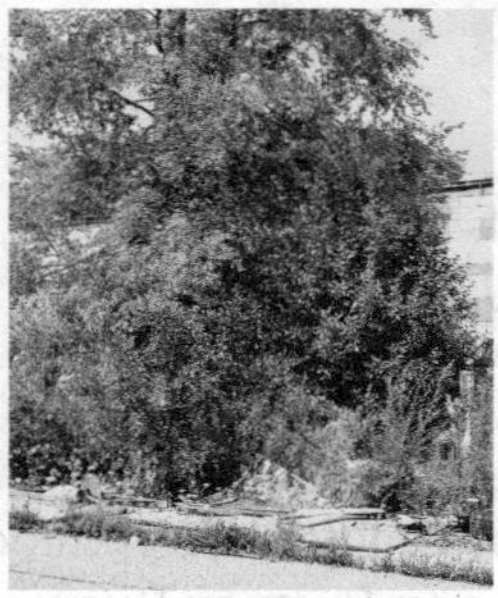

11/12

East Palmer Street (Balsam Poplar), 2015

Gratiot Town / Kettering Neighborhood

Auf beiden Bildern ist eine Balsam-Pappel zu sehen, überwachsen mit Weinreben und flankiert von Goldruten, Seidenpflanzen, Wilder Möhre und einer kleinen Sibirischen Ulme. Die Balsam-Pappel wird im Englischen auch hackmatack oder tacamahac poplar genannt. Beide Namen stammen aus der indigenen Algonkin-Sprache. Sie bedeuten dichter Wald bzw. Harz der Balsam-Pappel.

2018, drei Jahre nachdem ich die Fotografien gemacht hatte, war das flache Gebäude im Hintergrund übermalt und alle Pflanzen wurden entfernt. Allein die Balsam-Pappel ist übrig geblieben. Sie wächst benachbart zur Packard Automotive Plant.

→ 6/7 6437 East Palmer Street, 2015
→ 27/29 Packard Automotive Plant, 2015

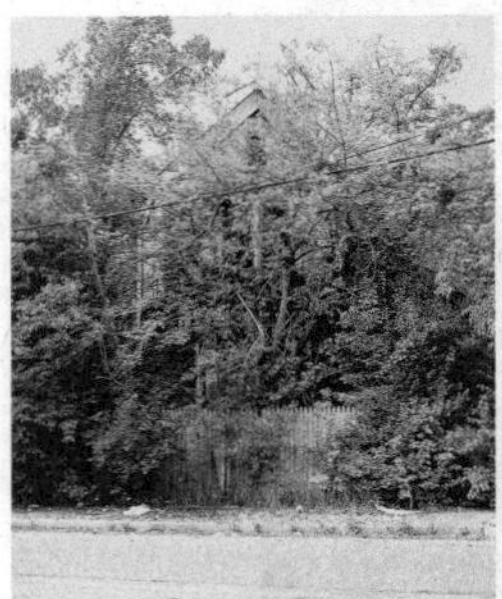

13

456 Harper Avenue, 2016

Medbury Park Neighborhood

Hinter Eschen-Ahorn, Sibirischer Ulme, Roten Maulbeer- und Wildapfelbäumen steht ein 1903 erbautes Mehrfamilienhaus in direkter Nachbarschaft zu Henry Fords erster Automanufaktur und der Fisher Body Plant 21. Besonders typisch für die ersten industrialisierten Stadtteile ist das dichte Nebeneinander großer Fabriken, Zulieferer-Werkstätten und Eisenbahnlinien zu Wohnhäusern, Kirchen und kleinen Restaurants, was in Stadtteilen wie Medbury Park, Milwaukee Junction oder Gratiot Town / Kettering noch zu sehen ist.

Das Grundstück ist im Besitz der Detroit Land Bank Authority. Verschiedene Immobilienmakler-Webseiten bewerben es als aufregendes Entwicklungsobjekt. Die Immobilie liegt fußläufig zum angesagten New Center, dem North End und der neu gebauten QLine, einer innerstädtischen Straßenbahnlinie entlang der Woodward Avenue. Diese hauptsächlich privat finanzierte Bahn ist nur eine Meile lang und verbindet das New Center mit Midtown und Downtown.

Öffentliche Straßenbahnen wurden in Detroit schon sehr früh eingeführt – die erste 1863 war noch von Pferden gezogen. Bis in die 1920er Jahre umfasste das innerstädtische Bahnnetz 187 Meilen und verband alle Stadtviertel sowie die Downtown mit Vorstädten wie Royal Oak. In den 1950er Jahren, als die Motor City zu einer Stadt der Autobesitzer wurde, stellte man die letzte Linie ein. Heute sind Busse die öffentlichen Verkehrsmittel.

Der Glaube, daß ein Industriestaat seine Industrien konzentrieren muß, ist nach meiner Ansicht unbegründet. Das ist nur in einem Zwischenstadium der Entwicklung nötig. … Die Industrie wird sich dezentralisieren.

Henry Ford (1934): Mein Leben und Werk, 217–218

Deindustrialisierung ereignet sich nicht einfach so. Manager müssen bewusste Entscheidungen treffen, um eine Fabrik von einem Standort an einen anderen zu verlegen, einen laufenden Betrieb aufzukaufen oder zu veräußern oder eine Anlage ganz zu schließen. Diese Dinge geschehen niemals automatisch, noch sind sie einfach eine passive Reaktion auf mysteriöse Marktkräfte. Die Planungen, die hinter solchen Entscheidungen stecken, sind in der Regel umfangreich, äußerst kompliziert und oft sehr kostspielig.

Harry Bluestone / Bennet Harrison (1982): The Deindustrialization of America, 15

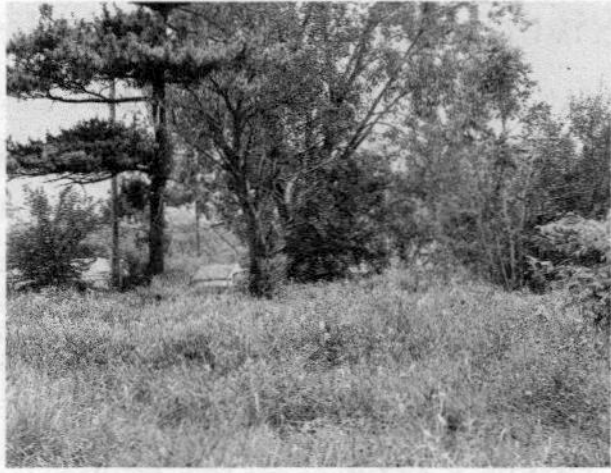

14

East Ferry Street, 2015

Poletown East Neighborhood

Dieses Bild zeigt leere Grundstücke im Stadtteil Poletown East. Breitblättrige Platterbsen und Rispen-Flockenblumen blühen vor einer Schwarzkiefer und den Pappeln im Hintergrund. Während ich fotografierte, mähte ein Nachbar den Rasen seines Vorgartens.

Der Stadtteil Poletown entstand ab 1870 auf Farmland, eingerahmt von zwei neu gebauten Eisenbahnlinien.

Bis 1900 waren bereits 48.000 Menschen hierher gezogen – viele von ihnen Einwanderer*innen polnischer Herkunft. Kurz vor der Weltwirtschaftskrise von 1929 erlebte Poletown seine Blütezeit. Zahlreiche Fabrikarbeiter fanden Arbeit in den benachbarten Fabriken von Packard, Dodge, Ford, Chrysler, Studebaker oder Fisher. Die Straßen waren von Kirchen, Geschäften, kleinen Restaurants und den typischen zweigeschossigen Holzrahmenhäusern mit kleinen Gärten gesäumt. 1955 teilte der Bau der Ford Edsel Freeway Autobahn (als Teil der Interstate 94) den Stadtteil. Die nördliche Hälfte wurde 1981 für eine neue Fabrik von General Motors enteignet und abgerissen (siehe Bilder 1/2). Der südliche Teil ist bis heute spärlich bewohnt und gleicht an vielen Stellen einer urbanen Prärie.

→ 1/2 2550 East Grand Boulevard, 2015
→ 41 5721 Dubois Street, 2015

Detroit leidet an einer der höchsten Armutsquoten des Landes. Gleichzeitig sind die Wassergebühren so hoch wie sonst fast nirgendwo. Detroiter zahlen auch die höchsten Grundsteuern des Bundesstaates und eine der höchsten Hypothekenraten. Darüber hinaus unternahm die Stadt nach der Großen Rezession nur geringe Anstrengungen zur Anpassung der Grundsteuern, was dazu führte, dass die Steuernachzahlungen oft den Marktwert des Eigenheims überstiegen. Es ist teuer, in einer armen Stadt zu leben.

→ Peter Hammer (2017): Detroit 1967 and Today: Spatial Racism and Ongoing Cycles of Oppression, 280

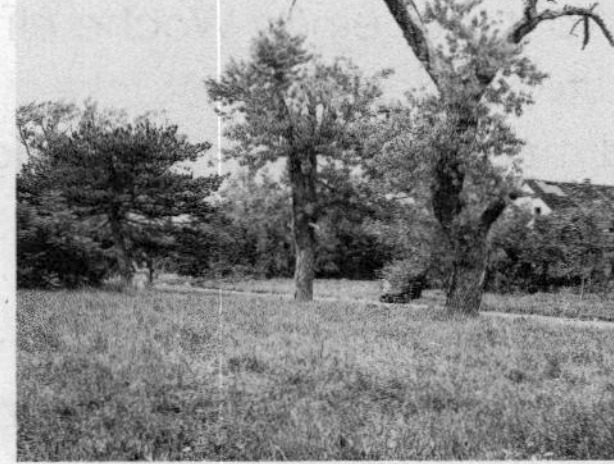

15

Eastlawn Street (Tires), 2016

Riverbend Neighborhood

Im Stadtteil Riverbend stehen an der Eastlawn Street über mehrere Blocks hinweg nur noch wenige Einfamilienhäuser, von denen selten eines bewohnt ist. Die Landschaft gleicht einer ländlichen Gegend oder einem urbanen Biotop, das von Straßen durchtrennt ist. Das zugewachsene Haus im Hintergrund wurde 1915 gebaut. Noch 2009 wurde es neu verkleidet, steht jedoch seit 2011 leer. Viele Brachen Detroits werden genutzt, um alte Boote oder wie hier Autoreifen zu entsorgen.

→ 44 Eastlawn and Lakeview Streets (Burned Down House), 2016

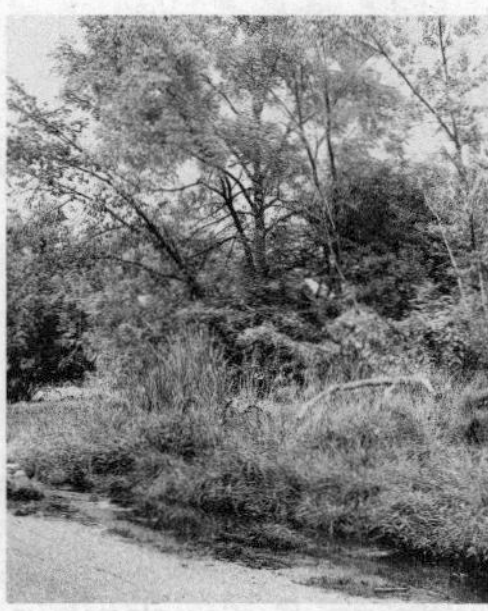

16

3034 Eastlawn Street (Water Leak), 2016

Riverbend Neighborhood

Wie in Bild 15 beschrieben, gleicht die Eastlawn Street eher einer ländlichen Gegend. Zwischen Jefferson und Warren Avenue wurden die meisten Wohnhäuser bereits abgerissen. Gut im Bild zu erkennen ist ein Wasserrinnsal entlang der Straße. Schilfrohr, verschiedene Weidenröschen und Floh-Knöterich haben sich als wasserliebende Pflanzen darin angesiedelt. Viele leer stehende Grundstücke und Häuser haben noch immer fließend Wasser, bei Rohrbrüchen tritt es ungehindert aus und verursacht ungedeckte Kosten.

Diesen Lecks stehen die sogenannten Water Shutoffs gegenüber. Seit der Detroit Bankruptcy von 2013 wurde mehr als 100.000 Privathaushalten wegen bereits geringster Zahlungsrückstände zeitweise das Wasser abgestellt. „Die Menschen wurden nicht gewarnt und hatten keine Zeit, Badewannen und Eimer zu füllen, sodass alle, auch Kranke, kein Wasser mehr zum Trinken, keine Toilettenspülung, keine Möglichkeit zum Baden und Kochen hatten." ° Bis heute treffen diese Maßnahmen vor allem einkommensschwache, alleinerziehende und ältere Bürger*innen sowie Familien mit Kindern. Denn neben hoher Arbeitslosigkeit hat Detroit gleichzeitig mit die teuersten Wasserpreise in den USA.

° Apel (2015): Beautiful Terrible Ruins, 31

→ 17 908 Clay Street (Water Leak), 2016

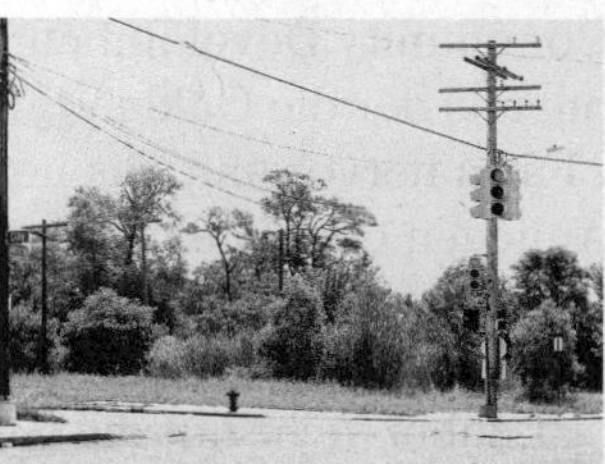

17

908 Clay Street (Water Leak), 2016

North End Neighborhood

Dieses Eckgrundstück an der Oakland Avenue liegt ca. eine Meile von der Innenstadt entfernt. 2009 wurde hier ein Backsteingebäude aus den 1920er Jahren abgerissen. Seither tritt aus der Kanalisation Wasser aus (was deutlich auf Google Maps Streetview zu sehen ist). Über die Jahre entstand ein Feuchtgebiet mit Schilf und verschiedenen Weiden. Wie in Bild 16 beschrieben, stehen diese Lecks auf unbewohnten Grundstücken, aus denen ungehindert Wasser austritt, im hartem Gegensatz zu den Water Shutoffs. Seit 2015 soll die mobile Improve Detroit App helfen, diese Wasserlecks den Stadtwerken zu melden.

→ 16 3034 Eastlawn Street (Water Leak), 2016

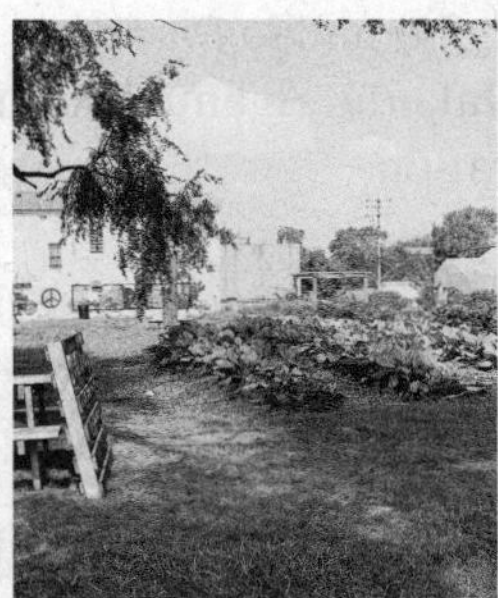

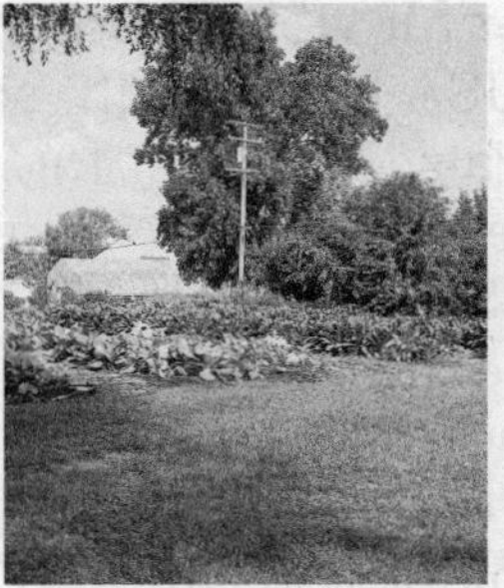

18/19

Oakland Avenue Urban Farm, 2016

North End Neighborhood

1999 begann Reverend Bertha L. Carter, von der Ladefläche ihres Kleinbusses aus Lebensmittel an Obdachlose in ihrem Viertel zu verteilen. Ein Jahr später gründete sie die North End

Christian Community Development Corporation, aus der die Oakland Avenue Urban Farm hervorging. Bis heute ist es das Anliegen der Oakland Farmer, das Stadtviertel nachhaltig und selbstbestimmt zu entwickeln. Urbane Landwirtschaft ist dabei nicht nur die Grundlage für Food Security, sondern auch um Jugendbildungsprogramme und Jobmöglichkeiten für die mehrheitlich afroamerikanische Community zu schaffen. Die Farm entwickelte sich aus einem Stadtgarten heraus, den Jerry Ann Hebron zusammen mit dem Youth Making a Difference Project an der Stelle anlegte, die auf den Bildern zu sehen ist. Im Laufe der Jahre wuchsen neben Obst, Gemüse auch Bildungsprogramme und Veranstaltungen heran, zu denen die Nachbarschaft regelmäßig zusammenkommt; einer der Detroit Community Markets, Garden on the Plate-Abendessen oder Kunstausstellungen finden regelmäßig statt. Die Oakland Avenue Urban Farm ist gut mit verschiedenen landwirtschaftlichen Projekten und Initiativen in der ganzen Stadt vernetzt und Teil des Detroit Food Policy Council. Bei meinen Besuchen 2016 und 2018 wurde die Farm von Jerry Ann und Bill Hebron, Bewohner*innen des Stadtteils und Freiwilligen betrieben.

Der Stadtteil North End grenzt nördlich an das ehemalige Paradise Valley und die Oakland Avenue ist eine seiner Hauptstraßen.

www.oaklandurbanfarm.org

→ 46 Oakland Avenue Urban Farm (Lacinato Kale), 2016

Detroit hat in der zweiten Hälfte des zwanzigsten Jahrhunderts als Metapher für vieles gedient, was in den USA falsch läuft, so wie es einst als Metapher für vieles diente, was positiv in den Vereinigten Staaten war. Aber Detroit ist viel mehr als eine Metapher. Detroit ist ein realer Ort, an dem echte Menschen leben. In zahlreichen Städten und Regionen im ganzen Land sind Amerikaner mit den gleichen Problemen konfrontiert, die Detroit heute plagen.

Dan Georgakas / Marvin Surkin (1975): Detroit, I Do Mind Dying, 232

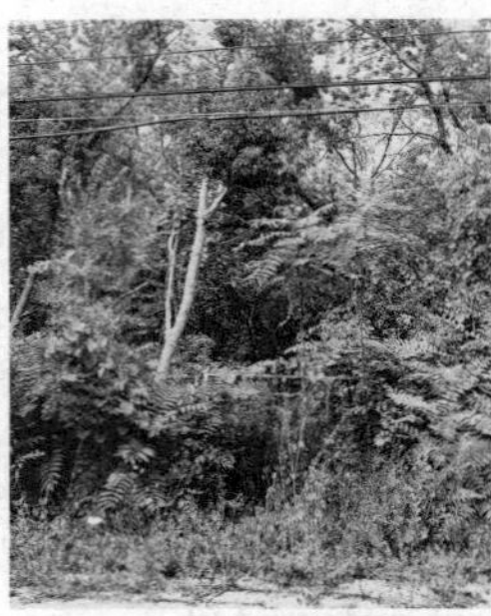

20

Ford Park (Ferris Street), 2015

Highland Park

„Als ich das erste Mal hierher kam, habe ich drei Monate bei Fisher Bodies gearbeitet. ... Aber dann ging ich zu Ford, wie alle anderen auch ... Du kriegst den Lohn, aber du verkaufst deine Seele bei Ford – du arbeitest jeden Tag wie ein Sklave und schläfst auf dem Heimweg im Auto ein. ... Du hast nie irgendeine Sicherheit in dem Job."

Englischer Einwanderer 1931, in: Wilson (1958), 219

Der Ford Park liegt nördlich der ehemaligen Ford Highland Park Plant, in der Henry Ford die industrielle Autoproduktion revolutionierte. 1910 ließ er seine erste große Fabrik in der Gemeinde Highland Park bauen, da die Grundstückspreise dort günstiger und die Steuern niedriger waren. Das Fabrikgebäude wurde von Albert Kahn entworfen und aufgrund der großen, innovativen Fensterfronten auch überschwänglich Crystal Palace – Kristallpalast genannt. 1913 wurde hier die bewegliche Assembly Line eingeführt – das Fließband, das bis heute die industrielle Produktion und Organisation prägt. Mechaniker konnten nun durch ungelernte, billige und leicht austauschbare Arbeiter ersetzt werden. Ohne feste Arbeitsverträge und die Monotonie am Fließband nicht gewohnt, wechselten die Ungelernten jedoch häufig die Fabriken, sodass Ford 1913 mehr als 52.400 Personen einstellte, um eine konstante Belegschaft von 14.000 aufrechtzuerhalten. Daraufhin wurde im Januar 1914 sehr medienwirksam der Five Dollar Day eingeführt – eine Verdopplung des Tageslohns auf fünf Dollar, um Arbeitskräfte an das Unternehmen zu binden und die Arbeitsmoral zu erhöhen. Nach wie vor wurde bei sinkenden Absätzen oder bei Umrüsten auf neue Automodelle die Produktion eingestellt und Arbeiter zeitweise entlassen. Henry Ford empfahl ihnen dann, in der Landwirtschaft zu arbeiten. Nach nur 18 Jahren verlegte Ford die Automontage von Highland Park in die Nachbarstadt Dearborn in den Ford River Rouge-Komplex.

Ein Teil des Crystal Palace steht bis heute. An der Stelle des Kraftwerks und der Bürogebäude befindet sich das niedrigpreisige Shopping Center Model T Plaza – benannt nach Fords erfolgreichstem Automodell.

Und dann hob sich das Rouge vom Himmel ab, stieg empor aus dem Rauch, den es erzeugte. Anfangs waren einzig die Spitzen der acht großen Schornsteine zu sehen. Ein jeder schickte seine eigene dunkle Wolke in die Welt. ... Es war wie ein Wäldchen: als hätten die acht Hauptschornsteine des Rouge Samen in den Wind gesät, aus denen nun zehn, zwanzig, fünfzig kleinere Stämme aus der unfruchtbaren Erde der Anlage sprossen.

Jeffrey Eugenides (2003): Middlesex, 138–139

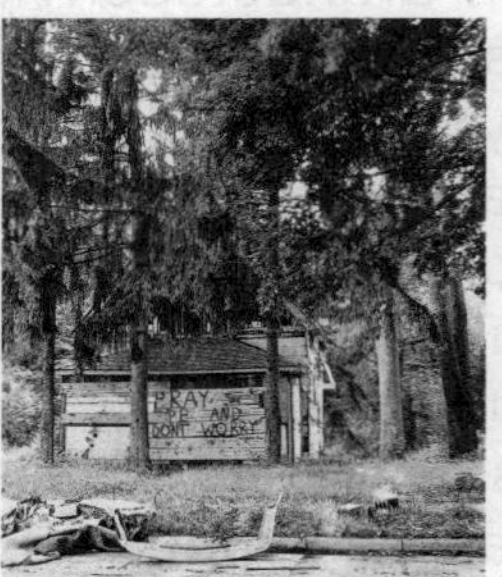

21

14409 Burgess Street (Pray Hope and Don't Worry), 2016

Brightmoor Neighborhood

„In den Anfangszeiten wurden überall in Brightmoor hektisch Wohnhäuser gebaut. ... Wo in der einen Woche eine Reihe leer stehender Grundstücke stand, fand man in der nächsten Woche Menschen, die in Häusern lebten. ... Zoneneinteilungen oder Auflagen waren nicht Teil der Planung. (Die einzige Beschränkung, die galt, war: keine farbigen Bewohner)."

John W. Carey (1940): Growth of Brightmoor, 1

Das Haus hinter den Tannen wurde 1922 gebaut, im selben Jahr, als der Bauunternehmer B. E. Taylor Brightmoor erschloss. Er kaufte Farmland, das damals außerhalb von Detroit lag, teilte es in Parzellen auf und verkaufte diese wieder, einige mit massengefertigten Häusern darauf. Kanalisation oder geteerte Straßen gab es keine. Wie viele der nach dem Ersten Weltkrieg entstehenden Stadtteile war auch Brightmoor nach Hautfarben getrennt – strikt weiß mit einem aktiven Ku-Klux-Klan. Brightmoor ist heute ein ungleichmäßig besiedeltes Viertel mit vielen Freiflächen. Um der Kriminalität etwas entgegenzusetzen, hat die Nachbarschaftsinitiative Neighbors Building Brightmoor 2012 etliche verlassene Häuser mit Brettern gesichert und zusammen mit Kindern und Jugendlichen des Viertels bemalt.

→ 62 Beaverland Street (Neighbors Building Brightmoor), 2015
→ 65/66 Bentler Street, 2018

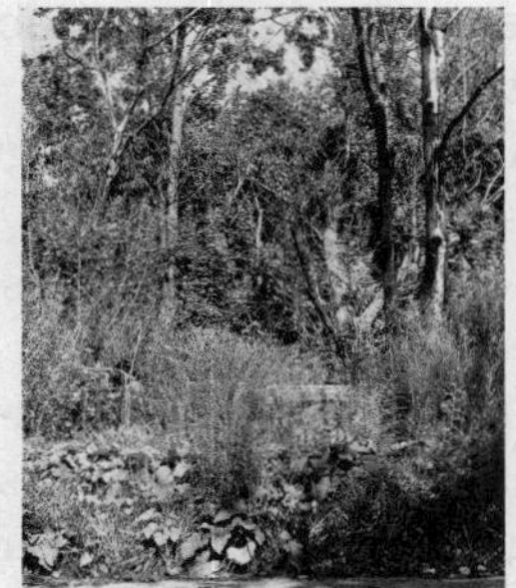

22

5972 Canton Street (Burned Down House), 2015

Gratiot Town / Kettering Neighborhood

Auf diesem Grundstück brannte im November 2014 ein zweistöckiges Wohnhaus von 1910 bis auf die Bodenplatte nieder, noch gut zu erkennen an den verkohlten Bäumen im Hintergrund. Hausbrände sind zahlreich in Detroit und haben unterschiedliche Ursachen. Kabelbrände und Brandstiftung sind die häufigsten. Besonders gefährlich sind die Brände für die Nachbarn in angrenzenden Häusern.

Wir standen an einem Fenster in der großen steinernen Burg der Firma General Motors. Vor unseren Augen eröffnete sich eine Szene der unsäglichen Hässlichkeit und des Chaos. Mitten in der Stadt gab es Fabriken, die dichten Rauch ausstießen, hohe Bürogebäude direkt neben Wohnhäusern in Holzrahmenbauweise, schmuddelige Garagen und trostlose Parkplätze für Autos. Schließlich fiel unser Blick auf ein kleines, unansehnliches Holzhäuschen mit geöffneten Jalousien auf der anderen Straßenseite. „Das ist ein ‚blind pig‘, eine illegale Bar“, sagte der Angestellte. „Ja, dies ist eine schreckliche Stadt. Ich möchte nicht, dass mein Sohn hier in dem Rauch und Dreck aufwächst. Wir leben auf dem Land. Ich habe einen Garten.“

Matthew Josephson (1929): Detroit: City of Tomorrow, 166

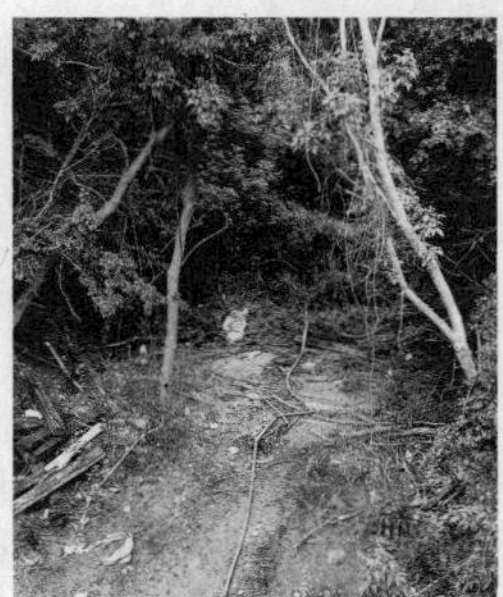

23

Uniroyal Tire Plant (East Jefferson Avenue), 2015

Rivertown Neighborhood

„Uniroyal stellt seit 1961 ununterbrochen Stahlgürtelreifen her. Gut 10 Jahre länger als jeder andere amerikanische Reifenhersteller.“

Werbeanzeige im Life Magazine, 06. Oktober 1972

1980 wurde das Uniroyal-Reifenwerk geschlossen und 5.000 Menschen wurden arbeitslos. 100.000 weitere Beschäftigte verloren ihre Jobs, nachdem auch die Zulieferer schlossen oder wegzogen. Das Werk war seit 1905 unter verschiedenen Namen und Unternehmen in Betrieb. 1981 kaufte die Stadt Detroit das Fabrikgelände für 5 Millionen Dollar und riss vier Jahre später alle Gebäude ab, um ein weitläufiges, attraktives Grundstück am Wasser zu erschließen. Leider war der Boden stark mit giftigen Chemikalien verseucht, die aus 70 Jahren Reifenproduktion übrig geblieben waren, und das Grundstück ist bis heute ungenutzt. Uniroyal produziert derzeit in Brasilien, der Türkei, Spanien und Australien. Das Foto entstand von einer Brücke aus mit Blick zum Fluss.

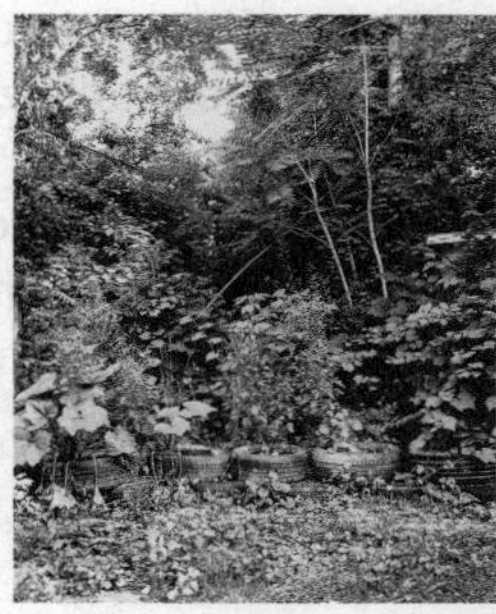

24

Beaverland Farms (Quinoa), 2016

Brightmoor Neighborhood

Zur Beschreibung siehe
→ 10 Beaverland Farms (Elderberry Trees), 2016

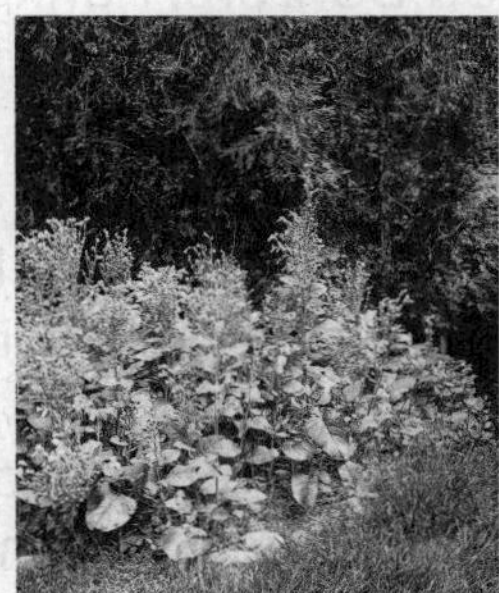

25

Sacred Roots Garden (Tobacco), 2018

Claytown Neighborhood

Das Bild zeigt ein Beet mit Tabakpflanzen im Sacred Roots Garden – einem kleinen didaktischen Garten des gemeinnützigen Gesundheitszentrums American Indian Health & Family Services. Das Gartenprogramm vermittelt Wissen zu traditionellen indigenen Pflanzen, zur gesunden Ernährung und Lebensweise.

Während der 1970er Jahre warb Detroits Autoindustrie Arbeitskräfte in den Reservaten der amerikanischen Ureinwohner an. Mitglieder unterschiedlichster Stämme zogen daraufhin in den Südosten Michigans, wo die neuen Autofabriken entstanden. 1978 gründeten sich die American Indian Health & Family Services, um die medizinische und psychologische Versorgung von indigenen und anderen Bevölkerungsgruppen zu gewährleisten, die vom Gesundheitssystem benachteiligt oder ausgeschlossen sind. Neben einer Klinik, die auch unversicherte Patienten aufnimmt, werden umfangreiche Gesundheitsberatungen sowie kulturelle Programme angeboten, um das körperliche, geistige, spirituelle und emotionale Wohlergehen der Menschen zu stärken und zu fördern. Das Zentrum befindet sich seit 1993 auf dem Gelände einer ehemaligen katholischen Kirche, in dessen Garten das Beet der Tabakpflanzen gelegen ist. Traditionell wird es von jungen Männern gepflegt. Die Pflanzen werden nach der Ernte getrocknet und für verschiedene Zeremonien verwendet.

www.aihfs.org

→ 54/55 Sacred Roots Garden, American Indian Health and Family Services, 2018

Ein Griff nach der Kette, Auflegen der Schraubenmutter, ein Griff nach der Kette, Einstecken der Schraube, ein Griff nach der Kette, zwei Hammerschläge, ein Griff nach der Kette, Ansetzen des autogenen Bohrers, Funken stieben, ein Griff nach der Kette, Befestigung der Bleilamelle, Paraffinpappe, eine Hülse, ein Bündel Kerzen, eine Kurbelwelle, und immer dazwischen ein Griff nach der Kette, ein Griff nach der Kette, Handbewegung und Ergebnis, Körperbewegung und Einsatz, Mensch und Maschine, immerfort gleich.

Egon Erwin Kisch (1929): Bei Ford in Detroit, 306

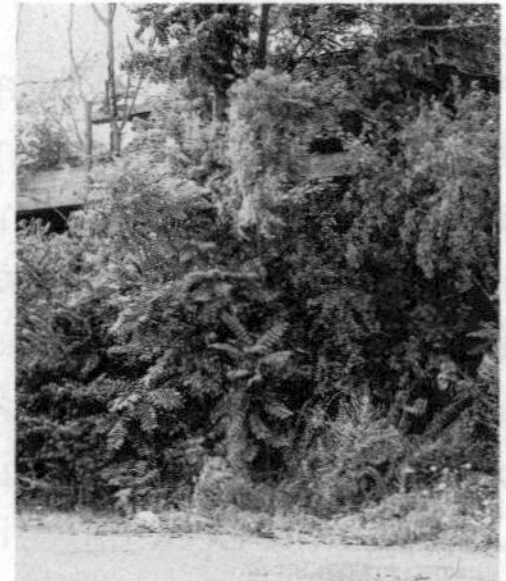

26

Kelsey-Hayes Wheel Company (McGraw Avenue), 2015

Chadsey Condon Neighborhood

Die Kelsey-Hayes Wheel Company stellte bei ihrer Gründung 1927 Räder für Automobile her (damals noch aus Holz) und wurde zum Hauptlieferanten für Ford, General Motors, Buick und andere Unternehmen. Während des Zweiten Weltkriegs und des Koreakriegs stellte man die Produktion auf Maschinengewehre, Panzerteile und Komponenten für Flugzeuge um. Nach den erfolgreichen 1950er Jahren entwickelte die Firma Bremssysteme, die in 85 Prozent aller amerikanischen Autos verbaut wurden. Ab 1978 wurde Kelsey-Hayes mehrmals von anderen Unternehmen übernommen und besteht seit 1998 nicht mehr als eigenständige Firma. Die Fabrikgebäude an der McGraw Street wurden 1920 erbaut und stehen seit den 1990er Jahren leer. 1936, während der Weltwirtschaftskrise und der Gründungszeit der Gewerkschaft United Auto Workers, kam es hier für zehn Tage zum ersten organisierten Sitzstreik Detroits.

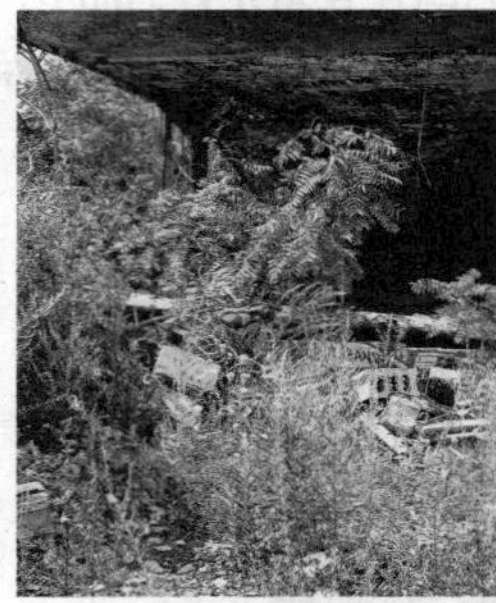

27

Packard Automotive Plant (Bellevue Street), 2015

Gratiot Town / Kettering Neighborhood

Zwischen 1903 und 1910 errichtete die Packard Motor Car Company einen von Albert Kahn entworfenen Produktionskomplex mit 47 Gebäuden auf einer Länge von 1,5 Meilen entlang der Eisenbahnlinie Detroit Belt Line. Eine zeitgenössische Zeitschrift lobte den „hellen, sauberen und fröhlichen Aspekt der verschiedenen Abteilungen. Es gehört zum neuen Stil der Fabriken ..., die allmählich die alten Gefängnisschuppen verdrängen ... ."° In der Fabrik wurden die hochpreisigen Packard-Automobile und im Zweiten Weltkrieg Motoren für Bomber und Patrouillen-Torpedoboote hergestellt. Infolge einer Rezession schloss die Fabrik 1956 und entließ 11.000 Arbeiter*innen. Nach kurzer Nutzung durch andere Unternehmen eroberten Raves, Technopartys, Sprayer und Skater das verlassene Gelände in den 1980er Jahren. Als größte Industrieruine Detroits wurde der Stahlbetonbau zur Ikone des Ruin Porn. Bis heute ist sie Kulisse für Endzeit-, Zombie- und Science-Fiction-Filme und illustriert Bildbände und zahllose Zeitschriftenartikel über den Verfall der Stadt. 2013 kaufte ein Investor aus Peru das Gelände in der Wayne County Tax Foreclosure Auction, um sie instand zu setzen. Seither ist es mit Brettern gesichert und rund um die Uhr von einer Sicherheitsfirma bewacht. 2018 konnte man für 40 Dollar eine begleitete Tour durch die Industrieruine buchen oder sie als verrückte, aufregende (crazy and amazing) Location für ein Hochzeitsfoto mieten.

Während der Kriegsproduktion im Zweiten Weltkrieg, als Detroit Arsenal of Democracy, die Waffenschmiede der Demokratie, genannt wurde, „fanden im Packard-Werk bei weitem die meisten, größten und längsten Hass-Streiks des Krieges statt, die 1941 begannen und bis 1944 andauerten. Die Zustände bei Packard waren geradezu eine Garantie für Rassenunruhen: Die überwiegende Mehrheit der Arbeiter waren Weiße aus dem Süden und polnische Amerikaner, zwei Gruppen, die Afroamerikanern feindlich gesonnen waren; die örtliche Gewerkschaft U.A.W. wurde angeblich von Mitgliedern des Ku-Klux-Klan kontrolliert; und der Personalchef bei Packard war offen rassistisch. Nach Dutzenden vorangegangener Streiks legten Packard-Arbeiter im Mai und Juni 1943 die Arbeit nieder, um dagegen zu protestieren, dass drei schwarze Gießereiarbeiter in die Flugzeugtriebwerkmontage befördert wurden."°° 25.000 weiße Arbeiter*innen beteiligten sich an einem sogenannten wilden Streik. Während desselben Sommers mit anhaltender Wohnungsnot und kriegsbedingter Warenknappheit, steigenden Rassenspannungen und Hass-Streiks in der ganzen Stadt brach der Detroit Riot im Juni 1943 aus.

° Ferry (1970): The Legacy of Albert Kahn, 11
°° Stone (2017): Detroit 1967, 50–51

→ 29 Packard Automotive Plant (Concord Avenue), 2015

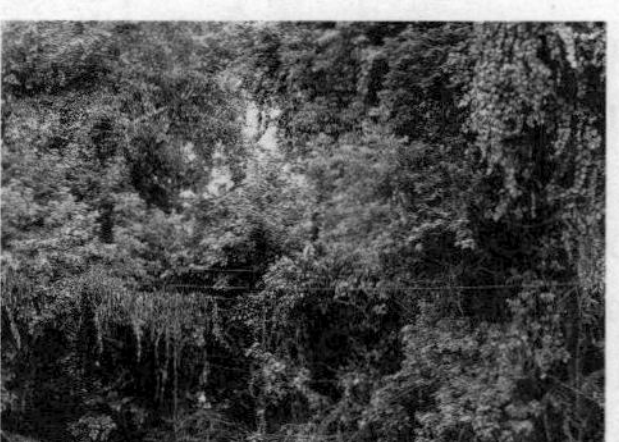

28

20037 Birwood Avenue (Eight Mile Wall), 2015

McDowell Neighborhood

Mit der Kriegsproduktion ab 1940 boomte Detroits Industrie und Tausende zog es in die Stadt, trotz Wohnungsnot und der in hohem Grad nach Ethnien und Hautfarben getrennten Wohnviertel. Die Mauer Eight Mile Wall ist ein Relikt dieser Zeit. Sie ist 1,8 Meter hoch und verläuft über eine halbe Meile zwischen den Häusern der Mendota Street und Birwood Avenue direkt unterhalb der Eight Mile Road, der nördlichen Stadtgrenze Detroits. 1941 von einem weißen Bauunternehmer errichtet, sollte sie neu erschlossene Grundstücke für ausschließlich weiße Käufer gegen den benachbarten ‚Slum' abgrenzen. Dieser ‚Slum' war eine afroamerikanische Eigenheimsiedlung, die 20 Jahre zuvor entstanden war. Die Wyoming/Eight Mile Pocket war eine der wenigen Enklaven gewesen, in denen Schwarze Land und Häuser kaufen konnten. Viele hatten kleine Gärten, um neben der unsteten Fabrikarbeit die Selbstversorgung zu sichern.

Seit den 1930er Jahren wurde der US-Immobilienmarkt durch Redlining und weiße homeowners' associations geprägt, deren strukturell rassistische Praktiken bis heute in der Stadtentwicklung nachwirken. Diese gewachsene Segregation wird gerade wegen ihrer Alltäglichkeit von vielen noch immer nicht wahrgenommen.

In Bild 28 ist die Eight Mile Wall einmal auf einem leeren Grundstück zu sehen, dessen Haus kurz zuvor abgerissen wurde, und in Bild 30 auf dem Alfonso Wells Memorial Playground. Das Wandbild zeigt neben Kindern der Nachbarschaft auch die Civil Rights-Aktivistin Rosa Parks.

→ Struktureller Rassismus

→ 30 Alfonso Wells Memorial Playground (Eight Mile Wall), 2015

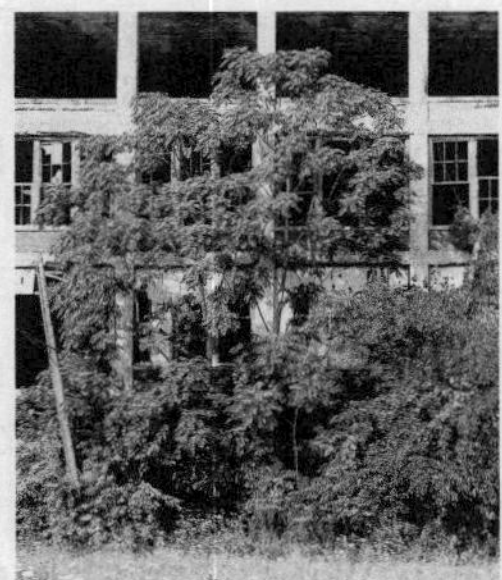

29

Packard Automotive Plant (Concord Avenue), 2015

Gratiot Town / Kettering Neighborhood

→ Zur Beschreibung siehe 27 Packard Automotive Plant (Bellevue Street), 2015

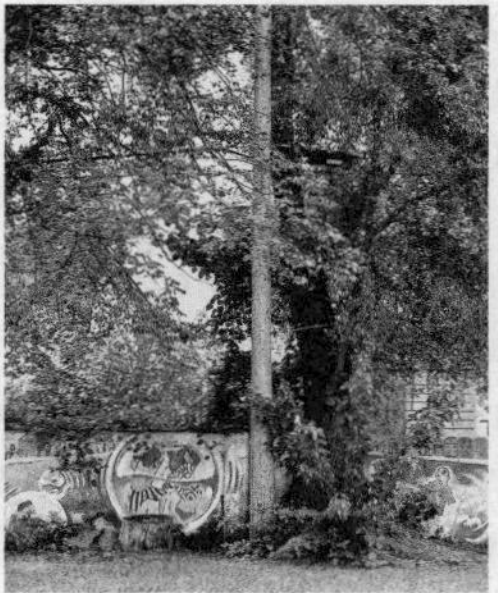

30

Alfonso Wells Memorial Playground (Eight Mile Wall), 2015

McDowell Neighborhood

→ Zur Beschreibung siehe 28 20037 Birwood Avenue (Eight Mile Wall), 2015

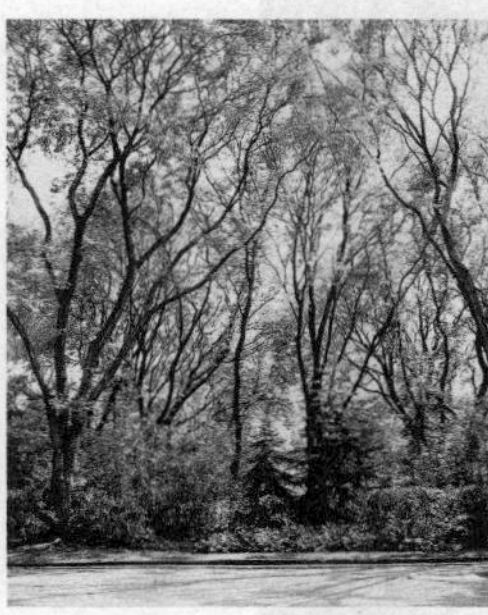

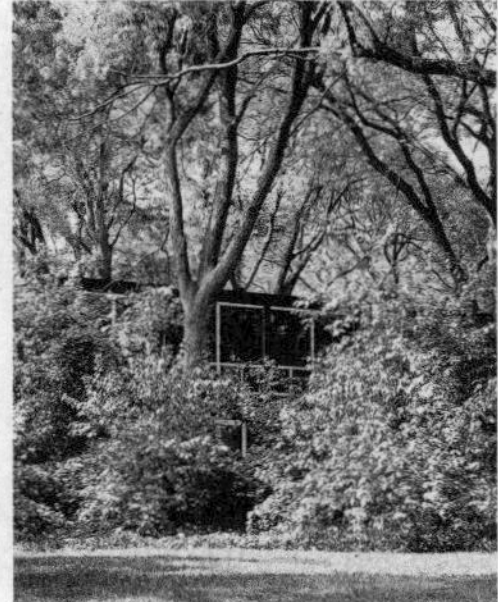

31/32

Lafayette Park (Parking Lot and Townhouse), 2015

Lafayette Park Neighborhood

Lafayette Park ist eine Wohnanlage für Menschen unterschiedlicher Einkommensgruppen, die im Zuge des Urban Renewal Stadterneuerungsprogramms ab 1955 von Ludwig Mies van der Rohe, Ludwig Hilberseimer und Alfred Caldwell als eine moderne Gartenstadt entworfen wurde. Bis 1969 entstanden mehrere Reihenhäuser als Wohneigentum, die Lafayette Twin Towers und Pavillon-Apartments sowie eine Schule, ein Einkaufszentrum und ein Park. Errichtet wurde es auf dem fünf Jahre zuvor abgerissenen Viertel Black Bottom, das zu den ältesten Detroits zählte. Vor dem Ersten Weltkrieg war es ein typisches Einwandererviertel. Neu angekommene Migrant*innen mieteten hier ihre ersten überteuerten Wohnungen, bevor sie weiterzogen und andere Neuankömmlinge nachfolgten. Zur Zeit der Great Migration und Industrialisierung trennten sich vormals ethnisch aufgeteilte Stadtviertel zunehmend nach Klasse und vor allem nach Hautfarbe. Black Bottom wurde zu einem der wenigen Wohnviertel für Afroamerikaner und People of Color. Die Häuser und Zimmer wurden zu hohen Preisen vermietet, von Besitzern, die sie gleichzeitig verfallen ließen. Im Zweiten Weltkrieg prägten Holzhäuser mit abenteuerlichen An- und Umbauten und größtenteils nur mit Außenlatrinen versehen das überfüllte Viertel. Alles nur einen Steinwurf von Downtown entfernt.

„Die Mies-Community hat Frieden gefunden, umgeben von Bäumen und Blattwerk, die aus der fruchtbaren, ursprünglichen Lehmerde des alten Black Bottom wachsen. … Der Frieden hier mag eine Belohnung sein, vielleicht verliehen durch die alten Zeiten, weil wir hier die Bereitschaft und Kühnheit besitzen, eine integrative Gemeinschaft zu leben in einer der am stärksten segregierten Städte der Vereinigten Staaten. … Wir haben bewiesen, dass die Nachbarschaft gemischter Hautfarben und Einkommen, von Mittelschicht und Arbeiterklasse möglich ist, in einer Ansammlung von architektonischen Schmuckstücken, so wie es von Anfang an beabsichtigt war."

Marsha Music (2012): Hidden in Plain Sight, 51

„Ganz ehrlich, anfangs kam ich mir bei so vielen Afroamerikanern um mich herum wirklich komisch vor. Verstehen sie mich nicht falsch, aber wo ich aufgewachsen bin, gab es hauptsächlich Weiße – hauptsächlich reiche, äußerst gepflegte Menschen. Ich wusste nicht, was mich erwartete. So eine Situation war komplett neu für mich. Aber nach und nach fühlte ich mich in dieser Gemeinschaft wohler. Ich lernte meine Nachbarn kennen, und ich habe diese Gedanken nicht mehr. Ich habe gelernt, dass sie einfach nur Menschen sind, die ihr Leben leben, so wie ich. Es gefällt mir jetzt sehr gut hier."

Eine Lafayette Park Pavilion Bewohnerin, in: Aubert (2012), 220

Urban Renewal kam relativ spät nach Detroit, doch von da an gab es kein Halten für die Bulldozer mehr. Ein breiter Gürtel um die Innenstadt … ist in einem ständigen Wandel begriffen, alte Gebäude werden geräumt, dann abgerissen, um nach und nach durch neue Wohnungen, Stadthäuser, Hotels, Motels und kleine Betriebe und Bürogebäude ersetzt zu werden. Nach Plänen, die ein Jahrzehnt oder länger zurückliegen, wird der gesamte verfallene Stadtkern schließlich eine große Ansammlung neuer bürgerlicher Wohnungen, Krankenhäuser, Museen, Parks, Schulen sowie städtische, kulturelle und kommerzielle Bauten umfassen.

Stanley H. Brown (1965): Detroit: Slow Healing of a Fractured City

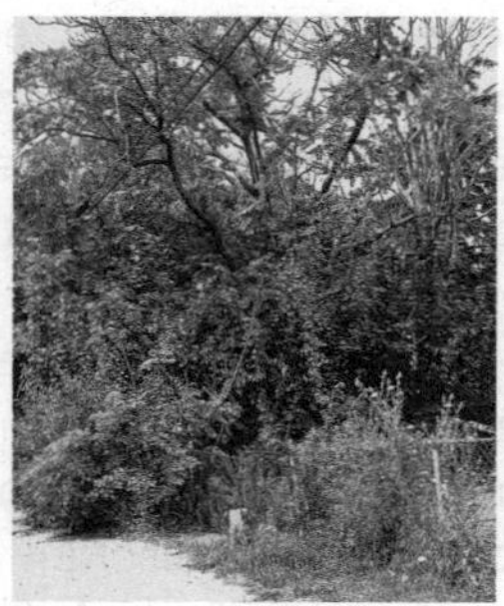

33

Alley in Midtown, 2015

Brush Park Neighborhood

Brush Park ist eines der wenigen Viertel Detroits, die derzeit einen regelrechten Bauboom erleben. Seit 2016 wird von unterschiedlichen Investoren ein völlig neues Viertel aus dem Boden gestampft. Auf den Brachen zwischen den aufwendig renovierten Villen entstehen komfortable Eigentumswohnungen. Während einzelne Stadtteile um Downtown von den Millionen privater Investoren profitieren, gibt es in anderen, weniger dicht besiedelten Gegenden die Tendenz, Infrastruktur abzubauen und Leerstand massiv abzureißen.

Brush Park wurde ab 1850 auf ehemaligen Ribbon Farms gebaut. Elijah Brush und später sein Sohn Edmund Askin teilten ihren Grundbesitz, benannten die Straßen nach Familienmitgliedern und verkauften das Land an die Detroiter Oberschicht. Die viktorianischen Villen wurden bereits um 1900 wieder aufgegeben, da die wohlhabenden Eigentümer*innen in ruhige Vororte zogen. Die schnell anwachsende Arbeiterklasse zog in das Viertel, bis auch sie in den 1970er Jahren ihren Jobs hinterherzogen. Mehrere Jahrzehnte prägten vernagelte Häuser, leer stehende Grundstücke, Kleinkriminalität und urbane Wildnis das Bild.

Das Foto entstand in einer kleinen Alley und zeigt einen blühenden Götterbaum.

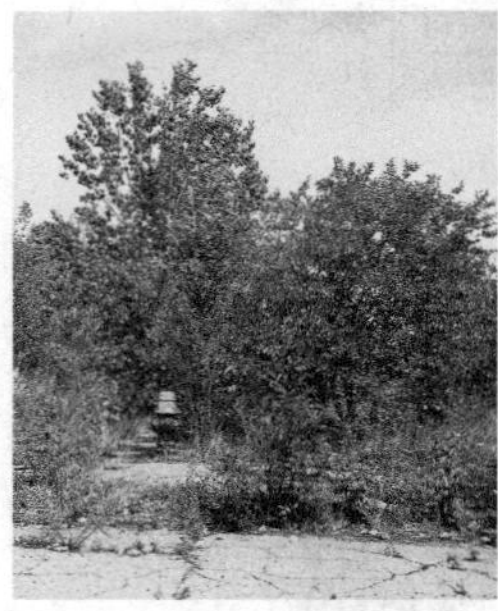

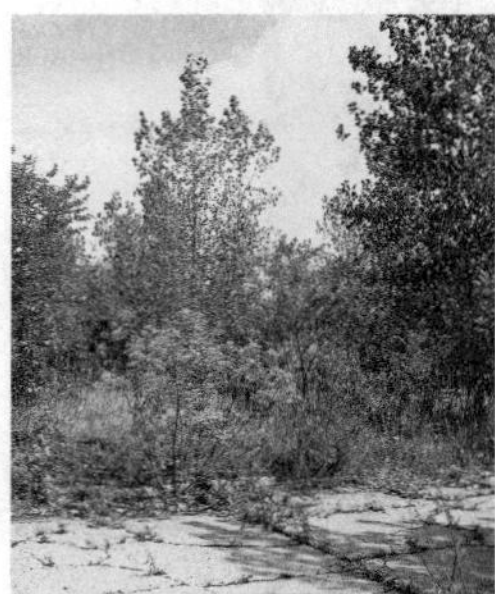

34 / 35

I-94 Renaissance Park, 2016

Airport Sub Neighborhood

„Seit Ende der 1990er Jahre habe ich miterlebt, wie dieses Viertel verlassen, abgerissen und durch Betonbarrikaden abgeriegelt wurde. Die letzten Bewohner zogen aus, ihre Häuser und die sie umgebenden ausgebrannten Ruinen wurden abgerissen; die geisterhafte Kirche St. Cyril's wurde bis zum Einsturz ausgeschlachtet; … die Bäume wurden herausgerissen, um potenzielle Bauherren zu beglücken; … Aber der Verkauf des Landes fand nie statt. Abgesehen von den massigen Wohnkomplexen entlang der Huber Street steht die Zone immer noch leer. Große entwurzelte Bäume liegen in Haufen herum. Wahllos aufgetürmte Erdhügel und abgerissener Schutt sind mit Gräsern und Wildblumen überwuchert. Überflutete Straßen sind zu Feuchtgebieten und Sümpfen geworden. Die Tierwelt gedeiht: Fasane, Kaninchen, Schlangen, Frösche, Falken, zahlreiche Vögel, aber auch streunende Katzen oder Hunde sind hier zu finden. Die I-94 Industrial Park Renaissance Zone ist versehentlich zu einer der natürlichsten Landschaften Detroits geworden."

Scott Hocking (2017): The Zone

Einige der weitläufigen Brachen Detroits entstanden durch den ehrgeizigen Abriss leer stehender Strukturen und Stadtviertel in Erwartung neuer Investoren. Die Strategie bestand darin, heruntergekommene Stadtviertel aufzukaufen, die Häuser abzureißen und hohe Steueranreize zu bieten. 1997 richtete die Stadt Detroit sechs industrielle Sanierungsgebiete ein, sogenannte Renaissance-Zonen, mit denen Unternehmen zurück in die Stadt gelockt werden sollten. Eine davon war der I-94 Renaissance Park in der Nähe des ehemaligen Stadtflughafens. Bis 2009 hatte die Detroit Economic Development Corporation rund 19 Millionen Dollar ausgegeben, um 75 Hektar Land zu erwerben und Gebäude wie die Jane Cooper-Grundschule abzureißen. Als die Investoren ausblieben, hat die Wildnis den Weg in das ehemalige Stadtviertel gefunden. Ich habe über 30 verschiedene Pflanzen gezählt: Pioniergehölze, Blumen und Kräuter wie Wiesenklee, Maulbeerbäume und Weinreben. Zu sehen ist die Kreuzung von Helen Street und Marcus Street.

Die Gentrifizierung in diesem Viertel begann vor etwa zehn bis zwölf Jahren. Und sie ist fast abgeschlossen. Einkommensschwache und arbeitende Menschen sind gerade erst vertrieben worden. Wir haben hier bald die teuerste Ansammlung von Eigentumswohnungen und Stadthäusern in der ganzen Welt. Es gibt diese Wohnanlagen hier zu meiner Linken und die obdachlosen Veteranen auf der anderen Straßenseite, die für ein paar Dollar alles versuchen, um Menschen auf einen Parkplatz zu lotsen. Ich meine, was für ein Gegensatz.

Maureen Taylor von der Michigan Welfare Rights Organization, in: Collapsing Auto Industry in Detroit (2013)

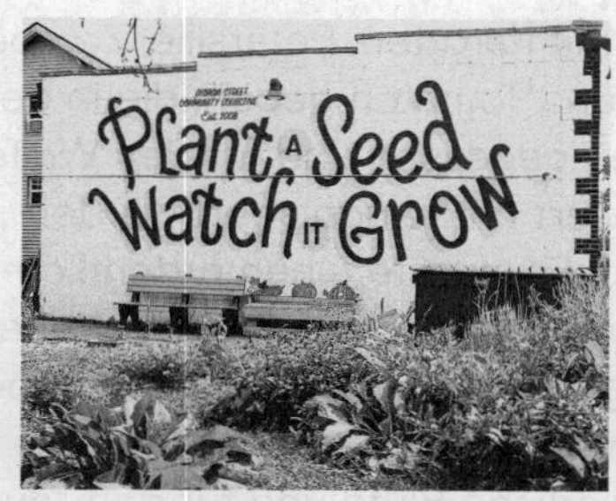

36

Georgia Street Community Collective, 2018

Airport Sub Neighborhood

Im Jahr 2008 pflanzte Mark Covington ein paar Blumen und Gemüse auf einer Ecke nahe des Hauses seiner Großmutter an, um Leute davon abzuhalten, Müll auf diesen Grundstücken abzuladen. Sehr schnell begrüßten sowohl Senior*innen als auch die Kinder der Nachbarschaft seine gärtnerische Initiative als willkommene Bezugsquelle frischer Lebensmittel und um ihre Lebenshaltungskosten zu senken. Menschen von außerhalb begannen, Schulmaterial für Kinder zu spenden, sodass einige Monate später die gemeinnützige Organisation Georgia Street Community Collective gegründet wurde mit dem Ziel, das Viertel zu stärken und zu beleben. Innerhalb der letzten zehn Jahre entstand um die ersten Gartenbeete herum ein Gemeindezentrum: ein Lern- und ein Obstgarten, ein Feld zum kostenlosen Selbsternten sowie eine Bibliothek mit Computerraum. Die Spenden wichen jährlichen Giveaway-Tagen – im Sommer für Schulrucksäcke, im Winter für Mäntel oder Truthähne. Geplant sind auch Reha-Häuser und ein Spendenzentrum in einer alten Lagerhalle. Leider wurde diese Halle zusammen mit zwei anderen Gebäuden 2018 in Brand gesteckt. Die Stadt Detroit hat sie nur wenige Wochen später abgerissen. Die zahlreichen Brandstiftungen, die Tatsache, dass sich die Stadt eine zweijährige Rückübertragung der erworbenen landwirtschaftlichen Flächen vorbehält, und die Gerüchte, die Nachbarschaft solle ein Industriegebiet werden, zeigen deutlich, dass die Bemühungen von Grassroots-Bürgerinitiativen in Detroit auf dünnem Boden zu wachsen scheinen.

Wie es Laura Lawson und Abbilyn Miller in ihrem Aufsatz 2013 über Gemeinschaftsgärten ausdrücken: „Der Umgang städtischer Beamter mit Gemeinschaftsgärten sagt viel darüber aus, was sie von Bürgerinitiativen halten. In Krisenzeiten werden gerne die Tugenden des Gartenbaus beschworen, aber wenn die Krise abklingt, verändert der Staat (meistens die Stadtverwaltung) oft die Interpretation des Gartens – er wird zu Land, das als Reserve für das ‚öffentliche Wohl' zu dienen hat, was wiederum sehr eng als privatwirtschaftliche Erschließung definiert wird.“°

www.georgiastreetcc.com

° Laura Lawson / Abbilyn Miller (2013): Community Gardens and Urban Agriculture as Antithesis to Abandonment, 39

→ 43 Georgia Street Community Collective (Free Picking Field), 2018

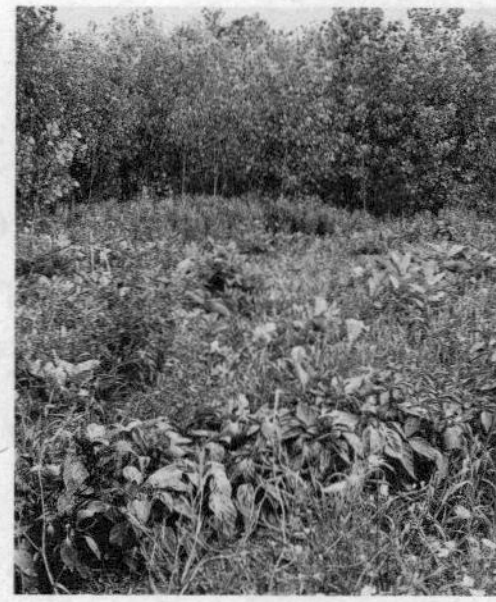

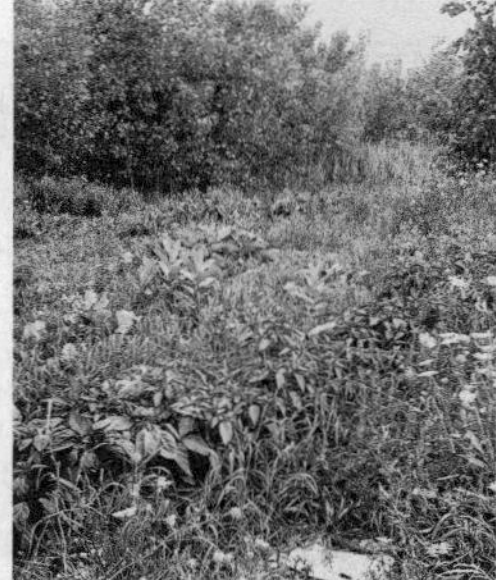

37 / 38

Guerilla Gardening, 2016

Um 2016 in Detroit Land für einen eigenen Garten kaufen zu können, musste man zumeist ein Haus besitzen. Die Stadt erlaubt dann den Ankauf angrenzender Grundstücke. Ausgenommen scheinen private Großinvestoren (siehe Bild 59). In Teilen der Stadt, die als Food Deserts gelten,werden immer wieder kleine Gärten illegal angelegt, um sich mit Gemüse zu versorgen. Sie sind von der Stadt geduldet, solange ihre Lage für die Stadtentwicklung und Grundstücksinvestitionen uninteressant bleibt. Somit gibt es gerade für einkommensschwache Bürger*innen (36,4 Prozent lebten 2018 unter der Armutsgrenze) und für kleinere Garteninitiativen keine Garantie, dass ihre Pflanzungen auch im nächsten Jahr noch genutzt werden können.

Einige Foodaktivist*innen besetzen daher Grundstücke mit Gärten und streiten bei der Stadt dafür, dass leere Brachflächen legal als Gärten genutzt und auch günstig erworben werden können – zur Selbstversorgung, aber auch als nachhaltige Wirtschaftsentwicklung und Arbeitsplätze für die Bürger*innen der Stadt.

Die Bilder zeigen ein solches Feld mit Kohlrabi, Basilikum und Chili, die zwischen Klee, Seidenpflanzen, Wilder Möhre, Gräsern und Disteln wachsen. Auf diesem Grundstück standen zuvor Wohnhäuser, die 2004 abgerissen wurden. Benachbart ist bereits eine neue geschlossene Wohnanlage entstanden.

→ Food Desert, Food Security, Detroit Food Policy Council

→ 59 Charlevoix Street (Dr. Sweet's House / Hantz Woodlands), 2018

Detroit ist das Endergebnis von Entscheidungen, die wir trafen, von Gesetzen, die wir verabschiedeten, von Wirtschaftsstrategien und kulturellen Haltungen, die wir unterstützten, auf unserem Weg in die suburbanisierte, auf Einkaufszentren fixierte, nach Hautfarben und Klassenzugehörigkeit getrennte Welt, in der wir heute leben. … Wenn Amerika einem einzelnen Ort widerfährt, ist das Ergebnis Detroit, mit allem, was dazu gehört, dem trostlosen städtischen Kern, den vorstädtischen Millionärsenklaven und allem, was dazwischen liegt.

Jerry Herron (2013): Motor City Breakdown

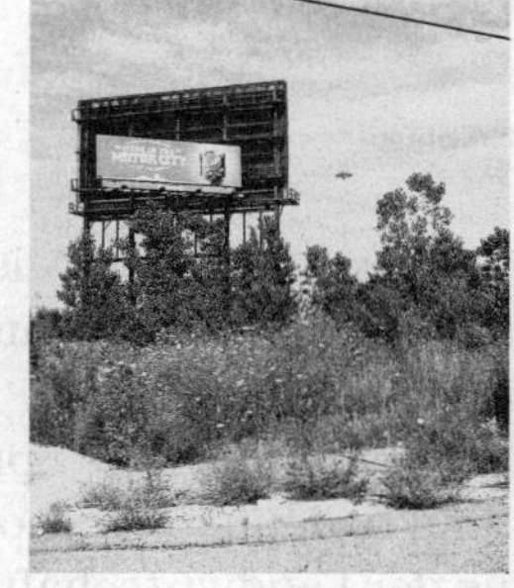

39

Hastings Street, 2015

Milwaukee Junction Neighborhood

Dieses Foto zeigt den verbliebenen Rest der Hastings Street, einst die belebteste Straße in Detroits afroamerikanischem Viertel mit Bars, Nachtclubs, Restaurants, Friseurläden und Geschäften. Blind Blake, John Lee Hooker und andere haben sie in ihren Songs verewigt. Im Zuge des Urban Renewal wurde die Hastings Street zusammen mit den Stadtteilen Black Bottom und Paradise Valley abgerissen. Sie liegt heute unter dem Chrysler Freeway begraben, der Teil der Interstate 75 Autobahn ist. Marsha Music, deren Vater einen Musikladen in der Hastings Street besaß, erinnert sich an den Abriss wie folgt: „Meine erste Erinnerung an Hastings war, dass mich mein Vater an einen Ort in der Nähe seines Plattenladens mitnahm. Ich war ein kleines Mädchen, etwa drei oder vier Jahre alt. Er führte mich von dem Ort, an dem wir standen, auf die andere Straßenseite zu dieser riesigen, in den Boden eingelassenen Erdgrube. Es sah für mich wie eine Schlucht aus. Er sah mich an und sagte: … ‚Hier war früher Hastings.' … Als ich älter wurde, wurde mir klar, dass es die ersten Erdarbeiten für die Interstate 75 waren. Was mein Vater verstand und so anschaulich mit diesem Satz ausdrückte, war, dass eine Lebensweise durch den Chrysler Freeway völlig zerstört worden war. Die Straße von Hastings existierte einfach nicht mehr." °

° Latzman Moon (1994): Untold Tales, Unsung Heroes, 361

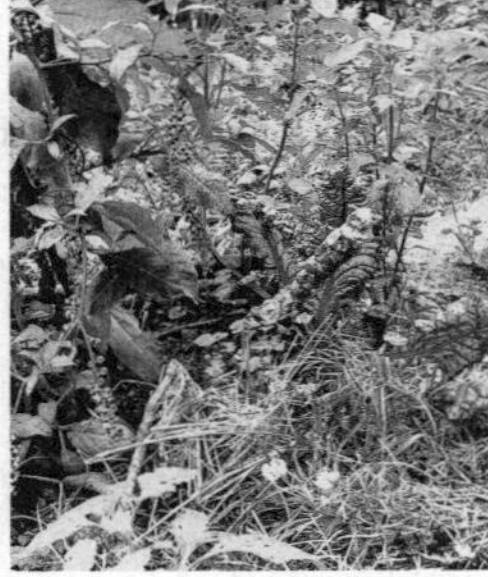

40

Ile Oko Farm (Swiss Chard), 2016

Jefferson Chalmers Neighborhood

Die Ile Oko Farm wurde 2012 von Atieno Nyarkasagam und Lorenzo Herron auf ihrem Hausgrundstück gegründet. Der Name Ile Oko kommt aus der Sprache der Yoruba und bedeutet etwa so viel wie das Haus der Landwirtschaft. Lorenzo ist in der Nachbarschaft aufgewachsen und Atieno in Nairobi, Kenia. Beide betreiben seit 2002 urbane Landwirtschaft, wobei sie Gemüse, Obstbäume und Medizinpflanzen anbauen. Neben der nachhaltigen Selbstversorgung ist das Anbauen für sie auch ein politischer Akt, der Fragen nach Food Security, Landverteilung, sozialer Gerechtigkeit und auch ihren kulturellen Wurzeln berührt. Urbane Landwirtschaft bedeutet für sie die Möglichkeit, einen Zugang zu angemessen, nährstoffreichen, nachhaltigen und kulturell relevanten Lebensmitteln zu gewährleisten. Zusammen mit anderen Initiativen und urbanen Farmern setzen sie sich dafür ein, dass die Stadt Detroit ihren Bürger*innen leere Grundstücke für urbane Landwirtschaft zur Verfügung stellt bzw. den Erwerb von Land erleichtert.

Das Bild zeigt das Beet vor ihrem Haus mit Mangold, Chili, Amerikanischer Kermesbeere, Gundermann und kleinen Nelken.

Wenn über urbane Landwirtschaft gesprochen wird, wird sie zumeist als etwas Neues dargestellt. Aber die Menschen betreiben hier schon seit langer Zeit Landwirtschaft. … wenn wir sie als eine neue Sache darstellen, machen wir die Anstrengungen der Menschen unsichtbar, die vor uns hier waren: Die Ribbon Farms, Victory Gardens, Liberty Gardens, das Farm-A-Lot Program in den 1970er Jahren, die Gardening Angels, Gerald Hairston. Und noch vor ihnen bauten die Ureinwohner dieses Landes, das Volk der Anishinabe, hier schon Nahrungsmittel an. In diesem Sinne ist die Landwirtschaft in diesem Gebiet also nicht neu. Was neu ist, ist die Stadt.

Shane Bernardo, damaliger Manager der Earthworks Urban Farm, in unserem Gespräch 2016

→ Anishinabe, Farm-A-Lot Program, Gardening Angels, Ribbon Farms, Victory Gardens / Liberty Gardens

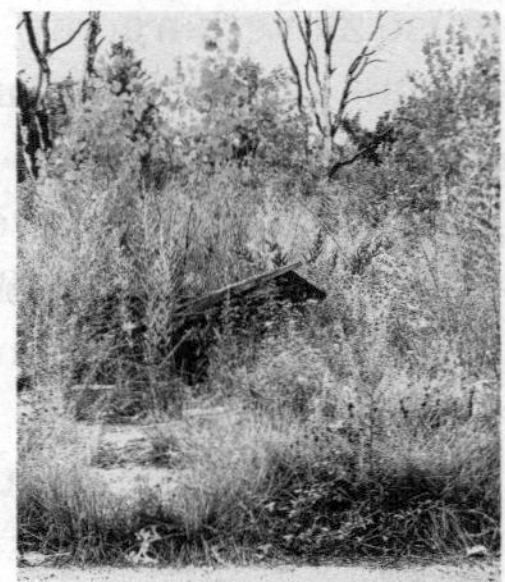

41

5721 Dubois Street, 2015

Poletown East Neighborhood

„Der Besitz eines Eigenheims in einer ‚polnischen' Nachbarschaft war von größter Bedeutung. … Es musste einen Garten mit Karotten, Petersilie, Zwiebeln, Rüben und Tomaten geben, die in der Erntezeit gegessen und für den Winter konserviert und eingelagert werden konnten. Es musste einen ordentlich getrimmten und von Unkraut befreiten Rasen geben. Es musste Blumen geben – viele verschiedene Sorten für eine kontinuierliche Blüte und für den Tausch mit den Nachbarn. Das Saatgut wurde gesammelt und für den nächsten Frühling gelagert – man konnte es sich nicht leisten, jedes Jahr Blumensamen zu kaufen! Damit dieses Gemüse, die Blumen und der Rasen blühen und gedeihen konnten, gab es im Frühling und Sommer das tägliche Ritual des Gießens, sogar an den Tagen, an denen es regnete."

Regina Kóscielski: Portrait of a Polish-American, in: Hartmann (1974), 115

Auf diesem Grundstück stand bis 2013 ein schlichtes Holzrahmenhaus von 1908. Vermutlich ist es niedergebrannt, verkohlte Reste des Dachs sind noch zu erkennen. Der Schmalblättrige Sonnenhut blüht nach wie vor im Vorgarten. Das Grundstück befindet sich im Stadtteil Poletown East, in dem sich bis 1900 viele polnische Migranten auf ehemaligen Ribbon Farms angesiedelt hatten.

→ 1 / 2 2550 East Grand Boulevard, 2015
→ 14 East Ferry Street, 2015

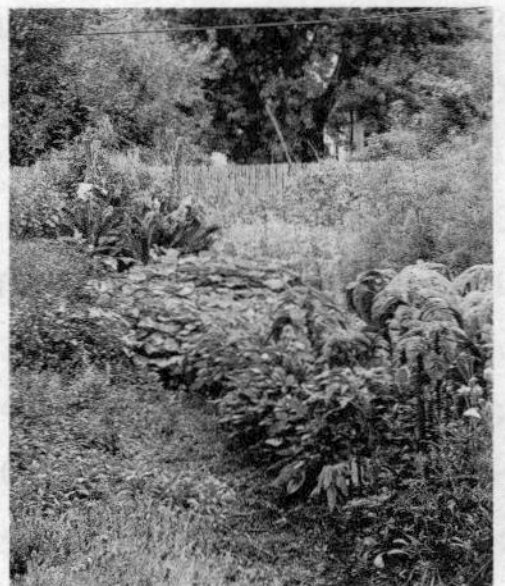

42

Molly and Mike's Garden, 2015

North End Neighborhood

Molly Hubbell und Mike Zuzolo betreiben einen Garten hinter ihrem Haus. Beide kamen 2014 nach Detroit. Während Mike an einem Aquaponik-System arbeitet – einem in sich geschlossenen Kreislauf von Fischhaltung in Aquakultur und Pflanzenanbau als Hydrokultur –, baut Molly Blumen und Gemüse auf klassische Weise an. Aufgrund der hohen Bleiwerte im Boden ihres Grundstücks wachsen die Pflanzen in Hochbeeten vom belasteten Unterboden getrennt in biologischem Kompost. Viele

Grundstücke in Detroit sind durch die früher verwendeten bleihaltigen Hausanstriche und wegen fehlender Umweltvorgaben für die Industrie mit Schwermetallen oder Öl kontaminiert. Gärten und Farmen lassen daher ihre Böden untersuchen, bevor sie etwas anbauen.

Neben ihrem eigenen Garten arbeitet Molly bei Keep Growing Detroit. Die Organisation versorgt mit ihrem Garden Resource Program urbane Farmer und Gärtner mit Saatgut und Setzlingen und vernetzt sie miteinander, um eine lebensmittelsouveräne Stadt zu schaffen, in der der größte Teil an Obst und Gemüse, das in Detroit konsumiert wird, innerhalb der Stadtgrenzen von den Bürger*innen selbst angebaut wird.

→ 48 Molly and Mike's Garden, 2018

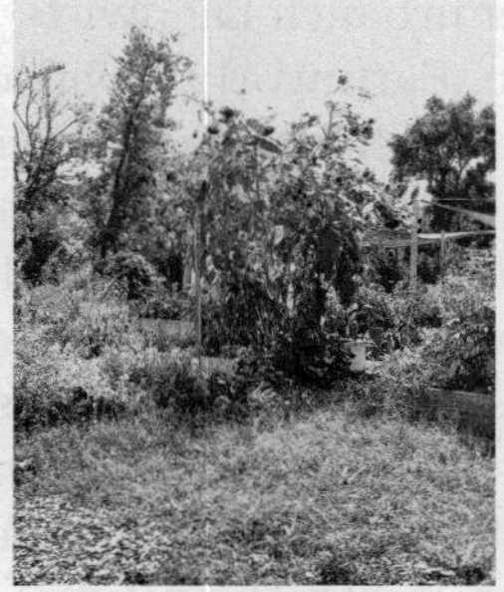

43

Georgia Street Community Collective (Free Picking Field), 2018

Airport Sub Neighborhood

Zur Beschreibung siehe
→ 36 Georgia Street Community Collective, 2018

Man kann auf ein leeres Grundstück schauen und nicht Verwüstung, sondern Hoffnung sehen. Die Möglichkeit, sein eigenes Essen anzubauen … Ein leer stehendes Grundstück steht für die Möglichkeiten einer kulturellen Revolution.

Grace Lee Boggs (2011) in einem Interview mit Democracy Now!

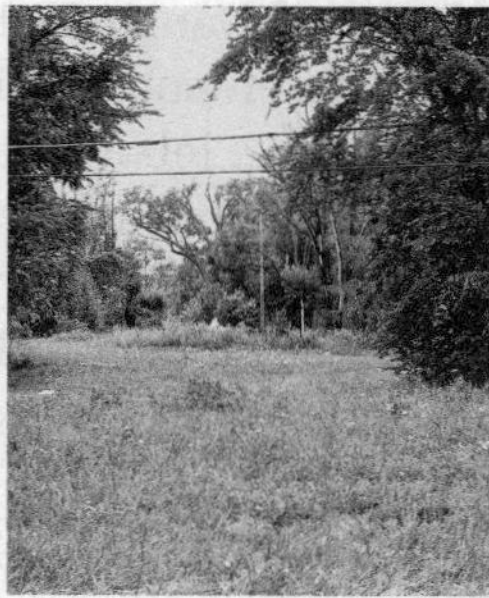

44

Eastlawn and Lakeview Streets (Burned Down House), 2016

Riverbend Neighborhood

Das Foto zeigt den Blick von der Eastlawn zur Lakeview Street. Neben blühenden Breitblättrigen Platterbsen und Wilder Möhre sind die Reste eines abgebrannten Hauses zu sehen. Es wurde 1924 gebaut und war als eines der letzten des Viertels bis 2009 bewohnt. Wie die Aktivistin Grace Lee Boggs in einem Interview betont, mögen die vielen Freiflächen Detroits als Nachteil erscheinen, bergen jedoch gleichzeitig die Möglichkeit, Stadt neu zu denken. Detroits Brachland kann Ausgangspunkt für eine urbane Landwirtschaft sein, die nicht nur die ganze Stadt ernähren könnte, sondern gleichzeitig auch sinnvolle, selbstverwaltete und nachhaltige Jobs für die Zukunft schafft.

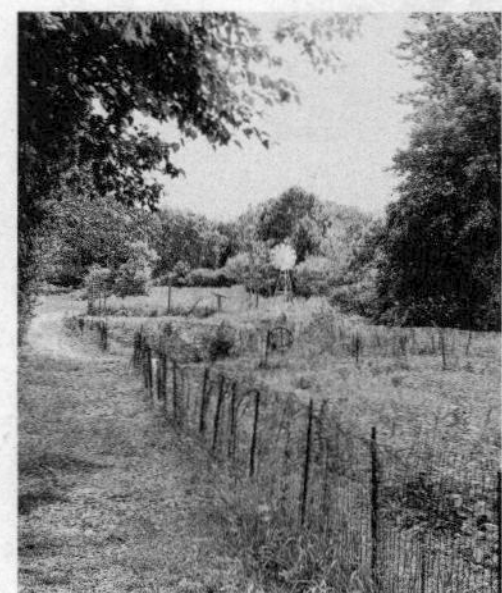

45

D-Town Farm, Detroit Black Community Food Security Network, 2016

Franklin Park Neighborhood

Detroits Bevölkerungszahl ist seit 1950 auf ein Drittel geschrumpft. Die Stadtfläche blieb jedoch gleich groß mit drastischen Folge für die Infrastruktur. Unter anderem gelten weite Teile der Stadt als sogenannte Food Deserts, Gebiete, in denen es auf Meilen keine Lebensmittelläden oder Supermärkte gibt, die man zu Fuß erreichen kann. Das Detroit Black Community Food Security Network (DBCFSN) wurde 2006 gegründet, um diese Unterversorgung zu bekämpfen. Das Netzwerk organisiert afroamerikanische Detroiter*innen, um eine selbstbestimmte und aktive Führungsrolle in der lokalen Food Security-Bewegung zu übernehmen. Das bedeutet, Besitz, Eigentum und Wohlstand für und in der eigenen Community zu schaffen, genauso wie das Aufgreifen der Fragen, welche Rolle Rassismus und Ungleichheit im Food System (dem System der Herstellung und Verbreitung von Lebensmitteln) und in der Stadtentwicklung spielen: Im mehrheitlich afroamerikanischen Detroit werden vorrangig weiße, finanzstarke Investoren bei Grundstückskäufen bevorzugt und vorrangig gut ausgebildete, weiße Neu-Detroiter*innen profitieren von der derzeitigen Neuordnung der Stadt. Auf Anregung des DBCFSN wurde 2009 das Detroit Food Policy Council gegründet. Es vertritt die Akteure urbaner Landwirtschaft gegenüber der Stadtverwaltung und fordert unter anderem: „Ungenutztes Land sollte für die landwirtschaftliche Nutzung zur Verfügung stehen. … Anwohnern sollte beim Kauf von leer stehenden Grundstücken Vorrang eingeräumt werden. … Die Stadt sollte die Bedeutung von Gemeinschaftsgärten anerkennen und sie als Ressourcen schützen, die nicht für andere Formen der Erschließung verdrängt werden dürfen."° Das Hauptprojekt des DBCFSN ist die D-Town Farm, eine der größten Farmen in Detroit. Neben biologischem Anbau und einem Detroit Community Market finden hier Ausbildungsprogramme für Kinder und Jugendliche statt. Ein kooperativer Supermarkt ist in Planung. Seit 2008 ist die Farm in Meyers Tree Nursery Baumschule in Rouge Park gelegen. Sie ist langfristig von der Stadt gepachtet, für einen Kauf fehlt bisher die gesetzliche Grundlage.

Das Windrad im Bild, hinter den Beeten mit Amaranth, Okra und Jalapeño, ist Teil der Regenwasserversorgung.

www.dbcfsn.org

° Detroit Food Policy Council (2012): Public Land Sale Process in Detroit: A Community Perspective

Hinter der Garage … befand sich ein Gemüsegarten – Tomaten in Reihen … mit Gartenstöcken und Metallstäben hochgehalten, gelber Sommerkürbis, Gurken, Paprika und ein Feigenbaum, der vor Jahren als Setzling aus dem Libanon geschickt worden war. Minzblätter und Oregano säumten den Rand zur Garage, und am Zaun, der das Haus von einem Nachbarn trennte, den niemand in der Familie kannte, hingen Zwiebelbündel.

Hayan Charara: Becoming the Center of Mystery, in: Abraham / Shryock (2000), 407

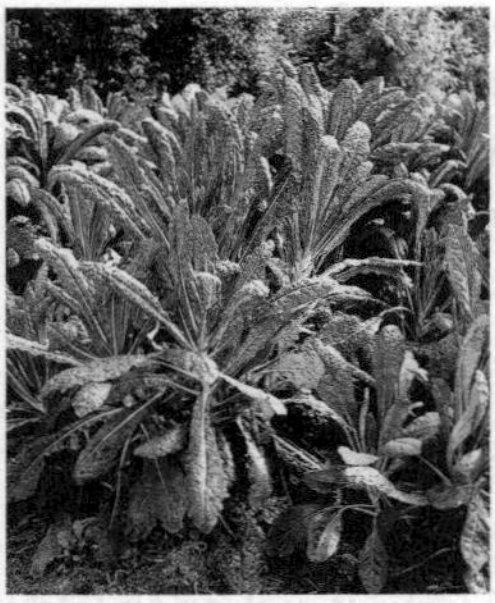

46

Oakland Avenue Urban Farm (Lacinato Kale), 2016

North End Neighborhood

Das Bild zeigt den in Detroit sehr beliebten Palmkohl, der in fast jedem Garten zu sehen ist. Diese Kohlart stammt aus der italienischen Toskana und wird dort seit Jahrhunderten angebaut. Sie wird auch toskanischer Grünkohl oder Cavolo Nero genannt, was Schwarzkohl bedeutet.

Das Bild entstand auf einem Feld der Oakland Avenue Urban Farm in North End Detroit, die ausführlich in Bildern 18 und 19 beschrieben ist.

→ 18 / 19 Oakland Avenue Urban Farm, 2016

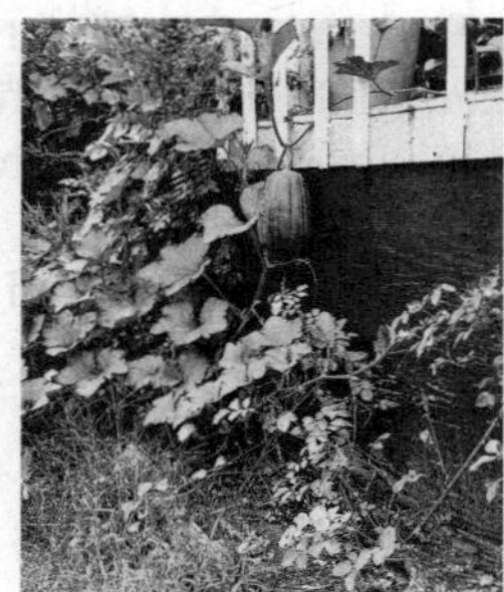

47

Bandhu Garden (Water Squash), 2018

Campau / Banglatown Neighborhood

Bandhu Gardens wurde 2015 von Emily Staugaitis und Minara Begum gegründet, als die beiden Nachbarinnen und Freundinnen wurden, obwohl sie kein Wort in der Sprache der anderen sprachen. Sie leben in Banglatown, einem Viertel mit mehr als fünftausend Bangladeshi-Amerikaner*innen. Frauen und Familien pflegen dicht bewachsene, lebendige Gemüsegärten in ihren Hinterhöfen, auf ihren Terrassen oder in der Nähe ihrer Häuser und bauen darin südasiatisches Gemüse an wie Bittermelone, Langbohne, Kabocha- und Wasserkürbis und vielfältigste Chilisorten.

Bandhu Gardens ist ein Kleinunternehmerinnen-Netzwerk für Gärten, die von bangalischen Frauen verwaltet werden und es ihnen ermöglichen, ihren Haushalt zu führen und gleichzeitig etwas Geld zu verdienen. Als Nachbarinnen arbeiten sie zusammen, um ihre Erzeugnisse zu verkaufen, Catering anzubieten, Pop-up-Veranstaltungen durchzuführen und Kochkurse zu geben. Als ich 2018 einige der Gärten besuchte, war ein Gemeinschaftshaus in Vorbereitung. „Bandhu Gardens“ ist halb Bangla, halb Englisch und bedeutet Garten der Freunde. Das Foto zeigt einen Kabochakürbis, der auf Emilys Veranda wächst.

www.bandhugardens.com

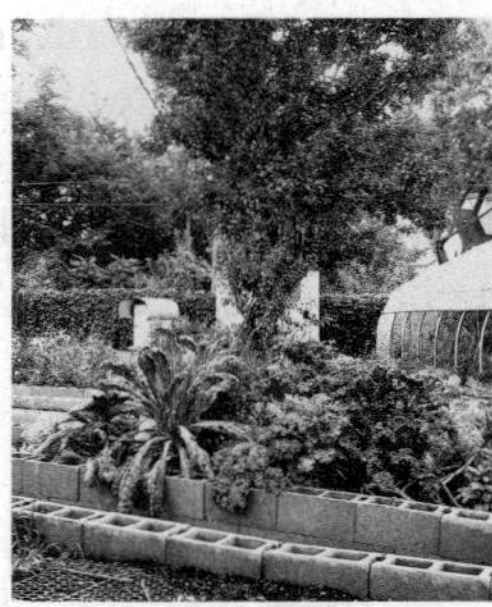

48

Molly and Mike’s Garden, 2018

North End Neighborhood

Zur Beschreibung siehe
→ 42 Molly and Mike’s Garden, 2015

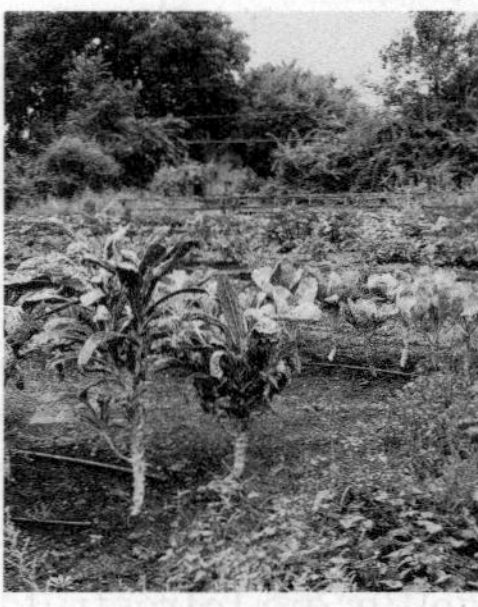

49

Earthworks Urban Farm, The Capuchin Soup Kitchen, 2018

Islandview Neighborhood

Earthworks Urban Farm ist Teil der Kapuziner-Suppenküche Capuchin Soup Kitchen in Detroit. Sie wurde 1929 während der Weltwirtschaftskrise im Kapuzinerkloster St. Bonaventure gegründet und schenkte pro Tag 2.000 Essensrationen aus. Diese Anzahl ist bis heute konstant geblieben. Hinzugekommen sind verschiedene Spendenkammern sowie Einrichtungen und Programme zur Unterstützung von ehemaligen Inhaftierten oder Drogenabhängigen.

1997 gründete der Kapuzinermönch Rick Samyn einen kleinen Gemüsegarten, nachdem er bemerkt hatte, dass die Nachbarschaftskinder ihr Essen an Tankstelle kauften (siehe Register für Food Desert). Mit der Zeit erwuchs daraus die Earthworks Urban Farm. Sie versorgt heute die Suppenküche mit Gemüse, viele Nachbarschaftsgärten mit Keimlingen und unterhält Gartenausbildungsprogramme, die Detroiter*innen dazu qualifizieren, ihr eigenes Unternehmen zu gründen oder einen Job in der urbanen Landwirtschaft zu finden. Earthworks sieht seine Aufgabe darin, durch urbane Landwirtschaft die Gemeindearbeit anzuregen, sie zu unterstützen und weiterzubilden sowie das Umweltbewusstsein wiederzubeleben. Dies ist in der Erkenntnis verwurzelt, dass sich Ungleichheit und Rassismus im derzeitigen Food System (der Versorgung und Qualität von Lebensmitteln) manifestiert haben.

Bild 49 und 52 zeigen beide ein Feld der Farm mit gelbem Gartenkürbis, verschiedenen Kohlsorten, Kartoffeln, Chili und Spargel. In Bild 52 ist zudem das Kloster im Hintergrund zu sehen.

www.cskdetroit.org/earthworks

→ 52 Earthworks Urban Farm (Church), 2018

Eigene Lebensmittel anzubauen bedeutet Selbstbestimmung, Saat, die man in die Erde legt, die man wachsen lässt und deren Früchte dann zubereitet … [das] nährt dich und befreit dich von der Notwendigkeit, eine Lebensmittelrechnung bezahlen zu müssen. Das eigene Essen anzubauen, sollte grundlegendes Können sein. Wenn du dir die Zähne putzen kannst, solltest du auch Kürbis anbauen können.

Bianca Danzy, eine Landwirtschaftsschülerin an der Earthworks Farm, in: Guzmán (2016)

Für dieses Viertel gibt es keinen konkreten Entwicklungsplan, aber die Stadt hat Überlegungen, es industriell zu nutzen. Also alle Häuser abzureißen und ein großes Industriegebiet daraus zu machen. … Als ich noch ein kleines Kind war, wurde spekuliert, dass der Flughafen erweitert werden würde. So entstand hier also unsere Immobilienkrise. Die Leute fingen an, wegzugehen, und zwar nicht wegen der Arbeitsplätze oder so, sondern weil sie in andere Viertel zogen, weil sie dachten, die Stadt würde hier bauen. Und es kam nie dazu. Es ist also so, als ob wir 30 Jahre später genau das gleiche Problem hätten.

Mark Covington, Anwohner in Airport Sub und Gründer des Georgia Street Community Collective, in unserem Gespräch 2018

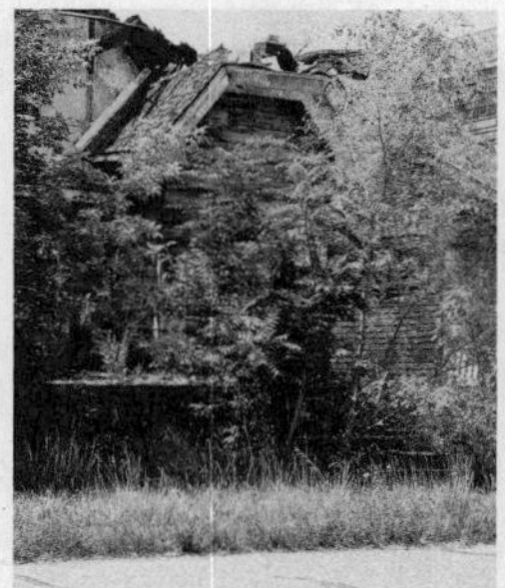

50

8120 Georgia Street, 2016

Airport Sub Neighborhood

Dieses Einfamilienhaus aus dem Jahr 1927 war überwachsen mit Götterbaum, Eschen-Ahorn und Maulbeerbäumen. Gelbrote Taglilien und Straucheibisch, von früheren Bewohner*innen gepflanzt, wuchsen noch wild im Vorgarten. Im Oktober 2018 wurde das Haus abgerissen. Das leere Grundstück gehört nun der Detroit Land Bank Authority.

Vor dem Abriss muss das Haus mehrmals in Brand gesteckt worden sein. Hinter den dichtgewachsenen Götterbäumen kann man ein Schild mit der Aufschrift „Arson Reward" erkennen. Es verspricht eine Belohnung von 5.000 Dollar für Informationen, die zu einer Verhaftung von Brandstiftern führen. Diese Belohnungen wurden 40 Jahre lang vom gemeinnützigen Michigan Arson Prevention Committee vergeben und von einer Versicherungsgesellschaft finanziert. Im Jahr 2017 stellte dieser einzige Geldgeber die Zahlungen ein, und das Komitee wurde aufgelöst. Die Zahl der Hausbrände belief sich in jenem Jahr auf 3.400.

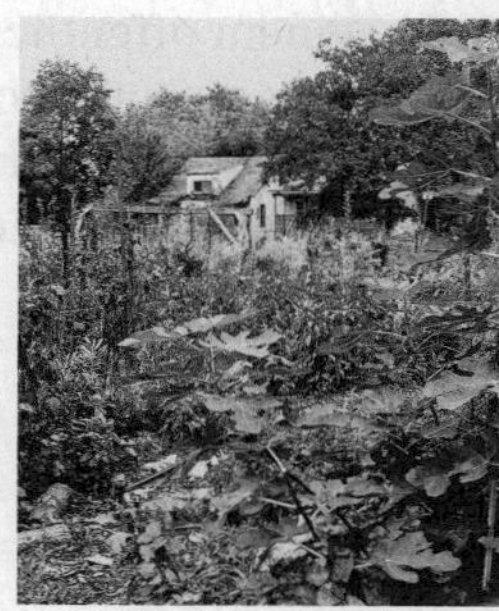

51

Faina and Graem's Garden (Popps Packing), 2018

Campau / Banglatown Neighborhood

Faina Lerman und Graem Whyte gründeten 2009 in einer ehemaligen Wurstverpackungsfabrik ihr gemeinnütziges Künstlerprojekt Popps Packing. Ihre Absicht ist es, wirksame Kunstprogramme zu entwickeln, den kulturellen Austausch zwischen lokalen und internationalen Künstlergemeinschaften zu fördern und dafür ihre eigene künstlerische Praxis und den einzigartigen Charakter ihres Stadtviertels zu nutzen. Popps Packing liegt an der Grenze von Banglatown und Hamtramck, in einem außergewöhnlich multikulturellen Teil Detroits. Hier treffen polnisch-katholische, verschiedene muslimische, bangalische und amerikanische Kulturkreise aufeinander. 2015 und 2016 habe ich neben meiner Residency in den Fortress Studios im North End auch jeweils einen Monat in Popps Packing gewohnt.

Der Popps Garten liegt auf einem Brachenstück neben ihrem neuen Bauspielplatz Camp Carpenter Kids Playland. Jedes Jahr wurde er anders genutzt: für Installationen, Pilzworkshops oder von Nachbarn bestellt. 2018 wächst hier neben Gemüse, Blumen und Birnen auch ein Feigenbaum.

www.poppspacking.org

→ 53 Dean's Garden, (Three Sisters), 2016

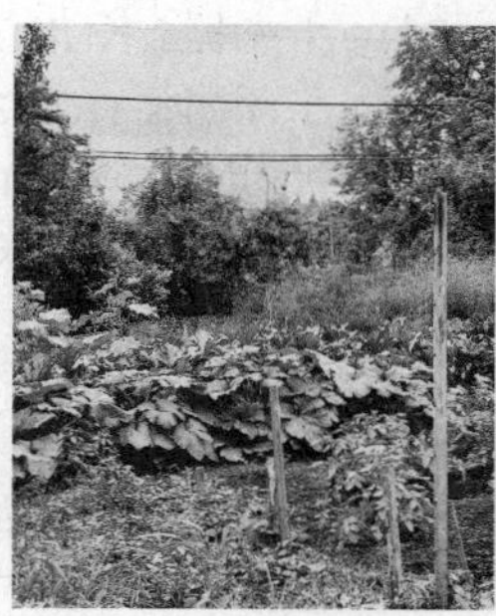

52

Earthworks Urban Farm (Church), 2018

Islandview Neighborhood

→ Zur Beschreibung siehe 49 Earthworks Urban Farm, The Capuchin Soup Kitchen, 2018

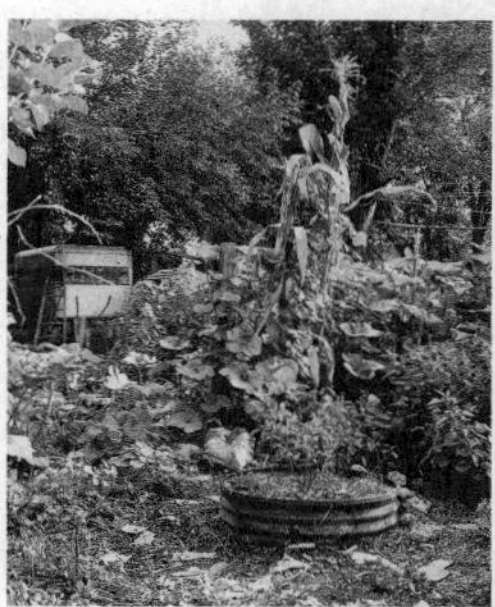

53

Dean's Garden (Three Sisters), 2016

Campau / Banglatown Neighborhood

2016 bestellte Dean Simionescu, ein Nachbar von Popps Packing, das Grundstück neben der Residency. Die meisten Samen der Gemüse- und Heilpflanzen hatte er von Reisen aus Südamerika mitgebracht. Im Bild sind neben Kapuzinerkresse, verschiedenen Chilisorten und Ringelblumen auch die Drei Schwestern zu sehen: Mais, Bohnen und Kürbis werden zusammen gepflanzt und unterstützen sich symbiotisch im Wachstum. Diese Anbauweise stammt aus Mexico und ist ca. 6000 Jahre alt.

Eine Woche bevor ich das Foto aufnahm, legten wir in einem Radical Mycology Workshop mit Marion Neumann und Geoffroy Grignon verschiedene Beete mit Speisepilzen an, die seitdem Gartenabfälle, Kaffeesatz und Zigarettenkippen verkompostieren.

→ 51 Faina and Graem's Garden (Popps Packing), 2018

Gärtnern – das bedeutet Kultur zu produzieren und nicht nur zu konsumieren, aktiv teilzunehmen, der Anbau von Essen ist bürgerschaftliches Engagement. ... Es bedeutet, Fortschritt eher zyklisch als linear zu denken, von daher ist der Garten ein sehr guter Lehrer für mich.

Emily Staugaitis von Bandhu Gardens in unserem Gespräch 2018

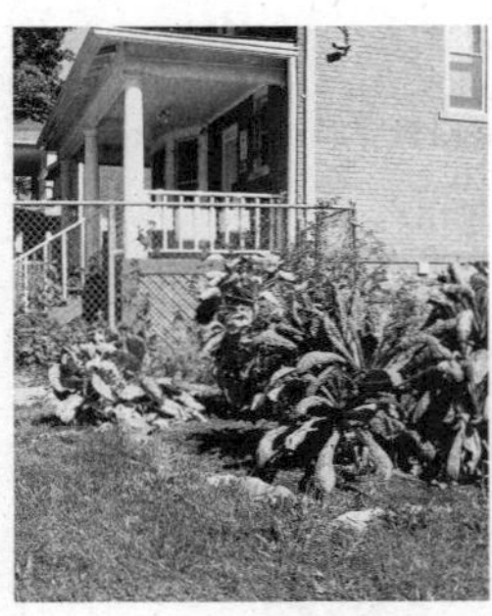

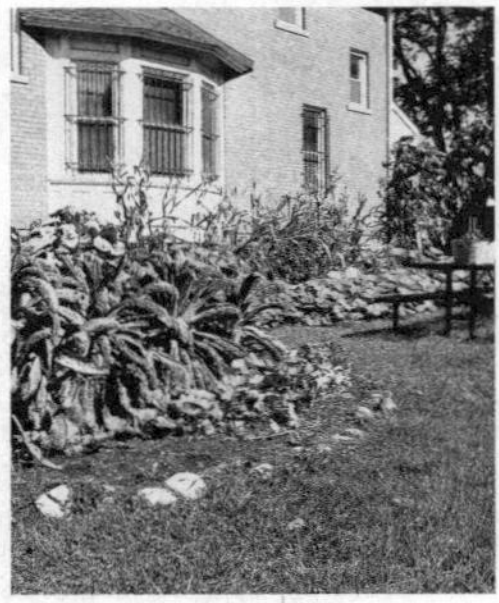

54 / 55

Sacred Roots Garden American Indian Health and Family Services, 2018

Claytown Neighborhood

Der Sacred Roots Garden ist Teil des Gesundheitszentrums American Indian Health and Family Services in Südwest-Detroit. Neben Gemüse und Blumen werden auch traditionelle medizinische Pflanzen wie Tabak, Süßgras und Eibe angepflanzt und die Anbauweise der Drei Schwestern praktiziert. Sie ist im Hintergrund an der Hauswand zu sehen. Mais, Bohnen und Squash werden dabei zusammen gepflanzt und unterstützen sich gegenseitig in ihrem Wachstum. Die Philosophie des sich nährenden Miteinanders wie auch des Gartenbaus und Essens als heilender Tätigkeit begegnete mir auch in anderen Farmen in Detroit. Sie ist gut zu verstehen, wenn man die Wunden anerkennt, die Entwurzelung, Zwangsumsiedlungen, Versklavung, Diskriminierung, Rassismus, Mord und Gewalt in der amerikanischen Geschichte an indigenen und nicht-weißen „Minderheiten" hinterlassen haben, deren Auswirkungen bis heute in Ungleichheit, Armut und ihren gesundheitlichen Folgen zu spüren sind.

Im Sommer 2017 wurde der Sacred Roots Garden um ein zwei Hektar großes Stück Land in einem öffentlichen Park erweitert, um die Ernährungssouveränität weiter auszubauen. Das Gartenprogramm wurde von Shilo Maples und Rosebud Schneider betreut.

→ 25 Sacred Roots Garden (Tobacco), 2018

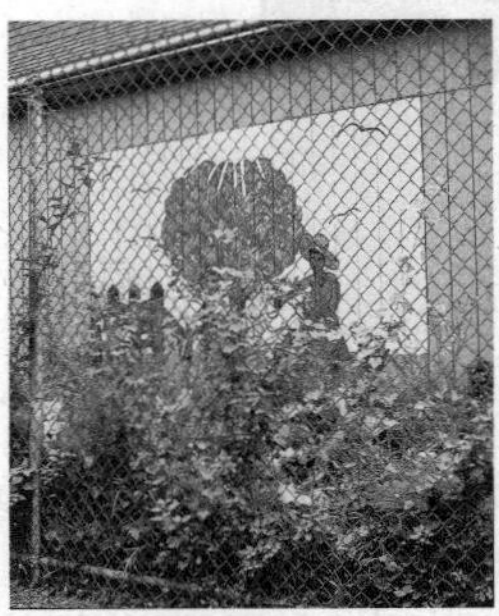

56

Catherine Ferguson Academy (Barn), 2018

Core City Neighborhood

„Wir haben überall auf diesem Spielplatz Samen gepflanzt, wir haben alle Arten von Gemüse angebaut, die in Michigan wachsen, sogar Süßkartoffeln. Aber noch wichtiger war, dass wir den Samen einer Persönlichkeit in unsere Mädchen gepflanzt haben. Wir haben Selbstvertrauen gepflanzt, wir haben Stärke gepflanzt, wir haben eine Scheune gebaut. Und wenn man eine Scheune bauen kann ... wissen sie, es ist wie: ich bin meine eigene Chefin, als Frau, ich kann erreichen, was immer ich will! ... Vermisse ich meine Schule? Ich vermisse meine Schule jeden Tag. Aber ich habe überall Mädchen. Ich habe Künstlerinnen und Musikerinnen und Geschäftsfrauen und Ärztinnen und Krankenschwestern und Anwältinnen, eine Politikerin ... Ich habe alle möglichen Mädchen überall. Jedes Mädchen, das die Catherine Ferguson Academy besucht hat, ist verpflichtet, eine Spur zu hinterlassen. Denn Catherine Ferguson war ein besonderer Ort."

Asenath Andrews (2017), ehemalige Direktorin der Catherine Ferguson Academy, in der Veranstaltung „School Days" Talk im Charles H. Wright Museum Detroit

Die Catherine Ferguson Academy war eine der sehr wenigen öffentlichen Highschools für schwangere Mädchen und Mütter im Teenageralter, die es in den Vereinigten Staaten gab. Die 1986 gegründete Schule bot Tagesbetreuung für die Neugeborenen und Vorschulerziehung für die Kleinkinder der Schülerinnen an. Urbane Landwirtschaft wurde ebenso gelehrt wie wirtschaftliche Kompetenzen für ein selbstständiges Leben. Jede Frau, die 2010 ihren Abschluss machte, wurde in ein zwei- oder vierjähriges College-Programm aufgenommen. Die meisten von ihnen waren Afroamerikanerinnen und kamen aus einkommensschwächeren Schichten. Nur ein Jahr später, im Jahr 2011, wurde die Schließung des einzigartigen Schulprojekts von einem Zwangsverwalter beschlossen, im Rahmen des landesweiten Deficit Reduction Plans für öffentliche Schulen, um öffentliche Gelder einzusparen. Als Privatschule konnte die Catherine Ferguson Academy für weitere drei Jahre unterrichten, bis sie 2014 endgültig schließen musste.

Das Foto zeigt das Wandgemälde auf der Scheune, die von den jungen Müttern an der Schule gebaut wurde.

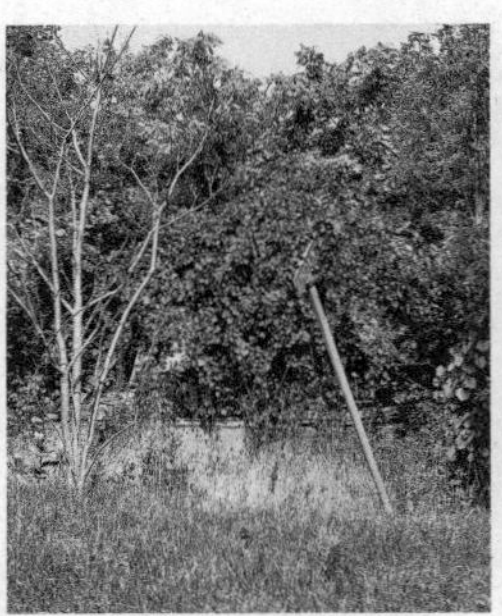

57

13603 Lincoln Street, 2015

Highland Park

Highland Park wurde 1889 als kleine Wohngemeinde mit solide gebauten mittelgroßen Häusern, schattigen Rasenflächen und ruhigen Straßen gegründet. 1910 eröffnete Ford hier seine erste Fabrik, die Ford Highland Park Plant. In nur wenigen Jahren explodierte die Einwohnerzahl von 400 auf 46.000. In dieser Zeit war die Wohnungsnot so groß, dass Vermieter einzelne Betten rund um die Uhr im Drei- bis Vier-Schichtsystem an Arbeiter jeden Alters und Herkunft vermieteten. Im Laufe der 1920er Jahre entwickelte sich Highland Park zu einem der am dichtesten besiedelten Orte der Welt. Bereits 1927 lagerte Ford seine Produktion in den neuen Ford River Rouge-Komplex aus. „Tausende von Angestellten und Arbeitern hatten sich in der Nachbarschaft der Fabrik angesiedelt – nun erwachen sie eines Morgens zehn Meilen weit von ihr entfernt."[8] Mittlerweile war Highland Park gänzlich von Detroit umgeben und blieb bis in die 1990er Jahre Arbeiterwohnbezirk für Chrysler und Dodge. Nach deren Abwanderung hatte die Kommune 35.000 Einwohner*innen und fast alle gewerblichen Steuereinnahmen verloren. 2001 folgte die Insolvenz, weiterführende Schulen wurden geschlossen und ein Großteil der Straßenbeleuchtung abgebaut. Die Stadtverwaltung riet den Menschen, das Licht auf der Veranda brennen zu lassen, um Kriminelle abzuschrecken.

Die Fotografie entstand am Labor Day in einem stillgelegten und abgerissenen Wohnviertel am Rande des Davidson Freeway. Die orangene Farbe stammt von der Kunstaktion „Detroit Demolition Disneyland", die die Aufmerksamkeit der Vorbeifahrenden auf den desolaten Zustand der Stadt lenken wollte und verfallene Häuser orange anmalte. Die Hausruine ist nur vom Freeway aus zu sehen – auf dem Weg in die Suburbs.

° Egon Erwin Kisch (1929): Bei Ford in Detroit, 301

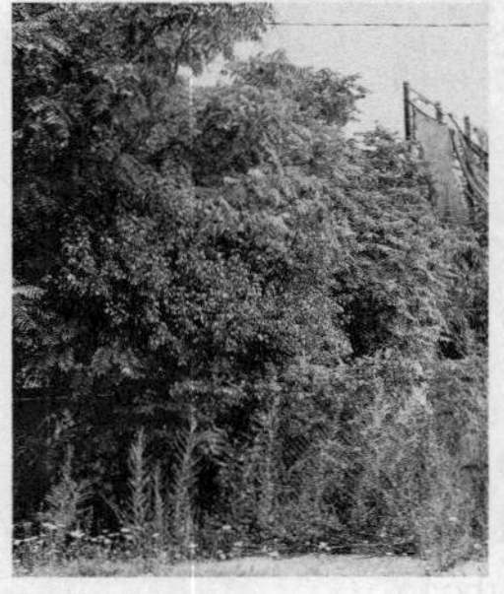

58

Trombly Street, 2015

Milwaukee Junction Neighborhood

Trombly Street liegt im Stadtteil Milwaukee Junction, in dem sich kleine Betriebe, Lagerflächen und Brachen mit Eisenbahnbrücken und Graffitiwänden abwechseln. Die Gegend gehört zu Detroits neuen Opportunity Zonen – für private Investitionen und Neugründungen bietet die Stadt Steuervergünstigungen. Die Nähe zur Gentrifizierung in Midtown, New Center und Tech Town lässt Zeitungen schon einmal vom „next hot neighborhood"° sprechen.

Auf einer Brache neben einem Maschinenbauunternehmen wachsen Götterbäume und Roter Hartriegel.

° Detroit Future City (2019), 4

→ 1/2 2550 East Grand Boulevard, 2015
→ 3 Fisher Body Plant 21 (Bucket), 2015

Obwohl wir in der Stadt Detroit eine riesige Fläche an brachliegenden Grundstücken haben, werden die Zuschläge zu diesem Land ungerecht vergeben. … Im Moment scheinen die Verantwortlichen der Stadt die Auffassung zu vertreten, dieses Land sollte an sehr wohlhabende Bauunternehmer gehen. Wir sind der Auffassung, dieses Land sollte perspektivisch unter den Einwohner*innen aufgeteilt werden, damit wir unsere Nachbarschaften und Communities stärken können.

Malik Yakini vom Detroit Black Community Food Security Network in einem Vortrag auf dem OuiShareFest, 2017

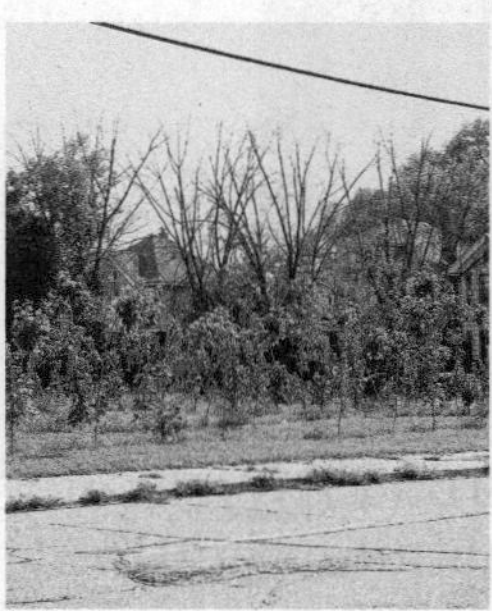

59

Charlevoix Street (Dr. Sweet's House/Hantz Woodlands), 2018

East Village Neighborhood

Das Bild zeigt den Blick vom ehemaligen Haus des Arztes Dr. Ossian Sweet auf Bäume von Hantz Woodlands.

Im Jahr 1925 zogen der Arzt Dr. Sweet und seine Frau Gladys als erste Afroamerikaner in das rein weiße Viertel an der Garland und Charlevoix Street. Nachdem sie ihr neues Haus bezogen hatten, wurden sie in der folgenden Nacht von einem Mob von Hunderten von Weißen angegriffen, die mit Steinen warfen und versuchten, sich Zugang zum Haus zu verschaffen. Zur Selbstverteidigung gab die Familie Sweet Schüsse vom Inneren des Hauses ab, woraufhin die Polizei ebenfalls mit Schüssen reagierte. Ein weißer Mann wurde getötet und ein weiterer verwundet. Alle elf Personen im Sweet-Haus wurden verhaftet und des Mordes angeklagt. „Das von der Anklage entworfene Bild schilderte einen warmen Sommerabend in einem ruhigen Gemeinwesen, wo jeder gute Nachbarschaft hält. … Plötzlich, unerwartet und ohne Herausforderung, knallte eine Salve von Schüssen an der Rückseite, den Flanken und der Front des Hauses."° Wohingegen der Angeklagte Otis Sweet erklärte: „Die Straße war ein Meer von Menschen. Die Menge war so dicht, dass man weder die Straße noch den Bürgersteig sehen konnte. Schon der Weg zur Haustür war wie ein Spießrutenlauf. Ich wurde von einem Stein getroffen, bevor ich hineinkam. …"°° Unterstützt durch die National Association for the Advancement of Colored People und nach zwei Verhandlungen, in denen sich Polizeibeamte und Zeugen wiederholt widersprachen, wurden alle Angeklagten freigesprochen. Heute ist das Haus Teil des National Register of Historic Places.

Gegenüber stehen, wie auf dem Bild zu sehen, neu angepflanzte Baumreihen von Hantz Woodlands, einer Hartholzfarm. Der Gründer John Hantz kaufte mit der Stiftung seiner Finanzdienstleisterfirma seit 2012 mehr als 2.000 Grundstücke von der Stadt Detroit zu einem Durchschnittspreis von nur 350 Dollar je Grundstück. Er wurde damit nach der Stadt und der Detroit Land Bank Authority der größte Grundstückseigentümer Detroits. Nach dem Entfernen von baufälligen Häusern und Müll wurden Bäume wie Eichen, Ahorn, Birken und Pappeln auf die Brachflächen gepflanzt. Verschiedene Initiativen kritisieren, dass die Stadt einem einzelnen Privatinvestor das Vorkaufsrecht für Tausende vergünstigter Grundstücke ohne die übliche Erschließungsvereinbarung einräumt, während Einwohner*innen und urbane Erzeuger*innen sich oft vergeblich um einen langfristigen Zugang zu Flächen oder deren Kauf bemühen.

° Hays (1929): Lasst Freiheitsglocken läuten!, 172–173
°° Widick (1989): Detroit: City of Race and Class Violence, 10–11

→ Redlining, Struktureller Rassismus

Detroits Zerfall ist jetzt sein Motor: Nirgendwo sonst im urbanen Amerika kann man mit so wenig Geld so viel erreichen.

Susan Ager (2015): Tough, Cheap, and Real, Detroit Is Cool Again

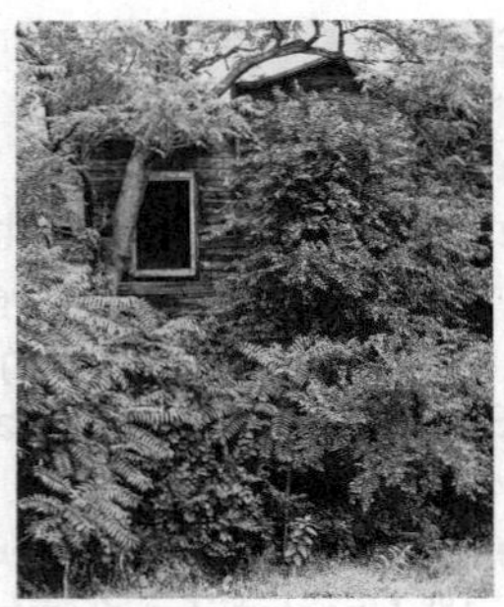

60
6000 16th Street, 2015
Northwest Goldberg Neighborhood

Dieses zweistöckige Familienhaus stand ungefähr zehn Jahre lang leer, bevor es im Zuge des Detroit Demolition Program im August 2018 abgerissen wurde. Es stand in einer Gegend, die ansonsten einer urbanen Prärie gleicht. Am Haus wachsen neben Götterbaum, Amerikanischer Ulme, einem Maulbeerbaum und Hartriegelstrauch auch Wilde Möhre, Spitzwegerich, Gemeine Brennnessel, Ufer-Rebe, Gewöhnlicher Löwenzahn und eine Gewöhnliche Seidenpflanze. Benachbart stehen die Apfelbäume der vormaligen Anwohner*innen.

Trotz der Erzählungen über ein wiederauflebendes Detroit ist es eine Stadt, in der im letzten Jahrzehnt ein Drittel aller Hausgrundstücke von Zwangsvollstreckung betroffen waren. Die Ecken mit neuen Wohnanlagen und kleinen Restaurants und die Anreize für Unternehmen aus den Vorstädten, neugestaltete Büros in der Innenstadt zu beziehen, machen etwas mehr als sieben Quadratmeilen einer 139 Quadratmeilen großen Stadt aus. Die wirkmächtigsten Kräfte auf dem Wohnungsmarkt der Stadt sind nach wie vor Verdrängung und Enteignung.

Joshua Akers (2017): Contesting Economies of Displacement and Dispossession, 1

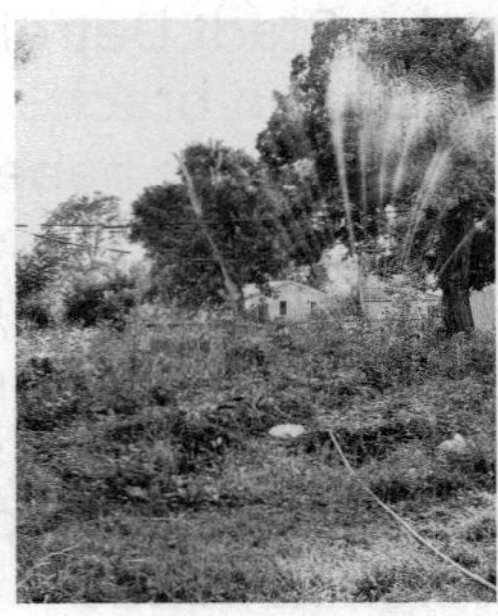

61
Beaverland Farms, 2016
Brightmoor Neighborhood

→ Zur Beschreibung siehe 10 Beaverland Farms (Elderberry Trees), 2016

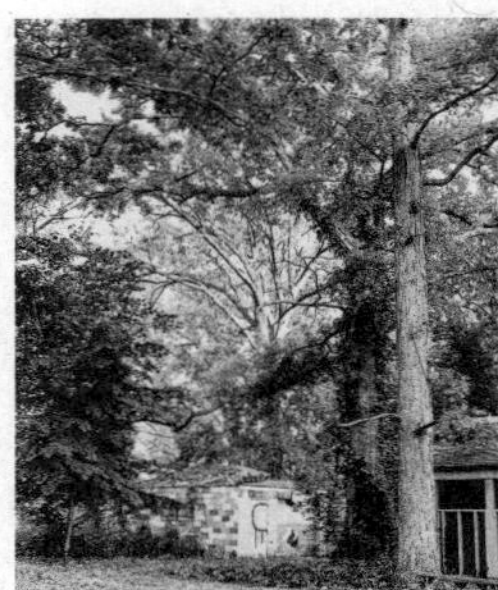

62
Beaverland Street (Neighbors Building Brightmoor), 2015
Brightmoor Neighborhood

Das kleine Haus im Bild wurde wie zahlreiche andere in Brightmoor 2012 von Jugendlichen, Kindern und Nachbar*innen des Viertels bemalt. 2009 gründeten Anwohner*innen die Neighbors Building Brightmoor und riefen einen Youth Market Garden ins Leben. Der Garten gehört den Kindern aus der Nachbarschaft, sie bauen das gesamte Gemüse an, verkaufen es auf dem Markt und erhalten die Gewinne. Die Gründerinnen Riet Schumack und Gwendolyn Shivers erzählten 2015 in einem Interview: Riet: „Aus unserem einen kleinen Garten sind Hunderte kleiner Gärten entstanden. Und was noch wichtiger ist: Aus ihm ist eine Gemeinschaft erwachsen. … In den 15 Häuserblocks, die zu Neighbors Building Brightmoor gehören, wo uns jeder kennt, gibt es praktisch keine Kriminalität mehr…“, Gwendolyn: „Wir haben jetzt eine Vielfalt, bei der es nicht mehr um Hautfarbe geht. Und das Größte daran ist, dass wir alle zusammen arbeiten.“°

Seither sind neben zahlreichen Gärten ein Detroit Community Market und das Community Center Brightmoor Artisans Collective entstanden. Letzteres „dient als sicherer Ort für die Gemeinschaft, als Café, als Inkubator für Food-Unternehmen und als Schulungsraum, in dem Nachbarn zusammenkommen können, um erschwingliche Produkte zu kaufen, sich gemeinsam gesund zu ernähren und Ideen auszutauschen.“°°

www.neighborsbuildingbrightmoor.org

° Healing Detroit One Garden at a Time (2015)
°° www.brightmoorartisans.org

→ 21 14409 Burgess Street (Pray Hope and Don't Worry), 2016
→ 65 / 66 Bentler Street, 2018

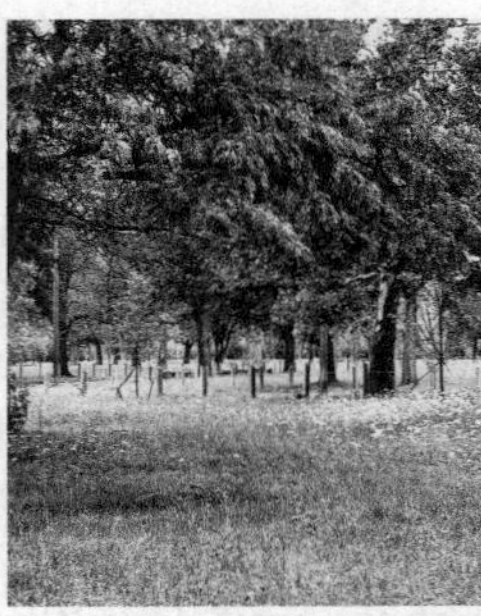

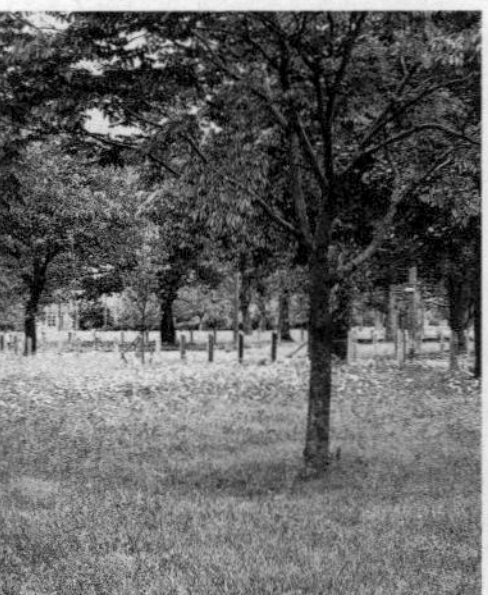

63 / 64
Brewster-Douglass Housing Projects, 2015
Brush Park Neighborhood

„Der Umzug in die Brewster-Sozialbausiedlung im Jahr 1956 war ein Wendepunkt in meinem Leben. … Viele Menschen hätten einen Umzug in die Sozialbauten als einen Rückschritt betrachtet. Aber für mich, die ich bereits aus einem bürgerlichen Viertel in verschiedene Wohnungen in der Innenstadt abgestiegen war, stellte es im Gegenteil einen Schritt zurück nach oben dar. Ich fühlte mich, als wäre ich gerade in einen Wolkenkratzer an der Park Avenue gezogen.“

Mary Wilson, Sängerin von The Supremes, in: Smith (1999), 157

Die Brewster-Douglass Homes waren eines der ersten öffentlichen Sozialbauprojekte des Landes und das größte im Besitz der Stadt Detroit. Es wurde nach Frederick Douglass benannt, einem afroamerikanischen Autor, Reformer und Kämpfer für die Abschaffung der Sklaverei. Zwischen 1935 und 1955 wurde der Wohnkomplex südlich der Hastings Street errichtet. Zu dieser Zeit war der Wohnungsmarkt in Detroit stark von der Rassentrennung bestimmt. Der Brewster-Douglass Homes Komplex wurde 1938 eingeweiht und zwar für afroamerikanische Arbeiter*innen „der unteren mittleren Einkommensschicht. ... Bewerber müssen eine Anstellung haben, in unzureichenden Wohnverhältnissen leben und seit mehr als einem Jahr in Detroit leben. Das Mindestfamilieneinkommen muss etwas mehr als das Vierfache, aber nicht mehr als das Fünffache der Miete betragen."° Bis zu 10.000 Bewohner*innen wohnten zu Spitzenzeiten in den Reihenhäusern, 6-stöckigen Wohnblöcken und 14-stöckigen Hochhäusern mit einem Erholungszentrum und Spielplätzen. Während der schwierigen Zeiten Detroits in den 1970er und 1980er Jahren begannen die Häuser zu verfallen, die Kriminalität nahm zu und die Siedlung verwahrloste. Die ersten Wohnblöcke wurden 1991 abgerissen. Als bis 2008 nur noch 280 Familien in dem Komplex verblieben waren, wurde die Wohnanlage vollständig geschlossen und stand weitere zehn Jahre leer. Zwischen 2013 und 2014 wurden alle restlichen Wohngebäude abgerissen und das Gelände in eine parkähnliche Fläche umgewandelt, die von Sicherheitskräften bewacht wird. Die Bilder zeigen die Stelle, an der früher die Hochhäuser und ein Basketballfeld standen.

Das Brewster-Douglass Gelände liegt direkt gegenüber dem Ford Field Stadion aus dem Jahr 2002 und benachbart zu Brush Park und Downtown, den beiden Vierteln mit den derzeit meisten Sanierungsaktivitäten in Detroit. Im Dezember 2019 wurde der Komplex von der Douglass Acquisition Community für 23 Millionen Dollar erworben. Wenige Monate später präsentierte deren Tochtergesellschaft Bedrock Detroit LLC erste Architekturentwürfe. Bedrock ist ein Immobilienverwaltungsunternehmen und Teil von Dan Gilberts Rock Ventures LLC, dem größten Bauträger, Arbeitgeber und Steuerzahler der Stadt.

° Michigan (1949): A Guide to the Wolverine State, 273

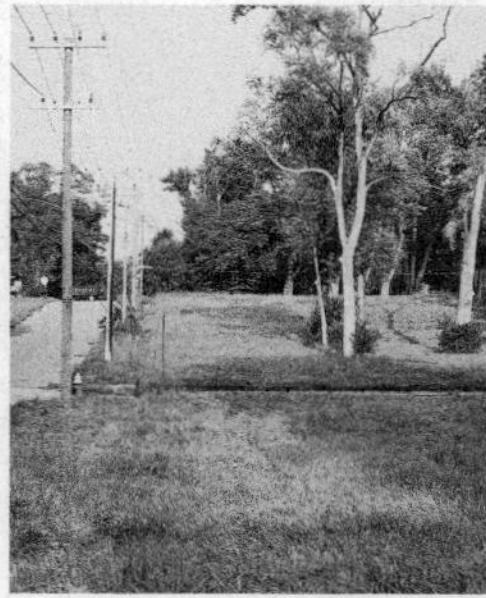

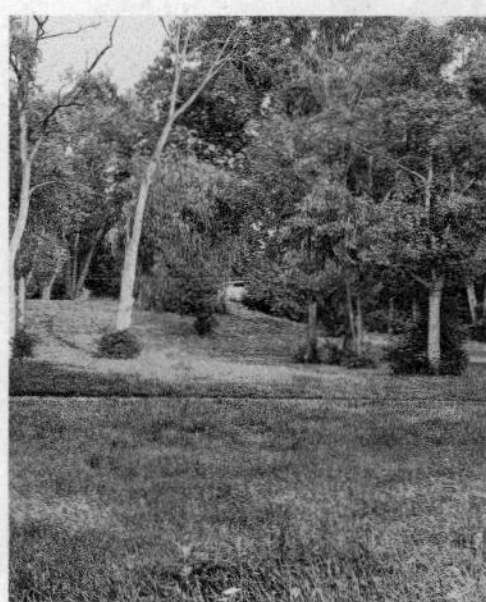

65 / 66

Bentler Street, 2018

Brightmoor Neighborhood

Der einst stark segregierte Stadtteil Brightmoor beherbergt heute unzählige kleine Gärten, Farmen und Nachbarschaftsnetzwerke. Die Bilder zeigen eine kleine hügelige Straße, und geben einen Eindruck, wie die Landschaft ausgesehen haben könnte, bevor sie 1922 erschlossen wurde.

→ 21 14409 Burgess Street (Pray Hope and Don't Worry), 2016
→ 62 Beaverland Street (Neighbors Building Brightmoor), 2015

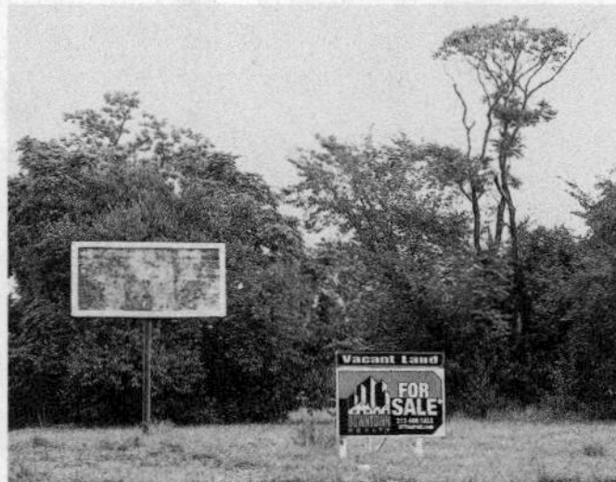

67

Oakland Avenue (For Sale Sign), 2018

North End Neighborhood

Detroit wandelt sich schnell. Bei meinem Besuch 2018 hatten viele Nachbarschaften ihr Gesicht verändert. Wie zuvor in Brush Park häuften sich auch anderswo die Verkaufsschilder auf leeren Grundstücken. Mit dem Detroit Demolition Program werden seit 2014 Tausende leer stehender Häuser abgerissen und neue Freiflächen entstehen. Sie bieten die Möglichkeit einer urbanen, selbstverwalteten Landwirtschaft, die Detroit als erste Großstadt der USA selbst versorgen und zivile Selbstbestimmung zulassen könnte. Nach wie vor sind diese Grundstücke jedoch zuallererst Grundbesitz, Spekulationsobjekt oder Geldanlage privater Investoren, besonders in Zeiten niedriger Grundstückspreise. Bereits um 1890 beschreibt ein Autor Detroit wie folgt: „Außergewöhnlich ist, dass die leeren Flächen der Stadt fast die Hälfte der verfügbaren Fläche ausmachten. ... Man kann nicht umhin, sich von der großen Menge an Freiflächen beeindrucken zu lassen, von denen ein Teil noch als Ackerland dient, der größte Teil aber ungenutzt ist und zu Spekulationszwecken frei gehalten wird ... ."°

Doch mit jeder zyklisch wiederkehrenden Rezession, Krise und erhofftem Comeback Detroits entstehen auch immer wieder Denkansätze, die eine aktive Teilhabe seiner unterschiedlichen Communities an der Stadtentwicklung ermöglichen können. Diese stete Entwicklung neuer Ideen zusammen mit dem Engagement der Detroiter*innen, ihre Stadt, oft aus der Not heraus, selbst zu gestalten, scheint mir eine Konstante in all dem Wandel zu sein. Es bleibt zu hoffen, dass auch die Stadtverwaltung dieses Potenzial erkennt. Bereits 1988 formulierte James Boggs: „Wir müssen anfangen, über die Gründung kleiner Unternehmen nachzudenken, die Lebensmittel, Waren und Dienstleistungen für den lokalen Markt produzieren, d. h. für unsere Allgemeinheit und für unsere Stadt ... Um diese neuen Unternehmen zu gründen, brauchen wir eine Sichtweise unserer Stadt, die sowohl die natürlichen Ressourcen unserer Gegend als auch die vorhandenen und potenziellen Fähigkeiten und Talente der Detroiter berücksichtigt."°°

° Unbekannter Autor (1890), in: Zunz (1982), 30
°° Guyette (2001): Down the green path

→ Gentrifizierung, Spekulation und Zwangsräumungen
→ 33 Alley in Midtown, 2015

> ... wir müssen uns mit dem Gedanken anfreunden, dass wir selbst die Führungspersönlichkeiten sind, die wir gesucht haben.
>
> Grace Lee Boggs (2011). The Next American Revolution, 159

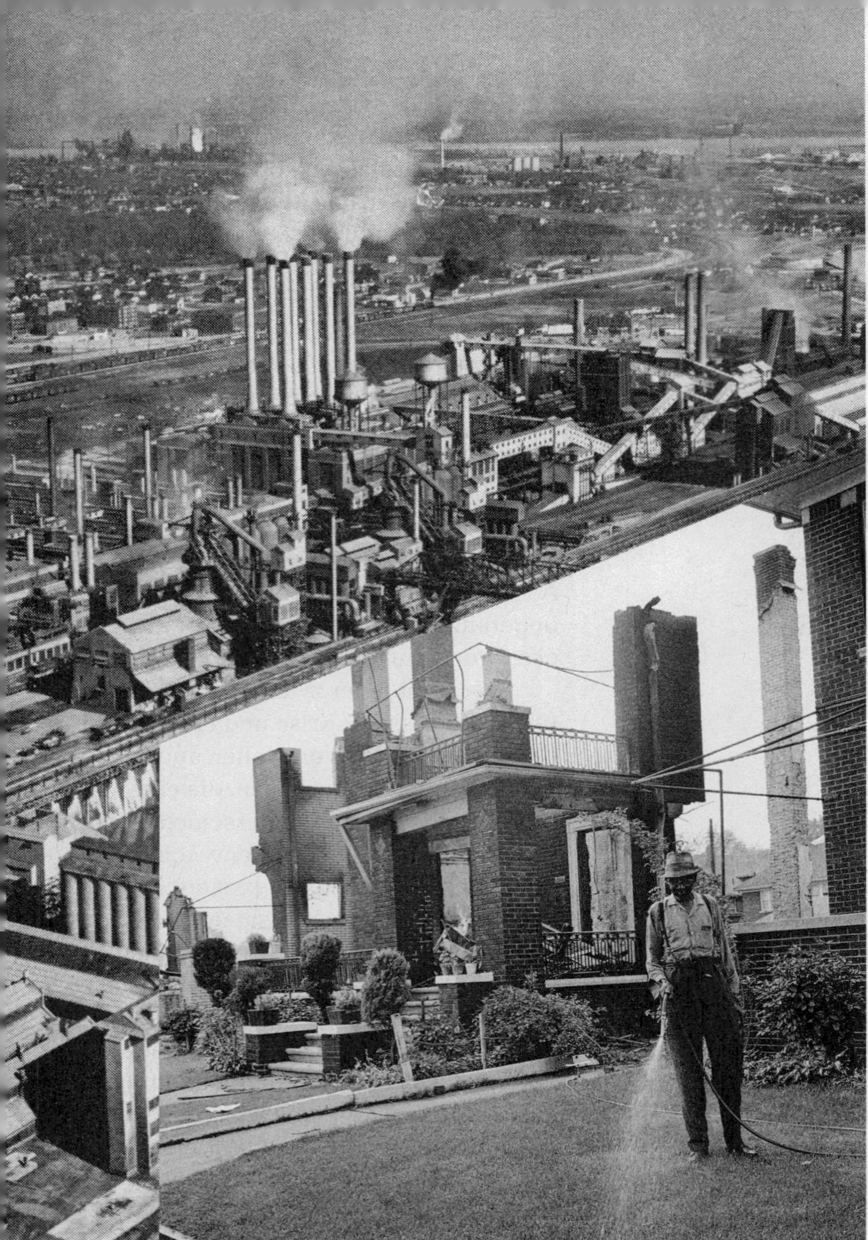

Abb. 1: Ford River Rouge Complex 1947 / Detroiter Anwohner wässert seinen Rasen nach den Unruhen der Detroit Rebellion im Juli 1967

Abb. 2: „Detroit ist Dynamit“, Arbeitsagentur 1942 / Munitionsmacherin in der Lincoln Motor Company 1918

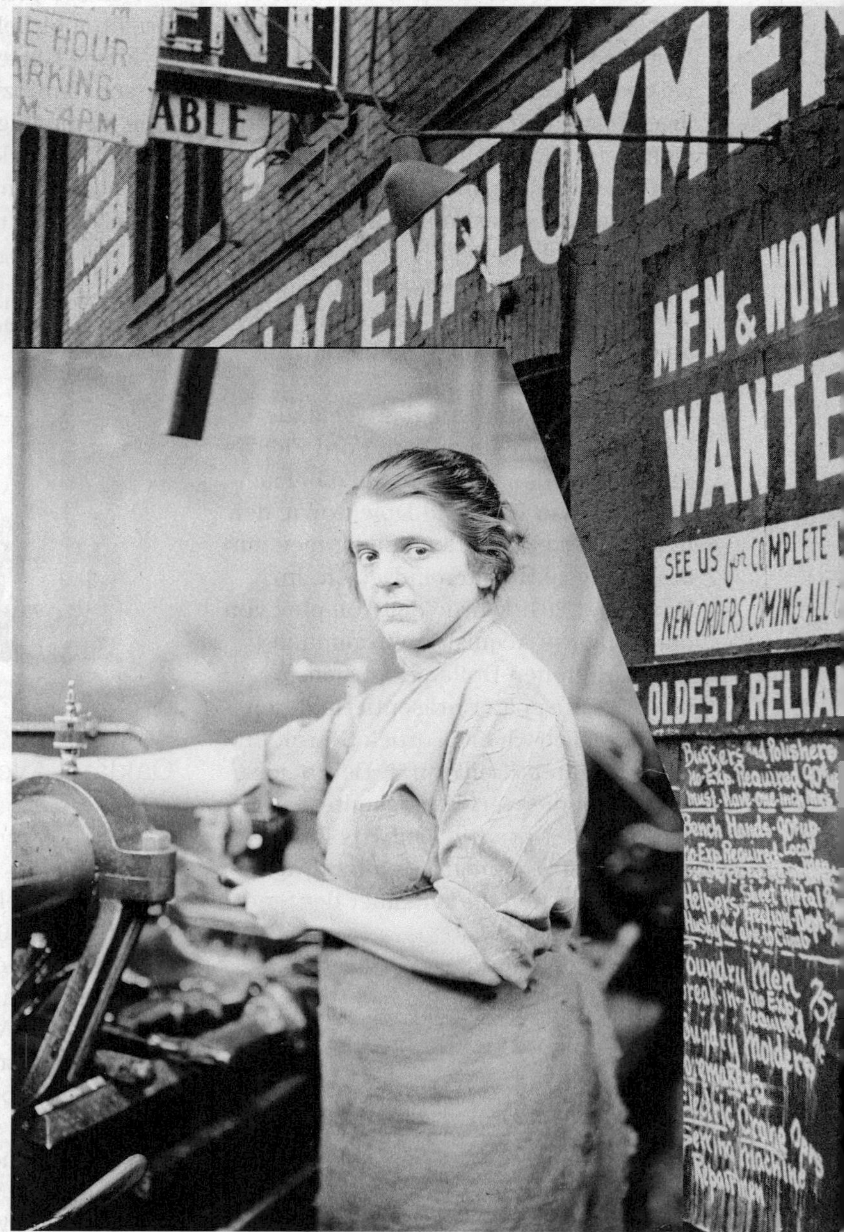

REGISTER

Albert Kahn
(1869–1942) war einer der bedeutendsten Industriearchitekten seiner Zeit. Zusammen mit seinem Bruder Julius entwickelte er innovative Stahlbetonkonstruktionen in Detroit, die im Jahr 1903 beim Bau der → Packard Automotive Plant zuerst Anwendung fanden. Kahn entwarf eine solche Vielzahl an Industriebauten und architektonischen Sehenswürdigkeiten der Stadt, dass man ihn oft als Architekt Detroits bezeichnet.

Algonkin
ist die Bezeichnung der am weitesten verbreiteten indigenen Sprachfamilie Nordamerikas und gleichzeitig der Name eines aus zahlreichen Lokalgruppen bestehenden Stammes nordamerikanischer Ureinwohner. Die Algonkin gehören zum östlichen Zweig des → Anishinabe-Volkes.

Amerikanischer Traum
ist die „Vorstellung von der individuellen Aufstiegsmöglichkeit, die auf Verdienst statt auf Klasse beruht und die allen Menschen offen steht, wenn sie nur hart genug arbeiten." (Apel (2015), 8) Diese Vorstellung blendet allerdings die statistische Tatsache aus, dass Geburtsort und soziale Herkunft eines Kindes seinen Lebenslauf mehr bestimmen als seine tatsächliche Arbeitsleistung.

Anishinabe
ist eines der heute größten indigenen Völker Nordamerikas, zu denen sich die Stämme der → Algonkin, Nipissing, Mississauga, Potawatomi, Odawa, Oji-Cree, Saulteaux und die Ojibwa zählen. Sie stammen ursprünglich aus der Region rund um die Großen Seen.

Arsenal of Democracy
(Waffenlager der Demokratie)
ist der Beiname Detroits während der Kriegsproduktion im Zweiten Weltkrieg. Die Autofirmen stellten ihre Produktion auf Panzer und Bomber um und neue Fabriken wurden im Umland aus dem Boden gestampft. Eine halbe Million Arbeitsmigrant*innen aus Europa, den Südstaaten und aus dem ländlichen Amerika strömte in die Stadt. Neuankömmlinge wohnten zeitweise in Zelten. Nach dem Kriegseintritt der USA rückten Frauen und ethnische „Minderheiten" in zuvor weiße Männerjobs. Ganz Detroit war in Vollbeschäftigung mit allen Unannehmlichkeiten, die dies mit sich brachte: Wohnungsnot, rassistische Ressentiments und Hass-Streiks. (→ Detroit Riot im Juni 1943)

Assembly Line
ist eine industrielle Fertigungsstraße, die auf dem Prinzip des Fließbands basiert. Sie wurde bereits in Schlachthöfen und vom Autobauer Ransom E. Old eingesetzt, als Henry Ford sie 1913 in seiner → Ford Highland Park Plant einführte und bekannt machte. Das Fließband ermöglicht eine rentable Massenproduktion, indem komplexe Montagevorgänge in einzelne einfache Handgriffe aufgeteilt werden, die von ungelernten, billigen und leicht ersetzbaren Arbeitskräften ausgeführt werden können. Heutige Fertigungsstraßen sind zumeist vollautomatisiert.

Big Three
steht für die drei größten amerikanischen Autohersteller → Ford, General Motors und Chrysler (heute Fiat Chrysler Automobiles). Sie werden in einem Atemzug mit der Motor City genannt, obwohl nur noch General Motors seinen Zentralsitz in Detroit hat.

Black Bottom und
Paradise Valley
gehörten zu den ältesten Stadtteilen Detroits und wurden im Zuge des → Urban Renewal Stadterneuerungsprogramms in der 1950er Jahren abgerissen. Black Bottom erhielt seinen Namen nach der fruchtbaren schwarzen Erde des Flussschwemmlandes. Während der Industrialisierung und der ersten Welle der → Great Migration strömten Zehntausende Afroamerikaner*innen aus dem Süden in die Stadt, um ihr Glück zu finden. Vormals ethnisch aufgeteilte Stadtviertel trennten sich nun nach Klasse und vor allem nach Hautfarbe und in beiden Stadtteilen entstand das afroamerikanische Ghetto. Paradise Valley war das kulturelle Ausgehviertel mit schicken Lokalen in der St. Aubin und → Hastings Street, Black Bottom im Süden die Wohn- und Geschäftsgegend. Während des Zweiten Weltkriegs wurde das ohnehin schon überfüllte Gebiet sehr stark überbevölkert und die bereits alten, heruntergekommenen Häuser boten miserable Lebensbedingungen. Im Rahmen der Detroiter → Urban Renewal wurde Black Bottom und ein großer Teil des Paradise Valley in den 1950er Jahren schließlich von Bulldozern planiert, um Platz zu schaffen für neue → Freeway-Autobahnen, den Lafayette Park und Brewster-Douglass Homes Wohnkomplexe (→ Bilder 31/32 und 63/64) und andere Bauvorhaben im heutigen Midtown. Zehntausende Menschen wurden verdrängt. Sie zogen auf die Westside in die Nähe der 12th Street – weitgehend unbeachtet, bis dort die → Detroit Rebellion im Juli 1967 ausbrach.

Detroit
ist die größte Stadt im Bundesstaat Michigan und Regierungssitz des Verwaltungsbezirks Wayne County. 82,7 Prozent der Bevölkerung sind Afroamerikaner*innen. Damit ist Detroit eine der größten schwarzen Communities in den USA. Die Stadt wurde 1701 von Antoine de la Mothe Cadillac als Ville d'Etroit (Stadt an der Wasserstraße) am Detroit River gegründet, der Lake St. Clair and Lake Erie verbindet. Bekannt wurde die sogenannte Motor City durch ihre schnell wachsende Autoindustrie. Nach 50 Jahren Blütezeit verließen die meisten Fabriken und 60 Prozent der Einwohner*innen die Stadt seit 1950 wieder.

Detroit Bankruptcy
Im Juli 2013 meldete die Stadt Detroit mit einem Schuldenstand von 18–20 Milliarden Dollar Insolvenz an. Bis Dezember 2014 kontrollierte der Bundesstaat Michigan die Finanzen der Stadt. Der eingesetzte Insolvenzverwalter Kevin Orr beauftragte neben Jurist*innen und Beraterfirmen auch seine ehemalige Kanzlei Jones Day. Alle Beratungsleistungen kosteten die Stadt insgesamt 170,2 Millionen Dollar. Um die Insolvenz zu überwinden, wurde dazu geraten, Pensionen städtischer Angestellter zu kürzen, städtische Unternehmen Grundstücke sowie wertvolle Kunstwerke des Detroit Institute of Art an Privatinvestoren zu verkaufen. In Vorbereitung auf den Verkauf der städtischen Wasserwerke begann die Stadt im Jahr 2014 mit den sogenannten → Water Shutoffs. Privaten Haushalten wurde wegen bereits geringer Schulden das Trinkwasser abgestellt. Im sogenannten Great Bargain (der Großen Vereinbarung) gelang es sowohl durch private und öffentliche Interventionen als auch durch Spenden, die städtischen Pensionen und Kunstwerke zu sichern und Schuldenschnitte zur Beendigung der Insolvenz zu vereinbaren.

Detroit Community Markets
sind Nachbarschaftsmärkte, Farmstände oder Food-Box-Programme, bei denen Detroiter Landwirt*innen ihre Erzeugnisse direkt an die Nachbarschaft verkaufen.
www.detroitmarkets.org

Detroit Demolition Program
ist ein staatlich gefördertes Abriss-Programm. Seit der Gründung 2014 wurden mit einem Budget von 250 Millionen Dollar 18.000 Gebäude abgerissen, die durch Zwangsvollstreckungen, Abwanderung, oder Brandschäden leer standen oder verfielen. Weitere 40.000 Gebäude sollen folgen. Neben dem lohnenden Geschäft für Abrissfirmen entstehen dadurch überall in der Stadt neue freie Grundstücksflächen.

Detroit Food Policy Council
wurde 2009 vom Detroit City Council nach Anstoß des Detroit Black Community Food Security Network (→ Bild 45) gegründet. Unter der Leitung von Detroiter*innen setzt sich die Organisation für die Schaffung eines nachhaltigen, lokalen Food Systems und für Ernährungssicherheit, -gerechtigkeit und -souveränität in der Stadt Detroit ein (→ Food Security). Sie vertritt die Interessen von urbanen Landwirt*innen und mahnt u. a. den fehlenden Schutz bzw. Zugang zu landwirtschaftlichen Flächen für die lokale Bevölkerung an, während suburbane Großinvestoren große Flächen zu Entwicklungszwecken kaufen können.

www.detroitfoodpolicycouncil.net

Detroit Future City
ist eine gemeinnützige Organisation, die 2012 von Architekt*innen und Stadtplaner*innen gegründet wurde. Nach einer zweijährigen Recherche veröffentlichte sie einen 50-Jahre-Entwicklungsplan für das post-schrumpfende New Detroit. Das Konzept sieht konzentrierte Geschäfts- und Wohnkorridore vor, während andere Gebiete der Stadt in Grünzonen umgewandelt werden sollen – in Parks, Wälder oder innovative Farmen und Obstgärten. Die derzeitige Stadtentwicklung mit Abriss und Rückbau, Steuererleichterungen für private Investoren in → Opportunity-Zonen, Nachbarschafts-Branding und → Gentrifizierung scheint diesem Konzept zu folgen. Andererseits fällt auf, dass es keine konkreten Planungen für sozialen Wohnungsbau gibt – in einer Stadt, die zurzeit eine Armutsrate von 36,4 Prozent aufweist.

Detroit Land Bank Authority
ist größter Grundstückseigentümer in Detroit (2019). Das staatliche Unternehmen wurde 2008 gegründet, um die Zahl der Grundstücke, die sich in öffentlichem Besitz befinden, zu verringern. Im Bestand sind unbebaute Grundstücke, verlassene Häuser und Gebäude, die nach Räumungsklagen leer stehen und durch die → Wayne County Tax Foreclosure Auction neu versteigert oder mit speziellen Programmen verkauft werden. Das „Side Lot Program" zum Beispiel ermöglicht Hauseigentümer*innen, leer stehende und direkt benachbarte Grundstücke zu ihrem Besitz hinzuzukaufen – eine Grundlage für viele Detroiter*innen, um Land für private Farmen und Gärten zu erwerben.

Detroit Renaissance
(Renaissance, französisch für Wiedergeburt). Dieser Slogan taucht zumeist in Zeiten einer wirtschaftlichen Krise auf und beschwört den Wiederaufschwung zu vorherigem Wohlstand, den es nachweislich nie für alle Bewohner*innen gab. Diese „Comebacks" bestehen zumeist aus privatwirtschaftlichen Bauprojekten, die mit Steuervergünstigungen einhergehen und sich zumeist auf Downtown oder Midtown konzentrieren.

Detroit Riots
Riot bedeutet Aufruhr und ist eine Form von gewaltsamen öffentlichen Unruhen gegen Staatsgewalt, Eigentum und/oder Menschen. Den meisten Riots in Detroit gingen kleinere Zusammenstöße zwischen Bevölkerungsgruppen oder mit der Polizei voraus, alle ereigneten sich in Zeiten eines enormen Bevölkerungswachstums, der wirtschaftlichen, sozialen Spannungen oder während eines Krieges. Nach dem Race Riot von 1863 wurde die Detroiter Polizei gegründet, 1929 kam es zum Angriff auf das Haus Dr. Ossian Sweets (→ Bild 59). Die größten Unruhen waren:

Detroit Riot im Juni 1943
mitten in der Kriegsproduktion (→ Arsenal of Democracy) eskalierten am 20. Juni 1943 Rassenunruhen, die zwei Tage anhielten und erst durch den Aufmarsch von Federal Troops beendet wurden. 34 Menschen wurden getötet. Weiße und schwarze Menschenmobs waren aufeinander losgegangen, griffen wahllos unbeteiligte Zivilist*innen an und zerstörten Häuser. Verschiedene Hass-Streiks in Fabriken (→ Bild 27) und 1942 gegen die Sozialwohnungen für Afroamerikaner*innen des Sojourner Truth Housing Project gingen den Ereignissen voraus.

Detroit Rebellion im Juli 1967
Am 23. Juli 1967 kam es nach der Razzia in einer illegalen Bar zu Massenunruhen, die fünf Tage andauerten und 43 Tote forderten. Tausende Menschen wurden verletzt, mehr als 7.000 verhaftet und 1.000 Gebäude niedergebrannt. Es kam zu Ladenplünderungen, Brandstiftung und Schießereien. Der Aufstand wurde von der Nationalgarde beendet, die innerhalb von vier Tagen über 150.000 Schuss Munition verschoss. Die Detroit Rebellion war eine der vielen Rassenunruhen, die zwischen 1963 und 1968 mitten im Vietnamkrieg in über 265 amerikanischen Städten ausbrachen und sich gegen Rassismus, Polizeigewalt und für bürgerliche und ethnische Gleichberechtigung einsetzten. In Detroit begannen die Unruhen in einem der am dichtesten besiedelten Stadtviertel, das ein paar Jahre zuvor von Afroamerikanisch*innen überschwemmt worden war, die aus → Black Bottom und Paradise Valley vertrieben wurden, nachdem ihre Häuser im Rahmen des → Urban Renewal planiert worden waren.

Detroit Summer
wurde 1992 von → Grace Lee und James Boggs zusammen mit anderen Detroiter Aktivist*innen gegründet. Das multiethnische, generationsübergreifende Kollektiv hat das Ziel, die Jugend vor Ort zu aktivieren, ihre Nachbarschaften und Communities zu verbessern und zu verändern. Gemeinschaftsgärten, Wandbilder, Abfallrecycling und Hausreparaturen sind Programme, um Verantwortung für die eigene Nachbarschaft und Führungsqualitäten der Jugendlichen ausbilden.

www.detroitsummer.wordpress.com

Drei Schwestern
ist eine ca. 6000 Jahre alte Anbauweise, die ihren Ursprung in der Landwirtschaft des indigenen Mexiko hat. Mais, Rankenbohnen und Squash-Kürbisse werden dabei so gepflanzt, dass die Bohnen am Mais emporwachsen und ihn dabei mit Nährstoffen und natürliche Pestiziden versorgen. Der Squash als Drittes bildet einen schützenden Ring, der Schatten spendet und vor dem Austrocknen schützt. Da jede Pflanzenart als Schwester verstanden wird, ergibt sich der Begriff der Drei Schwestern.

Eschen-Ahorn (Acer negundo)
ist ein Baum, der in Nordamerika beheimatet ist und auch Manitoba Maple genannt wird. Verschiedene indianische Kulturen nutzten Eschen-Ahorn unter anderem für medizinische Zwecke, für Zeremonien, um Zucker zu gewinnen oder um Essgeschirr, Trommeln oder Pfeifen herzustellen. Der schnellwachsende Baum wird nur an die 100 Jahre alt

und ist heute weltweit zu finden. Auch in Detroit ist er sehr häufig anzutreffen.

Farm-A-Lot Program
1975 rief Bürgermeister Coleman Young dieses Programm ins Leben. Ähnlich der wirtschaftlichen Rezession von 1894 und den → Pingree's Potato Patches wurden brachliegende Grundstücke für Gärten freigegeben. Die Stadt stellte Detroiter Familien Saatgut und technische Hilfe zur Verfügung und ermunterte sie, auf freien Flächen Obst und Gemüse anzubauen, um ihre Lebenshaltungskosten zu senken. Bis 1979 legten fast 7.000 Detroiter*innen in der ganzen Stadt kleine Gärten an. Nachdem die Unterstützung der Stadt nachzulassen begann, setzten andere wie die → Gardening Angels oder → Detroit Summer die Community Gardens bis heute fort.

Five Dollar Day
bezeichnet den Tageslohn, den die → Ford Motor Company am 4. Januar 1914 als Teil des „Profit Sharing Plan" einführte. Dieser sah die Verdopplung des bisher üblichen Lohns und die Einführung des Acht-Stunden-Arbeitstags vor (bei sechs Arbeitstagen die Woche). Profitieren konnten 10.000 Arbeiter, die länger als sechs Monate bei Ford arbeiteten und den Kriterien des „Ford Sociological Department" und des „Ford Service Department" entsprachen (fließendes Englisch, ein sauberes Eigenheim, pünktliches und tadelloses Arbeiten). Der Five Dollar Day machte weltweit Schlagzeilen. Tagelang strömten Zehntausende Arbeitssuchende vor die → Ford Highland Park Plant. Es entstanden Tumulte und Wasserspritzen wurden eingesetzt.

Food Desert
(übersetzt: Ernährungswüste) ist der Ausdruck für Wohngebiete mit eingeschränktem Zugang zu erschwinglichem und gesundem Essen. 75 Prozent aller US-amerikanischen Food Deserts liegen in Städten, oft in einkommensschwachen Gegenden. Ohne gesunde Ernährung steigt das Risiko von Erkrankungen bei Kindern, Familien und Älteren. In Detroit gibt es teilweise so wenige Lebensmittelläden, dass Einwohner*innen ohne Auto (ungefähr 20 Prozent) nur in Schnapsläden oder Tankstellen einkaufen können.

Food Security
(übersetzt: Ernährungssicherheit) bedeutet die Bedingung, dass alle Mitglieder einer Gemeinschaft jederzeit und in unmittelbarer Nähe Zugang zu ausreichenden Mengen von nahrhaften, kulturell angemessenen Nahrungsmitteln aus umweltverträglichen und gerechten Ressourcen haben.

Ford Motor Company
wurde als Automanufaktur 1903 von Henry Ford in → Milwaukee Junction gegründet. 1908 beschäftigte Ford rund 450 Personen und 1939 fast 90.000. Das Unternehmen führte die → Assembly Line und den → Five Dollar Day ein, unterhielt eine Ford English School, das Ford Sociological Department zur Kontrolle der Lebensumstände seiner Angestellten und das Ford Service Department, eine betriebsinterne Sicherheitsabteilung aus Ex-Polizisten, Spitzeln und Preisboxern. Als einer der letzten ließ Ford erst 1941 Gewerkschaften zu. Das Unternehmen formte die Stadt wie kein zweites, obwohl seit 1910 kein Fordmodell mehr in Detroit gefertigt wurde. Alle Fabriken entstanden außerhalb der Stadtgrenze. Die Ford Motor Company ist Teil der → Big Three.

Ford Highland Park Plant
war Henry Fords erstes Automobilwerk. Sie wurde von → Albert Kahn entworfen und 1910 in → Highland Park, einem Vorort von Detroit, eröffnet. Das Werk umfasste Büros, Fabriken, ein Kraftwerk und eine Gießerei. Hier produzierte Ford das Modell T und führte die → Assembly Line sowie den → Five Dollar Day ein. Bereits 1928 wurde die Automobilmontage in den → Ford River Rouge-Komplex verlegt; in den 1970er Jahren wurde die Produktion in Highland Park ganz eingestellt. Heute beherbergt die Fabrik Lagerplätze und ein Einkaufszentrum.

Ford River Rouge-Komplex
ist das zweite Automobilwerk von Ford. Es wurde südwestlich von Detroit in der Stadt Dearborn gebaut und war bei seiner Eröffnung im Jahr 1927 der größte zusammenhängende Fabrikkomplex der Welt. Das Werk wurde von → Albert Kahn entworfen und ist ein nationales historisches Wahrzeichen. Heute umfasst der Industriepark Ford Rouge Center sechs Ford-Fabriken und zwei Stahlwerke.

Freeway / Interstate Autobahnen
Im Zweiten Weltkrieg entstanden rund um Rüstungsfabriken und Militärstützpunkte neue Straßen, die Grundlage des heutigen Interstate-Autobahnnetzes wurden. Detroit baute die ersten Stadt- und Interstate-Autobahnen ab den 1950er Jahren im Zuge des → Urban Renewal. Bis 1958 wurden dafür über 5.000 Gebäude in Poletown und → Black Bottom zerstört. Die neuen Autobahnen erleichterten den Fortzug in die neuen Vororte und die → Suburbanisierung.

Gardening Angels
war ein informelles Netzwerk hauptsächlich afroamerikanischer Senior*innen, die in den Südstaaten aufgewachsen waren und die Gelegenheit leer stehender Grundstücke und das Saatgut des städtischen → Farm-A-Lot Program genutzt hatten, um überall in der Stadt zu gärtnern. Das Netzwerk entstand in den 1990er Jahren, als Gerald Hairston (1947–2001), ein ehemaliger Automobilarbeiter und gleichzeitig leidenschaftlicher Umweltschützer, damit begann, Gemeinschaftsgärten auf leerstehenden Grundstücken, an Schulen und auf Spielplätzen anzulegen.

Garden Resource Program
unterstützt rund 1.500 Familien-, Nachbarschafts- und Schulgärten sowie Gärtnereien in Detroit, → Highland Park und → Hamtramck mit Saatgut und Setzlingen. Außerdem werden Workshops, Weiterbildungen und Treffen angeboten, um Heimgärtnern und urbane Landwirtschaft zu fördern. 2003 gegründet, ist es seit 2013 Teil von Keep Growing Detroit.

http://detroitagriculture.net

General Motors Company
wurde 1908 als Holding gegründet, deren Betriebszweck die Kapitalbeteiligung an anderen Unternehmen ist. Bereits im Gründungsjahr erwarb GM die Autohersteller Buick und Oldsmobile und übernahm später Cadillac, Fisher Body, Chevrolet und viele weitere, die als eigenständige Marken geführt werden. GM ist einer der größten Autohersteller weltweit und hat als einziger der → Big Three seinen Hauptsitz in Detroit. 2009 meldete das Unternehmen mit 90 Milliarden Dollar Schulden Insolvenz an und wurde zur Rettung kurzzeitig verstaatlicht.

Gentrifizierung
ist der Prozess einer ökonomischen Wertsteigerung eines Stadtteils durch Sanierung oder Umbau. Eine Folge davon ist, dass langansässige Anwohner*innen von wohlhabenderen Bevölkerungsschichten verdrängt werden. Dieser Prozess beginnt oft mit der Zwischennutzung und Aufwertung von Leerstand durch die Nachbarschaft selbst oder der sogenannten creative class, einer meist gut ausgebildeten Mittelschicht, die Kultur etabliert oder Start-ups gründet.